The Life of Saint Clement

A translation of *La Vie de seint Clement*

MEDIEVAL AND RENAISSANCE
TEXTS AND STUDIES

VOLUME 488

———————

THE FRENCH OF ENGLAND TRANSLATION SERIES
(FRETS)

VOLUME 10

THE LIFE OF SAINT CLEMENT

A translation of *La Vie de seint Clement*

by
Daron Burrows

FRETS Series Editors
Thelma Fenster and
Jocelyn Wogan-Browne

ARIZONA CENTER FOR MEDIEVAL
ACMRS
AND RENAISSANCE STUDIES

Tempe, Arizona
2016

THE ARIZONA CENTER FOR
MEDIEVAL &
RENAISSANCE
STUDIES

Published by ACMRS (Arizona Center for Medieval and Renaissance Studies)
Tempe, Arizona
© 2016 Arizona Board of Regents for Arizona State University.
All Rights Reserved.

Library of Congress Cataloging-in-Publication Data

Names: Burrows, Daron Lee, 1973- translator.
Title: The Life of Saint Clement : a translation of La Vie de seint Clement / by Daron Burrows.
Other titles: Vie de seint Clement. | Vie de seint Clement. English.
Description: Tempe, Arizona : ACMRS, 2016. | Series: Medieval and Renaissance texts and studies ; Volume 488 | Series: The French of England translation series (FRETS) ; Volume 10 | Includes bibliographical references and index.
Identifiers: LCCN 2016015152 | ISBN 9780866985437 (hardcover : alk. paper)
Subjects: LCSH: Clement I, Pope. | Popes--Biography.
Classification: LCC BX1004 .V54 2016 | DDC 270.1092 [B] --dc23
LC record available at https://lccn.loc.gov/2016015152

Front Cover:
Cover image from f. 193r of Cambridge, Trinity College, R.3.46
Reproduced by kind permission of the Master and Fellows of Trinity College, Cambridge.

∞
This book is made to last. It is set in Adobe Caslon Pro,
smyth-sewn and printed on acid-free paper to library specifications.
Printed in the United States of America

TABLE OF CONTENTS

Series Editors' Preface

We are delighted to announce the publication in FRETS of the *Life of Saint Clement*, one of the most engaging and important works of 13th-century hagiography. The *Life of Saint Clement* positions itself, in its witty prologue, as a novel work of particular impact, a new way of making classic texts accessible to everyone, and not merely to the learned. And indeed, the poem, among other things, is one of the most complete and faithful pre-modern versions of an important text of early Church history, the Clementine *Recognitions*, attributed to Clement I, pope of Rome (88–99 CE), and translated into Latin from the Greek, ca. 400. But *Clement* also reframes this early papal figure and the work attributed to him in a saintly romance biography. Clement's family, shattered by accusations of incestuous sex, is dispersed and shipwrecked; following further loss, quest, and recovery, it is finally reconstituted as a spiritual *familia*. Biological family members are converted by Clement's spiritual father, St Peter, in part through a dramatic contest between Peter and Simon Magus. As part of debating Christianity, the text ranges widely through the spiritual ethnography and anthropology of the world. Its global reach makes it, among other things, a characteristic thirteenth-century encyclopaedic compilation: a verbal *mappa mundi*, and a predecessor to Mandeville's famous *Book* in its lively, virtual voyaging. This admirably executed hagiographic narrative is also an excellent example of the vigor of dialectic and *disputatio* in medieval doctrinal culture. Never previously translated, the *Life of St. Clement* now offers new material and new approaches for insular literary history's rich but under-explored thirteenth century.

Dr. Daron Burrows of St. Peter's College, Oxford, has produced a major edition of *La Vie de saint Clement* for the Anglo-Norman Text Society, ANTS 64–65, 66, 67 (publ. in three vols., 2006–2009). His prize-winning edition has greatly enriched knowledge of the sources, methods and significance of the *Vie de seint Clement*, both as an important hagiographic text and as a little known medieval re-working of early Church materials. We are very fortunate to have secured his expert translation for FRETS.

Acknowledgments

Completion of this translation marks the end of a project which began a number of years ago in the form of my edition of the *Vie de seint Clement*, and it is appropriate briefly to record once more my gratitude to some of the many who facilitated work on that edition. These include the staff of the Wren Library at Trinity College, Cambridge, and the Master and Fellows of the College who granted permission for publication of *Clement*; the Arts and Humanities Research Council, the British Academy, the Modern Humanities Research Association, and the former School of Languages, Linguistics, and Cultures at the University of Manchester, all of which offered essential financial support; and my esteemed colleagues Alison Williams, Marie-Laure Savoye, David Trotter†, Tony Hunt, and, in particular, Ian Short, all of whom have helped in various ways during my work.

For the present book, my particular gratitude is due to Thelma Fenster and Jocelyn Wogan-Browne, not only for agreeing to publish it in the French of England Translation Series, but especially for their patience in dealing with my many questions and for the invaluable feedback that they have offered.

My final thanks are due to my long-suffering family for their love and support. While I suspect that Stefanie, Antonia, and Daniel may feel that they have already heard far more about *Clement* than they would have wished, I hope that this translation will offer them all an opportunity to read and enjoy the text at their own pace, and will tide them over until they feel ready to tackle it in its original Anglo-Norman form.

LIST OF ABBREVIATIONS

AND   Rothwell, William, David Trotter, Stewart Gregory *et al. Anglo-Norman Dictionary* (electronic edition) [www.anglo-norman.net]

ANF   *The Ante-Nicene Fathers: Translation of the Writings of the Fathers down to A.D. 325*, ed. Alexander Roberts and James Donaldson, rev. Arthur Cleveland Coxe. 10 vols. Buffalo: Christian Literature Co., 1885–96.

ANTS   *Anglo-Norman Text Society*

BHL   *Bibliotheca hagiographica latina antiquae et mediae aetatis.* 2 vols. Subsidia hagiographica 6. Brussels: Socii Bollandiani, 1898–99; *Bibliotheca hagiographica latina antiquae et mediae aetatis.* Supplementum, Subsidia hagiographica 12. Brussels: Socii Bollandiani, 1911; Fros, Henricus. *Bibliotheca hagiographica latina antiquae et mediae aetatis.* Novum supplementum, Subsidia hagiographica 70. Brussels: Socii Bollandiani, 1986.

BL   *British Library*

Clement   *Vie de seint Clement*, ed. Daron Lee Burrows. 3 vols. ANTS 64–67. London: ANTS, 2007–10.

Dean   Dean, Ruth J. and Maureen B. M. Boulton. *Anglo-Norman Literature: a Guide to Texts and Manuscripts*, OPS 3. London: ANTS, 1999.

De origine   Leo Ostiensis. *De origine beati Clementis.* In *Excerpta ex Clementinis recognitionibus a Tyrannio Rufino translatis*, ed. Giovanni Orlandi. Testi e documenti per lo studio dell'antichità 24, 1–165. Milan: Istituto Editoriale Cisalpino, 1968.

EETS   *Early English Text Society*

Epistula   Rufinus of Aquileia. *Epistula Clementis ad Iacobum.* In *Die Pseudoklementinen II: Rekognitionen in Rufins Übersetzung*, ed. Bernhard Rehm. Die griechischen christlichen Schriftsteller der ersten Jahrhunderte 51, 373–87. Berlin: Akademie-Verlag, 1965.

FEW   Wartburg, Walther von *et al. Französisches etymologisches Wörterbuch: eine Darstellung des galloromanischen Sprachschatzes.* 25 vols. Bonn: Klopp, 1922-.

FRETS	*French of England Translation Series*
NPNF2	*A Select Library of the Nicene and Post-Nicene Fathers of the Christian Church, Second Series,* ed. Philip Schaff and Henry Wace. 14 vols. Oxford: Parker, 1890–1900.
OPS	*Occasional Publications Series*
Passio	Pseudo-Marcellus. *Passio sanctorum apostolorum Petri et Pauli.* In *Acta apostolorum apocrypha post Constantinum Tischendorf,* ed. Richard Adelbert Lipsius and Maximilian Bonnet, 1:119–77. Leipzig: Mendelssohn, 1891.
PL	*Patrologia Latina,* ed. Jacques-Paul Migne. 221 vols. Paris: Migne, 1844–1864.
PTS	*Plain Texts Series*
Recognitiones	Rufinus of Aquileia. *Recognitiones.* In *Die Pseudoklementinen II,* ed. Rehm, 1–371. [see *Epistula*]
SATF	*Sociéte des Anciens Textes Français*
St John	*The Life of St John the Almsgiver,* ed. Kenneth Urwin. 2 vols. ANTS 33–34. London: ANTS, 1980–81.
T-L	Tobler, Adolf, and Erhard Lommatzsch. *Altfranzösisches Wörterbuch.* 11 vols. Berlin / Stuttgart / Wiesbaden: Weidmann / Steiner, 1915–2002.
Vita	Johannes Hymmonides and Gauderic of Velletri. *Vita sancti Clementis.* In *Excerpta ex Clementinis recognitionibus,* ed. Orlandi, 1–165. [see *De origine*]

INTRODUCTION

Text

The *Vie de seint Clement*, written by an anonymous author in England in the first half of the 13th century, has a number of claims to fame.[1] Although the sole extant copy of the text is incomplete, it is still, at just short of 15000 lines in octosyllabic couplets, one of the longest hagiographical narratives in Anglo-Norman literature. Moreover, even though the text has received little attention from students of Pseudo-Clementine literature,[2] its first 14500 lines represent probably the most complete and faithful pre-modern translation of two key texts in the corpus,[3] namely the *Recognitiones* and the *Epistula Clementis ad Iacobum* of

---

[1] Dean no. 517; the base edition used is Daron Lee Burrows, ed., *La Vie de seint Clement*, 3 vols., ANTS 64–67 (London: ANTS, 2007–10). The first extracts from the text were published by Paul Meyer, "Notice d'un manuscrit de Trinity College (Cambridge) contenant les vies, en vers français, de saint Jean l'Aumônier et de saint Clément, pape," *Notices et extraits des manuscrits de la Bibliothèque Nationale* 38 (1903): 293–339, with the first full edition appearing in the unpublished doctoral thesis of Nora K. Willson, "Critical Edition of the *Vie de Saint Clement Pape*" (Ph.D., Newnham College, Cambridge, 1951). A text-only edition was published online by Delbert W. Russell, "La Vie de seint Clement, pape" (Waterloo: University of Waterloo, 2007) [http://margot.uwaterloo.ca/campsey/cmpclement_e.html].

[2] Bernhard Rehm, "Zur Entstehung der pseudoclementinischen Schriften," *Zeitschrift für neutestamentliche Wissenschaft* 37 (1938): 77–183, at 166 speaks of "eine altfranzösische Paraphrase in Versen," and Walter Ullmann, "The Significance of the *Epistola Clementis* in the Pseudo-Clementines," *Journal of Theological Studies* 11 (1960): 295–317, at 302, note 4 mentions "an Old French translation in metric form (14th century?)."

[3] Some parts of the disputations are incorporated into Edward Schröder, ed., *Die Kaiserchronik eines Regensburger Geistlichen*, Monumenta Germaniae Historica: Scriptores qui Vernacula Lingua Usi Sunt 1,1 (Hannover: Hahn, 1892); cf. Graeme Dunphy, "Die *wilsælde*-Disputation: zur Auseinandersetzung mit der Astrologie in der *Kaiserchronik*," *Zeitschrift für deutsche Philologie* 124 (2005): 1–22. Elements of the *Recognitiones* feature in Tirso de Molina's *Trionfos de la verdad*, of which the disputations are available in Luis Vázquez, ed., *Tirso de Molina: Diálogos teológicos y otros versos diseminados*, Teatro del Siglo de Oro: Ediciones Críticas 15 (Kassel: Reichenberger, 1988), 95–193, but this is a far less extensive version which presents a number of crucial differences; cf. André Nougué, *L'Œuvre en prose de Tirso de Molina: "Los cigarrales de Toledo" et "Deleytar aprovechan-*

Rufinus of Aquileia, both of great importance to early Church history and the question of Jewish Christianity.

While it is accurate to describe our text as a hagiographical narrative, since it provides an account of the deeds and words of saintly protagonists, the title of *Vie de seint Clement*— adopted for convenience of reference by modern scholarship in the absence of any *titulus* in the manuscript[1] — may be a little misleading if one approaches it with expectations predicated on previous experience of famous hagiographical legends such as the lives of Alexis, Laurence, or George. While the text does describe the early years of Pope St Clement I of Rome (d. c. CE 100), his conversion to Christianity, and the process of education and enlightenment which culminates in his eventual reluctant appointment as Bishop of Rome, it is not a conventional biographical *vita* focussing on his exemplary life and triumph over the trials of adversity or temptation. Nor, although the rich tradition associated with Clement would provide plentiful material in this vein, does our text include his glorious *passio*, the subsequent *miracula* witnessed and *visiones* experienced by those who survived him, or the *inventio* and *translatio* of his relics.[2] In fact, the main narrative action in which Clement is directly involved could be termed a family romance,[3] centred around the tragic separation and gradual reunion of his family, culminating in their integration into the larger family of the *corpus Christianorum*. Within this framework, the main protagonist and focus of attention is in reality the individual responsible for reuniting Clement and his family: St Peter.

---

do", Thèses, Mémoires et Travaux 1 (Paris: Centre de Recherches de l'Institut d'Etudes Hispaniques, 1962), 223–31. The early 13th-century *Clemens saga* presents a drastically abbreviated version of the *Recognitiones* (with numerous modifications), followed by a version of the passion of St Clement; cf. Helen Carron, ed., *Clemens saga: the Life of St Clement of Rome*, Viking Society for Northern Research Text Series 17 (London: Viking Society for Northern Research, 2005); Dietrich Hofmann, *Die Legende von Sankt Clemens in den skandinavischen Ländern im Mittelalter*, Beiträge zur Skandinavistik 13 (Frankfurt am Main: Peter Lang, 1997), 72–108.

[1] On the evolution of the modern title, see Burrows, *Clement*, 3:vii.

[2] The most comprehensive overview of the kinds and constituent elements of a saint's biography is offered by Walter Berschin, *Biographie und Epochenstil im lateinischen Mittelalter*, 5 vols., Quellen und Untersuchungen zur lateinischen Philologie des Mittelalters 8, 9, 10, 12, 15 (Stuttgart: Hiersemann, 1986–2004).

[3] Cf. Jocelyn Wogan-Browne, "'Bet . . . to . . . Rede on Holy Seyntes Lyves . . .': Romance and Hagiography Again," in *Readings in Medieval English Romance*, ed. Carol A Meale (Cambridge & Rochester: Brewer, 1994), 83–97. On the significance of the family in the principal Latin source for *Clement*, see Kate Cooper, "Matthidia's Wish: Division, Reunion, and the Early Christian Family in the Pseudo-Clementine *Recognitions*," in *Narrativity in Biblical and Related Texts*, ed. George J. Brooke and Jean-Daniel Kaestli, Bibliotheca Ephemeridum theologicarum Lovaniensium 149 (Leuven: Leuven University Press, 2000), 243–64.

Following the model offered by its Pseudo-Clementine sources, the bulk of the so-called *Vie de seint Clement* consists in an account of the campaign waged by St Peter, with the support of his loyal disciples, against the despicable heresiarch Simon Magus, with much of the text—although still significantly less than in the sources—devoted to the lengthy speeches in which St Peter imparts his moral and doctrinal wisdom. That St Peter is the true focus of our text is confirmed by the manner in which Clement, upon being appointed Bishop of Rome, simply disappears, as the narrative proceeds beyond the Pseudo-Clementine sources not by following the tradition of Clement's martyrdom and miracles, but instead by turning to the *Passio Petri et Pauli* of Pseudo-Marcellus, which offers an account of St Peter's ultimate victory over Simon and the martyrdom that this earns for him and St Paul at the hands of Nero.

Summary of Text

Despite the text's length, *Clement*'s narrative content can be summarised relatively succinctly. The tale begins by recounting the tragedy which befalls a powerful family in Rome when the brother of the paterfamilias Faustinianus attempts to seduce the latter's wife, Matthidia. To avoid scandal, Matthidia claims that she has been warned in a vision that she must sail from Rome with two of her sons, the twins Faustus and Faustinus, or face certain death. She leaves their youngest son, Clement, as a comfort for his grieving father in Rome, but disaster soon befalls the travellers when a storm wrecks the ship, killing the mariners and separating the mother from her twins. Matthidia is cast alone onto the island of Aradus, where, unable to find her sons, whom she presumes dead, she finds lodging with a kindly widow, but her sorrow drives her to maim her hands by gnawing them, and when her companion is stricken by palsy, she is constrained to beg for their sustenance. The brothers, by contrast, are hauled from the sea by pirates, who rename them Niceta and Aquila and sell them to a widow in Caesarea by the name of Justa, who ensures that they are educated. There the brothers befriend and support a wicked upstart called Simon Magus, who lays false claim to divinity, but they are saved from catastrophe by the intervention of Zacchaeus, who initiates their conversion to Christianity and sends them to join St Peter. In the meantime, Faustinianus, despairing at the lack of news regarding his wife and sons, sets out from Rome in search of them, leaving Clement there under guardianship.

As Clement matures, he is increasingly beset by religious doubts, until Barnabas, a follower of St Peter, happens to come to Rome to preach the word of God, thus revealing to Clement the truth that he has been seeking. Clement saves Barnabas from a hostile and impious crowd, and follows his new friend to Caesarea, where he meets St Peter on the eve of his scheduled disputation with Simon Magus. St Peter offers religious instruction to Clement, while his followers Niceta and Aquila reveal Simon's treacherous past; the changes wrought by the years which have passed since the twins last saw Clement prevent the three brothers from recognising each other. In the disputation with Simon, St Peter soundly defeats his opponent by exposing his treachery, and the necromancer flees to Tripolis. St Peter remains in Caesarea to convert the people, but sends followers ahead to counter Simon's evil machinations. By the time that St Peter reaches Tripolis, Simon has fled to Syria, granting to the apostle the opportunity to convert the city's inhabitants. Before they depart for Antioch, St Peter baptises Clement. When they reach Antaradus after a journey slowed by crowds of supporters, St Peter sends ahead to Laodicea all his principal followers except Clement, and it is at this point that Clement reveals what he knows of the disasters which befell his family. The next day, St Peter and his remaining entourage head to the nearby island of Aradus, where St Peter encounters a beggar woman with maimed hands who reveals the woes that she has suffered. When it becomes clear that the woman is Matthidia, St Peter reunites her with Clement, and when they proceed to Laodicea, the telling of her story inspires Niceta and Aquila to reveal their true identity, leading to a joyful reunion which is capped by Matthidia's baptism.

As Peter and his followers pray by the sea one day, an old labourer approaches them in order to apprise them of the futility of their actions. They begin a series of disputations centred on the old man's belief that genesis rather than providence governs the course of an individual's life. When the old man, repeatedly defeated in the debates, reveals the personal tragedies which have shaped his beliefs, it becomes clear that he is Faustinianus, and by steps the whole family is joyfully reunited. The disputation then continues, exposing the folly of classical mythology, until word comes that Simon Magus has arrived from Antioch, together with his followers Anubion and Appion, old acquaintances of Faustinianus whom he hastens to visit.

When Faustinianus returns, his family is aghast to see that he has acquired Simon's face, although St Peter can still see his true appearance. There then comes from Antioch a messenger who reveals that Simon's campaign of slander has turned the people against St Peter. He is soon followed by Anubion, who announces that Simon has fled to Judaea, and explains the means whereby Simon transformed Faustinianus. St Peter develops his own counter-ruse, and sends Faustinianus, with a reluctant Matthidia and the twins, ahead to Antioch, to disavow Simon's criticism of St Peter whilst he bears the necromancer's appearance. After their departure, allies of Simon come in search of Faustinianus, but St Peter and his followers pretend that the only visitor to the camp appeared to be Simon, who, when they refused to believe his claims to be Faustinianus, left disconsolate and threatening suicide.

In Antioch, Faustinianus executes St Peter's subterfuge; the people turn their hatred towards Simon, and wish for St Peter to come. As a reward, Christ restores Faustinianus's true face, and when Simon comes in an attempt to salvage his plot, the people eject him from the city. When news of this reaches St Peter, he completes his business in Laodicea and heads for Antioch. He works miracles there, and the people honour him by placing him on the chair in a newly consecrated church. The narrative involving Clement's family derived from the *Recognitiones* concludes with the baptism of the converted Faustinianus.

The text continues with the events of the *Epistula*, as St Peter leaves Antioch and heads for Rome. Having learnt from God that he is to die there, he appoints an unwilling Clement as his successor as Bishop of Rome, and dispenses plentiful advice to him and his new subjects. Clement's final part in the tale is to agree to send an account of his time with St Peter to St James the Less.

In the final section, based on the *Passio*, St Peter proceeds to convert many Romans, including a number of women whom he persuades to forsake their husbands' beds, much to the men's discontent. He is joined by St Paul, who is duly incarcerated. Also in Rome is Simon Magus, who through various deceptions, notably including a feigned resurrection involving the decapitation of a sheep, persuades the Emperor Nero that he is the Son of God. On Simon's request, Nero summons St Peter and St Paul, but Simon's attempts to discredit them and to prove his divinity are thwarted when he fails to demonstrate the omniscience required to read St Peter's thoughts, whereas St Peter shows himself quite capable of the contrary when he undertakes ingenious preparations which allow him to repel an attack by hellhounds that the humiliated Simon summons. The text breaks off after some 500 lines of the *Passio*, at a point where Nero acknowledges defeat, and Simon seeks to explain away his failure. The missing ending would presumably have been that of the *Passio*, in which Simon attempts to fly up to God, his purported father, from a tower built for this purpose, only to fall to his death when St Peter and St Paul through their prayers drive away the demons who bear him aloft, an act which earns them martyrdom through inverted crucifixion and decapitation respectively.

Manuscript

The sole extant copy of *Clement* survives on fols. 122r-357v of Cambridge, Trinity College, R.3.46.[1] The text is incomplete, breaking off without obvious reason halfway down fol. 356r. The consequent assumption that this copy is not the original is strengthened by two features potentially suggestive of recourse to multiple exemplars: first, the scribes include, in the margin or between lines, a score of alternative (but similar) readings, ranging in length from one word to several; and second, a marked change in the regularity of the poem's metre in the final third of the poem may be explained by use of a different copy (see below).

---

[1] For a full description of the manuscript, see Burrows, *Clement*, 3:1–7.

The manuscript dates from the mid-13th century, but nothing is known of its history prior to its donation to Trinity by Thomas Nevile (1568/9–1615), who became Master of the College in 1593, in the midst of an illustrious career which also saw him serve as Dean of Peterborough and of Canterbury, Master of Magdalene College, and Vice Chancellor of the University. Preserved in a 17th-century leather binding, the manuscript comprises 372 vellum folios in 32 quires, with pages of an average size of 103mm x 185mm presenting a single column usually containing 32 lines of text. There are no illustrations, and decoration throughout is minimal and functional, with the clear pragmatic aim of guiding reading. *Clement* begins with a 4-line blue majuscule followed by a 3-line red majuscule to indicate the start of the main narrative, both with pen-flourishing; major sections thereafter are introduced by 2-line initials (111 in total, with sporadic pen-flourishing), and sub-sections by 1-line initials (390 in total; 6 have been omitted), with red and blue usually alternating. Brown wash, or occasionally red, has been applied to majuscules in the initial column, and to some 600 letters outside this column, chiefly the first letter of proper nouns.

Clement is the second of three texts in the manuscript, all of them presented without *titulus*. It is preceded on fols. 1r–121v by the sole extant copy of the Anglo-Norman *Life of St John the Almsgiver*, an anonymous early 13th-century translation in 7702 lines of octosyllabic couplets of the widely disseminated Latin translation by Anastasius Bibliothecarius of the Greek *vita* authored by Leontius, Bishop of Neapolis.[1] *Clement* is followed on fols. 358r–372v by a copy of the *Passio Petri et Pauli* of Pseudo-Marcellus, the very same widely disseminated prose text which serves as the source for the final 500 lines of *Clement* and which through its inclusion provides, albeit in Latin, the narrative content—the ultimate defeat of Simon and the martyrdom of Peter and Paul—that the incomplete copy of *Clement* lacks.

The texts have been copied by three scribes: Scribe 1, who copied all of *St John* and fols. 278r–289v of *Clement* (quire 24 of the manuscript); Scribe 2, who copied the rest of *Clement*; and Scribe 3, who copied the *Passio*. While the three hands can be distinguished in their production of a relatively informal Gothic textualis rotunda, there are sufficient similarities across a range of features (e.g., patterns in use of variant letter forms, *litterae elongatae*, abbreviation, punctuation, diacritics on vowels, etc.) to suspect that they belonged to the same scriptorium, not least as one finds across the manuscript the same revisor signalling in plummet corrections which have then been effected in ink. In concert with the complementarity of the texts, this collaboration serves to create an impression of a deliberately conceived hagiographical anthology.

---

[1] Dean no. 535; Kenneth Urwin, ed., *The Life of Saint John the Almsgiver*, 2 vols., ANTS 33–34 (London: ANTS, 1980–81).

Sources

Clement does not stem from a single extant source.[1] The prologue states that it is translated from the *Livre Clement* ("*Book of Clement*," v. 58) or *Petri Itinerarium* ("*Journey of Peter*," v. 60), and from the accompanying description of this as a Latin narrative by St Clement about St Peter's travels, ministry, and disputation with Simon Magus, and about the separation and reunion of Clement and his family, it is clear that the source in question—which accounts for the majority of *Clement* (vv. 1–13184)—is the Pseudo-Clementine *Recognitiones*, translated in the early 5th century by Rufinus of Aquileia (c. 340–410) from a lost Greek source. The following account (vv. 13185–14500) of Peter's appointment of an unwilling Clement as Bishop of Rome and of the advice that he offers is no less recognisably another Pseudo-Clementine text, the *Epistula Clementis ad Iacobum*, translated from Greek by the same Rufinus shortly before he wrote the *Recognitiones*.[2] The closing, incomplete account of Peter and Paul's final conflict with Simon in Rome (vv. 14501–994) stems from the *Passio sanctorum apostolorum Petri et Pauli* conventionally attributed to Pseudo-Marcellus.[3]

Pseudo-Clementine Material

Both the *Recognitiones* and the *Epistula* belong to a larger corpus of texts, which includes the Greek *Homilies* and two later Greek epitomes, spuriously attributed to Pope St Clement I of Rome. While *Clement*'s translator claims that his source is *poi usez* ("little known," v. 57), the *Recognitiones* in reality enjoyed a vast dissemination, surviving in more than a hundred manuscripts dating from the 5th to the 14th century.[4] The *Epistula* was often transmitted together with the *Recognitiones*, but also on its own, and elements of it achieved even wider dissemina-

---

[1] Further specific details of the treatment of sources are provided in the Notes and Appendix.

[2] *BHL* 6644, 6645, 6646, 6647; both the *Recognitiones* and *Epistula* are in Bernhard Rehm, ed., *Die Pseudoklementinen II: Rekognitionen in Rufins Übersetzung*, Die griechischen christlichen Schriftsteller der ersten Jahrhunderte 51 (Berlin: Akademie-Verlag, 1965). It is generally assumed that the lost source of the *Recognitiones* was written in Syria during the 4th century, and that both it and the related *Homilies* were based on a common *Grundschrift*; cf. Frederick Stanley Jones, "The Pseudo-Clementines: a History of Research," *Second Century* 2 (1982): 1–33, 63–96. On fragments in other languages, see Franz Paschke, *Die beiden griechischen Klementinen-Epitomen und ihre Anhänge: Überlieferungsgeschichtliche Vorarbeiten zu einer Neuausgabe der Texte*, Texte und Untersuchungen zur Geschichte der altchristlichen Literatur 90 (Berlin: Akademie-Verlag, 1966), 74–78.

[3] *BHL* 6657; Richard Adelbert Lipsius and Maximilian Bonnet, eds., *Acta apostolorum apocrypha post Constantinum Tischendorf*, 3 vols. (Leipzig: Mendelssohn, 1891–1903), 1:119–77.

[4] Cf. Rehm, *Recognitiones*, xvii–cvii.

tion through their integration into the false decretals of Pseudo-Isidore, and subsequent use by such notables as Pope Gregory VII, Ivo of Chartres, and Gratian.[1]

One of the key questions is, however, in what form our translator consulted his Pseudo-Clementine sources, for although *Clement* in many respects follows Rufinus closely, there are some significant differences: the first-person *ego Clemens* is replaced by a third-person narrator; a lengthy expository narrative detailing the separation of Clement's family is inserted, thereby substituting *ordo naturalis* for the source's *ordo artificialis*; large portions of the *Recognitiones* are omitted; and the epistolary framework of the *Epistula* is suppressed. While each of these differences could be explained as direct modification of Rufinus's work by our translator, it is natural to wonder whether he might instead have been working from an intermediary source which already presented these differences.

There were numerous medieval Latin adaptations of Rufinus, the most widely disseminated being the *De sancto Clemente* found in the *Legenda aurea* of Jacobus de Voragine (c. 1230–98).[2] Although Jacobus's version resembles *Clement* in its use of the third person, insertion of an exposition, and omission of sermons and disputations, it can quickly be discounted as *Clement*'s source, since it was almost certainly written later than our text, contains but a fraction of Rufinus,[3] and ends not with Peter's conflict with Simon in Rome, but rather an account of Clement's exile and death,[4] followed by the discovery of his remains

---

[1] Cf. Ullmann, "The significance of the *Epistola Clementis*," 302–5.

[2] *BHL* 1852; Giovanni Paolo Maggioni, ed., *Legenda aurea*, 2nd ed., 2 vols., Millennio Medievale 6, Testi 3 (Tavarnuzze: SISMEL: Edizioni del Galluzzo, 1998), 2:1188–202. The translation of the *Legenda aurea* as the *Légende dorée*, first by Jean de Vignay in the mid-14th century and then by Jean Batallier in 1476, secured the widest circulation of the life of Clement in French; cf. Brenda Dunn-Lardeau, ed., *La Légende dorée: Edition critique dans la révision de 1476 par Jean Batallier d'après la traduction de Jean de Vignay (1333–1348) de la Legenda aurea (c. 1261–1266)*, Textes de la Renaissance 19 (Paris: Champion, 1997), 1091–103.

[3] On his sources, see Barbara Fleith, "Die *Legenda Aurea* und ihre dominikanischen Bruderlegendare: Aspekte der Quellenverhältnisse apokryphen Gedankenguts," *Apocrypha* 7 (1996): 167–92, at 182–84; Rémi Gounelle, "Sens et usage d'*apocryphus* dans la *Légende dorée*," *Apocrypha* 5 (1994): 189–210.

[4] The passion of Clement (*BHL* 1848) is widely disseminated, with an abbreviated form often appearing in Latin legendaries; cf. Boninus Mombritius, *Sanctuarium, seu Vitae Sanctorum*, 2nd ed., 2 vols. (Paris: [n.p.], 1910), 1:131–34. On French legendaries, see Jean-Pierre Perrot, *Le Passionnaire français au Moyen Age*, Publications Romanes et Françaises 200 (Geneva: Droz, 1992), 22, 99, 170–71, with extracts 218–20, 303–4. Clement's passion recounts that, having been exiled to the Chersonese by Trajan in the late 1st century, he was put to work in a quarry, where the plight of his thirsty fellow prisoners led him to pray for them. A lamb appeared on a nearby hill, and when Clement struck the ground where it had stood with a pickaxe, a stream of water poured forth. As people converted in droves, Clement was punished by being tied to an anchor and cast into the

and their translation to Rome. The source for this final section is the *Translatio Clementis* or *Legenda italica* of Leo of Ostia (1046–c. 1115), alias Leo Marsicanus, cardinal-bishop of Velletri from 1105.[1] The *Translatio* is, we learn from its prologue, the third part of a trilogy of which the second part, which would appear to have been a version of the *Epistula*,[2] has been lost, but of which the first part, *De origine beati Clementis*, survives in a single copy in the same manuscript as the *Translatio*. Like Jacobus's version, *De origine* presents third-person narration and an exposition, but is also substantially longer and at times very close to the *Recognitiones*. Yet while Leo's work is still too abbreviated to have served as a source for *Clement*,[3] the same cannot be said with such certainty of Leo's own principal source: the *Vita sancti Clementis* (*BHL* 1851).[4]

This *Vita* was written in the period 876–82, shortly after the discovery of Clement's relics and their return to Rome.[5] Its preface reveals that Gauderic, bishop of Velletri from 867–79 and an ardent supporter of the rising cult of Clement in Rome, had asked Johannes Hymmonides to compose a life of Clement from existing sources,[6] but when Hymmonides died before finishing the work,

---

sea, with the shrine which contained his bones being miraculously revealed every year by the withdrawing sea.

[1] *BHL* 2073; Paul Meyvaert and Paul Devos, "Trois énigmes cyrillo-méthodiennes de la *Légende italique* résolues," *Analecta Bollandiana* 73 (1955): 375–461, at 455–61. Leonard E. Boyle, "Dominican Lectionaries and Leo of Ostia's *Translatio s. Clementis*," *Archivum Fratrum Praedicatorum* 28 (1958): 362–94 argues that Jacobus may have worked from the abbreviated version of the narrative found in Dominican lectionaries.

[2] Cf. Meyvaert and Devos, "Trois énigmes," 412–13. A single introductory fragment of this *Sermo de ordinatione seu cathedra s. Clementis papae* (*BHL* 1851ad) survives; cf. Paul Meyvaert and Paul Devos, "Autour de Léon d'Ostie et de sa *Translatio S. Clementis* (légende italique des ss. Cyrille et Methode)," *Analecta Bollandiana* 74 (1956): 189–241, at 225–26.

[3] One assumes that the same would apply to the lost *Sermo de ordinatione*, and it is certainly so for the abridged accounts of Clement's ordination (*BHL* 6647d; cf. *BHL* 1847m) which do survive; cf. Meyvaert and Devos, "Trois énigmes," 432.

[4] On Leo's disingenuous claims that he in fact used Rufinus, see Meyvaert and Devos, "Trois énigmes," 433–34.

[5] During a mission amongst the Slavs in the company of his brother Methodius, Constantine the Philosopher (later St Cyril) re-discovered Clement's shrine, from which he rescued the relics in January 861. In 867/8, the brothers entered Rome with Clement's relics, which were received by Pope Adrian II and then transferred to the Basilica di san Clemente. Cf. Paul Meyvaert and Paul Devos, "La date de la première rédaction de la *Légende italique*," in *Cyrillo-Methodiana: zur Frühgeschichte des Christentums bei den Slaven 863–1963*, ed. Manfred Hellmann *et al.*, Slavistische Forschungen 6 (Cologne: Böhlau, 1964), 57–71, at 58–59; Bronwen Neil, "The Cult of Pope Clement in Ninth-Century Rome," *Ephemerides Liturgicae* 117 (2003): 103–13.

[6] Cf. Girolamo Arnaldi, "Giovanni Immonide e la cultura a Roma al tempo di Giovanni VIII," *Bullettino dell'Istituto storico italiano per il medio evo* 68 (1956): 33–89;

Gauderic completed the remainder and organised it into three books. A single large fragment of the *Vita* survives, with a preface which indicates that it stems from the first part of a trilogy which clearly resembled that written by Leo of Ostia. The fragment covers the *Recognitiones* to X.58, just fourteen chapters from its end, at greater length and with greater fidelity than Leo's *De origine*; the missing second part, the version of the *Epistula*, would presumably have been similar in approach. Since it also inserts an exposition and uses third-person narrative, and since a translation of its extended verbatim extracts from the *Recognitiones* would be indistinguishable from a direct translation of Rufinus, the *Vita* clearly merits consideration as a possible source for *Clement*.[1]

The first point of interest is naturally the exposition, which in both texts is derived from speeches by Clement, Matthidia, St Peter, and Niceta and Aquila which are not delivered until Book VII of the *Recognitiones*. While the basic content of both is very similar, *Clement* is generally more expansive and emotive, and presents a number of narrative details absent from the *Vita*, such as features of Simon's wonders (vv. 389–98), the rescue of the twins by Zacchaeus (vv. 403–16), a list of the items taken on board the ship (vv. 453–56), and comments on Clement's formative years (vv. 687–736). The *Vita* likewise contains features absent from *Clement*: a history of the Roman emperors (I.1); geographical information (I.3, I.6); Faustinianus's belief in astrological causes (I.16); and a duration of twenty years for the travails of Matthidia and Faustinianus (I.5, I.17). There are also structural differences: *Clement* recounts the fate of Niceta and Aquila (vv. 313–74) before that of Matthidia, whereas the order is reversed in the *Vita*; the *Vita* (I.8–13) alone places in the exposition the account of Simon's betrayal of Dositheus, which appears in the main body of *Clement* (vv. 2145–406); in *Clement*, the brother's lie (vv. 607–42) precedes Faustinianus's enquiries, whereas in the *Vita* (I.16) it follows them; and in the *Vita* (I.4) Matthidia gnaws her hands on an occasion prior to the act of self-mutilation described in *Clement* (vv. 507–10).

Turning to the main body of *Clement* and the *Vita*, a broadly similar pattern emerges in respect of the treatment of the *Recognitiones*. On the one hand, both texts omit or abbreviate with notable frequency the same major sections,[2] and they even present similar minor differences of detail, such as excluding St

---

Ferruccio Bertini, "Giovanni Immonide e la cultura a Roma nel secolo IX," in *Roma nell'alto medioevo*, ed. Adriano Prandi, Settimane di studio del Centro Italiano di Studi sull'Alto Medioevo 48 (Spoleto: Centro Italiano di Studi sull'Alto Medioevo, 2001), 897–919.

[1] The possibility was considered but dismissed by Meyer, "Notice d'un manuscrit," 310.

[2] E.g., *Rec.* I.22–74, II.1–2, II.17–18, IV.8–VI.15.1, VIII.9–33, VIII.41.2–43.4, VIII.45–56, VIII.59–60; see notes to vv. 1751–832, 1845–82, 2451–94, 5135–306, 5307–58, 7531–604, 8023–30, 8119–220, 8327–50.

Peter's establishment of an order of widows and his allusion to the removal of sinning members.[1] On the other hand, *Clement* also includes a number of sections that the *Vita* omits,[2] just as the *Vita* does not present certain omissions seen in *Clement*.[3] Moreover, vv. 1421–616 and 8693–818 of *Clement* present innovations which have no equivalent in the *Vita*, nor does *Clement* in vv. 7531–604 and 11925–12326 feature the reorganisation of material seen in *Vita* II.9 and II.72–80. There are also further differences stemming from the texts' relationship to the manuscript transmission of the *Recognitiones*,[4] with *Clement* clearly drawing on the English branch Θ,[5] while the *Vita* seems to be dependent on the Italian branch Λ.[6]

A final point of interest involves the figure of Anastasius Bibliothecarius (c. 810–79), the librarian of the Roman Church appointed by Pope John VIII, who appears to have been closely involved in the promotion of the cult of Clement in Rome.[7] He translated Greek material for Johannes Hymmonides,[8] and for Gauderic of Velletri he translated Constantine's brief account of the discovery of Clement's relics and a sermon by him, as he reveals in a letter of which the sole extant copy, in MS Lisbon, Biblioteca nacional 342 (*olim* Alcobaça 205), intriguingly precedes copies of the *Epistula* and *Recognitiones*.[9] Although these

---

[1] See notes to vv. 5355–56, 6919–22.

[2] E.g., *Rec.* VIII.40 (vv. 7885–946), IX.38 (vv. 9993–10130), X.15–51 (vv. 10897–11924), and much of II.20–IV.7 (vv. 2543–5134).

[3] E.g., of *Rec.* VII.26–27, X.7–12.

[4] For the stemmata, see Rehm, *Recognitiones*, xvii–c.

[5] On the score of manuscripts involved, see Rehm, *Recognitiones*, lxxii–lxxx. For the readings which prove this affiliation, see the notes to vv. 355, 2095, 2119, 4169–70, 5836, and 7546.

[6] Cf. Orlandi, *Vita*, xii–xv.

[7] Cf. Girolamo Arnaldi, "Anastasio Bibliotecario," in *Dizionario biografico degli italiani* (Rome: Istituto della Enciclopedia Italiana, 1961), 25–37; Claudio Leonardi, "L'agiografia romana nel secolo IX," in *Hagiographie, cultures et sociétés, IVe–XIIe siècles: Actes du colloque organisé à Nanterre et à Paris (2–5 mai 1979)*, ed. Evelyne Patlagean and Pierre Riché (Paris: Etudes Augustiniennes, 1981), 471–90; Bronwen Neil, *Seventh-Century Popes and Martyrs: the Political Hagiography of Anastasius Bibliothecarius*, Studia Antiqua Australiensia 2 (Turnhout: Brepols, 2006), 11–34.

[8] Epist. 9 (874), in Ernst Perels and Gerhard Laehr, eds., *Epistolae Karolini aevi*, Monumenta Germaniae Historica: Epistolae 7 (Berlin: Weidmann, 1928), 422–26; newly edited in Neil, *Seventh-Century Popes and Martyrs*, 148–61.

[9] Epist. 15 (875), in Perels and Laehr, *Epistolae Karolini aevi*, 435–38. Cf. Johann Friedrich, "Ein Brief des Anastasius Bibliothecarius an den Bischof Gaudericus von Velletri über die Abfassung der *Vita cum translatione s. Clementis Papae*. Eine neue Quelle zur Cyrillus- und Methodius-Frage," *Sitzungsberichte der Bayerischen Akademie der Wissenschaften, phil.-hist. Klasse* 1892 (1892): 393–442; Meyvaert and Devos, "Trois énigmes," 399–405; Neil, "The Cult of Pope Clement," 104.

translations are lost, it is very likely that they provided the material for the final part of the *Vita*.[1] While Anastasius's promotion of Clement may be attributable to 9th-century papal politics,[2] his particular importance for *Clement* stems from his activity as a translator of Greek religious texts, especially hagiography.[3] One of these translations is the *Vita sancti Joannis eleemosynarii*, from the Greek original by Leontius of Neapolis;[4] in other words, the very source for the Anglo-Norman *Life of Saint John the Almsgiver* which precedes *Clement* in Trinity, R.3.46. Anastasius's role in the production of Latin lives of SS John and Clement may constitute one of the reasons why the two translations appear side-by-side in our manuscript.

In conclusion, while it is not impossible that the authors of *Clement* and the *Vita* decided independently, and four centuries apart, to rework the *Recognitiones* in such similar ways, some kind of affiliation seems more likely. The translator of *Clement* might have used the *Vita*—perhaps even a copy of it which differed from the sole extant fragment—whilst choosing at times to suppress, amplify, and innovate, or he may have had access to a lost Latin adaptation of the *Vita*. He might equally have used a version of the *Vita*, but in conjunction with an Θ copy of the *Recognitiones*,[5] a possibility suggested by his frequent acknowledgement of omissions and abbreviations relative to Rufinus, which have no equivalent in the *Vita*, and by the summaries of omitted material, as in vv. 1751–1832 and 7533–604, which give the impression of being derived from a table of contents or from skim-read rubrics. In the absence of conclusive evidence, however, the precise role played by an intermediary in *Clement*'s composition must remain conjectural.

---

[1] They are mentioned by Leo of Ostia as a source for his *Translatio*; cf. Meyvaert and Devos, "Trois énigmes," 413.

[2] Neil, "The Cult of Pope Clement," 111–13 argues that Clement's particular importance for a papacy in the later 9th century seeking to assert its authority lay in the fact that Clement's direct appointment by St Peter, as described in the *Epistula*, supported a doctrine of papal primacy which relied on an interpretation of the pope as the proxy of Peter; indeed, Neil even suggests that Anastasius may have been involved in the production of the forged decretals into which the *Epistula* was incorporated.

[3] On Anastasius's corpus, see Neil, *Seventh-Century Popes and Martyrs*, 35–91. Interestingly, the sole copy of Leo's *Translatio* is followed by Anastasius's version of the life of St Stephen the Protomartyr (*BHL* 7858); cf. Orlandi, *Vita*, xix.

[4] *BHL* 4388; *PL* 73:337–84.

[5] Orlandi, *Vita*, xxiii–xxv argues that Leo of Ostia may similarly have used Gauderic, but with Rufinus to hand.

Passio Petri et Pauli

Although *Clement* differs from the *Legenda aurea*, and presumably the *Vita* and *De origine*, in that Clement's ordination is followed by an account not of his martyrdom and miracles, but rather of Peter and Paul's conflict with Nero in Rome, such a combination of Pseudo-Clementine material with the apostles' passion is by no means unprecedented. In the first book of the 6th-century *Historiae apostolicae* of Pseudo-Abdias,[1] for example, we find elements of the *Recognitiones* and *Epistula* followed by a version of the Pseudo-Linus passion of Peter,[2] and in vernacular legendaries, the prose *Passion de saint Pierre II* and *Passion de saint Pierre III* also offer broadly comparable combinations, although they clearly have no genetic affiliation to *Clement*.[3]

Amongst the numerous versions of the passion of Peter and Paul, the final section of *Clement* is most clearly related to that of Pseudo-Marcellus. The relationship between the two texts is, however, problematic. Initially, the differences are considerable: *Clement* replaces Peter and Paul's discussions with Jews and gentiles by a description of their arrival in Rome (vv. 14501–36); introduces the innovation that Paul is imprisoned while Peter roams free (vv. 14537–76); reworks the material included in vv. 14601–14 and 14677–86; repositions the tale of the decapitated sheep (vv. 14615–76); and omits the letter from Pontius Pilate. After approximately v. 14713, however, there are fewer differences, with the final lines of *Clement* being close to the *Passio*.

The reasons underlying *Clement*'s treatment of the *Passio* are unclear. Our translator may himself have chosen the *Passio* as a suitable vehicle for continuing his Pseudo-Clementine material, but preferred to adapt as he saw fit. More likely is that he used a lost source which already presented the changes to Pseudo-Marcellus that we find in our text. Indeed, this version might already have been appended to a narrative resembling the *Vita* of Gauderic and Hymmonides, with *Clement* a faithful rendering of a single lost composite source. Another mystery concerns why the copy of *Clement* is incomplete, with the translation breaking off when nearly forty chapters of the *Passio* still remain. If treated like the preceding chapters, this material could have required a further thousand lines of verse translation, far more than the hundred or so lines left blank in the final quire of *Clement*. Given the paucity of evidence available, it is unlikely that this conundrum will be solved.

---

[1] *BHL* 6663; John Allen Giles, ed., *Codex Apocryphus Novi Testamenti* (London: [Author's private press], 1852), 2:256–77.

[2] *BHL* 6655; Lipsius and Bonnet, *Acta apostolorum*, 1:1–22.

[3] On these and similar texts, see Burrows, *Clement*, 3:53–55.

Translation Technique

While the precise form in which our author consulted his sources remains uncertain, the strategy that he has adopted in translating them is described at some length in his prologue. He presents his work first and foremost as a stirring and action-packed tale of separation and reunion,[1] promising to abridge and reorganise the sermons and disputations of his source material for a variety of reasons: he has no knowledge of the discipline of *astronomie*; the speeches are too long and might prove tedious; and the vernacular cannot do justice to the complex beauty of Latin (vv. 47–118). While such a mixture of modesty and pragmatism is standard fare for a *captatio benevolentiae*, this is, in fact, the strategy to which our translator generally adheres.

When he omits a major section of the *Recognitiones*, our translator usually signals it explicitly, mostly in the first person and with a justification consonant with the reasons provided in the prologue: he is unwilling or unable to say any more, as in *Entur cest mult dist seint Pierre, / E plus que ci ne voille dire* (lit.: "St Peter said a great deal about this, and more than I am prepared to say here," vv. 3373–74; cf. vv. 4127–28, 5291–92, 6919–22, etc.); he wishes to avoid boring or vexing his audience, as in *Dit le ai des einz prolixement, / Partant le ai mis ci plus briefment, / Kar a ennui porreit turner / De trop suvent un rehercer* (lit.: "I said it at length previously, and so I have mentioned it here more briefly, for it could be a source of irritation to repeat the same thing very often," vv. 6447–50; cf. vv. 2485–86, 8215–20, 8559–74, etc.); and he omits material of no profit to the audience, such as pagan astrology and mythology, as in vv. 9045–50 and 11614–16. The resulting impression of painstaking fidelity is further enhanced by his readiness to profess his ignorance when faced with a gap in his sources, with the formulaic admission *Ne sai* ("I do not know") recurring with notable frequency (vv. 5067, 6140, 9958, etc.). Such is his fidelity that it is a surprise when, discovering that his much vaunted *essemplaire* ("source") does not specify whether Clement and the twins are happy to be reunited or whether St Peter saw fit to heal their mother's maimed hands, he has the audacity to speculate that all three were delighted and that St Peter, who performed miracles for strangers, would surely

---

[1] While adaptations such as *Clement*, *Vita*, and *De origine* manifest similar enthusiasm for the narrative content of the *Recognitiones*, Pseudo-Clementine scholarship has not always appreciated this aspect of the text. Notable exceptions include Mark J. Edwards, "The *Clementina*: a Christian Response to the Pagan Novel," *The Classical Quarterly*, N.S. 42 (1992): 459–74; Frederick Stanley Jones, "Clement of Rome and the Pseudo-Clementines: History and/or Fiction," in *Studi su Clemente Romano: atti degli Incontri di Roma, 29 marzo e 22 novembre 2001*, ed. Philippe Luisier (Rome: Pontificio Istituto Orientale, 2003), 139–61; Meinolf Vielberg, *Klemens in den pseudoklementinischen Rekognitionen: Studien zur literarischen Form des spätantiken Romans*, Texte und Untersuchungen zur Geschichte der altchristlichen Literatur 145 (Berlin: Akademie-Verlag, 2000).

have cured Matthidia as well (vv. 6483–502). Comparison between source and target text further confirms the impression of a translator who not only understands the language of his source material extremely well, but also pays careful attention to points of detail: for example, Simon and Peter's trading of the imperative *Indulge* in the *Recognitiones* is captured by *Releis demand* [. . .] *E vus de ceo me releissiez* (lit.: "I ask to be excused [. . .] And may you excuse me this thing," vv. 3471–77), while play on *creatura, creator* is rendered by *creatures, Creatur* ("creatures, Creator," vv. 1047–50; cf. vv. 2268–73, 4459–66, 7369–84).

Yet the translator's ostentatious and demonstrable fidelity should not lead one to overlook that while the major sections that he has omitted are chiefly, as promised, the sermons and disputations, they also happen to contain the material which is potentially most problematic in terms of contemporary orthodoxy. *Rec.* I.27–71, for example, well known for its Jewish Christian and anti-Pauline elements,[1] is replaced by a combination of conventional allusions to the Old Testament and a summary of the life and resurrection of Christ (vv. 1751–832). Similarly, in vv. 2543–5306, most of the disputation with Simon in *Rec.* II has disappeared, as have Peter's three sermons in *Rec.* IV-VI, and with them the discussions of polytheism, demons, idolatry, the nature of evil, and more. The result is the effective suppression of nearly every potentially controversial or heterodox section.

That this process occurs by design rather than by chance is strongly suggested by instances in which minor elements of Rufinus are modified whilst the surrounding material remains untouched. In vv. 2929–46, the translator suppresses Peter's argument that higher truths should be hidden from unworthy listeners, thus removing any doubt that the audience is receiving the unadulterated truth. In *Rec.* VII.38.3–4, Peter contentiously declares that chastity can be of benefit in this life even to unbelievers, but in *Clement* he states in more orthodox fashion that *De lur chasteé pru ne avrunt / Quant chastes pur Deu ne sunt* (lit.: "From their chastity they will receive no benefit if they are not chaste for God," vv. 6955–56). Peter's argument in *Rec.* VII.37.3–7 in favour of a figurative reading of the noto-

---

[1] Cf. Frederick Stanley Jones, *An Ancient Jewish Christian Source on the History of Christianity: Pseudo-Clementine Recognitions 1.27–71* (Atlanta, GA: Scholars Press, 1995); Nicole Kelley, *Knowledge and Religious Authority in the Pseudo-Clementines: Situating the Recognitions in Fourth-Century Syria*, Wissenschaftliche Untersuchungen zum Neuen Testament: 2. Reihe 213 (Tübingen: Mohr Siebeck, 2006); Georg Strecker, *Das Judenchristentum in den Pseudoklementinen*, 2nd ed., Texte und Untersuchungen zur Geschichte der altchristlichen Literatur 70 (Berlin: Akademie-Verlag, 1981); Annette Yoshiko Reed, "'Jewish Christianity' after the 'Parting of the Ways': Approaches to Historiography and Self-Definition in the Pseudo-Clementine Literature," in *The Ways that Never Parted: Jews and Christians in Late Antiquity and the Early Middle Ages*, ed. Adam H. Becker and Annette Yoshiko Reed, Texts and Studies in Ancient Judaism 95 (Tübingen: Mohr Siebeck, 2003), 188–231.

riously problematic instruction in Mt 5:28–29 to cut off sinning members is likewise excised, with vv. 6919–22 claiming disingenuously that *essamples* "examples"
have been omitted. At the same time, there is a clear tendency to present St Peter
as more militant than in the *Recognitiones*, as seen both in his encounters with Simon in vv. 1689–90, 3075–76, and 3909–20, and in his teachings on the delights
of eternal reward and the horrors of everlasting punishment, as in vv. 2553–70,
2585–96, and 7923–44.

These are not the only instances of minor reworking. While the *Recognitiones* alludes frequently and unambiguously to people possessed by demons, *Clement* speaks of *forsenez* and *desvez* (vv. 884, 2875, 4203, etc.), both of which primarily denote the insane. Although it is possible that these terms were for our
translator synonymous with diabolical possession, it is also the case that we find
the suppression of Peter's explanation of the actions of demons who reside in men
(vv. 2907–10), the comments on demonic forces which prevent repentance (vv.
4009–10), and the role of demons in inciting sin (vv. 8819–42), perhaps suggesting some degree of adjustment for the cultural context of the target text. Further
omissions also tend to reduce the importance of the theme of the True Prophet.[1]

There are also minor modifications which tend to accommodate the source
to 13th-century religious practice and experience. In a manner reflecting the development of excommunication in canon law,[2] explanations are added to clarify
the pagan Clement's exclusion from communal meals (vv. 1629–38, 2889–902),
and a list of those with whom the Christian must not commune is expanded (vv.
6549–50). Aspects of baptism less familiar to a medieval audience are also modified, with the explanation of the length of preparation for adult catechumens in
Rec. II.72.4–5 omitted, and an explanation for the use of the sea in the ritual
added (v. 6929).

Cultural transposition is apparent in other minor changes. An allusion in
Rec. III.64.3 to the implements of Simon's wicked magic is rendered by *sun ma-
humet* (lit.: "his idol," v. 4387), conflating his impiety with that of Mohammed.[3]
Further changes include the placing of Clement in a seated rather than incum-

---

[1] Cf. notes to vv. 1421–616, 8327–50, 8372.

[2] Cf. Eugène Vernay, *Le 'Liber de excommunicacione' du Cardinal Bérenger Frédol,
précédé d'une introduction historique sur l'excommunication et l'interdit en droit canonique de
Gratien à la fin du XIIIe siècle* (Paris: Rousseau, 1912); Elisabeth Vodola, *Excommunication
in the Middle Ages* (Berkeley: University of California Press, 1986); Josephus Zeliauskas,
De excommunicatione vitiata apud glossatores (1140–1350), Institutum Historicum Juris
Canonici: Studia et Textus Historiae Juris Canonici 4 (Zürich: Pas, 1967).

[3] On the link between Simon Magus and the denigration of Mohammed, see Alberto Ferreiro, "Simon Magus, Nicolas of Antioch, and Muhammad," *Church History*
72 (2003): 53–70; Alberto Ferreiro, *Simon Magus in Patristic, Medieval, and Early Modern Traditions*, Studies in the History of Christian Traditions 125 (Leiden: Brill, 2005),
159–62.

bent position for dining (v. 2882), an explanation for the presence of St Peter's wife, perhaps surprising for *Clement*'s audience (vv. 6377–80), and a clarification of the relevance to the current calendar of the chairing of St Peter in Antioch (vv. 13101–10). Intriguingly, while a relatively circumspect allusion in the *Recognitiones* to homosexuality is vitriolically amplified in vv. 9225–30, the source's subsequent explanation that it is amongst the Gauls that such unions are contracted is rendered by a vague allusion to it as a practice observed in *Un autre pais* (lit.: "a different country," v. 9237).

Other minor changes reflect the translator's stated intention to simplify his source. Names of people and places are often omitted, as in vv. 4567–72 and 6383–88. Metaphors, similes, and allegories are sometimes omitted, or replaced with a literal gloss, as we see in the treatment of ideas such as sins like smoke filling a house (vv. 1405–20), following the path of knowledge (vv. 3363–72), and the medicine of truth curing the sickness of uncertainty (v. 4046).[1] When figurative material is retained, the translator often seeks to clarify it through simplification or exegetical amplification, as in the rendering of the farmer who loses seed that he spreads (vv. 3049–66), the water of baptism against sins which are like tow covered in pitch (vv. 8819–42), the metaphors of the Bride of Christ (vv. 13605–52), and the analogy between vomiting and confession (vv. 14195–228). More exceptionally, the metaphor of Penelope's procrastinatory tactic of weaving and then unweaving a shroud for Laertes, drawn from Homer in order to evoke disputation which fails to progress because it constantly returns to and revises the same points, is replaced by the simile of a spider which expends great effort in working and reworking its web (vv. 10647–56).

Further minor modifications indicate a concern for the fluency, clarity, and immediacy of the tale. Numerous brief transitional narratives are added. Often, these introduce a speech, signposting its content at the risk of superfluity, as in *Il le apelat, tuz oiant, / Si lui dist que il venist avant: / "Venez avant!" ceo dist seint Pierre* (lit.: "He called to him with everybody listening and told him that he should come forward: 'Come forward!' he said," vv. 7873–75; cf. vv. 7297–304, 7723–28, 13867–70, etc.). Frequently these additions take the form of an allusion to the passage of time between the narrative events described, as in *Passat la nuit, vint le ajurnant* (lit.: "The night passed; daybreak came," v. 12001; cf. vv. 425, 1158, 2930, etc.). Deft use of these and similar techniques sometimes serves to mask instances of substantial omission or reorganisation, as in the treatment of *Rec.* III.20.2–30.5 and X.65–72.[2] As a general principle, the translator also honours the promise of entertainment made in the prologue by amplifying and focussing on scenes of narrative excitement, such as Clement's refusal of the chair (vv. 13295–306) or his minor altercation with Peter (vv. 5463–792).[3]

---

[1] Cf. also vv. 3173–76, 7121–30.
[2] Cf. notes to vv. 3037–38, 3187–200, 12675–92, 12693–772, 12775–820.
[3] Cf. Wogan-Browne, "'Bet ... to ... rede'," 91.

A final noteworthy feature of the translator's treatment of his sources is the occasional appearance of a wry sense of humour. Sometimes, this stems from a sympathetic rendering of a narrative which in the *Recognitiones* itself is not bereft of levity, including scenes such as Peter's amusement at Clement's desire to serve him (vv. 5553–70) and Aquila's hapless violation of his own interdiction of the use of *pere* "father" (vv. 7505–20), as well as the ongoing *Schadenfreude* at Simon's misfortunes. On other occasions, the translator also innovates for apparently humorous purposes. When Simon, as one of the thirty members of the sect of Dositheus on whom the course of the moon is supposed to depend, sleeps with Luna, his master's concubine, the translator allows himself some essentially untranslatable almanacal puns to evoke the aberrant behaviour (*Tute fud fause la luneisun, / Trop grant bisexte i fist Simun*, vv. 2037–38; see note to translation). Similarly, it smacks more of deliberate irony than of bumbling incompetence when he launches into a 44-line excursus on the importance of brevity (vv. 2775–818). It is also possible to detect occasional subtle mischief in the work. When Peter sends followers in pursuit of Simon, our translator claims: *Il furent duze cumpainnuns, / Ne sai pas numer lur nuns* (lit.: "There were twelve companions; I am unable to specify their names," vv. 4659–60). While other admissions of ignorance are genuine, this is disingenuous, for the names had appeared shortly before in the source in a section which was otherwise rendered so closely that one can only assume that our author deliberately omitted them (vv. 4567–72). The suspicion that the translator is enjoying a private joke only grows when, a short while later, he draws attention to his earlier failure by alluding apologetically and ostentatiously to *les duze cumpainnuns / Dunt jeo ne sai dire les nuns* (lit.: "The twelve companions whose names I am unable to say," vv. 4911–12), and then follows this with a couplet calculating the total number of people present in the scene, the banality of content and poverty of rhyme of which do not convince that it is to be taken seriously: *Ki met ensemble quatre e duze, / Si il bien cunte, ceo funt sedze* (lit.: "For anybody who adds together four and twelve, if he counts accurately, that makes sixteen," vv. 4913–14).

In conclusion, while Willson lamented that our translator had produced "a very unbalanced poem — a good story related with little regard for style, interspersed with long and tedious passages of theological and philosophical commonplaces, the didactic value of which is doubtful,"[1] her judgement betrays a lack of appreciation of his skill and, indeed, of the very purpose of such translations of religious material. He has succeeded admirably in realising the project outlined in his prologue, balancing the requisite respect for his venerable sources with the requirements of producing a palatable, suitably distilled text capable of engaging its target audience and transmitting important and fastidiously orthodox instruction.

---

[1] Willson, "*Vie de Saint Clement Pape*", xvii.

Style

A leitmotif in the *Recognitiones* is the importance of simplicity in speech: this is the laudable quality which distinguishes the pure and unadulterated discourse of Barnabas and Peter from the ostentatious artifice and obfuscation of the philosophers and Simon Magus. From the very outset, the translator aligns himself with this cult of accessibility. His *captatio benevolentiae* begins by dismissing the vainglorious efforts of contemporary clerics who—implicitly like Simon and the philosophers—strive for the sake of fame and recognition to produce ornately complicated Latin that the less educated cannot understand, whereas he—like Peter and Barnabas—intends to use what little learning he has acquired to produce a text which might be understood by those of modest education, for which reason he has undertaken to remove from his sources elements which may confuse through their complexity. While we have seen that there are other motives at work in the various modifications that he effects upon his sources, it is certainly true that in the transition from Latin prose to French verse, he generally avoids introducing particular embellishment, making modest use of a relatively small range of poetic and rhetorical devices commonly found in vernacular verse of this period.

Anaphora is particularly frequent, often in combination with isocolon. The repeated term may stand at the beginning of consecutive lines within a couplet or between couplets, as in *Dunc se changent les orez, / Dunc surdent tempestes asez* (lit.: "Then the winds change, then many storms arise," vv. 8133–34) or *Suvent le apelat nunsavant, / Suvent le rettat de folie* (lit.: "Often did he call him ignorant, often did he accuse him of foolishness," vv. 2836–37; cf. vv. 5665–66, 8133–34, etc.), or within a single line in which the repeated term emphasises a medial caesura, as in *Seient moles, seient dures* (lit.: "Be they pleasant, be they harsh," v. 9068) or *Tant i sistrent, tant i parlerent* (lit.: "So long did they sit there, so long did they talk there," v. 10819; cf. vv. 672, 8872, 10965, etc.). Such single lines often feature as the first in a couplet in which they are followed by a more flowing line, as in *Issi pensa, issi le fist, / E a Rume Clement remist* (lit.: "Thus he thought, thus he acted, and in Rome Clement remained," vv. 677–78) or *Tel le seignur, tel le serjant, / Le cuple en iert le plus avenant* (lit.: "Such is the lord, such is the servant; the pair will be all the more suited from this," vv. 11513–14; cf. vv. 705–6, 12103–4, 12551–52, etc.). The combination of anaphora and isocolon often serves to foreground a relationship between the following elements which is synonymic, as in *La demura, la se tint* (lit.: "There he stayed, there he remained," v. 731; cf. vv. 4731, 5287, 7263, etc.), or, a little more often, antithetical, as in the contentio that we see in *Suvent de aukes, suvent de nient* (lit.: "Often from something, often from nothing," v. 8872; cf. vv. 8240, 8384, 11829, etc.). On a few occasions, more extensive use of anaphora is found, most notably in vv. 4781–89, 8599–614, and 8728–38, and to lesser extents in vv. 4165–69, 5007–12, 5533–37, 8749–54, etc.

Synonymic binomials such as *sens e saveir* (lit.: "sense and knowledge," v. 5160) and *ordure e vileinie* (lit.: "filth and ignobility," v. 11477) occur with a frequency typical for this kind of narrative. By contrast, recourse to even modestly more elaborate devices is sparse. Amongst these we find occasional chiasmus, as in *Vulcan feu, le soleil Phebus, / Mars grant arsun, beauté Venus* (lit.: "Vulcan [represents] fire, the sun, Phœbus; Mars, great burning, and beauty, Venus," vv. 11409–10) and *Freiz sunt les autres, e cil est chaud* (lit.: "Cold are the others, and he is hot," v. 11404; cf. 14059, 14139, etc.); polyptoton, as in *Tute la doins e tute la ai, / Vus la avrez tute, e jeo la avrai* (lit.: "I give it all and have it all; you will have it all, and I shall have it," vv. 14255–56) and *Si il fist le plus, / Face le meins* (lit.: "If he did the greater, may he do the lesser," vv. 14901–2); and conduplicatio, as in *Mult demandast, mult enquist, / E de opposer mult se entremist* (lit.: "A great deal did he ask, a great deal did he enquire, and he strove a great deal to propose objections," vv. 8211–12; cf. 13164–65, 13218–19, 14538–39, etc.). While our author's use of rhetoric indicates his clerical education, sophistication and ostentation are clearly not his goal.

A number of syntactical features characterise our author's work. Parataxis involving the omission of coordinating conjunctions is as pervasive as one would expect in a narrative from this period, both within lines, as in *Passerunt jurs, passerunt anz* (lit.: "Days passed, years passed," v. 705), and within couplets, as in *N'aveit de rien dunc cunfort, / Mult desira que il fust mort* (lit.: "He had comfort from nothing, he greatly wished that he were dead," vv. 605–6). Hyperbaton of varying degrees of obtrusiveness is quite common, occurring most frequently when the main verb follows the subordinate clause that it governs, as in *E que fin eit si creire dei* (lit.: "And that it has an end whether I should believe," v. 1388) and *Purquei le out dit entendimes* (lit.: "Why he had said it we understood," v. 2404; cf. vv. 4045–46, 6194, 6611, 10493–94, etc.), but also in constructions such as *Kar nuls ne poet autrui penser / Senz celui kil pense saver* (lit.: "For nobody can the thoughts of other people without the one who thinks them know," vv. 8307–8; cf. vv. 2231–34, 8879–82, etc.). This often Latinate fluidity of word order is further apparent in the complex sentences that our author occasionally produces, most often when the main clause is delayed by nested subordinate clauses. The most remarkable example occurs in vv. 8495–512, in which the first subordinate clause appears some sixteen lines before the eventual main clause, but examples such as vv. 1128–42, 6302–14, and 6865–90 are also noteworthy. In order to clarify the syntax of such sentences, which meander towards anacoluthon in instances such as vv. 8159–76, our author sometimes adds redundant markers in order to remind his audience of clauses which had begun much earlier, as we see in vv. 3049–60, 4091–106, 5530–43, 7185–94, and 13323–39.

A partiality for repetition of particular words, phrases, and constructions is also characteristic of our author's style. The frequency of the appearance of *nepurquant* ("nonetheless"), often in combination with *meis* ("but"), crystallises the extent to which antithesis serves as the basis for coordinating clauses and sentences. A concern for balance is evident in the prevalence of the structure *que. . .que*, as in *Que cil de nef, que cil de batel* (lit.: "Both those from the ship and those from the boat," v. 657). The causal conjunction *kar* ("for") is found even more frequently, its appearance at the beginning of more than five hundred lines emblematic of the importance attached to logical exposition. An attachment to apophthegmatic absolute relative clauses involving a protasis headed by *ki* "whoever, anybody who" such as *Ki bien le sert avrat honur, / Ki malement chiet en dulur* (lit.: "Whoever serves him badly will gain honour; whoever [serves] badly falls into pain," vv. 1513–14) contributes noticeably to the sententious tone. There is a marked predilection for intensifiers such as *mult, asez, bien,* and *trop,* although the profusion of these terms may have as much to do with the requirements of metre as with any grand hyperbolic design. This proclivity for repetition is also manifest in more extensive form, with there being at least twenty pairs of identical lines (e.g., vv. 96 and 2788, 341 and 6666, 755 and 7997, etc.), and more than twice that number of very nearly identical pairs (e.g., vv. 299 and 9847, 318 and 6648, 325 and 14735, etc.).

Despite this repetitiveness, there is also a notable richness in a number of lexical fields, including sorcery, health and sickness, law and justice, seafaring, and in particular many aspects of religion and of activities related to the schools, such as science, literature, logic, and disputation. While this richness to some extent stems from the sources, there is no question that our author was familiar with a broad range of learned and Latinate terms, such as *allegorie* ("allegory"), *desputeisun* ("disputation"), *dieleticien* ("dialectician"), *diffiniciun* ("precise description"), *espositiun* ("explanation"), *prolixement* ("at considerable length"), *sentence* ("opinion, belief"), *sillogisme* ("syllogism"), and *tresposiciun* ("transposition"). Such vocabulary leads one to wonder whether the repetitiveness in other respects stems less from an innate poverty of expression than from our author's express goal of simplicity and accessibility.

Versification

The text is composed in octosyllabic couplets, the most common form for narrative at this time. Allowing for uncertainties regarding the effacement of consonants and the treatment of feminine *e*, around half of the rhymes are "sufficient" (i.e., phonemically comprising a vowel and a consonant), a third "poor" (i.e., an assonance comprising a single vowel phoneme), and a sixth "rich" (i.e., comprising three or more phonemes). Around 3% of the rhymes are disyllabic, mostly involving unexceptional endings such as *-ement, -erat, -ité,* and *-eisun,* with few instances of more extensive rhymes, such as *demurastes : urastes* (vv. 7081–82), *avrunt : savrunt* (vv. 10967–68), and *familier : humilier* (vv. 14383–84). More striking is the frequency of the occurrence of standard combinations such as *sunt : unt, -faire : -traire, bien : rien,* and *-pris : -mis,* with an inventory of fifty pairings accounting for a tenth of the total rhymes. Identical rhymes such as *eussent* (vv. 575–76), *un* (vv. 3531–32), *nun* (vv. 6211–12) are rare, although *est* rhymes with itself eight times (vv. 3037–38, 3897–98, 4425–26, etc.). On a number of occasions we find the same rhyme over four lines, as in vv. 191–94, 393–96, 2521–24, etc., but such monorhymed quatrains appear more coincidental than stylistically significant. There are a few instances where the sole basis for the admixture appears to be a shared final consonant, as in *duze* : *sedze* (vv. 4913–14), *ars* : *mors* (vv. 6981–82), *blasme* : *meisme* (vv. 7513–14), and *hume* : *femme* (vv. 14607–8).

The question of metre is somewhat more problematic. As one begins reading the text, it quickly becomes apparent that while the majority of lines would be octosyllabic by Continental criteria, a significant number would not, even after recourse to the minor interventions of which editors of Anglo-Norman verse typically avail themselves to compensate for scribal infidelity and the vagaries of transmission.[1] While this irregularity would hardly be uncommon for an Anglo-Norman text, what is remarkable is that the metre appears to be considerably more regular at the end of the text than the beginning. More precisely, in the first 9000 lines, we find consistently that a little over half of the lines of the manuscript text would scan as octosyllables against Continental criteria, with nearly a third being hypermetric by one syllable.[2] In the following thousand lines, however, there is a marked increase in the number of octosyllables, attained primarily through a decrease in hypermetric lines; in particular, from around v. 9400 onwards, around 75% of lines are octosyllabic. In the final third of the text, the octosyllable count exceeds 90%, averaging around 95% in the final three thousand lines even before any of the potential emendations at an editor's disposal. For an Anglo-Norman narrative poem of this period, the metrical regularity by the end of the text is noteworthy.[3] To compare this final section with some other religious texts composed in octosyllabic couplets, it is a little more regu-

---

[1] E.g., reading synaeresis or diaeresis, assuming elision or hiatus, adding or suppressing epenthetic *e*, substituting the appropriate member of a doublet (*cum* or *cume*, *or* or *ore*, *ne* or *nen*, etc.), adding or suppressing subject pronouns or other monosyllabic function words, removing or introducing agreements on epicene adjectives, etc.

[2] Assuming elision and synaeresis to occur regularly in accordance with what seems to be the author's usual practice, 2% of the lines have 6 syllables, 35% have 7 syllables, 8% have 9 syllables, and 4% have 10 syllables. There are two exceptional lines of potentially five syllables: *Jeo ai femme e enfanz* (v. 4341), and *U de Deu u de hume* (v. 8743).

[3] A comparable case from the mid-13th century (Dèan no. 626) is discussed by Glynn Hesketh, ed., *Rossignos*, ANTS 63 (London: ANTS, 2006), 26–28, who finds that only 2.67% of the author's lines fail to scan, a total which could be reduced even further with venial interventions. On account of this regularity, there seems little need in this instance take recourse to the hypothesis of accentual metre sometimes adduced in relation to Anglo-Norman verse; for the debate, cf. Jocelyn Wogan-Browne and Thelma S. Fenster, trans., *The Life of St Alban by Matthew Paris*, FRETS 2 (Tempe, AZ: ACMRS, 2010), 47–48.

lar than the *Vie de seint Laurent* from the later 12th century,[1] somewhat more so than the slightly later *Vie des set dormanz*,[2] and considerably more so than texts from the mid- and later 13th century such as the *Lumere as lais*,[3] the *Vie de seynt Fraunceys*,[4] the *Vie seint Richard*,[5] or, in particular, the Verse Apocalypse,[6] which epitomises the increasing syllabic irregularity of Anglo-Norman verse relative to Continental norms.

This development is puzzling. There are no other features which would suggest a change of author, nor would the relatively sudden nature of the transition seem to correspond with the thesis of a poet who, in the process of composition, had gradually learnt to write regular octosyllables.[7] An explanation may, however, lie in the transmission of the text. The significant increase in regularity near the beginning of the final third of the text coincides with the quire copied by Scribe 2, with this regularity sustained when Scribe 1 returns after this quire. Since the change in respect of metre therefore appears to be independent of the scribe, it seems quite possible that when Scribe 2 began work, he used a base exemplar different from the one used to that point by Scribe 1, and that when Scribe 1 continued with his work, he similarly used an exemplar which contained a metrically regular copy of the text.

---

[1] Dean no. 536; Delbert W. Russell, ed., *La Vie de saint Laurent: an Anglo-Norman Poem of the Twelfth Century*, ANTS 34 (London: ANTS, 1976), 19–21, estimates that 7.5% of the poem's lines cannot scan as octosyllables.

[2] Dean no. 534; Brian S. Merrilees, ed., *La Vie des Set Dormanz, by Chardri*, ANTS 35 (London: ANTS, 1977), 17, estimates that even after allowing for the "7 + *e*" hypometric "*Brendan* line" and "4 + *e* + 4" epic caesura, some 230 out of 1896 lines fail to scan.

[3] Dean no. 630; Glynn Hesketh, ed., *La Lumere as lais, by Pierre d'Abernon of Fetcham*, 3 vols., ANTS 54–57 (London: ANTS, 1996–2000), 3:60–62, finds 40.9% of a sample to scan as octosyllables before emendation.

[4] Dean no. 527; Delbert W. Russell, ed., *La Vye de seynt Fraunceys d'Assise (Ms Paris, BNF, fonds français 13505)*, ANTS 59–60 (London: ANTS, 2002), 13–14, demonstrates that in a sample of the text, after emendation, 77% can scan as octosyllables.

[5] Dean no. 545; Delbert W. Russell, ed., *La Vie seint Richard Evesque de Cycestre, by Pierre d'Abernon of Fetcham*, ANTS 51 (London: ANTS, 1995), 29–31, observes that 70% of the lines can be emended to scan, and hypothesises that this tally would rise when the text was read aloud—an observation which might equally obtain for the earlier sections of *Clement*.

[6] Dean no. 478; Brent A. Pitts, ed., *Revelacion (BL Royal 2.D.xiii)*, ANTS 68 (London: ANTS, 2010), 42–46, finds that before emendation only 21.6% of the lines correspond with the octosyllabic model to which they apparently aspire.

[7] This theory was proposed by Meyer, "Notice d'un manuscrit," 311–12, and was accepted by Johan Vising, *Anglo-Norman Language and Literature*, Language and Literature Series (London: Oxford University Press, 1923), 81, but questioned by Mary Dominica Legge, *Anglo-Norman Literature and its Background* (Oxford: Clarendon, 1963), 253. Willson, "*Vie de Saint Clement Pape*", xxxi also considered the improvement in the final third of the text to be a more drastic change.

Whatever the reason underlying the increase in metrical regularity, a feature which remains consistent across the text is the presence of a more or less clear medial caesura. A break after the fourth syllable occurs in two thirds of the octo-syllabic lines (e.g., *Vostre cunseil // ore dirrez*, lit.: "You will now say your opinion," v. 10302) and over half of the 7-syllable lines (e.g., *Mes partant que // li plusurs*, lit.: "But because many people," v. 8799).[1] For the 9-syllable lines, a break after the fourth syllable (e.g., *Pur faute de // vostre enseinnement*, lit.: "On account of a lack of your teaching," v. 13538) is less common than one after the fifth (e.g., *Que tutes les riens // ki sunt el mund*, lit.: "That all the things which are in the world," v. 8866), but since the fifth syllable is often an unstressed *e* (e.g., *En ciel, en terre, // fors lui n'ad nul*, lit.: "In heaven, on earth, there is none but He," v. 1444), it is not inconceivable that it was susceptible to elision, as in a so-called "epic" caesura. A less pervasive feature is the use of enjambement, which is found in around 10% of lines,[2] and more frequently within the couplet than between couplets. A *rejet* is found in fewer than 10% of cases of enjambement, and a *contre-rejet* appears a little less frequently, albeit more regularly in the form of four syllables, quite often at the beginning of a passage of direct speech. On a few occasions, the en-jambement may be quite noticeable, as in *Tel ad esté lur mescreance / Que ne crurent que purveance / Fust en Deu, meis tute lur cure / Meteient a aventure* (lit.: "Such was their heresy that they did not believe that providence was in God, but rather all their attention they devoted to chance," vv. 5207–10; cf. vv. 4982–84, 7612–14, 8549–51, 9847–51, etc.), but for the most part it remains unexceptional. There are fewer than twenty clear instances of breaking of the couplet (vv. 155–56, 1623–24, 2239–40, etc.)

In conclusion, it would be fair to say that while our poet's command of ver-sification is entirely adequate for the task of producing 15000 lines of verse with relatively few infelicities, clarity of communication was evidently of greater im-portance to him, as to the majority of authors of comparable Anglo-Norman religious verse of the time, than experimentation with the creative potential of rhyme and metre.[3]

---

[1] On this question, see Thomas M. Rainsford, "Dividing Lines: the Changing Syn-tax and Prosody of the Mid-Line Break in Medieval French Octosyllabic Verse," *Transac-tions of the Philological Society* 109, no. 3 (2011): 265–83.

[2] For the approach adopted, see Tony Hunt, "A Forgotten Author - Péan Gatineau," *French Studies* 58 (2004): 313–26, at 324.

[3] Cf. e.g., the conclusion drawn by Hesketh, *Lumere as lais*, 3:63, that the text's au-thor "had no pretensions to write anything other than functional verse, and that his ver-sification is subservient to his task of imparting information."

Authorship

The sole extant copy of *Clement* is preceded in Trinity, R.3.46 by the sole extant copy of the *Life of St John the Almsgiver*. At first glance, aside from their hagiographical content, there is no compelling similarity between the texts in terms of subject matter, with the adventures of St Peter and St Clement in the 1st century having little obvious in common with the series of anecdotes evoking the humble and charitable ministry of the Patriarch of Alexandria in the 7th.[1] Nonetheless, the fact that these *unica* are anonymous verse translations of Latin hagiographical narratives in whose production Anastasius Bibliothecarius was involved leads one to wonder whether there may be any other reason for their juxtaposition in their manuscript; and given that both would appear at first glance to be similar in age and style, the question which inevitably raises itself is whether they might have been written by the same author.[2] While enquiries of this kind are not without their problems and pitfalls, in this case the investigation proves especially fruitful.[3]

The linguistic similarities between the texts are profound and profuse.[4] In terms of phonology, both texts present rhymes which are more or less common in Anglo-Norman in the earlier 13th century: in *e*, between the products of Latin tonic free A (including after a palatal), tonic free and blocked /ɛ/, tonic blocked /e/, the reflexes of -ARIU and -ERIU, -*er* derived from the verbal termination -*eir*, and the reduced diphthongs /ai/, /ei/, and /ue/; between *en* and *ien*, and *en* and *ein*; in /u/, between the products of Latin tonic free and blocked /o/, standard Old French /y/, preterites featuring earlier /ɔ/ < /ɔu/, and levelled /eu/, /ieu/, and

---

[1] A possible exception—although certainly not a decisive one, given its overall minor significance—might be the dangers posed in both texts by the stormy sea and the *utlages* ("pirates") who sail on it, as seen in *Clement* in the fate of Matthidia and her sons and in *St John* in various of the maritime misfortunes which befall the Patriarch and his associates.

[2] This possibility was first mooted by Meyer, "Notice d'un manuscrit," 312. Noting considerable similarities, with the principal difference being the initially less regular versification of *Clement*, he concluded that if the texts were by the same author, *Clement* would have been composed first, whilst the poet was still learning his trade. Willson, "*Vie de Saint Clement Pape*" stated without further explanation that there were "good grounds" for assuming joint authorship; conversely, but with an equal lack of evidence, Legge, *Anglo-Norman Literature*, 253 dismissed the possibility as "unlikely."

[3] For a more fully substantiated discussion, see Daron Lee Burrows, "Die anglonormannischen *Life of St John the Almsgiver* und *Vie de seint Clement*: Werke ein und desselben Autors?," *Zeitschrift für romanische Philologie* 129, no. 1 (2013): 3–23.

[4] For discussion of the features identified, see Ian Short, *Manual of Anglo-Norman*, 2nd ed., OPS 8 (Oxford: ANTS, 2013); Mildred Katharine Pope, *From Latin to Modern French, with Especial Consideration of Anglo-Norman*, 2nd ed. (Manchester: Manchester University Press, 1952).

/ueu/; and between non-palatal /n/ and /l/ and what in standard Old French would be palatalised /ɲ/ and /ʎ/. The metre in both texts indicates generalised reduction of hiatus in *eu* and *ei*, and that the demonstrative pronoun *ceo* can elide before *a* and *o*. More distinctive phonological features encountered in both texts include rhymes between /i/ and *e* (e.g., *dire : maniere, Clem.* 1911–12; *St John* 741–42) and between *ei* and /i/ (e.g., *peril : cunseil, Clem.* 13375–76; *cil : soleil, St John* 2935–36); the product of MELIUS rhyming only in *-iez* (e.g., *siez : mieuz, Clem.* 6091–92; *liez : miez, St John* 6669–70); rhymes suggesting more typically Continental developments of *oi* (*cuntraire : gloire, Clem.* 12833–34; *faire : memoire, St John* 3559–60) and *uin* (*esluine : enseinne, Clem.* 13781–82; *deinne : busuinne, St John,* 387–88); the rhymes *mot : out* (*Clem.* 6633–34; *St John* 5445–46) and *povre(s : oevre(s* (*Clem.* 5823–24; *St John* 3105–6); and the effacement of pre-consonantal *r* (*floz : efforz, Clem.* 14067–68; *turne : lune, St John* 4475–76). *St John* also resembles *Clement* in offering a handful of admixtures on the basis solely of shared final consonants (e.g., *haste : feste* 5277–78, *Alisandre : ordre* 6111–12, *Constantinoble : deable* 6191–92).

Morphological similarities include patterns in the declension of masculine nominative forms, the exclusive use of the personal pronoun *vus* instead of *tu*, the frequency of Western forms for the third person singular and plural imperfect indicative (e.g., *osout, Clem.* 226; *St John* 1261), the consistent appearance of a *-ge-* infix in the present subjunctive (e.g., *tienge, Clem.* 1221; *St John* 5184), the frequency in future stems of contraction (e.g., *durrat, Clem.* 13903; *St John* 737), epenthesis (e.g., *viver-, Clem.* 2436; *St John* 6950), and metathesis (e.g., *suffer-, Clem.* 2259; *St John* 600), and the appearance of forms such as *feimes* (*Clem.* 4919; *St John* 6340), *truissez* (*Clem.* 12920; *St John* 6993), *duinst* (*Clem.* 117; *St John* 78), *sentu* (*Clem.* 14669; *St John* 1968), monosyllabic *chae(i)t* (*Clem.* 3528; *St John* 41), and genitive *Moÿsi* (*Clem.* 2829; *St John* 1097).

Syntactical similarities include the frequency of juxtaposed oblique constructions denoting possession (e.g., *le regne Deu, Clem.* 870; *St John* 155), including with preceding pronominal *autrui* (e.g., *Clem.* 8304; *St John* 1267), of absolute constructions headed by *ki* without antecedent (e.g., *Clem.* 43–44; *St John* 41–42), of redundant cataphoric and anaphoric pronouns such as *ceo, le,* and *en* (e.g., *Clem.* 595–96; *St John* 2385–86), of periphrases involving *aler* + gerund (e.g., *veit querant, Clem.* 8669; *St John* 7558), of concession through *tut* + subjunctive (e.g., *tut seit, Clem.* 6951; *St John* 1596), of parataxis after constructions including *quel(e ure* (e.g., *Clem.* 11910; *St John* 2294) and *guardez* (e.g., *Clem.* 10632; *St John* 2820), of agreement of a past participle with the subject when conjugated with *aveir* (e.g., *Clem.* 223; *St John* 5816), and of singular *gent* taking a plural verb (e.g., *Clem.* 183; *St John* 164). *St John* also resembles *Clement* in its marked penchant for the *que. . .que* structure (e.g., *Que de vesture, que de chiere,* lit.: "both of clothing and of appearance," *St John* 794; cf. 987, 1243, 1446, etc.), frequent positioning of the main verb after the subordinate clause (e.g., *E qu'el ceo seit qu'esteim ne sai,* lit.: "And that it should be other than tin I do not know," *St John* 1070; cf.

1230–31, 1542, 2636, etc.), and occasional syntactical complexity through the nesting of subordinate clauses (e.g., *St John* 377–96, 601–16, 6141–52, etc.).

Lexical similarities include the use of fairly distinctive words and phrases such as *beaubelet* "trinket," *cungeter* "conjecture," *demener vilment* "treat terribly," *en povres* "to the poor," *enjurnant* "dawn," *espaer* "castrate," *jur festival* "day of celebration," *maluer* "pollute," *marbres* "stones," *planch(e)iz* "floor of planking," *prosprement* "well," and *vezdie* "cunning," as well as dual forms denoting Syria (*Sire, Sirie, Clem.* 4942–43; *Syre, Siria, St John* 758, 508). Also noteworthy is the very frequency with which certain terms occur in both texts, such as *acheisun* "opportunity," *al veir dire* "truth to tell," *beal fiz* "dear son," *chaudpas* "immediately," *mettre a nunchaler* "not care about," *mettre a reisun* "question," *mes nepurquant* "but nonetheless," *pru* "profit" in combination with *turner a* "be a source of" and *surdre de* "result from," and many more, including the ubiquitous intensifiers *mult, trop, asez,* and *bien*. More striking still are the similarities which encompass whole lines. There are six completely identical lines, such as *Issi pensa(t, issi le fist* (lit.: "In this way, he thought, in this way he acted," *Clem.* 677; *St John* 1593; cf. *Clem.* 899–900, *St John* 625–26; *Clem.* 2409, *St John* 2036; *Clem.* 8943, *St John* 7196; *Clem.* 11683, *St John* 5772; *Clem.* 13554, *St John* 6965). Lines which are very nearly identical (e.g., *Des biens que Deu vus/nus ad presté*, lit.: "Of the good things that God has granted to you/us," *Clem.* 13748; *St John* 3103) number into the dozens, but these are in turn eclipsed in frequency by lines featuring formulaic expressions such as *Quant tant out dit* (lit.: "Once he had said this much," *Clem.* 7885, 11257, 12605; *St John* 675, 1831, 2839, 3037, 3761), *A ces paroles* (lit.: "Upon these words," *Clem.* 3111, 3392, 12077, 14743, 14987; *St John* 1461, 5219, 6990), and numerous others.

St John's author further resembles *Clement*'s in his obtrusive fidelity to his *essemplaire* (e.g., *Mun essamplaire plus n'en dit / Ne jeo n'en met plus en escrit*, lit.: "My source says no more about this, nor shall I write any more about it," *St John* 1299–1300; cf. 501–2, 2736–38), and he also does not hesitate to confess his ignorance when his source is silent (e.g., *Mes ne sai puis qu'ele devint; / De sa femme quele iert la fin / Ne truis en rumanz n'en latin*, lit.: "But I do know what then became of her; regarding the fate of his wife I find nothing in French or in Latin," *St John* 104–6; cf. 107–12, 537–40, 762, etc.). He likewise repeatedly expresses his own opinion (*St John* 336–48, 557–58, 1760, etc.), adds his own didactic comments and provides explanations of unfamiliar customs and terms, points of religious significance, metaphors, and the like (*St John* 1567–76, 1803–4, 2173–76, etc.), and manifests a tendency towards prolixity and amplification when translating (*St John* 289–300, 1091–1120, 1519–36, etc.).

Further stylistic similarities are no less compelling. While devices such as conduplicatio and chiasmus are used as sparingly as in *Clement* (*St John* 1855–58, 2653–64, 3141, etc.), anaphora is equally frequent, appearing in similar circumstances: within a single line, often with isocolon (e.g., *Dreit fust le mui, dreit le sestier*, lit.: "true was the measure, true the sester," *St John* 210; cf. 1258, 1856,

2375, etc.), and usually in conjunction with synonymia (e.g., *Tut turne a mal, tut turne a ennui*, lit.: "Everything becomes a source of woe, everything becomes a source of vexation," *St John* 240; cf. 768, 1215, 1537–38, etc.) or contentio (e.g., *Issi duné, issi vendu*, lit.: "Thus given, thus sold," *St John* 2526; cf. 2973, 4058, etc.); in the first line of a couplet followed by an uninterrupted line (e.g., *Iloec sëeit, iloec parlout / A ki qu'a lui la venir vout*, lit.: "There he sat, there he spoke / To anybody who wished to come to him," *St John* 321–22; cf. 413–14, 427–28, 1239–40, etc.); at the beginning of each line of a couplet (e.g., *Nient autrement la s'acusat, / Nient autrement merci crïat*," lit.: "In no other way did he excuse himself there, / In no other way did he cry for mercy there," *St John* 1477–78; cf. 985–86); and occasionally in more extensive form (e.g., *St John* 21–27, 5575–77, 5630–32, 6747–50, etc.).

The evidence that the authors of *Clement* and *St John* were one and the same person is therefore compelling. Unfortunately, we know little more about this individual who, by virtue of his 22,000 surviving lines of verse, ranks as one of the most prolific translators and hagiographers writing in Anglo-Norman in the 13th century.[1] That he resided in England, or at least was writing for an English audience, is confirmed in *St John* when, confessing his ignorance of the word *esophoire* that he finds in his *essamplaire*, he waggishly invites anybody wishing to discover the sense of the term to go Greece, but warns that it is a very long journey from England (vv. 2736–46). If at this point he admits that he does not understand Greek, the claims that he makes in the *captatio benevolentiae* of *Clement* regarding his lack of learning should be recognised as a modesty topos. His work attests an excellent command of Latin and French across a diverse range of lexical fields, and demonstrates an easy familiarity with areas including the Eastern liturgy, classical mythology, and, in particular, contemporary theology and ecclesiastical practice. That he had received a clerical education seems beyond doubt; whether he was more specifically a monk, as his apparent sympathy with the regular clergy in *St John* has led some to assume,[2] is less certain.

Context

Clement supplies no indication of patronage, but it does reveal something about its target audience: it comprises both laity and clergy (v. 39) who are not proficient readers of Latin (v. 15), but who are not so uncouth that they are incapable of understanding the vernacular—that is, French (vv. 41–42)—in written or spoken form (v. 102). This is, however, potentially a very diverse audience,

---

[1] On the time potentially involved in writing a corpus of material of this size, with a focus on a comparably prolific contemporary of our author, see Ian Short, "Frère Angier: Notes and Conjectures," *Medium Ævum* 80, no. 1 (2011): 104–10.

[2] Cf. Urwin, *St John*, 2:24; Meyer, "Notice d'un manuscrit," 295.

comprising women and men whose circumstances and privileges have granted them access to an education which includes at least French language, but not the kind of specialised study of Latin material conducted by clerics working in the schools; within such a broad congregation one might find nuns, noblemen, parish priests, and many others, but the text itself offers no indication as to which of these or other groups our author might have had in mind.[1]

In the absence of precise information regarding the identity of the author or his audience, hypotheses regarding his potential motives for choosing the *Recognitiones* as a source to translate are naturally all the more speculative, but it is possible to imagine resonances that the text might have had in 13th-century Britain. For example, in the context of new contacts and engagement with foreign lands through enterprises such as the Crusades, one can imagine, given the fascination indicated by later cultural artefacts such as the Hereford Mappa Mundi[2] and Mandeville's *Travels*,[3] that an audience may have been just as enthralled as are we by *Clement*'s fantastic anthropological and ethnographical account (vv.

---

[1] On the vast question of Insular speakers of French in the Middle Ages, see amongst others: Richard Ingham, ed., *The Anglo-Norman Language and its Contexts* (Woodbridge: York Medieval Press / Boydell, 2010); Douglas Kibbee, "La Romania submersa dans les îles britanniques: après 1066," in *Romanische Sprachgeschichte: ein internationales Handbuch zur Geschichte der romanischen Sprachen*, ed. Gerhard Ernst *et al.*, Handbücher zur Sprach- und Kommunikationswissenschaft 23 (Berlin / New York: de Gruyter, 2003), 717–26; Serge Lusignan, *La Langue des rois au Moyen Age: le français en France et en Angleterre* (Paris: Presses Universitaires de France, 2004); Michael Richter, *Sprache und Gesellschaft im Mittelalter: Untersuchungen zur mündlichen Kommunikation in England von der Mitte des elften bis zum Beginn des vierzehnten Jahrhunderts*, Monographien zur Geschichte des Mittelalters 18 (Stuttgart: Hiersemann, 1979); Richard Sharpe, "People and Languages in Eleventh- and Twelfth-Century Britain and Ireland: Reading the Charter Evidence," in *The Reality behind Charter Diplomatic in Anglo-Norman Britain*, ed. Dauvit Broun (Glasgow: University of Glasgow, 2010), 1–119; Ian Short, "Patrons and Polyglots: French Literature in 12th-Century England," *Anglo-Norman Studies* 14 (1992): 229–49; Ian Short, "L'anglo-normand au siècle de Chaucer: un regain de statistiques," in *Le Plurilinguisme au Moyen Age: Orient - Occident*, ed. Claire Kappler and Suzanne Thiolier-Méjean, Coll. Méditerranée Médiévale (Paris: L'Harmattan, 2009), 67–77; Ian Short, "'Anglice loqui nesciunt': Monoglots in Anglo-Norman England," *Cultura Neolatina* 69 (2009): 245–62; Jocelyn Wogan-Browne et al., eds., *Language and Culture in Medieval Britain: the French of England c.1100-c.1500* (Woodbridge: York Medieval Press, 2009).

[2] Cf. Paul Dean Adshead Harvey, *Mappa Mundi: the Hereford World Map* (London: Hereford Cathedral & the British Library, 1996); Naomi Kline, *Maps of Medieval Thought: the Hereford Paradigm* (Woodbridge: Boydell & Brewer, 2001); Jocelyn Wogan-Browne, "Reading the World: the Hereford Mappa Mundi," *Parergon* 9 (1991): 117–35.

[3] On the likely Anglo-Norman context of Mandeville, see Michael J. Bennett, "Mandeville's *Travels* and the Anglo-French Moment," *Medium Aevum* 75, no. 2 (2006): 273–92.

9101–482),[1] derived from the *Recognitiones'* adaptation of Bardaisan's *Book of the Laws of Countries*,[2] of the unusual customs practised by exotic peoples such as Persians, Amazons, Bactrians, Brahmans, and Seres, including anthropophagy, incest, promiscuity, homosexuality, polygamy, exposure of infants, and self-immolation. Given the specific interest in Byzantium and the Eastern Church that our author manifests in his *Life of St John the Almsgiver*, one might also imagine that a tale centred on Peter and Clement, as the first Bishop of Rome and his appointed successor, involved in exploits in Eastern cities such as Laodicea, Caesarea, and Antaradus which culminate in his founding of the See of Antioch, could have been especially poignant at a time when the Great Schism between East and West had been hardened by events such as the sacking of Constantinople during the Fourth Crusade and the appointment in the Crusader states of Latin rivals to the Sees of Constantinople, Antioch, and Jerusalem already occupied by Orthodox patriarchs. Amongst many such features of *Clement* which could have been of particular relevance in the context of 13th-century Britain, I shall for reasons of space limit the discussion to three.

The Cult of Clement

Since our author foregrounds Clement in his *captatio benevolentiae* by identifying the saint's story as a source of moral improvement and by hinting at the exciting events which befall him and his family (vv. 43–56) before even mentioning St Peter, the true focus of the *Recognitiones*, it is natural to wonder whether the figure of Clement might have held a particular appeal for his audience. Certainly, the cult of Clement had thriven in Britain long before the composition of our text. In terms of written evidence,[3] Clement's feast day (November 23rd) is recorded in the vast majority of the Anglo-Saxon liturgical calendars,[4] including the earliest

---

[1] Further evidence of Insular interest in this question is provided by the examples of geographical texts and itineraries involving the Holy Land covered in Dean nos. 330–337. For a recent edition, see Brent A. Pitts, ed., *Barthélemy l'Anglais: Le Livre des regions*, Plain Texts Series 15 (London: ANTS, 2006).

[2] Cf. Franz Winter, *Bardesanes von Edessa über Indien: ein früher syrischer Theologe schreibt über ein fremdes Land*, Frühes Christentum: Forschungen und Perspektiven 5 (Thaur: Druck- und Verlagshaus Thaur, 1999).

[3] A very useful overview of Clement's appearance in early English literature is provided by Michael Lapidge, "The Saintly Life in Anglo-Saxon England," in *The Cambridge Companion to Old English Literature*, ed. Malcolm Godden and Michael Lapidge (Cambridge: Cambridge University Press, 1991), 243–63.

[4] Rebecca Rushforth, *An Atlas of Saints in Anglo-Saxon Calendars* (Cambridge: Department of Anglo-Saxon, Norse and Celtic, 2002), Table XI, lists 27 calendars, in 22 of which Clement is named (his absence in those cases where he does not appear is generally due to the fragmentary nature of the manuscript). Most of the calendars are printed in Francis Wormald, ed., *English Kalendars before A.D. 1100*, Henry Bradshaw Society 72

extant liturgical calendar, the 8th-century Calendar of St Willibrord,[1] and the Old English Metrical Calendar, in which Clement's appearance amongst twenty-eight liturgical feasts includes an allusion to the drowning described in his passion.[2] A lengthier description of Clement's *passio* and *inventio* is provided in the martyrology of Bede,[3] while the later 9th-century Old English Martyrology expands this further to include pre- and post-death miracles.[4] A fuller account still of Clement's passion and miracles is provided in the Cotton-Corpus Legendary, which supplied the hagiographical material for Ælfric's homily on his feast day.[5] Numerous churches were also dedicated to the saint. If the churches of St Clement Danes and St Clement, Eastcheap in London and St Clement in Oxford are amongst the best known today, they were but three amongst some fifty which stood in medieval England, more than half of which were located to the east of the River Thames, in the southern part of the Danelaw, with most of the rest scattered towards the coast in the south-east and far south-west.[6]

(London: Henry Bradshaw Society, 1934). On Clement's inclusion in liturgical books, see Joyce Hill, "Ælfric's Homily for the Feast of St Clement," in *Ælfric's Lives of Canonised Popes*, ed. Donald Scragg, Old English Newsletter Subsidia 30 (Kalamazoo: Medieval Institute Publications, 2001), 99–110, at 101, note 8.

[1] Cf. Henry Albert Wilson, ed., *The Calendar of St Willibrord from MS Paris. Lat. 10837: Facsimile with Transcription, Introduction and Notes*, Henry Bradshaw Society 55 (Woodbridge: Boydell, 1918), 13.

[2] Edited as *Menologium* in Elliott Van Kirk Dobbie, ed., *The Anglo-Saxon Minor Poems*, Anglo-Saxon Poetic Records 6 (London: Routledge, 1942), 49–55; this edition has been superseded by Kazutomo Karasawa, ed., *The Old English Metrical Calendar (Menologium)*, Anglo-Saxon Texts (Cambridge: Brewer, 2015).

[3] Cf. Jacques Dubois and Geneviève Renaud, eds., *Edition pratique des martyrologes de Bède, de l'anonyme lyonnais et de Florus* (Paris: Editions du CNRS, 1976), 212.

[4] Cf. Günter Kotzor, ed., *Das altenglische Martyrologium*, 2 vols., Abhandlungen der Bayerischen Akademie der Wissenschaften, philosophisch-historische Klasse, n.F. 88 (Munich: Beck, 1981), 2:255–56.

[5] Cf. Peter Clemoes, ed., *Ælfric's Catholic Homilies: the First Series. Text*, EETS SS 17 (Oxford: EETS, 1997), 497–506. On Ælfric's sources, see Malcolm Godden, ed., *Ælfric's Catholic Homilies: Introduction, Commentary and Glossary*, EETS SS 18 (Oxford: EETS, 2000), 308–18 (esp. 308). On Ælfric's use of the Legendary, see the unpublished thesis of Patrick H. Zettel, "Ælfric's Hagiographic Sources and the Latin Legendary Preserved in BL MS Cotton Nero E i + CCCC MS 9 and Other Manuscripts" (DPhil, University of Oxford, 1980) (on Clement, esp. 162–66 and 241–44).

[6] Fewer churches were dedicated to St Clement elsewhere in the British Isles: while there were four in Scotland, there was only one in Ireland, and none in Wales. For a brief overview, see Barbara E. Crawford, "The Saint Clement Dedications at Clementhorpe and Pontefract Castle: Anglo-Scandinavian or Norman?," in *Myth, Rulership, Church and Charters: Essays in Honour of Nicholas Brooks*, ed. Julia Barrow and Andrew Wareham (Aldershot: Ashgate, 2008), 189–210, at 189–92. The extent of Clement's cult, with investigation of individual churches in Britain and consideration of the potential relationships

Yet while these facts attest to Clement's popularity as a saint in Britain, the extent to which they might elucidate the reasons underlying the decision to compose our *Vie de seint Clement* is less compelling. First, Clement was a much venerated saint through much of northern and western Europe, and the scope of his cult in Britain is not remarkable. Second, the focus in these early texts is not on the events recounted in the *Recognitiones*, but rather on those described in Clement's *Passio*, in particular his watery demise and subsequent marine miracles: that he was seen primarily as a saint who could protect those at risk from water is reflected by the overwhelming concentration of churches dedicated to him in areas by the coast or at risk from flooding.[1] Third, the evidence cited stems noticeably from the earlier medieval period: by the assumed time of our text's composition in the early 13th century, Clement's popularity would seem rather to have waned, with Nicholas having gained ground as a mariners' saint.[2] Although it could be argued that our author was seeking to promote or revive Clement's cult, or that the foregrounding of the maritime mishaps of Matthidia and her sons through the expository narrative might be viewed in the light of an awareness of Clement's martyrdom and miracles, there is little to suggest that our text either responded to or initiated a resurgence of interest in the saint.

While the Anglo-Norman *Clement* seems to have experienced only very limited dissemination, this stands in stark contrast to the Middle English verse account of his life incorporated into the various redactions of the late 13th-century *South English Legendary*.[3] This is, at 552 lines, a vastly shorter version of Clement's life than found in our *Clement*,[4] which stays much closer to the text incorporated into Jacobus de Voragine's *Legenda aurea* than is the case with some of the lives in the *SEL*.[5] While the *SEL* life of Clement presents occasional points

---

with the cult in Scandinavia, is explored in fascinating detail in Barbara E. Crawford, *The Churches Dedicated to St. Clement in Medieval England: a Hagio-Geography of the Seafarer's Saint in 11th-Century North Europe*, Scripta ecclesiastica 1 (St Petersburg: Axiōma, 2008).

[1] Cf. Crawford, *Churches Dedicated to St. Clement*, 52–55.

[2] Cf. Robert William Henry Miller, *One Firm Anchor: the Church and the Merchant Seafarer, an Introductory History* (Cambridge: Lutterworth, 2012), 61–64.

[3] Opinions regarding the date of composition vary, but the most widely accepted is probably still the period of c. 1270–85 suggested by Manfred Görlach, *The Textual Tradition of the South English Legendary*, Leeds Texts and Monographs, N.S. 6 (Leeds: University of Leeds School of English, 1974), 37–38.

[4] The edition cited is that available in Charlotte D'Evelyn and Anna Jean Mill, eds., *The South English Legendary*, 3 vols., EETS 235, 236, 244 (London: EETS, 1956), 2:515–33; the copy in Bodleian, MS Laud 108 is edited by Carl Horstmann, ed., *The Early South-English Legendary, or, Lives of Saints*, EETS 87 (London: EETS, 1887), 322–40.

[5] On the *Legenda aurea*, see above, p. 8, note 2. On its influence on the *SEL*, see Klaus P. Jankofsky, "*Legenda aurea* Materials in *The South English Legendary*: Translation, Transformation, Acculturation," in *Legenda aurea: sept siècles de diffusion*, ed. Brenda

of textual interest — for example, whereas our translator suffices himself with speculating, when faced with silence in the *Recognitiones*, that St Peter would undoubtedly have healed Matthidia's hands, the *SEL* Clement fills the similar gap in the *Legenda aurea* by declaring unequivocally that as soon as she was reunited with Clement, *Hire honden þat hire were bynome : anonriȝt hole were* (v. 189) — these are purely coincidental. More potentially significant is the extent of the diffusion of the life of Clement via the *SEL*. Surviving in over sixty manuscripts compiled between c. 1300 and the mid- to late 15th century, the *SEL* ranks amongst the most widely disseminated works in Middle English,[1] and amidst the shifting contents of the compilations subsumed for the convenience of scholarship under the banner of the *SEL*, the life of Clement is second only to that of St Peter in frequency of appearance.[2] Together with the translation of Jean de Vignay's French version of the *Legenda aurea* as the *Gilte legende* in the 15th century,[3] and subsequently Caxton's printing of the *Golden Legend* in 1483,[4] the *SEL* ensured that Clement's abridged life will have reached a far wider audience in medieval Britain than the Anglo-Norman *Clement* ever achieved.

Dunn-Lardeau (Montreal / Paris: Bellarmin / Vrin, 1986), 317–29. For a comparison of the versions of Clement's life in the *Legenda aurea* and the *SEL*, see Anne B. Thompson, *Everyday Saints and the Art of Narrative in the South English Legendary* (Aldershot: Ashgate, 2003), 163–71.

[1] Cf. Heather Blurton and Jocelyn Wogan-Browne, "Rethinking the *South English Legendaries*," in *Rethinking the South English Legendaries*, ed. Heather Blurton and Jocelyn Wogan-Browne, Manchester Medieval Literature and Culture, 3–19, at 3. On the manuscript transmission, see Görlach, *Textual Tradition*, esp. 77–130; Thomas R. Liszka, "The *South English Legendaries*," in *The North Sea World in the Middle Ages: Studies in the Cultural History of North-Western Europe*, ed. Thomas R. Liszka and Lorna E. M. Walker (Dublin: Four Courts Press, 2001), 243–82, reprinted in Blurton and Wogan-Browne, *Rethinking the South English Legendaries*, 23–65.

[2] Cf. Jocelyn Wogan-Browne, "Bodies of Belief: MS Bodley 779's *South English Legendary*," in Blurton and Wogan-Browne, *Rethinking the South English Legendaries* (Manchester: Manchester University Press, 2011), 403–23, at 407. Görlach, *Textual Tradition*, 306–9, records the presence of Clement in 17 of a sample of 24 manuscripts.

[3] Cf. Richard Frederick Sanger Hamer and Vida Russell, eds., *Gilte legende*, 3 vols., EETS 327, 328, 339 (Oxford: EETS, 2006–12), 2:863–74; the manuscripts are mid-15th century and later, but the colophon of one dates the translation to 1438 (cf. ibid., 3:47). On Jean de Vignay, see above, p. 8, note 2.

[4] Cf. Manfred Görlach, *The South English Legendary, Gilte Legende and Golden Legend*, Braunschweiger anglistische Arbeiten 3 (Braunschweig: Institut für Anglistik und Amerikanistik, 1972); Auvo Kurvinen, "Caxton's *Golden Legend* and the Manuscripts of the *Gilte Legende*," *Neuphilologische Mitteilungen* 60 (1959): 353–75.

Simon Magus

Another possible point of interest lies in the figure of Simon Magus.[1] Simon is introduced in Acts 8:9–24 as a man who through his magical deeds has deceived the people of Samaria into believing him to be the power of God, until the preaching of Philip convinces both Simon and the people to be baptised. The apostles send Peter and John to Samaria to confer the Holy Ghost by the imposition of their hands, and when Simon sees this wonder, he offers money in an attempt to buy the power for himself; Peter refuses firmly, and Simon asks Peter to pray on his behalf. On the basis of this meagre scriptural narrative, Simon was soon to become one of the most maligned figures in Christian writing. Church historians and heresiologists were quick to identify him as the leader and author of all heresies, associated with the adulteration of truth and the promotion of idolatry, including worship of effigies of himself and his concubine, Helena.[2]

The Clementine literature plays a crucial role in fleshing out the nature of Simon's crimes.[3] While there is perhaps a certain irony, given the increasing preoccupation with simony in the Middle Ages, that *Clement* does not depict Simon reprising the crime of bartering in spiritual things named after him for his scriptural transgression,[4] his characterisation as a heretic is clear. He is presented as a

---

[1] On the development of the image of Simon, see Ferreiro, *Simon Magus*; William R. Cook and Ronald B. Herzman, "Simon Magus and the Medieval Tradition," *Journal of Magic History* 2 (1980): 28–43; James Nohrnberg, *The Analogy of The Faerie Queene* (Princeton: Princeton University Press, 1976), 247–60.

[2] Cf. e.g., Irenaeus, *Adversus haereses*, I.23 (*ANF* 1:347–48); Philaster of Brescia, *Liber de haeresibus*, xxix (*PL* 12:1137D-1141A); Tertullian, *Apologia adversus gentes*, xiii (*PL* 1:347A-348A); Eusebius, *Historia ecclesiastica*, II.xiii-xiv (*NPNF2* 1:113–15); Augustine, *De haeresibus*, i (*PL* 42:25–26).

[3] On the texts' general treatment of heretics, see Annette Yoshiko Reed, "Heresiology and the (Jewish-)Christian Novel: Narrativized Polemics in the Pseudo-Clementines," in *Heresy and Self-Definition in Late Antiquity*, ed. Eduard Iricinschi and Holger M. Zelletin, Texts and Studies in Ancient Judaism 119 (Tübingen: Mohr Siebeck, 2008), 273–89. On Simon in particular, see Dominique Côté, "La fonction littéraire de Simon le Magicien dans les Pseudo-Clémentines," *Laval Théologique et Philosophique* 57 (2001): 513–23.

[4] The earliest attestations of *simonie* and related forms date from the 12th century, derived from the Church Latin *simonia*; cf. *FEW* 11:633b-634b. On the process whereby simony gained particular prominence, see e.g., Uta-Renate Blumenthal, *Der Investiturstreit*, Kohlhammer Urban-Taschenbücher 335 (Stuttgart: Kohlhammer, 1982); John Gilchrist, "*Simoniaca haeresis* and the Problem of Orders from Leo IX to Gratian," in *Proceedings of the Second International Congress of Medieval Canon Law, Boston College, 12–16 August 1963*, ed. S. Kuttner and J. J. Ryan, Momenta iuris canonici, series C: subsidia (Vatican: S. Congregatio Semionariis et Studiorum Universitatibus, 1965), 209–35; Jean Leclercq, "Simoniaca heresis," in *Studi Gregoriani per la storia di Gregorio VII e della riforma Gregoriana*, ed. Giovanni Battista Borino (Rome: Abbazia di San Paolo, 1947),

disciple of Dositheus, who has persuaded people that he is God by claiming that he is an eternal power, that his concubine Luna is the moon, and that his thirty acolytes represent the days of the lunar cycle. Having infiltrated the sect, however, Simon soon begins an affair with Luna and starts to undermine Dositheus, eventually usurping his position (vv. 2005–204). If this episode underlines Simon's treacherous and deceptive nature, it also portrays his rise to power as a heresiarch and the manner in which heresy can spread. Within the context of the late 12th and early 13th century, amidst fears about popular heretical sects such as the Waldensians and Cathars, one can imagine that this evocation of the propagation of heresy and its polluting effects could have held a particular interest and resonance for the audience of *Clement*.[1] Nonetheless, it should be noted that the heretical component of Simon's portrayal is in fact diminished in our text relative to the *Recognitiones*. While Simon's pretentions to godhead and his desire for worship are certainly retained, the thoroughgoing abridgement of his disputations with Peter effectively removes the vast majority of his heretical doctrine and arguments: we are assured in summary that he recounted many heresies (v. 2839), but the details of his heterodoxy are suppressed.

The treatment of Simon's magical practices is, however, quite different. *Clement*'s adoption of the exposition allows for Simon to make an early appearance as a ne'er-do-well companion to Niceta and Aquila during their formative years. Simon is introduced as a *nigromancien* ("necromancer," v. 387), and we are immediately treated to the first of a number of catalogues of his vain wonders: he adopts the appearance of an old man and then a child; he makes statues move; he gives stone the appearance of bread; he makes brazen dogs bark; he causes mountains to shake; he flies from one place to another, borne aloft by devils (vv. 391–98). As the text progresses, these deeds are repeatedly evoked, and are complemented by an ever expanding list of other wonders. He claims the ability to make himself invisible; pass through mountains and rocks; fall from

---

522–30; Hans Meier-Welcker, "Die Simonie im frühen Mittelalter," *Zeitschrift für Kirchengeschichte* 64 (1952–53): 61–93; Joseph Weitzel, *Begriff und Erscheinungsformen der Simonie bei Gratian und den Dekretisten*, Münchener theologische Studien, 3: Kanonistische Abteilung 25 (Munich: Hueber, 1967).

[1] For a brief introduction to medieval heretical movements, see Malcolm David Lambert, *Medieval Heresy: Popular Movements from the Gregorian Reform to the Reformation*, 3rd ed. (Oxford: Blackwell, 2002); Gordon Leff, *Heresy in the Later Middle Ages: the Relation of Heterodoxy to Dissent, c.1250–c.1450* (Manchester: Manchester University Press, 1967); Robert Ian Moore, *The Formation of a Persecuting Society: Power and Deviance in Western Europe* (Oxford: Blackwell, 1987); Jeffrey B. Russell, *Religious Dissent in the Middle Ages* (New York / London / Sydney / Toronto: Wiley & Sons, 1971); Lucy J. Sackville, *Heresy and Heretics in the Thirteenth Century: the Textual Representations*, Heresy and Inquisition in the Middle Ages 1 (Woodbridge: York Medieval Press, 2011); Walter Leggett Wakefield and Austin Patterson Evans, *Heresies of the High Middle Ages* (New York: Columbia University Press, 1991).

a mountain without harm; escape from chains and bind his captors; make trees bear fruit; place himself in fire without burning; cause children to grow beards; appear as a sheep or goat; exhibit gold; and make kings and depose them; and he also says that he once commanded a sickle to reap such that it reaped ten times more than any harvester (vv. 2051–120). His victory over Dositheus is secured by causing the blows with which the enraged heresiarch seeks to avenge himself to pass through his body as if through smoke, and he soon celebrates by performing a wonder which involves Luna leaning out from a tower and appearing to be visible from all sides (vv. 2157–200). When he has been so humiliated by Peter in disputation that only one of his followers remains, Simon places about his shoulders undefined instruments of foul magic with unspecified but clearly nefarious intent (vv. 4299–308).

While the theological component of the conflict between Peter and Simon tends to be lessened through the abridgement of the disputations of the *Recognitiones*, *Clement* very much foregrounds the decisive role that magic plays in settling their arguments. Following the exposition, we find Clement beset by religious doubts, in particular concerning the immortality of the soul, so much so that he contemplates consulting necromancers in Egypt who might conjure forth a soul to reveal the truth (vv. 737–852). When Peter and his followers are later preparing for the disputation with Simon in Caesarea, the twins recount that during their time with the necromancer, he had revealed that he had killed a virgin child for the very purpose of summoning it forth to divulge information (vv. 2209–20); when challenged, he had then amended his story, claiming divinity and omnipotence and explaining that the image of a child that he possessed was not connected with necromancy, but rather represented the human that he had created from air and water before returning it to the air (vv. 2385–402). In the following disputation, Peter then triumphs when he proves that the soul is immortal—thus echoing the existential crisis in which we originally found Clement—by citing as evidence the image of the child that Simon uses in his necromancy. Later in the text, when Simon seeks to evade punishment for his sorcery and to avenge himself on the twins by placing his own face on Faustinianus, Peter again triumphs by using Simon's own magic against him, by having Faustinianus in the guise of Simon make a public confession which leads the people to reject Simon and turn to Peter: he acknowledges that all Simon's wonders were vain and futile, performed *par enchantement* ("through sorcery," v. 12750) and the Devil's art—just as the narrator had said when introducing Simon in the exposition (vv. 391, 398)—whereas Peter's miracles bring health, life, and salvation, and are performed in the name of Him whose message he bears (vv. 12675–774).

Faustinianus's words serve to underline the extent to which the conflict between Simon and Peter is one between illegitimate and legitimate magic.[1] Peter,

---

[1] Cf. Valerie Irene Jane Flint, *The Rise of Magic in Early Medieval Europe* (Oxford: Clarendon, 1991), 338–44.

following Christ his master, is no less a magician than Simon when performing miracles such as curing the sick, the deaf, the mute, the blind, the lame, and the insane: the crucial difference concerns method and intent. Peter explains this to Niceta when the latter asks how people should avoid being deceived by Simon's magic, admitting that he himself would have had difficulty distinguishing between the wonders performed in Pharaoh's court by Moses and the sorcerers: the bad king, the Devil, would like to perform true wonders, but can only perform vain and pointless illusions, while the good king alone has the power to perform beneficial miracles (vv. 4047–196). Simon performs empty wonders through diabolical agency, yet claims magical power for himself in pursuit of fame and glory (cf. vv. 4353–56); Peter performs true miracles, but clarifies explicitly that he is but a mortal man through whom Christ can bring salvation (vv. 13017–46), seeking no gain other than zealous converts to Christ (cf. vv. 10957–68). While the episode involving the changing of Faustinianus's face marks the culmination of this battle between forms of magic in the *Recognitiones*, in *Clement* the addition of the *Passio* material develops it further and brings it to a crescendo through the final battle in Nero's court: in the extant section, we see Peter defeat Simon in a mind-reading challenge and at the same time repel the necromancer's hell-hounds by producing some consecrated bread hidden in his sleeves; the abrupt ending of our copy deprives us of Peter's ultimate triumph, when he and Paul thwart Simon's attempts to fly up from a tower to his alleged father when through prayer they drive away the devils carrying him, leaving him to fall to his death.

While our translator was evidently enthused by his sources' presentation of Simon's magical activities, the significance of their inclusion is more difficult to ascertain. Although Simon's heretical pronouncements are curtailed, the full treatment of his necromantic transgressions might be seen as a topical attempt to evoke the aberrant practices in which contemporary heretics might be suspected of engaging. The focus on magic might more specifically be seen as reflecting a contemporary interest in, or concern regarding, illicit magical and necromantic practices,[1] or an attempt to clarify for the audience in contradistinction to such

---

[1] The field of magic in the Middle Ages is vast, and currently enjoying a surge in scholarship. For an introduction, see Jean-Patrice Boudet, *Entre science et nigromance: astrologie, divination et magie dans l'occident médiéval (XIIe–XVe siècle)*, Histoire Ancienne et Médiévale 83 (Paris: Publications de la Sorbonne, 2006); Charles Burnett, *Magic and Divination in the Middle Ages: Texts and Techniques in the Islamic and Christian Worlds*, Variorum Collected Studies 557 (Aldershot: Variorum, 1996); Claire Fanger, *Conjuring Spirits: Texts and Traditions of Late Medieval Ritual Magic* (University Park, PA: Pennsylvania State University Press, 1998); Graziella Federici-Vescovini, *Le Moyen Age magique: la magie entre religion et science du XIIIe au XIVe siècle*, Etudes de Philosophie Médiévale 97 (Paris: Vrin, 2011); Richard Kieckhefer, *Magic in the Middle Ages* (Cambridge: Cambridge University Press, 1989); Frank F. Klaassen, *The Transformations of Magic: Illicit*

practices the orthodoxy and legitimacy of the miraculous works performed by Peter's successors in rituals such as the consecration of the Eucharist. None of these explanations, however, need preclude the possibility that the translator recognised in Simon's deviant exploits not only an essential part of his characterisation, but also a feature consonant with the strategy of retaining exciting elements while omitting those which might prove tedious.

Simon's portrayal as a heretic and worker of vain wonders may have held a further relevance for *Clement*'s audience, as we can see if we consider, for example, his outburst following his defeat during the disputation with Peter (vv. 3839–78). Here he denies that Jesus is the Christ; he declares himself to be God and the Son of God, claiming a miraculous incarnation in the womb of Rachel, the power to live for ever and to grant eternal life, and the ability to turn stones to bread and to be borne down from a mountain by angels; and he boasts of the wonders that he has performed, such as flying through the air, mingling his body with fire, and making statues move. While the *Recognitiones* does not include from the Pseudo-Clementine *Homilies* the explanation by Peter to Clement that his own arrival to counter the deceiver Simon prefigures the eventual arrival of Christ after Antichrist,[1] it is abundantly clear that Simon's depiction is conditioned by scriptural allusions to the deceivers who would deny Christ, falsely claim to be the Messiah, and perform vain wonders.[2] This association between Simon and Antichrist is made all the more clear in *Clement* through the addition of the *Passio Petri et Pauli*, in particular the episode in which Simon strives to prove to Nero that he is the Son of God by requesting that he be decapitated in order that he might prove his divinity by rising from the dead three days later: Simon's success in this fraudulent resurrection by substituting for himself a sheep that the hapless executioner decapitates was identified by some medieval writers as a magical deception emblematic of Antichrist.[3] *Clement*'s sources and their reception thus play an important part in the development of a venerable custom of identifying Simon Magus as the first representative of a succession of heretics

---

Learned Magic in the Later Middle Ages and Renaissance, Magic in History (University Park, PA: Pennsylvania State University Press, 2013).

[1] *Homilies*, 2.17.3–5; cf. Bernhard Rehm and Georg Strecker, eds., *Die Pseudoklementinen I: Homilien*, 3rd ed., Die griechischen christlichen Schriftsteller der ersten drei Jahrhunderte 42 (Berlin: Akademie Verlag, 1992), 42.

[2] Cf. e.g., 1 Jn 1:7, 2:22, 4:3; Lk 21:8, Mk 13:6, Mt 24:5; Mt 4:3–6; Mk 13:22, Mt 24:24.

[3] The connection is made in an 11th-century interpolation in the *Libellus de Antichristo* of Adso of Montier-en-Der (Daniel Verhelst, ed., *Adso Dervensis De ortu et tempore Antichristi*, Corpus Christianorum: Continuatio Mediaevalis 45 [Turnhout: Brepols, 1976], 45; also found in the commentary attributed to Haymo of Auxerre, in *PL* 117:782a), and likewise in the Middle English *Cursor Mundi* (Richard Morris, ed., *Cursor Mundi: a Northumbrian Poem of the XIVth Century*, Vol. 4, EETS 66 [London: Trübner for EETS, 1877], vv. 22161–64).

professing to be Christ which would ultimately culminate in Antichrist,[1] such that "By the late Middle Ages it had become thoroughly ensconced in tradition that Simon [. . .] was Antichrist, actually, or at least his chief member."[2]

This association between Simon and Antichrist is vividly expressed in the mid-13th-century Abingdon Apocalypse (London, BL Ms Add. 42555), which presents a Latin text of the Apocalypse of St John and a facing-page prose commentary in Anglo-Norman, with the top half of each page filled by lavish illustrations.[3] Chapter 13 of the Apocalypse famously recounts the arrival of two beasts on earth: the first, rising from the sea, has seven heads and ten horns, and when one of its heads appears fatally wounded, it is healed, and the people worship it; a second beast, with two horns, then rises from the earth, and causes people to worship the first beast and to bear its mark, the number 666. Fol. 43v of the Abingdon Apocalypse presents the Latin text of Apoc. 13:14–15, which tells of the wonders that the second beast performs to deceive the people, and of his instruction to make an image of the beast, which it then brought to life and caused to speak. The Anglo-Norman commentary explains: "The fact that the beast is said to be wounded by the sword, and yet still to live, may mean that Antichrist pretends to be dead, and then rises again through the art of the Devil, and thereby causes the people to be deceived more easily. And it is said that

---

[1] Cf. e.g., Bede's interpretations of Mt 4:24, Mk 13:5–6, Mk 13:21–22, Lk 17:22, Lk 21:8 (*PL* 92:102C, 260A, 263B, 545C, 585D). For the developing tradition of associating Simon and Antichrist, cf. Jerome on Mt 24:5 (*PL* 26:176A-B); Gregory, *Moralia*, 29.17.15, on Job 38:15 (*PL* 76:484C). Bede's comments on the line extending from Simon Magus to Antichrist are repeated in, for example, the gloss on Lk 17:23 by Hincmar of Rheims (*De Praedestinatione Dei et libero Arbitrio dissertatio posterior*, ep. cap. 6, in *PL* 125:462C), Rabanus Maurus (*Homilia* 144, in *PL* 110:424C), and Bonaventure (Adolphe-Charles Peltier, ed., *S.R.E. Cardinalis S. Bonaventurae ex Ordine Minorum Episcopi Albanensis, Eximii Ecclesiae Doctoris opera omnia* [Paris: Vives, 1867], 11:62), and in the interpretations of Mt 24:11 and Mk 13:6, 21 in the *Glossa ordinaria* (*PL* 114:161B, 226D, 227C). Bruno of Segni's interpretation of Mt 24:4 (*PL* 165:269B) identifies Simon and Antichrist as deceivers claiming to be God, and in his comments on Lk 10:16 (*PL* 165:385B) he links Nero, Simon Magus, Diocletian, Maximian, and Antichrist.

[2] John Parker, *The Aesthetics of Antichrist: from Christian Drama to Christopher Marlowe* (Ithaca / London: Cornell University Press, 2007), 228. Further on Simon and Antichrist, see Richard Kenneth Emmerson and Ronald B. Herzman, "Antichrist, Simon Magus, and Dante's *Inferno* XIX," *Traditio* 36 (1980): 373–98; Richard Kenneth Emmerson, *Antichrist in the Middle Ages: a Study of Medieval Apocalypticism, Art, and Literature* (Manchester: Manchester University Press, 1981), 27–31, 75–76, 93, 122–24.

[3] Dean no. 474; my edition of the text is forthcoming. The manuscript was given to Abingdon Abbey by Bishop Giles de Bridport shortly before 1262; cf. Suzanne Lewis, "Giles of Bridport and the Abingdon Apocalypse," in *England in the Thirteenth Century: Proceedings of the 1984 Harlaxton Symposium*, Harlaxton Medieval Studies 1 (Woodbridge: Boydell, 1986), 107–19.

Simon Magus did the very same thing."[1] The association is underlined in the accompanying image, which depicts a hooded Simon standing above the resurrected dead beside a seated Antichrist, equipped with wings which presage his fateful flight in Rome.[2]

While the cited Anglo-Norman commentary is found only in the Abingdon Apocalypse, this is anything but the case with the Latin text from which it is derived: the Apocalypse commentary by Berengaudus.[3] This enjoyed a vast transmission, in no small part due to an important development which may be of particular relevance to our interpretation of the significance of Simon's portrayal as an Antichrist figure in *Clement*. The middle of the 13th century witnessed the beginning of a vogue of richly illustrated Apocalypse manuscripts, of which some eighty produced in England and France over the next two centuries still survive.[4] Half of these contain solely Latin material, usually includ-

---

[1] *Ce k'est dit la beste aver playe de l'espee, e vivere, ce poet estre ke Auntecrist se feingne mort, e pus relever par l'art del Diable, e par cest fet plus legerement desceyvre* [MS *desceyne*] *la gent. E si est dit ke Symon Magus feseit cele memes* (fol. 44r; transcription regularised).

[2] The painting of the image has not been completed in the Abingdon Apocalypse, but it has been in the Gulbenkian Apocalypse (Lisbon, Museu Calouste Gulbenkian MS L.A. 139, fol. 36v), a closely affiliated English manuscript of similar age in which the commentary is in Latin. For discussion of this image, and also of the depiction of Simon on fol. 20r in connection with Apoc. 8:1, including analysis of the explicitly Jewish features of Simon's portrayal, see Suzanne Lewis, *"Tractatus adversus Judaeos* in the Gulbenkian Apocalypse," *The Art Bulletin* 68, no. 4 (1986): 543–66, at 554–59. These images are likewise discussed by Emmerson and Herzman, "Antichrist, Simon Magus, and Dante's *Inferno* XIX," 379–82, who also describe the iconographical associations which developed between depictions of Simon's fall from the sky in Rome and the fall of Antichrist, on which also see Charles Zika, *The Appearance of Witchcraft: Print and Visual Culture in Sixteenth-Century Europe* (London: Routledge, 2007), 173. Some sense of the popularity of the representation of Simon's fall across a range of media can be gleaned from the inventory of images compiled by Ferreiro, *Simon Magus*, 323ff.

[3] *Expositio super septem visiones libri Apocalypsis*, in *PL* 17:763–970. On Berengaudus, see Achim Dittrich, *Mater Ecclesiae: Geschichte und Bedeutung eines umstrittenen Marientitels*, Bonner dogmatische Studien 44 (Bonn: Echter, 2009); Guy Lobrichon, "L'Apocalypse en débat: entre séculiers et moines au XIIe siècle (c. 1080–c. 1180)," in *L'Apocalisse nel medioevo: atti del Convegno Internazionale dell'Università degli Studi di Milano e della Società Internazionale per lo Studio del Medioevo latino (Gargnano sul Garda 18–20 maggio 2009)*, ed. Rossana E. Gugliemetti (Florence: SISMEL, 2011), 403–26; Derk Visser, *Apocalypse as Utopian Expectation (800–1500): the Apocalypse Commentary of Berengaudus of Ferrières and the Relationship between Exegesis, Liturgy, and Iconography*, Studies in the History of Christian Thought 73 (Leiden: Brill, 1996).

[4] On the Apocalypse manuscripts, see Léopold Delisle and Paul Meyer, eds., *Apocalypse en français au XIIIe siècle (Bibl. Nat. fr. 403)*, 2 vols., SATF 44 (Paris: Didot, 1900–1); Richard K. Emmerson and Suzanne Lewis, "Census and Bibliography of Medieval Manuscripts Containing Apocalypse Illustrations, ca. 800–1500: II," *Traditio* 41 (1985):

ing the Berengaudus commentary, while the rest contain Anglo-Norman and French texts. Within this vernacular corpus, the Abingdon Apocalypse is one of a small group of Anglo-Norman unica, including the Trinity Apocalypse[1] and William Giffard's rhymed Apocalypse,[2] with the majority of the manuscripts belonging to one of two major traditions: the Anglo-Norman verse Apocalypse,[3] which survives in ten copies, and the French Prose Apocalypse,[4] which survives in over thirty copies, the majority of which, including the earliest witnesses, are of English origin.[5] While the precise reasons why Apocalypse manuscripts became popular in the mid-13th century remain unclear,[6] one factor may involve

---

367–409; Montague Rhodes James, *The Apocalypse in Art*, Schweich Lectures in Biblical Archaeology 1927 (London: Published for the British Academy by H. Milford, Oxford, 1931); Peter K. Klein, "The Apocalypse in Medieval Art," in *The Apocalypse in the Middle Ages*, ed. Richard Kenneth Emmerson and Bernard McGinn (Ithaca, NY: Cornell University Press, 1992), 159–99; Suzanne Lewis, *Reading Images: Narrative Discourse and Reception in the Thirteenth-Century Illuminated Apocalypse* (Cambridge / New York: Cambridge University Press, 1995); Nigel J. Morgan, *Early Gothic Manuscripts II: 1250–1285*, A Survey of Manuscripts Illuminated in the British Isles 4 (London / New York: Harvey Miller / Oxford University Press, 1988); Nigel J. Morgan, "Latin and Vernacular Apocalypses," in *The New Cambridge History of the Bible: from 600 to 1450*, ed. Richard Marsden and E. Ann Matter (Cambridge: Cambridge University Press, 2012), 404–26; Nigel J. Morgan, "Some French Interpretations of English Illustrated Apocalypses c. 1290–1330," in *England and the Continent in the Middle Ages: Studies in Memory of Andrew Martindale*, ed. John Mitchell, Harlaxton Medieval Studies 8 (Stamford: Shaun Tyas, 2000), 137–56.

[1] Dean no. 473; edited by Ian Short in David McKitterick *et al.*, *Die Trinity-Apokalypse: Faksimile und Kommentar*, 2 vols. (Lucerne: Faksimile Verlag, 2004), 2:197–356.

[2] Dean no. 477; cf. Olwen Rhys and John Fox, eds., *An Anglo-Norman Rhymed Apocalypse, with Commentary: from the Giffard Ms. Formerly in the Possession of Sir John Fox and Now in the Bodleian*, ANTS 6 (Oxford: Blackwell, 1946).

[3] Dean no. 478; cf. Pitts, *Revelacion (BL Royal 2.D.xiii)*.

[4] Dean no. 475. Editions based on individual manuscripts are printed by Paul Meyer in Delisle and Meyer, *Apocalypse en français*, 2, and by Daron Burrows in Nigel Morgan, Peter Kidd, and Daron Lee Burrows, *Apocalipsis Yates Thompson (MS. 10) / Apocalypse Yates Thompson: Libro de estudios / Book of Studies* (Madrid: AyN Ediciones, 2010), 99–192.

[5] Cf. Daron Lee Burrows, "'Vers la fin croistra la religion': the End of the World According to the Medieval French Prose Apocalypse," in *Visions of Apocalypse: Representations of the End in French Literature and Culture*, ed. Leonie Archer and Alex Stuart (Bern / Oxford: Peter Lang, 2013), 15–42; John C. Fox, "The Earliest French Apocalypse and Commentary," *Modern Language Review* 7 (1912): 444–68.

[6] On the possible influence of the *Bibles moralisées*, see Günter Breder, *Die lateinische Vorlage des altfranzösischen Apokalypsenkommentars des 13. Jahrhunderts (Paris, B.N., ms. fr. 403)*, Forschungen zur romanischen Philologie 9 (Münster: Aschendorff, 1960); John Lowden, "The Apocalypse in the Early-Thirteenth-Century *Bibles Moralisées*: a Reassessment," in *Prophecy, Apocalypse and the Day of Doom: Proceedings of the 2000 Harlax-*

the influential Apocalypse commentary written in the late 12th century by the
Calabrian Abbot, Joachim of Fiore, which was interpreted by some as indicating
that the third and final age of the world would begin following a great catastro-
phe set to occur around 1260.[1] Indeed, the famous Benedictine chronicler of St
Alban's, Matthew Paris, had brought the date of the advent of Antichrist for-
ward to 1250, as he considered that the invasion of the East by the Mongols (or
Tartars) in the late 1230s and early 1240s represented the gathering of Gog and
Magog for the final battle prophesied in Apoc. 20:7.[2]

   While it is questionable whether the context adumbrated would suffice as
proof of a surge in eschatological preoccupations in mid-13th-century Britain, there is no doubt that *Clement* provides strident reminders of the terrors
of the impending Judgement. The *juise Deu* ("judgement of God," v. 2243) is
nigh, bringing rewards to the righteous and punishment to the impious (cf. vv.
1121–24, 1381–85, 1513–22, 2289–92, 2417–18 etc.); those who fail to heed the
word of God will suffer eternal torments in Hell (vv. 5267–72, 6815–24); those
soaked in sin and not cleansed by baptism will ignite all the more quickly (vv.
8819–64). The message may impress more through its insistent repetition than
its originality, but its importance to our translator is evident from his tendency
to amplify the pertinent material supplied by the *Recognitiones*,[3] and it is possible
that the presentation of Simon as an avatar of Antichrist could have had the additional salutary benefit of impressing upon his audience the imminence of the
Last Judgement.

---

ton Symposium, ed. Nigel Morgan, Harlaxton Medieval Studies 12 (Donington: Shaun
Tyas, 2004), 195–219.

   [1] On Joachim and his influence, see Bernard McGinn, *The Calabrian Abbot: Joachim
of Fiore in the History of Western Thought* (New York / London: MacMillan, 1985); Mar-
jorie Ethel Reeves, *The Influence of Prophecy in the Later Middle Ages: a Study in Joachimism*
(Oxford: Clarendon, 1969); Marjorie Ethel Reeves, "The Originality and Influence of
Joachim of Fiore," *Traditio* 36 (1980): 269–316. For discussion of the parallel drawn by
Joachim between Simon and Antichrist, see Richard Kenneth Emmerson and Ronald
B. Herzman, *The Apocalyptic Imagination in Medieval Literature*, The Middle Ages Series
(Philadelphia: University of Pennsylvania Press, 1992), 21–22.

   [2] Cf. Henry Richards Luard, ed., *Matthæi Parisiensis, monachi Sancti Albani, Chronica majora*, 7 vols., Rerum Britannicarum Medii Aevi Scriptores 57, i-vii (London: Long-
man, 1872–84), 1:81, note 1, and 6:80. On Matthew's prophecy and its reception, see
Morton Wilfred Bloomfield and Marjorie E. Reeves, "The Penetration of Joachism into
Northern Europe," *Speculum* 29 (1954): 772–93, at 787–88; Hans-Eberhard Hilpert, "Zu
den Prophetien im Geschichtswerk des Matthaeus Paris," *Deutsches Archiv für Erforsc-
hung des Mittelalters* 41 (1985): 175–91; Suzanne Lewis, *The Art of Matthew Paris in the
Chronica Majora*, California Studies in the History of Art 21 (Berkeley / Los Angeles:
University of California Press, 1987), 102–4.

   [3] Cf. notes to vv. 3931–46, 7391–44, 9551–72.

Fourth Lateran Council

One of the most forceful influences on our author's decision to write *Clement*—and doubtless an important factor in the popularity of the Apocalypse manuscripts—may be deduced from his prologue. Having lamented the vainglorious exploits of clerics who write in Latin solely in order to secure praise from their brethren, he declares that it would be preferable if works written by venerable authors known to be of unimpeachable virtue were adapted into the vernacular so that laypeople and clerics with a knowledge of French and a desire to avoid sloth might derive *pru* ("profit," v. 34) and *amendement* ("improvement," v. 46) from them.

In this declaration of intent, we may detect the far-reaching effects of the Fourth Lateran Council (1215). In convoking this Council, Pope Innocent III had identified as his primary aims the extirpation of vices and the reform of morals within the Christian Church.[1] This dual ambition is writ large across the body of momentous canons promulgated by the Council, as is the awareness that education of the *corpus Christianorum* would be essential to its realisation.[2] In the following decades, the canons of Lateran IV were to enjoy a wide dissemination and frequent reiteration in England, as elsewhere in Europe.[3] One of the important consequences of this programme of moral reform was the creation of a vast body of instructional literature which distilled into an appropriately accessible form essential moral and theological teachings, such as the ten commandments, the seven sins, and the seven sacraments;[4] and while much of this was in Latin, and aimed particularly at the clergy entrusted with the responsibility of

---

[1] Augustus Potthast, ed., *Regesta pontificum romanorum inde ab a. post Christum natum MCXCVIII ad a. MCCCIV*, 2 vols. (Berlin: Rudolf de Decker, 1873–75), 1:407–8 (no. 4706).

[2] For the canons, see Giuseppe Alberigo, ed., *Conciliorum oecumenicorum decreta*, 3rd ed. (Bologna: Istituto per le Scienze Religiose, 1973), 227–71; Antonio García y García, ed., *Constitutiones Concilii quarti Lateranensis una cum commentariis glossatorum*, Monumenta Iuris Canonici, Series A: Corpus Glossatorum 2 (Vatican: Biblioteca Apostolica Vaticana, 1981).

[3] Cf. e.g., Marion E. Gibbs and Jane Lang, *Bishops and Reform, 1215–1272, with Special Reference to the Lateran Council of 1215*, Oxford Historical Series (London: Oxford University Press, 1934).

[4] Cf. Leonard E. Boyle, "The Fourth Lateran Council and Manuals of Popular Theology," in *The Popular Literature of Medieval England*, ed. Thomas J Heffernan, Tennessee Studies in Literature 28 (Knoxville: University of Tennessee Press, 1985), 30–43; Joseph Ward Goering, "Pastoralia: the Popular Literature of the Care of Souls," in *Medieval Latin: an Introduction and Bibliographical Guide*, ed. Frank A. C. Mantello and Arthur George Rigg (Washington: Catholic University of America Press, 1996), 670–76; Joseph Ward Goering, "Leonard E. Boyle and the Invention of 'Pastoralia'," in *A Companion to Pastoral Care in the Late Middle Ages (1200–1500)*, ed. Ronald James Stansbury, Brill's Companions to the Christian Tradition 22 (Leiden: Brill, 2010), 7–20.

taking confession,[1] there was also a substantial market both for parishioners and for their ministers who preferred to receive similar edification in the vernacular.[2]

During the 12th century, Anglo-Norman literature had already distinguished itself through the precocity, richness, and diversity of the religious material which was produced:[3] beside scriptural translations such as the Oxford Psalter,[4] the *Proverbes de Salemon*,[5] and the *Quatre Livre des Reis*,[6] and the Marian miracles of Adgar and his anonymous successor,[7] we find a remarkable

---

[1] On the *summae confessorum*, see Leonard E. Boyle, "*Summae confessorum*," in *Les Genres littéraires dans les sources théologiques et philosophiques médiévales: définition, critique et exploitation*, ed. Robert Bultot (Louvain-la-Neuve: Institut d'Etudes Médiévales, 1982), 227–37; Joseph Ward Goering, "The Internal Forum and the Literature of Penance and Confession," in *The History of Medieval Canon Law in the Classical Period, 1140–1234: from Gratian to the Decretals of Pope Gregory IX*, ed. Wilfried Hartmann and Kenneth Pennington (Washington: Catholic University of America Press, 2008), 379–428; Pierre Michaud-Quantin, *Sommes de casuistique et manuels de confession au moyen âge (XIIe-XVIe siècles)*, Analecta Mediaevalia Namurcensia 13 (Louvain: Nauwelaerts, 1962).

[2] Cf. George H. Russell, "Vernacular Instruction of the Laity in the Later Middle Ages in England: Some Texts and Notes," *Journal of Religious History* 2 (1962): 98–119; Andrew Taylor, "Manual to Miscellany: Stages in the Commercial Copying of Vernacular Literature in England," *The Yearbook of English Studies* 33 (2003): 1–17.

[3] Cf. Mary Dominica Legge, "La précocité de la littérature anglo-normande," *Cahiers de civilisation médiévale* 8 (1965): 327–49. Particularly compelling evidence of the importance of 12th-century Anglo-Norman literature in Francophone literary history is provided by Maria Careri, Christine Ruby, and Ian Short, *Livres et écritures en français et en occitan au XIIe siècle: catalogue illustré*, Scritture e Libri del Medioevo 8 (Rome: Viella, 2011), xxxiii–xxxv, who demonstrate that two-thirds of the extant material copied in the century is of Insular provenance.

[4] Dean no. 445; Ian Short, *The Oxford Psalter*, ANTS 72 (Oxford: ANTS, 2015). Amongst recent insights into the importance of the Psalter tradition, see Geoff Rector, "An Illustrious Vernacular: the Psalter *en romanz* in 12th-Century England," in *Language and Culture in Medieval Britain: the French of England c. 1100–c. 1500*, ed. Jocelyn Wogan-Browne *et al.* (Woodbridge: York Medieval Press, 2009), 198–206; Christine Ruby, "Les psautiers bilingues latin / français dans l'Angleterre du XIIe siècle: affirmation d'une langue et d'une écriture," in *Approches du bilinguisme latin-français au Moyen Age: linguistique, codicologie, esthétique*, CNRS C.E.M. 11 (Turnhout: Brepols, 2010), 167–90; Ian Short, Maria Careri, and Christine Ruby, "Les Psautiers d'Oxford et Saint Albans: liens de parenté," *Romania* 128 (2010): 29–45.

[5] Dean no. 458; Claire Isoz, ed., *Les Proverbes de Salemon, by Sanson de Nantuil*, 3 vols., ANTS 44–45, 50 (London: ANTS, 1988–94).

[6] Dean no. 444; Ernst Robert Curtius, ed., *Li Quatre Livre des Reis: die Bücher Samuelis und der Könige in einer französischen Bearbeitung des 12. Jahrhunderts*, Gesellschaft für romanische Literatur 26 (Dresden: Niemeyer, 1911).

[7] Dean nos. 558, 559; Pierre Kunstmann, ed., *Adgar: le Gracial* (Ottawa: Editions de l'Université d'Ottawa, 1982); Hilding Kjellman, ed., *La Deuxième Collection anglo-normande des Miracles de la Sainte Vierge et son original latin; avec les miracles correspondant des*

wealth of hagiographical material, including texts dealing with St Catherine,[1] Edward the Confessor,[2] St Edmund,[3] Thomas Becket,[4] St Giles,[5] St George,[6] and many more.[7] In the wake of Lateran IV, the 13th century was to bear witness to a further surge in the production of religious material.[8] If the Council's impact is perhaps most obvious in both the form and the profuse dissemination

---

mss. fr. 375 et 818 de la Bibliothèque nationale (Paris / Uppsala: Champion / Akademiske Bokhandeln, 1922).

[1] Dean no. 567; William MacBain, ed., *Life of St Catherine, by Clemence of Barking*, ANTS 18 (Oxford: Blackwell, 1964); cf. Jocelyn Wogan-Browne and Glyn S. Burgess, trans., *Virgin Lives and Holy Deaths: Two Exemplary Biographies for Anglo-Norman Women* (London: Dent, 1996), 1–43.

[2] Dean no. 523; Östen Södergård, ed., *La Vie d'Edouard le Confesseur, poème anglo-normand du XIIe siècle* (Uppsala: Almquist & Wiksell, 1948); cf. Jane Bliss, trans., *"La Vie d'Edouard le Confesseur" by a Nun of Barking Abbey* (Liverpool: Liverpool University Press, 2014).

[3] Dean no. 520; Delbert W. Russell, ed., *La Vie seint Edmund le rei*, ANTS 71 (Oxford: ANTS, 2014).

[4] Dean no. 509; Börje Schlyter, ed., *La Vie de Thomas Becket par Beneit, poème anglo-normand du XIIe siècle*, Etudes Romanes de Lund 4 (Lund: Gleerup, 1941). It would be churlish not to mention Dean no. 508, written by a Continental author but revised in England; Emmanuel Walberg, ed., *La Vie de saint Thomas le martyr par Guernes de Pont-Sainte-Maxence: Poème historique du XIIe siecle (1172–1174)*, Acta Reg. Societas Humaniorum Litterarum Lundensis 5 (Lund: Gleerup, 1922).

[5] Dean no. 529; Gaston Paris and Alphonse Bos, eds., *La Vie de saint Gilles, poème du XIIe siècle publié d'après le manuscrit unique de Florence*, SATF 16 (Paris: Didot, 1881); cf. Delbert W. Russell, trans., *Verse Saints' Lives Written in the French of England*, FRETS 5 (Tempe, AZ: ACMRS, 2012), 87–142.

[6] Dean no. 526; John Ernst Matzke, ed., *Les Œuvres de Simund de Freine* (Paris: Champion, 1909), 61–117; translation in Russell, *Verse Saints' Lives*, 143–64.

[7] One might mention the hagiographical works of Wace, hailing from Jersey: Dean nos. 537.1 and 571: Hans-Erich Keller, ed., *La Vie de sainte Marguerite par Wace*, Beihefte zur Zeitschrift für romanische Philologie 229 (Tübingen: Niemeyer, 1990); Einar Ronsjö, ed., *La Vie de saint Nicolas par Wace, poème religieux du XIIe siècle*, Etudes Romanes de Lund 5 (Lund: Gleerup, 1942). Cf. Jean Blacker, Glyn S. Burgess, and Amy Victoria Ogden, trans., *Wace, the Hagiographical Works: the 'Conception Nostre Dame' and the Lives of St Margaret and St Nicholas*, Studies in Medieval and Reformation Traditions 169 (Leiden: Brill, 2013).

[8] On this vast question, see Hesketh, *Lumere as lais*, 3:5–11; Legge, *Anglo-Norman Literature*, 206–42. Very useful selections of pastoral and devotional material are included in Tony Hunt, ed., Jane Bliss, trans., Henrietta Leyser, intro., *"Cher alme": Texts of Anglo-Norman Piety*, FRETS OP 1 (Tempe, AZ: ACMRS, 2010) and Maureen B. M. Boulton, ed. and trans., *Piety and Persecution in the French Texts of England*, FRETS 6 (Tempe: ACMRS, 2013). Recent studies meriting particular attention are Claire M. Waters, *Translating "Clergie": Status, Education, and Salvation in Thirteenth-Century French Texts* (University Park, PA: Pennsylvania State University Press, 2015) and Maureen B. M.

of relatively unadulterated catechetical works such as the *Mirour de Seinte Eglise*,[1] *Lumere as lais*,[2] and *Manuel des pechiez*,[3] which, in their systematic treatment of a range of themes including the sacraments, virtuous conduct, and, in particular, the nature of sin and its remedy through confession and penance, attest in varying ways to the influence of the manuals for confessors, it is equally apparent in less patently scholastic works of doctrinal instruction, such as Robert of Greatham's *Corset*[4] and Robert Grosseteste's allegorical *Chasteau d'Amour*.[5] As richly demonstrated by the rise of the exemplum,[6] edifying narratives were also recognised as an ideal form for educating audiences and inspiring them to virtue, and Insular hagiography continued to thrive in this context, as seen in the

---

Boulton, *Sacred Fictions of Medieval France: Narrative Theology in the Lives of Christ and the Virgin, 1150–1500*, Gallica 38 (Cambridge: Brewer, 2015).

[1] Dean no. 629; Alan D. Wilshere, ed., *Mirour de seinte Eglyse (St. Edmund of Abingdon's Speculum ecclesiae)*, ANTS 40 (London: ANTS, 1982).

[2] Dean no. 630; Hesketh, *Lumere as lais*.

[3] Dean no. 635; unfortunately there is still no full critical edition of the *Manuel*, but useful material is contained in Emile Jules François Arnould, '*Le Manuel des péchés': étude de littérature religieuse anglo-normande (XIIIe siècle)* (Paris: Droz, 1940).

[4] Dean no. 590; Keith Val Sinclair, ed., *Corset, by Rober Le Chapelain: a Rhymed Commentary on the Seven Sacraments*, ANTS 52 (London: ANTS, 1995).

[5] Dean no. 622; Jessie Murray, ed., *Le Château d'amour de Robert Grosseteste, évêque de Lincoln* (Paris: Champion, 1918); translated in Boulton, *Piety and Persecution*, 61–89. On the importance of Grosseteste for the dissemination of Lateran IV's precepts, see Leonard E. Boyle, "Robert Grosseteste and the Pastoral Care," *Medieval and Renaissance Studies* 8 (1979): 3–51; James R. Ginther, "Robert Grosseteste's Theology of Pastoral Care," in *A Companion to Pastoral Care in the Late Middle Ages (1200–1500)*, ed. Ronald James Stansbury, Brill's Companions to the Christian Tradition 22 (Leiden: Brill, 2010), 95–122; Matthias Hessenauer, "The Impact of Grosseteste's Pastoral Care on Vernacular Religious Literature: *La Lumière as lais* by Pierre de Peckham," in *Robert Grosseteste: New Perspectives on his Thought and Scholarship*, ed. James McEvoy (Turnhout: Brepols, 1995), 377–91.

[6] On this vast area, see Jacques Berlioz and Marie-Anne Polo de Beaulieu, *Les Exempla médiévaux: introduction à la recherche* (Carcassonne: Garac/Hésiode, 1992); Claude Brémond, Jacques Le Goff, and Jean-Claude Schmitt, *L'Exemplum'*, Typologie des Sources du Moyen Âge Occidental 40 (Turnhout: Brepols, 1982); Markus Schürer, *Das Exemplum oder die erzählte Institution: Studien zum Beispielgebrauch bei den Dominikanern und Franziskanern des 13. Jahrhunderts*, Vita Regularis Abhandlungen 23 (Berlin: Lit, 2005); still indispensable is Jean Thiébaut Welter, *L'Exemplum dans la littérature religieuse et didactique du Moyen Âge*, Bibliothèque d'Histoire Ecclésiastique de France (Paris: Guitard, 1927).

composition of lives of saints such as Richard of Chichester[1] and Francis of Assisi[2] and the work of authors such as Frère Angier[3] and, notably, Matthew Paris.[4]

Clement's fidelity to its much earlier sources is such that there is naturally no question of the text serving as a programmatic narrativisation of the canons of Lateran IV. For example, while great importance is attached to the act of Christians communally partaking of food provided by God's grace in the absence of false believers (vv. 1629–52, 2881–924, 6543–62), there is no direct reflection of the Council's affirmation of the doctrine of transubstantiation (c. 1), its prescription of annual communion (c. 21), or its related preoccupation with the protection of the Eucharist (c. 20). Nonetheless, the nature of the text is such—particularly by reason of St Peter's speeches, strategically amplified by our translator—that it proves an excellent vehicle for didactically complementing and reinforcing numerous of the Council's pronouncements. The previously discussed preoccupation with the dangers of deception by heresiarchs such as Simon and Dositheus echoes the Council's attempts to extirpate all heretics and their supporters (c. 3). Peter's explanation of the therapeutic benefits of confession (vv. 14195–228), notably longer than in the *Epistula*, and of the importance of penance (vv. 11729–38) could clarify for an audience the benefits of the obligation of annual confession and penance that the Council imposed (c. 21); this canon's recommendation that the confessor should proceed like a physician is also the method advised by Peter to those entrusted with the *cura animarum* (vv. 13289–94). Peter's constant preaching, and its invariable success, demonstrates the wisdom of the importance that the Council attached to the word of God (c. 10), just as his willingness to entrust his preaching to worthy men (vv. 10947–86) is consonant with the Council's instruction in the same canon that bishops should, where necessary, pass their preaching responsibilities to suitable parties. Peter's insistence on the importance of education and of speaking only about things in which one has been well instructed (e.g., vv. 11633–75, 11991–12000, 13247–54, etc.) and his advice concerning the training of deacons (vv. 13971–14002) concord with the Coun-

---

[1] Dean no. 545; Russell, *Vie seint Richard*.

[2] Dean no. 525; Russell, *Vye de seynt Fraunceys*.

[3] Dean nos. 513 and 514; Paul Meyer, "La Vie de saint Grégoire le Grand par Frère Angier," *Romania* 12 (1883): 145–208; Renato Orengo, ed., *Les Dialogues de Grégoire le Grand traduits par Angier, publiés d'après le manuscrit Paris, BNF, Fr. 24766 unique et autographe*, 2 vols., SATF (Abbeville: SATF, 2013).

[4] E.g., Dean nos. 506, 521, 522; Arthur Robert Harden, ed., *La Vie de seint Auban: an Anglo-Norman Poem of the Thirteenth Century*, ANTS 19 (Oxford: Blackwell, 1968) (trans. Wogan-Browne and Fenster, *The Life of St Alban by Matthew Paris*); Alfred Thomas Baker, "La Vie de saint Edmond, archevêque de Cantorbéry," *Romania* 55 (1929): 332–81; Kathryn Young Wallace, ed., *La Estoire de seint Ædward le rei, Attributed to Matthew Paris*, ANTS 41 (London: ANTS, 1983) (Thelma S. Fenster and Jocelyn Wogan-Browne, trans., *The History of St Edward the King by Matthew Paris*, FRETS 1 [Tempe, AZ: ACMRS, 2008]).

cil's prescriptions regarding the education of clerics (c. 11) and the acquisition of sufficient learning as a prerequisite for elevation to the priesthood (c. 27). Peter's concern that his followers should behave in decorous fashion (vv. 5845–60) and, in a notable amplification of the *Epistula*, that the clergy should endeavour to avoid any concupiscent behaviour (vv. 13705–12) is no less in accordance with the Council's aim of reforming clerical conduct (cc. 14–16). More generally, Peter's homiletic activity proves ideally suited to the purpose of religious instruction, as he explains to his various audiences a range of moral, theological, and doctrinal issues, such as the dangers of adultery (vv. 13597–600, 13657–74) and avarice (vv. 13791–98), the efficacy of baptism (vv. 8831–64), the manifold benefits of alms-giving (vv. 11731–38) and chastity (vv. 6939–60), and much more. Indeed, at one point our translator replaces a discussion in the *Recognitiones* about the nature of the True Prophet with a little primer from Peter covering Creation, the expulsion of Lucifer, and the importance of good conduct in the face of the coming judgement (vv. 1421–616). Whether the programme of religious instruction launched by Lateran IV was directly responsible for our translator's decision to undertake this project is unclear, but that the result, with its palatable didactic combination of *delectatio* and *utilitas*,[1] is entirely compatible with the Council's ambitions is beyond doubt.

---

[1] On the theme of combining instruction and enjoyment, see Glending Olson, *Literature as Recreation in the Later Middle Ages* (Ithaca / London: Cornell University Press, 1982); Joachim Suchomski, *Delectatio und Utilitas: ein Beitrag zum Verständnis mittelalterlicher komischer Literatur*, Biblioteca Germanica 18 (Bern / Munich: Francke, 1975).

Suggested Further Reading

Primary sources

1. Editions of Clement

Burrows, Daron Lee, ed. *La Vie de seint Clement*, 3 vols., ANTS 64–67. London: ANTS, 2007–10.

Russell, Delbert W. "La Vie de seint Clement, pape." University of Waterloo, 2007. http://margot.uwaterloo.ca/campsey/cmpclement_e.html

Willson, Nora K. "Critical Edition of the *Vie de Saint Clement Pape*." Ph.D., Newnham College, Cambridge, 1951.

2. Primary Material Relevant to Clement

Guillaume, Paul, ed. *Istoria Petri et Pauli: mystère en langue provençale du XVe siècle*. Gap/Paris: Maisonneuve, 1887.

Lipsius, Richard Adelbert, and Maximilian Bonnet, ed. *Acta apostolorum apocrypha post Constantinum Tischendorf*, 3 vols. Leipzig: Mendelssohn, 1891–1903.

Orlandi, Giovanni, ed. *Excerpta ex Clementinis recognitionibus a Tyrannio Rufino translatis*, Testi e Documenti per lo Studio dell'Antichità 24. Milan: Istituto Editoriale Cisalpino, 1968.

Rehm, Bernhard, ed. *Die Pseudoklementinen II: Rekognitionen in Rufins Übersetzung*, Die griechischen christlichen Schriftsteller der ersten Jahrhunderte 51. Berlin: Akademie-Verlag, 1965.

Urwin, Kenneth, ed. *The Life of Saint John the Almsgiver*, 2 vols., ANTS 33–34. London: ANTS, 1980–81.

3. Other Anglo-Norman Religious Texts

Arnould, Emile Jules François. *'Le Manuel des péchés': étude de littérature religieuse anglo-normande (XIIIe siècle)*. Paris: Droz, 1940.

———, ed. *Le Livre de seyntz medicines: the Unpublished Devotional Treatise of Henry of Lancaster*, ANTS 2. Oxford: Blackwell, 1940.

Baker, Alfred Thomas. "An Anglo-French Life of St Osith." *Modern Language Review* 6–7 (1911–12): 476–502, 74–93, 157–92.

———. "Vie anglo-normande de sainte Foy par Simon de Walsingham." *Romania* 66 (1940–41): 49–84.

———, and Alexander Bell, ed. *St Modwenna*, ANTS 7. Oxford: Blackwell, 1947.

Paris, Gaston, and Alphonse Bos, ed. *La Vie de saint Gilles, poème du XIIe siècle publié d'après le manuscrit unique de Florence*, SATF 16. Paris: Didot, 1881.

Harden, Arthur Robert, ed. *La Vie de seint Auban: an Anglo-Norman Poem of the Thirteenth Century*, ANTS 19. Oxford: Blackwell, 1968.

Hesketh, Glynn, ed. *La Lumere as lais, by Pierre d'Abernon of Fetcham*, 3 vols., ANTS 54–57. London: ANTS, 1996–2000.

———, ed. *Rossignos*, ANTS 63. London: ANTS, 2006.

Hunt, Tony, ed., Jane Bliss, trans. *"Cher alme": Texts of Anglo-Norman Piety*, MRTS 385; FRETS OP 1. Tempe, AZ: ACMRS, 2010.

Murray, Jessie, ed. *Le Château d'amour de Robert Grosseteste, évêque de Lincoln*. Paris: Champion, 1918.

Russell, Delbert W., ed. *La Vie de saint Laurent: an Anglo-Norman Poem of the Twelfth Century*, ANTS 34. London: ANTS, 1976.

———, ed. *Légendier apostolique anglo-normand*, Etudes Médiévales. Montreal: Presses de l'Université de Montréal, 1989.

———, ed. *La Vie seint Richard Evesque de Cycestre, by Pierre d'Abernon of Fetcham*, ANTS 51. London: ANTS, 1995.

———, ed. *La Vye de seynt Fraunceys d'Assise (Ms Paris, BNF, fonds français 13505)*, ANTS 59–60. London: ANTS, 2002.

———, trans. *Verse Saints' Lives Written in the French of England*, FRETS 5. Tempe, AZ: ACMRS, 2012.

———, ed. *La Vie seint Edmund le rei*, ANTS 71. Oxford: ANTS, 2014.

Sinclair, Keith Val, ed. *Corset, by Rober Le Chapelain: a Rhymed Commentary on the Seven Sacraments*, ANTS 52. London: ANTS, 1995.

Wallace, Kathryn Young, ed. *La Estoire de seint Ædward le rei, Attributed to Matthew Paris*, ANTS 41. London: ANTS, 1983.

Wilshere, Alan D., ed. *Mirour de seinte Eglyse (St. Edmund of Abingdon's Speculum ecclesiae)*, ANTS 40. London: ANTS, 1982.

Secondary Sources

4. General Studies of Hagiography

Ashley, Kathleen, and Pamela Sheingorn. *Writing Faith: Text, Sign and History in the Miracles of Sainte Foy*. Chicago / London: University of Chicago Press, 1999.

Brunel-Lobrichon, Geneviève, Anne-Françoise Leurquin-Labie, and Martine Thiry-Stassin. "L'hagiographie de langue française sur le Continent: IXe–XVe siècle." In *Hagiographies: Histoire internationale de la littérature hagiographique latine et vernaculaire en Occident des origines à 1550*, ed. Guy Philippart, 2:291–371. Turnhout: Brepols, 1996.

Calin, William C. "Saints' stories: the literary quality of Anglo-Norman martyr hagiography." In *The Shaping of Text: Style, Imagery, and Structure in French Literature. Essays in Honor of John Porter Houston*, ed. Emanuel J. Mickel, 24–44. Lewisburg, PA: Bucknell University Press, 1993.

Campbell, Emma. *Medieval Saints' Lives: the Gift, Kinship and Community in Old French Hagiography*. Gallica 12. Cambridge: Brewer, 2008.

————. "Saints' Lives, Violence and Community." In *The Cambridge History of French Literature*, ed. William E. Burgwinkle, Nicholas Hammond and Emma Wilson, 38–46. Cambridge: Cambridge University Press, 2011.

Cazelles, Brigitte, and Phyllis Johnson. *Le vain siecle guerpir: a Literary Approach to Sainthood through Old French Hagiography of the 12th Century*. North Carolina Studies in the Romance Languages and Literatures 205. Chapel Hill: University of North Carolina Press, 1979.

Dembowski, Peter F. "Traits essentiels des récits hagiographiques." In *La Nouvelle: Formation, codification et rayonnement d'un genre médiéval. Actes du Colloque International de Montréal (McGill Univ., 14 - 16 oct. 1982)*, ed. Michelangelo Picone, Giuseppe Di Stefano and Pamela S. Stewart, 80–88. Montreal: Plato Academic Press, 1983.

Goodich, Michael. *Vita Perfecta: The Ideal of Sainthood in the Thirteenth Century*. Monographien zur Geschichte des Mittelalters 25. Stuttgart: Hiersemann, 1982.

————. *Lives and Miracles of the Saints: Studies in Medieval Latin Hagiography*. Variorum Collected Studies 798. Aldershot: Ashgate, 2004.

Gumbrecht, Hans Ulrich. "Faszinationstyp Hagiographie: ein historisches Experiment zur Gattungstheorie." In *Deutsche Literatur im Mittelalter: Kontakte und Perspektiven. Hugo Kuhn zum Gedenken*, ed. Christoph Cormeau, 37–84. Stuttgart: Metzler, 1979.

Heffernan, Thomas J. *Sacred Biography: Saints and their Biographers in the Middle Ages*. Oxford: Oxford University Press, 1988.

Kay, Sarah. "The Sublime Body of the Martyr: Violence in Early Romance Saints' Lives." In *Violence in Medieval Society*, ed. Richard W. Kaeuper, 3–20. Woodbridge: Boydell & Brewer, 2000.

Laurent, Françoise. *Plaire et édifier: les récits hagiographiques composés en Angleterre aux 12e et 13e siècles*. Nouvelle Bibliothèque du Moyen Age 45. Paris: Champion, 1998.

————. "La précocité de l'écriture hagiographique et l'identité normande: les vies de saints composées par Wace." In *La Fabrique de la Normandie. Actes du colloque international organisé à l'Université de Rouen en décembre 2011*, ed. Michèle Guéret-Laferté and Nicolas Lenoir. Rouen: Publications Numériques du CÉRÉdI, 2013.

Leonardi, Claudio. "L'agiografia romana nel secolo IX." In *Hagiographie, cultures et sociétés, IVe-XIIe siècles: Actes du colloque organisé à Nanterre et à Paris (2–5 mai 1979)*, ed. Evelyne Patlagean and Pierre Riché, 471–90. Paris: Etudes Augustiniennes, 1981.

Meyer, Paul. "Légendes hagiographiques en français I: Légendes en vers." In *Histoire littéraire de la France*, 33:328–78. Paris: Imprimerie nationale, 1906.

————. "Légendes hagiographiques en français II: Légendes en prose." In *Histoire littéraire de la France*, 33:378–458. Paris: Imprimerie nationale, 1906.

Mooney, Catherine M. *Gendered Voices: Medieval Saints and Their Interpreters*. Philadelphia: University of Pennsylvania Press, 1999.

Perrot, Jean-Pierre. *Le Passionnaire français au Moyen Age*. Publications Romanes et Françaises 200. Geneva: Droz, 1992.

Robertson, Duncan. *The Medieval Saints' Lives: Spiritual Renewal and Old French Literature*. Edward C. Armstrong Monographs on Medieval Literature 8. Lexington, KY: French Forum, 1995.

Thiry-Stassin, Martine. "L'hagiographie en anglo-normand." In *Hagiographies: Histoire internationale de la littérature hagiographique latine et vernaculaire en Occident des origines à 1550*, ed. Guy Philippart, 1:407–28. Corpus Christianorum: Hagiographies. Turnhout: Brepols, 1994.

Townsend, David. "Anglo-Norman Hagiography and the Norman Transition." *Exemplaria* 3 (1991): 385–433.

Wogan-Browne, Jocelyn. "'Clerc u lai, muine u dame': Women and Anglo-Norman Hagiography in the Twelfth and Thirteenth Centuries." In *Women and Literature in Britain: 1150–1500*, ed. Carol M. Meale, 61–85. Cambridge Studies in Medieval Literature 17. Cambridge: Cambridge University Press, 1996.

———. *Saints' Lives and Women's Literary Culture c. 1150–1300: Virginity and its Authorizations*. Oxford: Oxford University Press, 2001.

Yarrow, Simon. *Saints and Their Communities: Miracle Stories in Twelfth-Century England*. Oxford: Clarendon, 2006.

5. Anglo-Norman Language: Context

Ingham, Richard, ed. *The Anglo-Norman Language and its Contexts*. Woodbridge: York Medieval Press, 2010.

Lusignan, Serge. *La Langue des rois au Moyen Age: le français en France et en Angleterre*. Paris: Presses Universitaires de France, 2004.

Rothwell, William. "The Role of French in Thirteenth-Century England." *Bulletin of the John Ryland Library* 58 (1976): 445–66.

———. "Glimpses into our Ignorance of the Anglo-Norman Lexis." In *Medieval French Textual Studies in Memory of T.B.W. Reid*, ed. Ian Short, 167–79. OPS 1. London: ANTS, 1984.

———. "The Missing Link in English Etymology: Anglo-French." *Medium Ævum* 60 (1991): 173–96.

———. "Chaucer and Stratford Atte Bowe." *Bulletin of the John Ryland Library* 74 (1992): 3–28.

———. "The 'faus franceis d'Angleterre': Later Anglo-Norman." In *Anglo-Norman Anniversary Essays*, ed. Ian Short, 309–26. OPS 2. London: ANTS, 1993.

———. "The Trilingual England of Geoffrey Chaucer." *Studies in the Age of Chaucer* 16 (1994): 45–67.

————. "English and French in England after 1362." *English Studies* 82 (2001): 539–59.

————. "Stratford atte Bowe Revisited." *Chaucer Review* 36 (2001): 184–207.

Short, Ian. "On Bilingualism in Anglo-Norman England." *Romance Philology* 33 (1979–80): 467–79.

————. "Patrons and Polyglots: French Literature in 12th-Century England." *Anglo-Norman Studies* 14 (1992): 229–49.

————. "*Tam Angli quam Franci:* Self-Definition in Anglo-Norman England." *Anglo-Norman Studies* 18 (1996): 153–75.

————. "Language and Literature." In *Companion to the Anglo-Norman World*, ed. Christopher Harper-Bill and Elisabeth van Houts, 191–213. Woodbridge: Boydell & Brewer, 2003.

————. "L'anglo-normand au siècle de Chaucer: un regain de statistiques." In *Le Plurilinguisme au Moyen Age: Orient – Occident*, ed. Claire Kappler and Suzanne Thiolier-Méjean, 67–77. Coll. Méditerranée Médiévale. Paris: L'Harmattan, 2009.

————. "*Verbatim et literatim*: Oral and Written French in 12th-Century Britain." *Vox Romanica* 68 (2009): 156–68.

————. "'Anglice loqui nesciunt': Monoglots in Anglo-Norman England." *Cultura Neolatina* 69 (2009): 245–62.

————. "Another Look at 'le faus franceis'." *Nottingham Medieval Studies* 54 (2010): 35–55.

Trotter, David A., ed. *Multilingualism in Later Medieval Britain*. Cambridge: Brewer, 2000.

————. "Not as Eccentric as it Looks: Anglo-French and French French." *Forum for Modern Language Studies* 39 (2003): 427–38.

————. "L'anglo-normand: variété insulaire ou variété isolée?" *Médiévales* 45 (2003): 43–54.

————. "'Deinz certeins boundes': Where Does Anglo-Norman Begin and End?" *Romance Philology* 67 (2013): 139–77.

Wogan-Browne, Jocelyn, Carolyn Collette, Maryanne Kowaleski, *et al.*, eds. *Language and Culture in Medieval Britain: the French of England c.1100-c.1500*. Woodbridge: York Medieval Press, 2009.

6. Anglo-Norman Language: Reading Aids

Baldinger, Kurt, Georges Straka, Jean-Denis Gendron, *et al. Dictionnaire étymologique de l'ancien français*. Tübingen: Niemeyer, 1971-.

Buridant, Claude. *Grammaire nouvelle de l'ancien français*. Paris: Sedes, 2000.

Godefroy, Frédéric Eugène. *Dictionnaire de l'ancienne langue française et de tous ses dialectes du IXe au XVe siècle*. 10 vols. Paris: Vieweg, 1881–1902.

Ménard, Philippe. *Syntaxe de l'ancien français*. 3rd ed. Etudes Médiévales. Bordeaux: Bière, 1988.

Pope, Mildred Katharine. *From Latin to Modern French, with Especial Consideration of Anglo-Norman*. 2nd ed. Manchester: Manchester University Press, 1952.

Short, Ian. *Manual of Anglo-Norman*. 2nd ed. OPS 8. Oxford: ANTS, 2013.

Tanquerey, Frédéric Joseph. *L'Evolution du verbe en anglo-français (XIIe–XIVe siècles)*. Paris: Champion, 1915.

Tobler, Adolf, and Erhard Lommatzsch. *Altfranzösisches Wörterbuch*. 11 vols. Berlin / Stuttgart / Wiesbaden: Weidmann / Steiner, 1915–2002.

Wartburg, Walther von. *Französisches etymologisches Wörterbuch: eine Darstellung des galloromanischen Sprachschatzes*. 25 vols. Bonn: Klopp, 1922-.

Zink, Gaston. *Phonétique historique du français*. 3rd ed. Linguistique Nouvelle. Paris: PUF, 1992.

7. General Introductions to Anglo-Norman Literature

Calin, William C. *The French Tradition and the Literature of Medieval England*. Toronto / Buffalo: University of Toronto Press, 1994.

Crane, Susan. "Anglo-Norman Cultures in England: 1066–1460." In *The Cambridge History of Medieval English Literature*, ed. David Wallace, 35–60. Cambridge: Cambridge University Press, 1999.

Dean, Ruth J., and Maureen Barry McCann Boulton. *Anglo-Norman Literature: a Guide to Texts and Manuscripts*. OPS 3. London: ANTS, 1999.

Lecco, Margherita. *Storia della letteratura Anglo-Normanna (XII–XIV secolo)*. I Manuali. Milan: Edizioni Universitarie di Lettere Economia Diritto, 2011.

Legge, Mary Dominica. *Anglo-Norman in the Cloisters: the Influence of the Orders upon Anglo-Norman Literature*. Edinburgh: Edinburgh University Press, 1950.

———. *Anglo-Norman Literature and its Background*. Oxford: Clarendon, 1963.

———. "La précocité de la littérature anglo-normande." *Cahiers de civilisation médiévale* 8 (1965): 327–49.

Pensom, Roger. "Pour la versification anglo-normande." *Romania* 124 (2006): 50–65.

Short, Ian. "Literary Culture at the Court of Henry II." In *Henry II: New Interpretations*, ed. Christopher Harper-Bill and Nicholas Vincent, 335–61. Woodbridge: Boydell, 2007.

Note on the Translation

I have chosen prose for the translation not only because any attempt to write in verse would entail manifold difficulties and compromises, but also because prose is as common a medium for narrative nowadays as were octosyllabic couplets at the time of *Clement*'s composition. My aim has been as far as possible to produce a translation which respects modern idiom, but which will still permit anybody reading with the source text at hand to identify and understand key aspects of its grammar and style; it need scarcely be said, however, that such an approach is far from unproblematic, and that it has necessitated various concessions in terms both of fluency and of fidelity. While I have generally tried to maintain stylistically significant features of word order and repetition, certain modifications have been necessary. I have often omitted essentially redundant anaphoric and cataphoric pronouns (*ceo*, *le*, *en*, etc.). and deictics (*i*, *en*, *la*, etc.), and in order to avoid what in English would be unjustifiably obtrusive hyperbaton I have frequently altered word order. Tenses such as historic present and verbal constructions such as the *aler* + gerund periphrasis have been standardised and simplified for idiom where appropriate. I have tried to reflect the general extent of repetition and relatively limited vocabulary of the text, although sense and idiom have sometimes prevented this; this approach also obtains in respect of the treatment of the source text's characteristically hyperbolic penchant for *bien*, *mult*, *asez*, and similar. I have likewise respected to some extent the source text's predilection for parataxis by linking clauses through semi-colons, but have also on occasion added appropriate coordinating conjunctions. I have as far as possible followed the same disposition of paragraphs as found in my edition of *Clement*, in which a new paragraph begins each time that a line commences with a large red or blue initial, with a two-line or larger initial indicated by an additional line break above the new paragraph. In some cases where this approach would in the translation have yielded paragraphs of unwieldy length or in contravention of modern English conventions for the use of paragraphs in organising direct speech, I have divided them into smaller sections, following the chapter division of the *Recognitiones* where appropriate.[1] In the notes I have not, unless specifically relevant, sought further to justify any corrections to the manuscript reading which have already been explained in the edition, or repeated discussion of particular points of philological interest or difficulty.

---

[1] The single paragraphs from the edition which have been treated in this way are: vv. 159–272, 737–830, 1075–146, 1441–556, 2005–2100, 2411–84, 3511–96, 3757–838, 3931–4014, 4117–254, 4255–336, 4417–82, 4817–92, 4905–78, 5135–290, 5463–97, 5671–792, 5951–6102, 6643–744, 7533–604, 7699–722, 8111–92, 8287–392, 8445–512, 8575–722, 8723–818, 9503–88, 9807–944, 10221–302, 10415–526, 10727–810, 11007–238, 11355–448, 11453–530, 11681–924, 12091–188, 12281–380, 12427–508, 12509–28, 12675–772, 13221–94, 13307–562, 13579–866, 13871–14014, 14015–240, 14294–414, 14423–96.

The Life of Saint Clement

The clerics from the schools who have studied enough to have a measure of learning take great pains to write books and spin out lengthy opinions both to show their knowledge and to earn praise from the world. They write brand new books and present them very well; they write well and compose them well, but the laypeople derive little benefit from them, and clerics who are not steeped in learning[1] benefit little from them. The same clerics who write these books are neither ready nor willing to help those unable to read Latin[2] to learn and to understand in the common vernacular[3] what it is that they have said in the books that they have written, for it is quite enough for them to be praised by other clerics, and for it to be able to be said: "Anybody who writes like this is a fine cleric!" Since it is a foolish idea to squander a good intellect in this way, and since there are plenty of books which cater well for those who can read Latin,[4] in my opinion it would be much better and would be of greater benefit if the ancient books which are composed of the truth, and whose authors have been clearly recognised to have found favour with God, were translated into a language which would allow many people to profit. I am not one of those Latin readers[5] who are steeped in learning, but I nonetheless have in mind to write that little that I do know in such a way that clerics and laypeople who hear it will be able to understand it clearly,

---

[1] 12 **learning** *lettrure*: This term can also denote specifically writing in Latin (cf. *AND*, s. *lettrure*). See note to v. 15.

[2] 15 **those unable to read Latin** *nunlettrez*: The illiteracy indicated by the Old French term denotes the inability to read Latin. On this point, see Franz Heinrich Bäuml, "Varieties and Consequences of Medieval Literacy and Illiteracy," *Speculum* 55 (1980): 237–65; Yves Congar, "Clercs et laïcs au point de vue de la culture au Moyen Age: *laicus* = sans lettres," in *Studia medievalia et mariologica P. Caroli Balic OFM septuagesimum explenti annum dictata*, ed. Carolus Balic (Rome: Antonianum, 1971), 309–32; Herbert Grundmann, "*Litteratus - illiteratus*: der Wandel einer Bildungsnorm vom Altertum zum Mittelalter," *Archiv für Kulturgeschichte* 40 (1958): 1–65.

[3] 16 **in the common vernacular** *en vulgar cumun*: This remarkably early use of *vulgar* to denote the language of the people (cf. *FEW* 16:642a-643b) refers in context to French rather than English; cf. note to v. 41.

[4] 26 **for those who can read Latin** *as lettrez*: See note to v. 15.

[5] 35 **Latin readers** *lettrez*: See note to v. 15.

provided that they are not so completely uncultivated[1] that they have not learnt any French. May anybody who wishes to avoid idleness make an effort to listen to this so that what I shall say about St Clement might be of benefit for him!

Who wants to hear about where St Clement was born and into what kind of family, about the way in which his father, his mother, and his brothers were separated from each other and how they later recognised each other, and how they turned to St Peter, thanks to whom they all found each other?[2] Anybody who wishes to know all this will certainly learn it through this story. (1–56)

There is a book, albeit little known, which is called the *Book of Clement*,[3] and it also has another name — the *Journey of Peter*[4] — for St Clement wrote this book, and in the book he describes how St Peter the apostle roamed the earth and how he spoke of Jesus Christ, how those who heard the apostle preaching converted to God, how he debated with Simon — the one with the surname Magus — and how he himself and his brothers debated with their father, and were all baptised thanks to the teaching of St Peter. Since the speeches are long, and the disputations are long, I cannot translate it all, for there is a great deal of astronomy;[5] I have learnt nothing of this science, and I cannot explain what I do not know. It would take a very long time to write that whole book from beginning to end, for that book, written in Latin, fills a great deal of parchment. The story would likewise be too tedious and too long if all of the disputations

---

[1] 41 **uncultivated** *vilains*: The Old French term is particularly rich in connotations. The adjective *vilain* essentially captures everything which is base and ignoble, with the noun denoting "peasant"; the antonym is *cortois*, the manifold positive connotations of which stem from its basic sense of "of the court."

[2] 47–54 **Who wants. . .found each other** *Ki veut. . .se entretruverent*: These lines could be read as declarative rather than interrogative, with *Ki* used as an absolute relative ("Anybody who wants to hear. . ."), as it often is in the text. The lines would then be a protasis which becomes so lengthy that the author for clarity restates its essence (*Ki tut cest saver vuldra*, v. 55, "Anybody who wishes to know all this") before finally providing the apodosis. While such delaying of the main clause through subordinate clauses is not uncommon in the text (cf. vv. 3049–60, 4091–106, 5530–43, etc.), the scribe's use of the *punctus interrogativus* here suggests that he also read the sentence as a question.

[3] 58 **Book of Clement** *Livre Clement*: The *Recognitiones* is identified particularly in southern French and German manuscripts as the *Liber Clementis*; cf. Rehm, *Recognitiones*, xviii. The closest equivalent amongst the titles found in English manuscripts is *Historia Clementis*; cf. Rehm, *Recognitiones*, lxxiii.

[4] 60 **Journey of Peter** *Petri Itinerarium*: It is particularly German manuscripts of the *Recognitiones* which feature the title *Itinerarium beati Petri*; cf. Rehm, *Recognitiones*, l.

[5] 76 **astronomy** *astronomie*: From a modern perspective, a combination of astrology, astronomy, cosmology, and mythology. Cf. Nicole Kelley, "Astrology in the Pseudo-Clementine *Recognitions*," *Journal of Ecclesiastical History* 59, no. 4 (2008): 607–29.

were translated, for those familiar with Latin know very well how difficult it is to translate fine Latin well and preserve all of its beauty, for sometimes an idea which is highly regarded when it is finely presented in Latin will be treated rather flippantly when expressed in another language. I shall therefore leave out the long speeches and the long disputations and shall write down that which may bring pleasure. From the whole book I shall gather that with which I shall bore nobody, but rather those who read and those who hear it will be able to take great pleasure. I cannot retain the ordering of material and the beginning found in the book of St Clement on account of the speeches, which put things into an unexpected order, and having things in an unexpected order tends to cause nothing but vexation; I shall therefore follow the best ordering of material that I can provide.[1] We shall now start saying what we have in mind thanks to God, who started at the beginning[2] and proceeded in order. May He who created the world from nothing be with us at the beginning of our story, and may He grant us to reach the end as it pleases Him! (57–118)

When Our Lord Jesus Christ took flesh in the Blessed Virgin and came to earth for the salvation of the whole world, which was on the path to damnation, there was in Rome at that time a very rich and powerful man: he was called Faustinianus and was pagan in his beliefs. I cannot recount anything about him other than what I have found in the book: that he was on very good terms with the emperor, for anybody who was on good terms with such a powerful man as was the emperor of Rome at that time could not have been lacking in status. He was on good terms with him and his kin, and all this turned to his advantage. He was also on good terms with the people of the city of both the lowest and the highest ranks. By the standards of that society he was well educated and well versed in the seven arts.[3] To increase his status considerably the emperor gave him a wife who was of very great beauty, great wealth, and great goodness, and she was also of noble lineage in terms of the ancient peerage that the Romans had back then when they held dominion over the whole word that they had conquered when

---

[1] 103–10 **I cannot...I can provide** *Le ordre...purverai*: The source refers to the *granz trespociuns* "great transpositions" caused by the speeches, which seems to evoke the effect on the coherence of the narrative exerted by the length and organisation of the speeches. In essence, the author appears here to be justifying his imposition of *ordo naturalis* by placing the expository narrative about the family tragedy at the beginning of his text, whereas the *Recognitiones* follows an *ordo artificialis*, since the tragedy which occurred years before the main narrative is not revealed until a series of speeches in Book VII.

[2] 113 **started at the beginning** *primes la chose cumença*: The source is slightly obscure, but presumably evokes the act of Creation.

[3] 138 **well versed in the seven arts** *a[s] set arz asez fundez*: While the seven liberal arts had been codified by the late Classical period, for our translator and his audience, *set arz* would certainly have evoked primarily the medieval curriculum of the Trivium (grammar, rhetoric, logic) and the Quadrivium (arithmetic, geometry, music, astronomy).

they were at the height of their power. The lady was called Matthidia and loved her husband very much. They had three children together, of whom two were twins: one of them was named Faustus, the other was called Faustinus, and the third son bore the name of Clement. Their father and mother loved them very dearly and raised them without suffering any kind of harm. (119–58)

Faustinianus had a brother, but he was not like him; he made a most terrible show of brotherly love when he sought to dishonour his brother. He sought to disgrace him through his wife when he made improper advances; he engaged in wickedness when he asked her to fornicate with him. But she was a virtuous lady and was not prepared to besmirch her reputation,[1] nor was she prepared to consent to the fornication into which he was urging her. He did not then stop pursuing wickedness, but rather the more he solicited her, the more she resisted him. The lady suffered greatly from the lecher's lustful behaviour, and thought a great deal about how she might save herself from him. She did not wish to tell her husband lest he be furious at his brother, for it would cause great disgrace for them and their kin, and people would talk about it a great deal if there were seen to be strife between them, and it would cause shame if people knew the reason. The lady thought very carefully about how to protect herself effectively and how to protect her husband and his brother from dishonour. When she saw that the lecher would not desist on account of any entreaty, and that he had no concern whatsoever for his or his brother's honour, and that all the righteous things that she said to him would be to no avail, in order to avoid disgrace she made up a dream with great cunning and revealed to her husband the dream that she fabricated. The lady said to her husband: "My lord, listen to my vision! A god appeared before me whilst I was asleep, and through words and signs he ordered and warned me that if I wish to save my life and yours, and also our children, I should obey him. I am to leave here immediately and take both of our twins with me, and stay away for ten years, and then return when permitted. He also ordered that the third child should stay with you until it pleases him that we should return. And if there should be any refusal such that his order is not executed, there is no doubt that we ourselves and our three children shall all die in pain and in torment: there will we be no way of preventing this." (159–222)

Once the lady had said this, and that she was quite intent on this course of action, Faustinianus was extremely upset by it and did not dare to resist her. He loved his wife very faithfully and his children very dearly, and he did not dare offer any resistance which might harm them, for he believed that everything that the lady had related was the truth; but everything that the lady had said was complete fabrication. Faustinianus was very unhappy, but nonetheless he had

---

[1] 168 **her reputation** *sa fame*: It is not entirely clear to whom the possessive adjective refers; while it could indicate Matthidia, it could also refer to the evil brother or even Faustinianus.

readied everything that those who are to travel by sea tend to carry with them. He gathered provisions and servants for his wife and children; he gathered plenty of horses, packhorses, and palfreys with fine equipment, and gave to the little children plenty of toys and trinkets, and provided them so generously with everything that they lacked nothing. He then accompanied them to the sea and saw to it that all the servants, horses, and their equipment, as well as everything that they were to take with them, went on board. Then he tearfully[1] helped his wife and children on board, and told them that upon landing once they reached the other side of the sea, they should go straight to Athens, and stay at the schools for the children to be educated for a full ten years. He then sincerely thanked the god of which the lady had dreamt for being so compassionate as to let one of his children remain with him. The wind was favourable, and the weather calm; presently the ship left the port and, with its sail raised, they travelled well for as long as they had favourable wind and fair weather. Once Faustinianus had completely lost sight of the ship, he did not know what else to do other than to return to his house. He derived such comfort as he could from the son who remained with him. (223–72)

The lady began to find such solace as may a woman who is at sea. She and her companions sailed on well as long as they had a favourable wind, but they remained at sea until the weather changed completely. After the day there came a dark night which brought a terribly cruel event, for such a great storm arose that even the most experienced seafarer despaired. The ship could not withstand the force of the sea: neither mast nor rope nor oar could offer any protection there; neither the skill nor the strength of any sailor was of any avail in saving them. The ship broke apart into pieces, and absolutely everything which had been placed in the ship was wrecked so that nothing remained. Of that whole fellowship not a single one escaped with his life, except for the lady and her two sons, who were only just spared: all drowned except for these three, but they lost all their equipment. The lady was cast alone onto a rock and thus saved: the fabrication of her dream certainly caused her great sorrow. She had lost everything, and had few clothes with which she might be covered; she sat on the rock all night and had no pleasure or delight. She would have drowned herself in the sea if the hope of seeing her two children had not restrained her; she would have killed herself if this were not the case. She thought that she would see them either alive or dead, and from this derived a measure of solace. (273–312)

It so befell the two children that when the ship fell apart, and their young lives were set to come to an end through the power of the storm, they were both suddenly cast onto a plank which had worked free from the ship, and they clung

---

[1] 252 **tearfully** *tut pluranz*: Grammatically the tears could belong to the wife and children or to Faustinianus, but the choice in the translation is influenced by the fact that *tut pluranz* in v. 680 unambiguously refers to nominative singular Faustinianus.

on top of this against both winds and waves until there came some pirates who
with brutality and violence were ravaging the coastline and with lawlessness and
wickedness were living entirely from their plunder. When they saw the children
bobbing along in the sea, they set sail straight for them and took them on board
their ship. They did not let the storm stop them from departing, and by sailing
as hard as they could they endeavoured to draw near to a famous city which was
called Caesarea; with its full name, this city was known as Caesarea Stratonis.
The pirates terribly tormented the children whom they had abducted through
hunger, thirst, beatings, and many other cruel deeds, and through threats and
fear the robbers subdued them to the extent that they did not dare to reveal
from where they came or who they were. And lest those who might ask after
them should suspect anything and lest they should be recognised, the pirates
made them change their names, and called one of them Niceta and named the
other Aquila. Once they reached Caesarea, they sold them to a lady—she was a
widow[1] and was called Justa—who since her husband's death had lived chastely
and, for a pagan, with great goodness. The lady bought them, and from her own
resources provided them with plenty of drink, food, and clothing, and cared for
them very much: she loved them as her own sons and held them no less dear.
She then wanted them to be educated and sent them to school. They were both
bright and carefully remembered what they learned. Once they had thoroughly
studied the liberal arts, they turned to philosophers, for through philosophy they
thought that they would learn about the next life, and what should and should
not be done in respect of true religion. (313–74)

They had a companion who was called Simon Magus. He led a thoroughly
evil life, but the two brothers did not join him in his wickedness, for they loved
God in their own way. Nevertheless they loved Simon because they had been
raised together; on account of their childhood fellowship they had a bond with
him. They followed him long enough that he nearly deceived them, for he was a
necromancer and devoted himself to very little good. He performed many wonders before people, but he did everything through sorcery. He often changed his
appearance: one minute he was an old man, and the next a child; he made images move by themselves and made stone look like bread; he made dogs of brass
bark and great mountains shake; he flew through the air from one place to the
next—truth to tell, a devil carried him. The brothers saw him perform many a
wonder of this kind. As a result they thought that he was a god, and he would
have completely deceived them if it had not been for the mercy of God, who sent
Zacchaeus to them, who was a companion of St Peter who told them that Simon
was a deceiver. He made them leave Simon and sent them to St Peter. Once they
reached St Peter, he welcomed them with great joy. On account of the goodness
that they saw in him and the words that they heard, and on account of the mir-

---

[1] 355 **widow** *vedve*: Justa is only a *vidua* "widow" in the readings of branches ΘΦΨ
for *Rec.* VII.32.2, with the other branches identifying her as a *Iudaea* "Jewess."

acles that he performed, they converted to Jesus Christ. They were subsequently baptised, and from then on remained with St Peter. The place where they had been shipwrecked was called Antaradus;[1] it was an island surrounded by the sea, and nobody could reach it without a ship. (375–420)

The lady who had been shipwrecked had remained utterly distraught. She remained sitting on the rock, lamenting terribly all by herself. The night passed; when the day came, she no longer stayed on the rock: she went searching along the shore and looking everywhere for her children. She devoted all her effort to searching, bewailing their young lives all the while. If she was unable to have her sons alive, she wanted to see their dead bodies, but she found no sign of them which offered anything approaching certainty. People came running to her, and in particular women from nearby, who felt great pity for her, hurried to her, for they saw that she was extremely upset and overwhelmed by anguish. She repeatedly asked everybody whether they had seen two children who had been washed up at the port, be they alive or dead, but there was nobody who could say that he had heard or seen anything of them. Her suffering then increased when she saw no hope of finding them. The women who had come there endeavoured to comfort her; they recounted to her the misfortunes that they had experienced through the sea. They said a great deal about their husbands and their sons and their brothers who had died, and about other friends who had drowned at sea. By recalling their suffering they wished to lessen hers, but she was not so foolish as to derive any relief from her suffering by hearing such words; rather, it increased as a result. When they were unable to console her, they offered her lodging, but she cared little about everything that all the women said to her because they revealed nothing to her from which she might gain any certainty regarding her sons. (421–68)

Amongst these women there was one who felt great pity for her; she was a widow, but of little wealth, and she resided on that island. She came to the shipwrecked woman and recounted her story to her: that she had been the wife of a young man who used to go out to sea; he had happened to drown, but since then she had had no interest in taking up with another husband, whereby the first might be dishonoured. For a woman who is a widow is very lukewarm in her love for her husband when she takes up with another man and has no regard whatso-

---

[1] 418 **Antaradus** *Andarad*: There appears to be some geographical confusion in *Clement* (also in vv. 5840, 9849, and 9897). Antaradus (now Tartus, Syria) is the port city which faced the island of Aradus (now Arwad); since Matthidia was cast onto an island, v. 418 should allude to Aradus. This confusion is not without parallel in the *Recognitiones*, for while it usually accurately separates *Aradum* and *Antaradum*, in IX.36.3 and IX.36.7 *Antaradum* appears to designate Aradus, and in VII.26.5 different branches of the transmission offer either *Aradum* or *Ant(h)aradum*.

ever for the first: then it becomes clear that she loved him very little or that she has forgotten him very quickly.

Even though Matthidia had lost the wealth that she had had, she was very pleased by what the widow had told her, for she was very attached to virtue and valued very highly the chastity that the widow had observed since her husband had died, and that she had done him the honour of not taking another husband. She therefore departed with her and lodged at her house. They remained together for a long time, working to support themselves, and they shared everything that they earned through their labour. (469–502)

After such great adversity, both the lady who had come and the widow who had welcomed her were beset by infirmity, for the lady was unable to do anything whereby she might assuage her grief other than to harm herself by wringing and gnawing at her hands. As a result she lost the use of her hands, from which very great hardship then befell her, for she could no longer do any work with her hands whereby she might earn anything. When she was then incapable of working, there was nothing left to do but beg, for all those who had promised her support in the first place, as well as all those who had offered their houses to her and much more besides, had now gone back on their promises and kindness. The widow who had welcomed her was stricken by palsy, and lay so utterly incapacitated that she could not rise from her bed. They were thus completely helpless once they had lost their health; previously they had had little wealth, and now they were so poor that they had nothing. There was not a single neighbour who looked in or sent anything to the house; as a result, they had to search round outside if they wanted anything to eat or drink. The crippled woman sought sustenance for them by begging outside, and from what she gathered together she fed herself and her hostess. This makes it very clear that it is no joke when people say: "The higher you are, the further you fall!"[1] when that lady who had been so rich went sorrowfully seeking her daily bread.

Faustinianus, who knew nothing of all this, was in Rome. He had with him his son Clement, who was very nearly five years old. His father raised him tenderly, and when Clement's age so permitted, he sent him to school to be educated, and Clement devoted himself to his learning. He studied well and had a good intellect, and had no desire to waste his time. (503–52)

Faustinianus very much wished to hear good news about his wife and his sons, for his heart was very heavy for not having heard any news since his wife had left. A whole year had already passed without any man returning to tell him any good news which might bring a little cheer to his heart. At the end of the

---

[1] 540 **The higher. . .you fall** *Si haut, si bas*: A well-known proverb; cf. Joseph Morawski, *Proverbes français antérieurs au XVe siècle*, Classiques Français du Moyen Age 47 (Paris: Champion, 1925), no. 557.

year he readied messengers to cross the sea. Because he was very concerned, he wanted enquiries after them to be made in the old schools which were in Athens at that time. He thought that his wife was there and that she had his two sons with her. In order to cover all their debts and for them to spend without borrowing, he gave the messengers a great deal of gold and silver and money, and lest they should lack anything, he sent enough for them to have plenty. The messengers departed, but never subsequently returned, nor was it ever subsequently known what had become of a single one of them. (553–80)

Faustinianus very much wished to hear news from his messengers, both the first ones and the last ones, but he heard an equal amount from all of them: this was absolutely nothing from the whole lot of them. It was no surprise that he was upset; he did not know what to do, but nonetheless he once more readied messengers and sent them to Athens. These departed in the third year and returned in the fourth year, but they found nothing of that on account of which they had been sent. They said that they had searched thoroughly at sea, on land, and in many countries, and that they had been in Athens, but they had found no news there regarding his wife, sons, messengers, equipment, ships, or sailors; they could not learn from anybody what had become of a single one of them. As a result, Faustinianus's spirits dropped terribly; he had no solace from anything and very much wished that he were dead. His brother, who had been the cause of all the unhappiness when through wicked lechery he had made improper advances to the lady, increased his sorrow. He came to Faustinianus and told him something far from pleasant, for through deceptive cunning and in order to hide his wickedness he accused the lady of the insane lust of what he himself sought from her, claiming that she had in ignoble fashion solicited lecherous behaviour from him, and saying that he had not been prepared to consent to the desire to dishonour his brother. To his lie he added more which greatly pained his brother: that when he had refused and was not prepared to fornicate with her, the lady had taken up with her servant and begun a relationship with him. But since she would have been disgraced if she had fornicated in her own country, and it would have caused great shame for her and all of her family, she had with falsehood and lies fabricated a dream in order to carry out her wishes elsewhere in such a way that her kin should not know of it: she went elsewhere with her servant, who consented entirely to her, and once she had fornicated, she had perished with everything that she had. The scoundrel fabricated this and told it all to his brother, as a result of which he experienced greater sorrow than he had before. (581–642)

For a good while Faustinianus remained buried deep in thought; he did not know what to do or where to go so that he might find any of his family. When he could not think of any source of solace, he headed towards the port. He took his son Clement with him, and asked the sailors whether in the last four years they had themselves heard or seen or by hearsay learnt whether a woman and two children had been shipwrecked at sea, and their bodies washed up on shore.

Those both from ships and from boats told him a good deal about one thing and another: from some he took hope, and from others he remained in doubt, and he learned nothing there from which he derived any joy and happiness. He nevertheless still had hope; I do not know how or why unless it came to him from the desire of hearing good news. Presently it occurred to him—and he followed this plan in all respects—that he would hand his son Clement to his friends so that they could look after him, and would himself go and search both at sea and on land for his wife and children, and likewise for his servants, so that he might be certain of either losing or finding everything. Thus he thought and thus he acted, and Clement remained in Rome. Clement was twelve years old at that time, and his father tearfully set sail and departed. For a long time he did not return.

Now the father, mother, and their sons are all separated. From now on it is up to God to help in such a way that they might be reunited! (643–86)

Clement had remained in Rome, and he strove hard to be a man. He endeavoured diligently to study well and to use his intellect for good,[1] and he made a start in this by wishing to live chastely. This provided compelling evidence to hope that he would grow in goodness through great virtue, given that he was a young man who was pagan. He learned his grammar[2] very thoroughly and then moved to the arts;[3] he learned a great deal about astronomy and then concentrated on philosophy. From then on his mind was entirely fixed on morality, on how to live and what to do and what he should avoid. Days passed, and years passed. Clement grew and matured, and when he reached an age at which he was capable of looking after his inheritance, and no news or messenger came to gladden his heart by offering any more consolation regarding his father than regarding a man who were dead, he claimed his inheritance and dealt with it as a man responsible for what he owned. (687–714)

The Son of God, Our Saviour Jesus Christ, was on earth at that time, but His enemies had not yet put Him on the cross; or if it was the case that He had been put on it, this was not known in Rome. The apostles who followed Him and who saw His miracles were not aflame with the Holy Spirit, nor yet trained in preaching; there was nobody who roamed the lands or said anything to the people from which they might be reassured regarding the things about which they had doubts. The Son of God had looked only upon the land of Judaea; there He stayed and there He remained, for He came there only for the Jews. The whole

---

[1] 690 **use his intellect for good** *sun sens en bien despendre*: The author through lexical repetition is here contrasting Clement with the foolish clerics who are criticised in the prologue for squandering their intellect (*despendre en nient bon sens*, v. 24).

[2] 697 **grammar** *pars*: The Old French term refers specifically to the parts of Latin grammar; cf. T-L 7:352–53; *FEW* 7:672a.

[3] 698 **arts** *arz*: That is, the seven liberal arts; cf. note to v. 138.

world was in error, nobody was sure of the truth, and the small and the great alike all erred in their belief.[1] (715–36)

Clement was utterly perplexed; he saw nothing which pleased him as he did not know with any certainty what would become of him. With all his mental resources he thought a great deal about his end and what his beginning had been, and whether he[2] came from something or nothing. In addition to this he also thought about whether his soul[3] was mortal, and whether it would completely die with his body or would live for ever without his body. He thought about whether the world had been created, and if it had been created, about who had created it,[4] for he was quite certain that if it had been created, it would not be everlasting. He very much wished to know this, but he could not resolve it, and he particularly wanted guidance about this: whether his soul was mortal, for he focussed all his speculation on this; or whether it was to live for ever, and how, and in which land; and whether he had been anything before he had been born, and whether he would be anything once he died.[5] He undertook many a disputation and heard many a lesson from philosophers in order to learn this, but he could not manage it on his own. He was so perplexed in this that he nearly despaired completely of endeavouring to live well, since he had no absolute certainty of whether he would receive a reward for it or whether it would be a good one or not, nor of whether he would enter another life once he had finished this one. He took great pains to remove this thought from his mind, but it was fixed all the more firmly in his heart the more he endeavoured to remove it. He then thought that he would put all this behind him in a different way — and he would wait such a long time for it, since he could not understand it until he reached the end of his days — if he could find it out elsewhere and know the truth about whether the soul has immortality, for he would be thoroughly at peace if he were sure of this, and waiting around had not brought him much peace so far in this matter. (737–90)

He therefore thought most foolishly that he wanted to find out through necromancy what he had been unable find out with his own mind. He thought about going to Egypt to talk to the necromancers so that they might, if he gave gener-

---

[1] 687–736 **Clement. . .belief** *Remis. . .mescreant*: The description of Clement's formative years may draw on *Rec.* I.1, but the comments on the religious context have no obvious source.

[2] 744 **he** *il*: The pronoun could also refer to Clement's "beginning," in which case one would read "it."

[3] 746 **soul** *aume*: In *Rec.* I.1.3, the soul is not stated as the central issue.

[4] 749–50 **He thought. . .created it** *Del mund pensa. . .feit le eit*: In *Rec.* I.1.4, Clement does not consider who might have created the world.

[5] 753–62 **He very much wished. . .died** *De ceo saver. . .finez*: These lines do not have a clear source. They may amplify *Rec.* I.1.3 or take their inspiration from elements of *Rec.* I.2.

ously of his wealth, by sorcery summon a soul from Hell for him which might reveal to him the truth concerning everything that he might ask regarding his areas of doubt. He thought this, and would have done this if it had not been for one of his friends to whom he revealed his intention, but who completely dissuaded him from it. This friend presented a convincing argument for abandoning such presumption, for he would bring upon himself a terrible sin against God and religion, and it would be an act of terrible cruelty if he were involved in such an outrage, for it often tends to happen that necromancers tend to fail in their conjuration and fail completely in their investigation, and therefore are in greater doubt. And if this were to happen to him in his planned investigation, and the sorcerer were to fail so that what he summoned did not come, he would from that point on for ever remain in doubt regarding the investigation in which he had failed, and would fall into such despair that he would never, on account of the failure of the investigation, believe it to be true that there is any other life besides this one, and then he would never yearn for great virtue or great goodness. (791–830)

Or if it were by chance the case that a figure appeared there which through sorcery revealed what it was ordered to, nothing but ill could come of it, for a weak beginning gives rise to very weak faith unless God provides betterment, for committing evil in order to obtain something better seldom tends to lead to good. Anybody who torments a soul with sorcery once it leaves the body is considered terribly cruel and commits an utterly mortal sin. It was a philosopher friend of Clement who warned of all this, and through his advice he managed to dissuade him from acting wrongly, and made Clement abandon all the evil that he had in mind. He was nonetheless not free from the thing about which he had so often thought. (831–52)

Presently some news emerged; never had such news been heard! It came from the East, where it originated, and spread until it was known throughout the whole world. At that time Tiberius of Lombardy[1] was in power; the emperor Tiberius Caesar was acknowledged as lord of the world. The news was good and brought a good message; God did not wish it to remain hidden such that the whole world should not know it. The rumour was that there had come to Judaea a Prophet who was a Jew[2] and spoke of the kingdom of God. He would cause to enter the kingdom of God all those who were prepared to listen wholeheartedly to what He wished to say about God and to follow His teaching wholeheartedly. In order to prove that what He had said was not a deception, He performed many miracles and wonders in front of everybody. Entirely by His command and by no other means whatsoever, He made the deaf hear and the blind see, and He made

---

[1] 860 **Tiberius of Lombardy** *Tiberius de Lumbardie*: This means of referring to Tiberius Julius Caesar Augustus has no equivalent in *Rec.* I.6.1.

[2] 869 **Jew** *Jueu*: *Rec.* I.6.1 does not state that Christ was a Jew, but rather that He preached the kingdom of God to the Jews.

the lame stand upright; He restored the power of speech to the mute; all the madmen[1] and lepers who asked Him for their health were cured by His word. He cured every infirmity and brought the dead back to life, and He had such great power that His word alone would be done. This news had come and was deemed quite true by many people who had come and knew the full truth of it. People were already talking about this man throughout Rome. Groups gathered in parts of the city and considered what they had heard to be a great wonder: about who that man was, and from where He had such power, and in whose service He professed to be in the words that He said and the deeds that He performed, and about the promise that He made to those to whom He spoke. (853–906)

Whilst they were talking and marvelling in this way, a man entered the city and stopped in a place in which he could be seen and clearly heard and understood by everybody, and then from the place where he stopped he asked for attention and to speak to the people. He began thus:

"Listen to me, lords, countrymen, and citizens of Rome: the Son of God is in Judaea and He has shown His power there! Those who are prepared to hear Him and who are prepared to mend their ways and to follow His teaching in accordance with the will of God, His Father, who has sent Him, will have everlasting life. Therefore convert to Him; renounce evil and embrace good so that by forsaking temporal possessions you might live for ever in heaven! Recognise one true God and follow Him alone! Heaven and earth and everything connected with them are entirely at His command. He created this world that you see: it is unjust that you remain there when you reside in His property and do not obey Him. If you are prepared to convert to Him completely and do His bidding, you will live in never ending joy in the next world, which has no end! That life is everlasting, and the fellowship of all those who will be there is everlasting; never will they be able to die!"

That man said this and a great deal more. He did not speak as if he were learned, but rather he spoke very simply, and he never constructed any sophistic arguments. That man who had spoken in this way was called Barnabas; he was a Jew, as was his kin, and he had come from the East. According to him he was a disciple of that man who had come to the land of Judaea and performed miracles in that country. He had come on a journey to deliver in Rome the message of that man who had sent him, and was promising the kingdom of God to those who were prepared to accept His teaching as a way of life. (907–64)

---

[1] 884 **madmen** *forsenez*: This is the first of numerous instances in which a term which in Old French conventionally denotes a person afflicted by madness renders what in *Rec.* (here I.6.4) is an unequivocal allusion to diabolical possession.

There were many people crowded there. Clement was in the crowd, and he had taken great pains to understand this messenger properly. From his words, Clement clearly understood that he was not a dialectician, but rather he said in a simple fashion whatever he had in his heart. He did not add any embellishment to any word that he said, but rather he presented the good that he had learnt from the Son of God so that his argument could be clearly understood without any disputation. He had ample proof that what he said was neither falsehood nor fabrication, for there were many present in the crowd of people who bore witness to what he said regarding the miracles which had been performed. Everybody listened very intently in order to understand the miracles properly, and they listened very gladly because he spoke in a simple fashion. (965–88)

Then came the philosophers, who considered themselves to be wise. These men utterly scorned the stranger and all his words; they derided and mocked him a great deal, countered him in various ways, and constructed many sophistic arguments in order to discomfit him. But he, like a man without fear, paid no heed to anything that the hecklers said, and was not prepared to offer a single response to their nonsense. He continued talking and did not deign to respond to them. Presently one of them stepped forward and asked him numerous questions about the flea and the elephant, one of which is small, and the other large: "Why is it that the smaller has six feet, and the larger only four, and why is it that fleas have wings with which they fly? The elephant has no wings with which it might fly!"

Barnabas paid no heed to any question that he asked. He did not deign even to look at him or to stop speaking on his account; he continued speaking as if he heard nothing from him. Nonetheless, he repeatedly said the same thing when speaking when a question was asked of him in order to undermine his argument: (989–1022)

"My lords," he said, "Our Lord, in whose service we left our countries in order to convey to you what it pleased Him to communicate though us, does not want us to convey His commandments through sophistic arguments. I am quite certain that there are many people here who are quite certain of what I am saying, and will be able to testify to what they have seen and heard. It will now be up to you to choose which path you wish to follow, be it to persist or to refrain, for there is no question of compulsion. We cannot remain silent regarding what we believe, for we will incur harm by remaining silent, and you will incur loss if you do not hear our words. I could find plenty of solutions to your foolish questions about the flea and the elephant with which you keep countering me if you were asking for no other reason than to learn the truth about it. But it would be nothing but foolishness to make a speech about creatures when you do not recognise your Creator as Lord!"

Everything that Barnabas had said was considered a joke, and everything that he had said in speaking his mind became a source of ridicule. With pride and arrogance they all harangued him; they judged him worthy of derision and declared that he should not be listened to any more. He was a foreigner and completely unknown, and so was considered less wise. (1023–60)

Clement did not hesitate when he saw that Barnabas could not have any opportunity to speak and that people wished to abuse him. Everything that Barnabas had said pleased Clement greatly, as did what he had seen of his demeanour; he himself stepped forward in support of Barnabas and acted with great bravery. All on his own he spoke bravely against the whole crowd; he was aflame with a passion which came upon him through the love of God, whereby he began to speak in order to rescue the stranger:

"God," he said, "has most justly hidden His will from you so that you cannot know it, for you prove yourselves unworthy, as any man who has any understanding can clearly see! You seek to inflict shame and disgrace upon the messenger of truth because he says to you in a completely simple fashion the good that he has in mind. He did not present his case to you with any polished words, nor did he show you what you ought to do by using any art of grammar, but rather he said his message to you with everybody listening in such terms that everybody can clearly understand it, and great and small and educated and uneducated alike can all easily understand it. But you, who consider yourselves wise, bring shame upon yourselves when you seek to discredit him and have no case against him. You, who are eloquent and consider yourselves wise in comparison to others, will fall into damnation, and this will be entirely justified when you see these simple people who have set their minds on learning what the truth is, which you have so thoroughly rejected that once this truth has come to you, which ought to be a permanent resident and hailed as supreme amongst you, if only your pride could allow the rightful thing to happen, it is not even welcomed as a guest! You, who call yourselves philosophers, are thereby proven thoroughly guilty of not loving the truth, but rather of constantly seeking empty words, since you keep the truth hidden away in the kinds of statement which are in great need of a gloss, and say a thousand pointless words which are not worth as much as a single good one. What will happen to you wretches[1] if the judgement of God should come as this messenger, whom you deem so lacking in wisdom, indicates? (1061–124)

But may your mockery and mirth be put aside now, and may whoever it might be answer this for me: when you, through envy and pride, disturb with your blustering the good people who are gathered here, who have their hearts ready to welcome the truth, and cause them to fall back into the error that they wish to leave behind, what mercy will you ever find when you act so arrogantly that you wrongfully challenge with rebukes and insults this man who has come to show you the way to your salvation and who promises the certainty of knowing God without any doubt? Even if it were the case that he were saying nothing

---

[1] 1121 **wretches** *cheitifs*: *Rec.* I.9.8 refers to Greeks rather than wretches.

from which there was any hope of good, one should at least be grateful to him for his good intentions!" (1125–46)

The uproar was enormous once Clement had said this. With this and other things having been said, many became quite furious and conceived hatred for Clement as they had for the stranger. Some of the others who were there held Clement's words in high regard, and felt pity for the stranger because they saw that he was far from home. Clement asked him insistently to lodge with him when evening began to draw in. Barnabas refused, but this did not stop Clement from leading him away by force, even though he indicated that this upset him. He clearly indicated his wish to leave and said that he had business elsewhere, but Clement did not allow him to leave; he forced Barnabas to come with him and took him under his care lest harm be done to him. Clement asked him, while he was with him, about those things regarding which he had doubts, and the other man replied convincingly. With few words he showed him what the path of truth was. Clement listened to him gladly and carefully; it pleased him greatly, and he understood it clearly. Barnabas stayed there for a few days, and then said that he wanted to go elsewhere; he had to leave and return to Judaea. It could not be otherwise, for he had to go; he was due to attend a feast belonging to their religion, and so he had cause to leave.[1] Once he reached his country, he would thenceforth stay there for good; his brothers and friends there shared the same faith. He could not remain in Rome; he was appalled at the thought of staying there because he had encountered very cruel people in the city who had wrongfully and sinfully poured scorn on him. (1147–94)

In response to this, Clement said to him: "I implore you: stay here and reveal to me the teaching of your master of whom you speak! And I shall embellish your words and make them so appealing that all those who hear them will listen to them gladly. I shall preach the kingdom of God and His justice[2] and shall devote all my service to doing this, and then I shall depart with you for Judaea, your homeland, which I have long wished to see. I shall leave with you to stay there, perhaps never to return."

Barnabas replied: "If you wish to get a proper grasp of what you are seeking and wish to see my country, may there be no delay, but rather come with me immediately and cross the sea with me! For there you will find St Peter, who will be able to tell you absolutely everything that you will be able to ask: then there

---

[1] 1179–84 he had. . .leave *Mestier out. . .acheisun*: Cf. Acts 20:16, where Paul returns to Jerusalem for Pentecost.

[2] 1203–4 I shall preach. . .justice *Le regne Deu. . .precherai*: Cf. Mt 6:33.

will be no more doubting for you![1] And if it is the case that there is any obligation which makes it necessary for you to remain, I shall leave clear directions for
you when I depart from you so that when you wish to come to us, you will easily
find us. May it now be as you choose, for tomorrow I am leaving without fail!"
(1195–228)

Clement could no longer keep him from wishing to depart from there. He
escorted him towards the sea, and went with him as far as the port. He took clear
directions from Barnabas so that he could find him when he wished to come, for
he had to stay on account of debts which were owed to him. And he told Barnabas clearly that if this were not the case, he would go with him, and there would
be no delay, but instead he would hasten after him once he was better prepared.

Once Clement had spoken to him, he then entrusted him to the sailors. He
asked them to take good care of him; they then set sail, and Clement remained.
He returned home gloomily and sorrowfully; he could scarcely think of anything
other than his guest who had departed, from whom he had received great consolation. He considered him a very good friend and so thought a great deal about
him, for all aspects of Barnabas's behaviour had pleased him greatly. (1229–52)

Little more than a few days passed. Clement claimed from his debtors as
much as he could claim at that time, and then was not prepared to wait there
any longer. He completely forsook a large part of his wealth in order to leave his
country and cross into Judaea. He headed off to sea and set sail for there. After a
fortnight he landed at the city of Caesarea, which is the best and most important
of the cities in the country which is called Palestine; it was that city which with
its full name was called Caesarea Stratonis. When he landed and took lodging,
he heard some news in the city: that a man by the name of Peter was to debate
with a certain Simon who had been born in Samaria, and this was to take place
in Caesarea; and that this Peter was a disciple of that man about whom people
were talking so much, who had come to Judaea and performed miracles in the
country; and that this disputation between Peter and Simon was to take place
there on the following day. There it would become clear who would be the win-
ner. (1253–82)

Once Clement had found all this out, he asked after Peter's lodging. He
came to the doors and stopped there, as a man who knew nobody there. He then
spoke to the doorkeeper and revealed to him who he was and whence he came.
Presently Barnabas came, who, as soon as he had seen him, knew full well that
it was Clement. Weeping for joy, he kissed him and led him to St Peter. Before
he had led him all the way to him, Barnabas showed Peter to Clement, and said
to him: "Behold the man about whom you have heard so much! This is Peter, of

---

[1] 1217–20 **For there. . .for you** *Kar la. . .duter*: An addition to *Rec.* I.11.3 which foregrounds Peter's ability to provide solutions.

whom I told you that he is utterly aflame with God. I have spoken to him about you a great deal; come to him as his friend! He knows you well, and is well aware of the goodness and honour that you did to me, and is well aware of your purpose, for I have revealed everything to him. He wishes to see you, and will be very content with my bringing you here. I shall make a great offering to him today when I bring you before him!" When they came to him, Barnabas said very succinctly: "This is Clement." (1283–312)

Clement was now with St Peter, and so were his two brothers, Niceta and Aquila, whom Zacchaeus had sent there. The two brothers knew each other, but knew nothing of the third brother, nor did he know anything of them, except that there was nobody except those two.[1]

St Peter did not hesitate in the slightest once Clement had arrived; as soon as his name was mentioned, he kissed him with great joy. He had him sit beside him and then began to speak in this way: (1313–26)

"Clement," he said, "welcome! You received the messenger of truth most auspiciously, and for this you will be blessed! You did not fear the people who treated him most ignominiously; you gave Barnabas good lodging and saved him from harm. Through the goodness and honour that you did to him for the love of God, you have reached the truth which will bring you to salvation. You have come this way as a guest and a traveller, but through this journey of yours you will secure a great legacy. You have not come here in vain, for you will be a citizen of the city which has no end, for it is such that it will last for ever. Your wise action should be highly esteemed, for from the brief service that you did to God's servant you will have everlasting life. The joy there will be so great that no man alive can describe it. There is no need for you to tell me what is in your heart, for Barnabas, who mentioned you frequently, has revealed everything to me; every day, indeed often each day, we have spoken about you. If you have nothing else to do on account of which you must leave us, and if you wish to hear from me what you so greatly desire, come with us to the place to which we are going and listen to what we shall say! For if it pleases God, we shall proceed until we reach Rome. Nonetheless, tell me now what it is about which you have doubts!"[2] (1327–68)

Clement replied: "Thanks be to God that I have found you here! Because of you I left my country, and did so to remain with you permanently; I shall gladly go with you and shall tell you everything which is on my mind. I have been greatly preoccupied and am very troubled both by difficult questions and by com-

---

[1] 1313–20 **Clement was. . .two** *Clement fud. . .dous*: An added clarification relative to *Rec.* I.12.9.

[2] 1367–68 **Nonetheless. . .doubts** *Nepurquant. . .dutez*: Relative to *Rec.* I.13.6, our text foregrounds Clement's doubt, and thereby the didactic aspect of the exchange.

plicated disputations:[1] whether the soul is such that it is mortal, or such that it is never to die; and if it can never die, whether it will have to face judgement to receive the reward that it deserves, or to fall into perdition on account of sin; and whether righteousness is something from which good might come; whether the world was created, and why, and whether I am to believe that it has an end; and whether the world will change for the better or become nothing. I wish to know the truth about this and other things." (1369–92)

St Peter replied: "Listen, Clement! I shall tell you what you ask. God has hidden His grace and His will so that people cannot know them, and there are many reasons for this: first of all on account of wicked thoughts, and thereafter for wicked speech; on account of deliberate misdeeds, and committing them habitually; and on account of wicked fellowships and treacherous discussions. Through this, man falls into error and contempt for God, his Lord, and from there he falls into disloyalty and wickedness and greed. As a result he then starts to boast, and then falls into ignorance so that he cannot see God, his Lord, or know anything of His will. What will the wretch who has placed himself in such suffering then do except cry out from his heart to God and implore His help so that He, who sees all things, might grant him light and grace so that he might be able to see himself and recognise his Lord?[2] But he will strive in vain to know anything worthwhile unless God, who can grant sense and wisdom, should cause him to know it. He who does not learn cannot know anything, and so it is necessary from the outset to seek a master who is certain of everything that a man ought to know. It is necessary to believe him in all respects, even if one cannot understand him immediately; he is not to be contradicted in anything that he says, nor should one debate it, but rather one should fervently implore him to make comprehensible that which cannot be learnt without him. In faith lies the foundation of everything which pertains to our salvation: now hear what it is that you must believe of this faith! (1393–440)

God always was, is, and will be; what has been will always exist. He alone is the true God; in heaven and on earth there is none but He. He created the world through His goodness as befitted His will. In creating the world, He had nothing from which it might take form or matter: He did not create it from anything which was or is; by His word alone everything was created. He created both space and time in the world, and devoted much thought to the act of creation. He created a variety of creatures of various kinds. He created angels and placed them in heaven, but did not make them of mortal flesh: He created them all as

---

[1] 1369–78 **Clement replied. . .disputations** *Clement respunt. . .desputeisuns*: These lines replace *Rec.* I.14.1, in which Clement points James (the ostensible recipient of his account) to his earlier mention of the questions.

[2] 1405–20 **Through this. . .recognise his Lord** *Par cest. . .sun Seignur recunuisse*: A simplification of *Rec.* I.15.34, which likens the crimes to smoke in a house which can be cleared only by God.

spirits, but they did not remain in heaven; many of them grew proud and through pride fell from heaven. With overweening pride they ranged themselves against their Lord, who had created them; they were not prepared to obey Him, and so He was not prepared to support them any longer. They fell down into Hell, and never will they be rescued from there. Pride is a most wicked thing: it always desires to rise up, but in climbing, it stumbles down; it makes a poor exchange, and in place of good takes bad. God created many creatures in various forms, which have multiplied greatly in this world in which they were created. Above the others He created one in which is brought together all the goodness that all the others which are in heaven and on earth have within themselves. He called this form 'man' and fashioned him in such a way that he placed body and soul together; and after man He created woman, who was there for him as company, comfort, and assistance. He gave them life, and the power to act according to their will, and reason whereby they might know what should be done and what should be avoided. He created the body such that it might die, and the soul that it might live without suffering death. (1441–90)

When body and soul are together, they have in themselves the free choice to think well and act well and to refrain from all wickedness; or if they wish to turn to wickedness and are not prepared to discipline themselves, their Lord will not compel them, for He wishes to be served lovingly and willingly. Then the reward will be great, for anybody who has to serve his lord and performs the service unwillingly will receive little recompense or thanks when he has not served him willingly; anybody who owes service and deliberately serves his lord badly cannot receive recompense or thanks, but rather will have to pay for it dearly. In just the same way Our Lord God wishes to be served lovingly. He will never compel anybody: may anybody who wishes to serve Him do so! Anybody who serves Him well will receive honour, and anybody who does so badly will fall into suffering. When the soul leaves the body, the body will be dead, and the soul will live: then their hearts will be judged for better or for worse. If it turns out well, the joy is great, and if it turns out badly, the fire that they will have to suffer will be blazing, and then there will be no question of repenting! Anybody who has done his service to Him rightly and justly will receive great benefit from His righteousness, for righteousness is a great power. God does not want the world that He created from nothing to last for ever. Heaven and earth will come to a complete end, and the whole world will become nothing; all the things which are in the world will pass with the world. All things then will be new, some foul, and some fair: fair the ones for those who fare well, and foul the ones for those who fare badly. The bodies will then rise from the earth, for the souls will enter the bodies, and body and soul together will come to judgement. Their fellowship will be rewarded in accordance with whether they have deserved good or ill: the good people will receive everlasting reward, and the wicked eternal punishment. No ear can hear, and no eye can see, and no man's heart can imagine the good that God has prepared for all those who have loved Him. Of the ill and the torment that the wicked will suffer no man can say anything more than that anybody who is condemned to suffer will be utterly wretched. This is the faith in which one must believe: anybody who wishes to attain the truth will find his way through this path; without this there is no salvation." (1491–556)

The essence of what St Peter had said pleased Clement greatly. He had clearly understood the argument and most joyfully committed it to memory; by what he had said and by many other things Clement was already very satisfied. That which had for so long caused him doubt he now understood as clearly as if he could see it with his eyes or touch it with his two hands. He considered it quite unbelievable that he had not understood it previously when the proof which removed his doubt from him was so simple. He thanked God that he had understood it so well, and he was already very eager for St Peter to tell him more. (1557–74)

When he saw Clement so keen, St Peter did not hesitate to tell him what he ought to believe, what he ought to avoid, and what he ought to do; about the True Prophet Jesus Christ, who came to earth and took flesh there in order to lead the whole world to salvation through His humanity; and how He suffered death wrongfully and unjustly; what He did and what He said as long as He walked on earth; and that He first revealed what was false and what was true; and that He himself put into practice the good that He spoke from His mouth. Never was any man found who proved Him guilty of sin. All the prophets spoke of Him and bore witness to Him that when He came to earth, truth would be born with Him. He is true and the truth: in Him there is no disloyalty, for His words and His deeds are in complete harmony. He spoke well and acted well, and so nothing was discordant. He should be heeded all the more when none is found to be His equal. On account of such proofs and many others which bear ample witness to Him, He must be heeded and believed all the more; and since He performed great miracles and such ones as had never been heard of before, and which no man performed except Him, and which will never again be performed unless they are performed by Him, syllogisms and sophistic arguments are of no avail whatsoever against Him, for anybody who does not have authority from Him cannot be in a state of truth.[1] (1575–616)

St Peter's words pleased Clement greatly, and he was now quite certain regarding the things about which he had been in doubt. They both spoke, one asking questions and the other answering, until evening began to draw in. St Peter did not wish to let Clement go; he did not want him to lodge elsewhere, and told

---

[1] 1421–616 **But...truth** *Meis...auctorité*: These lines bear little resemblance to *Rec.* I.16–18, with the conventional comments on faith and creed replacing the discussion of the True Prophet and prophetic virtue.

him to stay with him to hear the disputation the next morning between him and Simon. For the meal he seated Clement on his own, and he explained the reason why, for St Peter and his followers were all Christian, and Clement was still a pagan, for he had come that very day: neither religion nor reason, since he was not of their faith, could allow him to eat or drink with them before he had become Christian.[1] Once they had all eaten, St Peter thanked God, and he explained to Clement the thanks that he gave to God. Clement did not lodge elsewhere, but rather stayed with St Peter. When it was time to go to bed, St Peter said this prayer for Clement: "May God grant us to see the day when we might commune with you, and when you might be baptised so that you might eat and drink with us!" Once he had said this, they went to bed, and they slept and rested well. (1617–52)

Once night had passed, one of St Peter's companions by the name of Zacchaeus came at daybreak to tell him that Simon Magus was sending word to him that he would not be able to keep the date that he had agreed with him until he had more leisure. But after the seventh day he would definitely present himself; then he would come to debate, and would not seek any more delay. Zacchaeus gave thanks for the delay once he had delivered his message, and said that it would be good to grant it. They would be better able to plan and to prepare more thoroughly what should be said and what should be kept quiet; it would be good for the companions to ask questions amongst themselves, to discuss various topics, and to argue points against each other. If they did this for the next seven days, they might be better prepared and more secure against Simon when it came to the disputation. By asking and replying in this way, they could defeat Simon, for in this way they would familiarise themselves with what Simon's arguments would be, and would be able to be on their guard against that with which he would counter.[2]

Once Zacchaeus had given this advice, St Peter replied: "In the name of God, may the delay be granted to him! And say this to Simon: may he come when he wishes to come, for he will find us ready at any time!"[3] Zacchaeus headed to Simon to deliver this response to him. Clement remained with St Peter, and he looked very despondent, for the delay that St Peter had granted greatly dis-

---

[1] 1629–38 **For the meal. . .Christian** *Al manger. . .Crestien devenu fust*: Our text clarifies the reasons for Clement's exclusion relative to *Rec.* I.19.3.

[2] 1665–84 **Zacchaeus gave thanks. . .counter** *Zacheu bien load. . .opposer*: A considerable abbreviation of *Rec.* I.20.4–11, which states the questions at stake, the eventual discussion of which is mostly omitted from *Clement*.

[3] 1689–90 **may he come. . .time** *Vienge. . .truvera*: Peter speaks rather more forcefully than in *Rec.* I.21.1.

pleased him. St Peter clearly noticed that Clement was upset, and that the delay that he had granted had vexed him. (1653–700)

St Peter then said: "Clement, my friend, do not take it amiss that I allowed Simon to have this delay! Anybody who loves God and believes that He ordains all things well must not believe that anything happens to which He does not pay close attention, particularly regarding anything which involves His friends. He arranges all things carefully, both great and small, and both sooner and later. Even if a thing does not please us as much as we wanted, and even if the opposite happens of something that we are thinking of doing, we must not think that God, who ordains all things well and knows what everybody needs, does it in order to make things worse. For however something might come to pass and whatever its outcome might be, everything is through His providence and for our betterment, for He is able to ordain everything better than we can imagine it. Therefore do not be upset, Clement, for this delay is to your advantage! And I fully believe and fully understand that everything is for your benefit, for in these seven days of delay I shall have complete freedom to explain to you the origins of things which have passed, and which will follow, and which are now present, and how and why God created everything which was, is, and will be. Everything that I briefly mentioned here has been written down, but a man cannot learn it by himself unless he has a master who might help him to understand it. Therefore in the same way as I learned it, I shall teach it to you, just as our master, without whom nobody can be certain, told it. He alone is the True Prophet and causes everything which is, will be, and has been to be understood immediately, for He alone knows the truth of it." (1701–50)

Clement paid careful attention to what St Peter said, and St Peter strove all the more to say what he thought. He then began freely to expound divine Scripture to him, and he began with the book which is called Genesis:

"In the beginning," he said, "God created heaven and earth from nothing. Light and the firmament and all four elements came into being through Him." And to summarise briefly, he recounted in order everything that God created in seven days according to the book. He told him a great deal about Adam, Noah, and Abraham, about Isaac and Jacob, about Joseph, Moses, and Job; about the law that God gave on the mountain which is called Sinai, and he explained in full what the law and the allegory represent; about the ancient patriarchs, and the events of their time; about the deeds and words of the kings, and the prophets and their writings. He recounted the Scriptures in order until he came to Jesus Christ and explained the meaning both of His words and of His deeds, and that everything concerning Jesus Christ, the Son of God, was prophecy. He then told him how the Son of God was born on earth, and that He was God through His Father and became man through His mother. God and man, one person: neither before nor since was any person ever so good, for God is and was His Father, and His Mother was and is the Virgin. St Peter told Clement all about the mira-

cles and wonders that Jesus Christ performed with everybody looking on, about
His words and His teaching, and how He was put to death most unjustly and
through envy; how He rose from death on the third day, and revealed Himself
alive in flesh and bone; and that with His disciples looking on, He most joyfully
ascended to heaven, and the Holy Spirit then descended and filled all the apostles; about the woes experienced by those who professed to be in His service; and
about the Jews who so assailed Him, and their outrageous behaviour. St Peter explained how and in what way he himself had then roamed the lands, and how he
had spoken of God, and that he had journeyed until he reached Caesarea; there
Simon had challenged him to conduct a disputation with him. St Peter recounted
all this—but by no means with such excessive brevity—in order and very clearly,
and then he said to Clement: "You have found this out through the delay which
has been taken. These seven days of the delay which was granted have been of
great benefit to you!"

Once Clement had heard everything, he was absolutely overjoyed, and it
also gave St Peter great joy that he strove to understand, for by repeating things
frequently and asking about his doubts, St Peter fully understood that Clement
was anything but half-hearted.[1] (1751–832)

The seven days had now passed, and the day came on which St Peter and
Simon had agreed to debate their beliefs. St Peter was not slothful; he rose very
early, for he did not sleep long, and this resulted entirely from habit and from the
practice of his profession when he was a sailor and when he was a fisherman with
St Andrew, his brother.[2] He roused all his companions—there were thirteen[3]
of them—and then said to them: "We must talk about what we have to do, and
particularly about whether Simon will reform, and whether he is such that he
might be prepared to understand what is right in order to learn effectively. And
we must enquire of him which he prefers, peace or war; whether he is sober and
merciful, whether he is compassionate and sociable, and whether his conduct is
such that he has no outrageous behaviour in him; whether he hates deadly sins
and loves works commonly recognised as good, and whether he commits deliberately any sinful or good deed that he performs. For if he has sufficient good
intention that he is prepared to understand the truth and does not deliberately
commit the sins which are called deadly, through the argument that we present
to him we will guide him to true faith. And if he is such that through wickedness he flees virtue and loves vice, we would waste time and effort in everything

---

[1] 1751–832 **Clement. . .half-hearted** *Clement. . .de rien*: These lines contain but a
few isolated elements of *Rec.* I.22–74, which is otherwise simply omitted.

[2] 1839–44 **for he. . .brother** *Kar il. . .frere*: This explanation has no equivalent in *Rec.*
II.1.1. Further comments on Peter and Andrew's earlier lives are provided in vv. 5601–14.

[3] 1846 **thirteen** *tredze*: *Rec.* II.1.2 specifies their names.

that we might say to him.[1] Therefore it will be good to be prepared with material whereby he might be defeated,[2] for we cannot avoid our obligation to talk to him, for otherwise the people would consider us ignorant and that we were afraid of him, and thereby they would remain in error. I therefore want you to apprise me of what you know of his nature."[3] (1833–82)

Niceta then urgently requested permission to speak his mind. Once St Peter had granted this to him, he then spoke in this way:

"My lord Peter, I am extremely upset about today's undertaking! I am very concerned about the disputation with Simon that you have undertaken; I am very unhappy about it and very worried, and am very fearful about it. I am very anxious about it, for Simon is very cunning. Simon is very cruel and knows a very great deal of sorcery. Simon is a dialectician, and is inclined strongly towards evil, and little towards good. Simon has frequented many schools, and is very skilled in speaking; he is of very great eloquence, and can present his opinion very effectively. In addition to all this he is a sorcerer, and so does whatever pleases him. It is therefore very much to be feared that he might defeat us, for it is quite often the case in a large gathering of people that for various reasons not everybody understands the argument, nor does everybody have the same way of judging what they hear being said: either they have not understood it properly, or not remembered it properly, or on account of love or hate or bribery or fear they are drawn more to wrong than to right: all this has often happened.[4] Simon is a very wicked deceiver: as far as concerns my brother and me, I can say that he would have completely deceived us if we had not become aware; he would have completely tricked us and drawn us into his wickedness if we had not by watching and listening become aware of his treachery." (1883–926)

Niceta had said his piece. Aquila then urgently requested permission to speak and be heard, and St Peter consented entirely.

Aquila said: "Listen to me, my dear lord Peter! I am extremely worried and extremely concerned for you, and am very anxious for you. This comes entirely

---

[1] 1869–72 **And if...say to him** *E si...od lui parlerium*: These lines omit Peter's comment in *Rec.* II.4.4 that he will refrain from discussing the more secret and sacred aspects of divine knowledge, perhaps lest the audience suspect that they are not receiving the unadulterated truth.

[2] 1873–74 **Therefore it will be...defeated** *Dunc iert...cunfundu*: Peter's goal here is rather more combative than in *Rec.* II.4.5, where he seeks evasion.

[3] 1845–82 **He roused...his nature** *Ses cumpainnuns...savez*: These lines omit most of *Rec.* II.1–2, and modify what is retained from *Rec.* II.3–4 (e.g., omitting the metaphor of placing pearls before swine from *Rec.* II.3.5).

[4] 1907–18 **for it is...happened** *Kar avenir...feit*: These lines stem from *Rec.* II.5.3, which otherwise would have appeared earlier (after v. 1893.)

from my great love for you, for I very much desire your honour. For anybody who loves his friend will be caused by love to think about him, and anybody who neglects him clearly demonstrates that he hates him. May it not vex you if I say this; I very much want you to be forewarned! But I do not nonetheless say this because I consider you less worthy, for you are far more justified in word and in deed than Simon. But I call God as my witness: since I have not been in any place where you have debated, I have feared for you all the more, for I know Simon well to be an educated man, and I know his manner very well because I have experienced it. From childhood on he has studied sorcery and necromancy: this is why he is confident in committing such outrageous misdeeds. I am concerned that the people who will come and hear you debate should all profit from it, and that the truth should emerge, and above all else that I might say, that your reputation should not be besmirched. My brother and I knew Simon well from childhood, and accompanied him as friends and helpers, and were very much accomplices in his wrongdoings. Had God not saved us, we would have still remained with him, but by reason and nature we utterly detested his outrageous behaviour; we had it in our hearts to love God, in accordance with what we are given to understand. God, I believe, ordained precisely for our benefit that we should spend time in his company in order to learn of his wicked life and that he does nothing with God's support, but rather does everything through sorcery. As far as concerns me[1] I can certainly say that if I had not seen and heard things whereby I became aware, he would without doubt have completely deceived me. And if you wish to know about where Simon was born, and about his deeds and his manner, I can tell you the certain truth. (1927–88)

Simon was born in Samaria, and his kin lives there. His father was called Antonius, and his mother was called Rachel. He is very well educated in Greek and he wishes to be considered to be God. He has learnt a great deal of necromancy and has practised sorcery; his mind is very much set on evil, and he is very full of vainglory. He claims to be higher and greater than God the Creator, and wants it to be believed that he can live for ever. He claims to be so great and so powerful that he calls himself the 'Standing One.'[2] (1989–2004)

In order to win acclaim, he had first joined a certain Dositheus; Dositheus was a heretic whose heresy was against God. He had thirty companions, and Simon was one of these thirty. Dositheus was their master, and in his circle he kept a mistress whom he loved very much; out of love he called her Luna. In order to

---

[1] 1981 **As far as concerns me** *Pur mei meisme*: Prior to this line, *Clement* omits *Rec.* II.6.9, in which Aquila admits that one with Simon's powers could easily be taken for a god.

[2] 2004 **Standing One** *Vertu Estant*: The Old French more literally means "Standing Power," but my rendering for clarity follows the conventional translation of the Latin name *Stans*, which describes the one who cannot die through any corruption (cf. *Rec.* II.7.2–3).

gain fame this Dositheus made people believe that he was God and a great power which would remain standing for ever. He said that the mistress whom he kept was the moon, and because the moon follows a course numbering thirty days, he accordingly had this number of companions: there was never one more or fewer, for when one of them died, another was immediately added; attention had to be paid to who was to be added to their number. In this way they deceived simple folk who believed that the moon could otherwise not follow its course, and that those thirty were the days. By his own efforts and those of his friends, Simon had joined that number; he was one of that number of thirty, but he did not follow his course properly.[1] The lunar month went completely awry, for Simon completely disturbed its cycle; he sped far from his course when he lay with Luna![2] He began a relationship with his master's mistress, but did not wish to reveal it immediately, for he preferred to wait until he could claim her in such a way that he might take her with greater glory and without incurring dishonour. He nonetheless revealed his entire subterfuge to my brother and me, and implored us to conceal the secret that he revealed to us. (2005–50)

He promised us very great love, great rewards, and great honours if we were prepared to follow him and in no way reveal his relationship. He admitted to us openly what it was that he was seeking: vainglory, and to be believed to be more powerful than he was; and in private he revealed to us everything about his sorcery. He promised to reward us generously if we were prepared to stay with him and consent to his magic and follow him as master, for he could perform many wonders whereby he would make it be truly believed that everything that he said was true on account of the wonders that he would perform. For, he said, if one were to seek him, and he were to avail himself of magic, he would be neither seen nor found until it so pleased him. Then when he wanted, he would be seen, and he would penetrate though mountains and rocks; he would let himself fall from the top of a mountain without suffering any injury or harm.[3] If it so happened that he should be captured and placed in sturdy chains, he would quickly be freed and would cause his captors to be chained: he would open every lock.[4] He would make graven images move by themselves in such a way that they could be

---

[1] 2005–36 **In order to. . .properly** *Il pur primes. . .tenu*: These lines include most of *Rec.* II.8, but exclude mention of the death of John the Baptist.

[2] 2037–40 **The lunar month. . .Luna** *Tute fud fause. . .acosta*: *Clement* contains paronomasia which cannot be adequately captured in translation. The *luneisun*—the dubious "lunar month" represented by the members of Dositheus's sect—goes awry because of Simon's passion for *Lune* "Luna," and through his actions, he commits a *bisexte*—which can denote a leap-year, keeping with the theme of time, but also some kind of aberrant action.

[3] 2075–76 **from the top. . .harm** *Del sum. . .suffrir*: Cf. Mt 4:6.

[4] 2081 **he would open every lock** *Il desclorreit tute serrure*: Cf. Acts 5:19, 12:7–10, 16:26.

thought to be alive; he was quite able to make new trees and great orchards bear fruit. He would place himself in fire without being burnt and would change his appearance in such a way that he would not be recognised; he would make little children grow beards. Through sorcery he would also give himself two faces; he would become a sheep or goat, and, if it pleased him, he would fly through the air. He would be able to exhibit a large amount[1] of gold, and make kings and then depose them.[2] He would cause himself to be considered and worshipped and served as God, so that those who considered him to be God would make images of him. (2051–100)

One time it so happened that he had gone out into the fields; his mother, Rachel, had told him that he had to reap crops in the fields. He saw where the sickle lay, but did not move to pick it up; rather he ordered it to reap without anybody touching it. The sickle did not hesitate in the slightest to execute his command; he reaped ten times more than any companion who was reaping during that harvest! Anybody who wanted to record everything that he said he could do and had recently done[3] would have a great deal to recount, for he had recently penetrated into a great mountain and passed through the middle, and had recently made an orchard[4] which was blossoming wonderfully. (2101–20)

Once we had heard this, we were quite astonished by it, and we were quite amazed about the orchard and the penetrated mountain, for what he said regarding the mountain he had, he said, done twice.[5] My brother and I understood by what we heard from him that he led a most wicked life, and we feared his company. We knew full well that he had not said anything from which any good might come, and we were quite sure that it was all the work of a sorcerer. Even though he told us this and a great deal worse, we had nonetheless joined him. We accompanied him and consented to his wicked deeds, and lied for him a great deal, and allowed him to deceive as many people as he wished. We lied for him so much that some considered him to be God without him having demonstrated any of the things of which he had boasted. (2121–44)

In the beginning, when he had joined the followers of Dositheus, he began to calumniate his master and disparage what he did. He said that he was ignorant and that everything that he said achieved nothing; he said repeatedly that his master was not what he claimed to be. But when Dositheus learned that Simon had calumniated him, he grew angry towards Simon and feared losing his

---

[1] 2095 **a large amount** *asez*: This renders the *plurimum* found only in the ΛΠΘΦ readings of *Rec.* II.9.5.

[2] 2096 **make kings and then depose them** *Faire reis e puis degraer*: Cf. Dn 2:21.

[3] 2113–16 **Anybody who…done** *Mult i avereit…fait out*: These lines seem to represent *Rec.* II.9.7, which should have appeared after v. 2100.

[4] 2119 **orchard** *vergier*: This resembles only the Θ^r reading for *Rec.* II.9.9.

[5] 2125–26 **for what…twice** *Kar ceo que…aveit*: In *Rec.* II.10.1, the amazement stems rather from the fact that the claimed deeds had been performed by their ancestors.

reputation because of him. He spoke to Simon when they came to school. There he had him stripped naked;[1] he wanted to beat him in order to avenge himself, but as he struck with the scourge, the blow fell as if into smoke: Simon had cast a spell on his master so that he did not hurt him in any way when striking him! Dositheus was quite astonished when he had been unable to avenge himself on Simon or hurt him by beating him, and on account of what he had seen he thought that Simon was God. Then he asked Simon whether he was the one who was called The Standing One, for if he was, Dositheus would immediately worship him.[2] Simon replied: 'I am he!' And when Dositheus heard this, he immediately fell at Simon's feet and handed over his power to him. He worshipped him as God and made him master in his stead; he himself took Simon's position and became one of the number of thirty. Dositheus did not live long after this; once he had died, Simon claimed Luna,[3] his mistress, as his own, and has kept her up to this day. Simon performed a great wonder involving this Luna with many people looking on: he made her stand in a tower and look out of a window, and then through sorcery made it seem to the people who were standing all around and looking at the tower that there was not a single window out of which Luna was not leaning. It seemed to everybody that they were all looking directly at her face; she was seen from all sides, and Simon did this through his magic. He performed many such wonders, and we who were his close associates consented to him and assisted his wicked deeds in every way.[4] (2145–204)

He revealed his secrets to us, as a result of which it once so happened that we implored him to describe how his deeds worked. He admitted to us privately a deed of exceptional cruelty, for he was doing everything for which he received acclaim through the soul of a child who had been most outrageously murdered and cruelly slain. The child whom he had thus killed was innocent and a virgin; Simon cast a spell on the soul and conjured it forth so forcefully that he compelled it to come and tell him what he wished.

Once he had admitted this to us, I inquired whether the soul could know and tell about a given thing once it had been separated from the body. (2205–24)

Simon then said: 'Be sure that once body and soul are separated, the soul is first in line after God to know everything! And because it knows everything which is to happen in the future, the sorcerers coerce it through necromancy into appearing at their bidding, in order to learn that what they are unsure of.'

---

[1] 2159 **naked** *neu*: Simon's nudity is an exciting innovation relative to *Rec.* II.11.2.

[2] 2171–74 **Then he asked. . .worship him** *Dunc demandat. . .le aurreit*: Cf. Mt 11:3.

[3] 2186 **Luna** *Lune*: The further details regarding Luna found in *Rec.* II.12.2 are omitted.

[4] 2201–4 **He performed. . .way** *Tels merveilles. . .aidant*: In place of *Rec.* II.12.5, which describes people's belief that Simon is God, the essence of vv. 1967–68 is repeated; cf. note to v. 1981.

I then asked why those who have been slain, given that they are so powerful, do not avenge themselves against their enemies and take revenge for the bodies from which they have been cast by force. In response to this, Simon said to me: (2225–40)

'Once the soul has left the body, it has immediately understood that God's judgement will come, in which every man will receive his just reward, for better or for worse, for it will know clearly what it has deserved; and because it has understood that the judgement will avenge everything, it has no desire to avenge itself, for the last judgement awaits, in which the murderer will receive worse than if he were slain here. And even if it were the case that the soul wanted to avenge itself, it could not do so, for it does not have the power to do as it will, for the angels which preside over it and have authority over it will not permit it to go forth or to do as it pleases.'

I immediately replied: 'Why does the soul appear and do the bidding of the sorcerer who is so cruel and harsh to it when the angels who hold power over the soul do not permit it?' (2241–66)

'It is by great force,' said Simon, 'and through a very powerful invocation that the angels allow the soul to leave once they have received it into their care, for we invoke them so powerfully by the name of the supreme being whom they acknowledge as their lord and exert such force upon them that they cannot resist the compulsion to let the soul go. The angels commit no sin whatsoever in this, but we sin most grievously, for they are excused by reason of our invocation when we force them to do what is against their will.'

Once Simon had said all this, Niceta very quickly jumped forward and said what I had in mind, but I wanted to wait a little in order better to examine and investigate and better to probe his wickedness.

Niceta said: 'Are you then not afraid that that judgement and that day of which you speak will come and judge the entire world, given that you invoke the angels in such a way that you force the souls away from them, and lead people astray in order to win honour here, and wish to claim for yourself the honour due only to God? What about your teaching that no judgement will come once this world has expired, which you deliver to us and other people, whom you also cause to believe that man's soul is mortal, when you have now revealed to us what you have seen with your own eyes, and have admitted that you yourself have heard that the soul itself has told you that it lives for ever without dying, and that it will receive such reward as it has deserved here?' (2267–312)

Simon became completely pale and considered himself quite confounded; he would have much rather preferred to have remained silent about what he had admitted at such length. He did not welcome Niceta's words, for he had no idea of how to respond. Nonetheless he thought it over when he did not have a response ready, and then he completely disavowed everything that he had treacherously said. He went back on everything that he had said and offered us the following response:[1]

'I am not what you believe me to be! I am of a quite different nature, for Antonius was not my father, nor am I a sorcerer, nor is Luna my mistress: I am of a completely different status. Before Rachel married Antonius or there was any union between them, I was conceived in Rachel whilst she was a virgin, and it was then in my power to be born as I wished.[2] It was completely at my command whether to be born small or big, and to reveal myself to people as it so pleased me. But you were the first that I took to my bosom and made my friends in order to test you first to see whether you were prepared to have faith in me, and to bring you such honour that you might have a special place in heaven. In the guise of a man I lied in everything that I said to you previously in order to ascertain whether you love me with the faith that you owe to me.'

I considered him an utter wretch once he had replied to me in this way; I saw his wickedness so clearly that I was quite astonished. I was ashamed for him and very afraid that he might seek to harm us. I therefore indicated to my brother that he should pretend to disavow what he had said. (2313–58)

I then said to Simon: 'Lord God, we did not know that you were so. Do not despise us; you have us and our hearts with you! Accept us and our love, for we have been striving as ignorant mortals to understand what God was. We have now fully grasped that you are the one whom we have been seeking.'

I said a great deal like this to him, and then the deceiver thought that we had been completely duped on account of our pretence. 'I shall,' he said, 'have mercy on you: I know full well that you love me as God. You loved me and knew nothing of it; you were not aware of this whilst seeking me. But I do not want you to doubt any longer: I am God, whom you have sought! He is God who can be small or big when he wishes; it cannot be more clearly known by anything else that I am powerful and God. But now I shall tell you the truth of the wonder that I performed. (2359–84)

One time, air was changed into water through my power; I turned that water into flesh and blood and formed a new man from it. I created him as a child and brought him to life with far greater skill than that shown by God the Creator, whom people acknowledge as Lord: He made His man from earth, and I made mine from air, and it is much more difficult to create a form from air than from earth! Once my man had been created from air, I returned him to the place from which he had been taken, but nonetheless I captured this form in painting in order to provide people with evidence and a reminder of my creation.'

---

[1] 2313–24 **Simon. . .response** *Simun. . .rendi*: A considerable amplification of *Rec.* II.14.1, highlighting the drama of Simon's predicament.

[2] 2331–36 **Before Rachel. . .wished** *Einz que. . .volenté*: Cf. Mt 1:18.

We who heard this from him understood why he had said it: on account of the child whom he had killed and through whom he was committing his wicked deeds." (2385–406)

St Peter had listened carefully to everything that Aquila had recounted. He could not keep himself from crying, and presently he began to speak in this way:

"I find it absolutely astonishing that God is so patient; the foolhardiness of many people is also astonishing. When will a reason ever be found which might make Simon understand that the judgement of God will come, in which God will judge the wicked, when he himself fully understands it through his own experience, and he himself admits that the soul obeys him and appears at his bidding and has said that it is not mortal, and he declares and states his questions word for word, and once he has ascertained the truth, he has subsequently devoted himself to deliberately acting wickedly, whereby he sins terribly against God? Truth to tell, it is to his great misfortune that he was born, for he is deceived by devils, for he will never admit that thing of which he is absolutely certain. He will never stop acting wickedly as long as he remains alive in this world! It often so happens, and it is very true, that some people have received knowledge and understanding from God, whereby they have fully understood through the evidence of compelling reason what is to be believed and what is not to be believed, who then through the sin and vice with which they are burdened have through wickedness grown so full of pride and hardened against God that through wicked obduracy they are not prepared to acknowledge the truth, even though they have understood it as well as if they had seen it with their own eyes. (2407–50)

It would be quite sufficient for a man if he were prepared to love his Lord in accordance with the law of nature which is set in justice, for that love is so great that it suffices for salvation. But the Devil has stolen the love that man owes to God, and he turns into enemies those who should be friends of God, for it greatly annoys the Devil when man is grateful to God and recognises as Lord the one who is his Creator. I gladly call without any further delay heaven and earth as witness that if the Devil could do as much evil as he wished, the earth would have been damned a long time ago, but the mercy of God has prevented it. And if all were so disposed that they loved God as they should, they would all be saved without fail; then there would be no need for them to fear the Devil, even if it were the case that they sinned and nonetheless imposed justice upon themselves in such a way that through chastisement they might be reformed.[1] But the Devil has seized the hearts of many and placed himself in them, and has made them enemies of God by abandoning good in order to do worse, and has claimed for himself the love that man should render to God." (2451–84)

---

[1] 2474–78 **then there would be. . .reformed** *Mar puis. . .amendement*: An addition to *Rec.* II.17.3 reflecting the development of penance into the 13th century.

St Peter said more than I have said, but for fear of tedium I shall not include it here. And Aquila asked questions, in response to which St Peter said a great deal; to each question he gave a very fitting answer.[1] Then St Peter asked to be told what Simon did after the two brothers had noticed that Simon was so deceptive.

Niceta then said: "Once it was the case that Simon had realised that we had seen through both him and his wickedness, and we realised the same thing, we discussed leaving. We talked a great deal about his wicked deeds; we completely abandoned him and came to Zacchaeus, who kindly received us. We told him what reasoning we had found with Simon; we told him the whole truth as we have told it to you. Zacchaeus joyfully taught us what the faith of Jesus Christ was; he placed us in the fellowship of God's faithful, and there we have remained."

Once Niceta had said this, Zacchaeus, who had gone out a little earlier, then entered and said that Simon had come. A large crowd had come with him, and Simon stood in the middle; all of them followed him on account of the wonders of which they had heard. St Peter could delay no more; he had to come and debate. (2485–522)

St Peter then wanted to pray, and so he asked Clement to step to one side, for Clement was the only pagan, and all the others were Christian.[2] Then he said to the other companions: "Let us say prayers to God that He might help me today, as I am His servant, for I go forth for the sake of the salvation of all the men who have come!"

Once he and his companions had finished their prayer, St Peter proceeded to the square, where he saw the large crowd. In the middle of them stood Simon as if he were carrying their banner. St Peter stood and remained silent until he saw that he might be heard; once he could be heard, he then began speaking in this way: (2523–42)

"My lords who have come here, may the peace of God be with all of you who have prepared yourselves to receive the truth! To those who wish to welcome it and do this favour to God for it, God will grant such a reward for this as will never end if as a result of the truth that they have acquired they wish to act in accordance with righteousness. Everybody must therefore begin this by inquiring into what the righteousness is which pleases God and which He esteems, and there-

---

[1] 2485–90 **St Peter. . .answer** *Plus dist. . .reisun*: An indication of the abridgement of *Rec.* II.17.5–18.10.

[2] 2525–26 **for Clement. . .Christian** *Kar Clement. . .Crestien*: *Rec.* II.19.5 explains rather that Clement is not yet cleansed of the sins that he had committed in ignorance.

after into His kingdom, that we might be worthy of attaining it.[1] Righteousness
is a fine virtue by which it will be clearly understood what should be done and
what should be avoided. In the kingdom of God will be the reward for those
who are toiling here and suffering patiently for God: those who endeavour to do
good will receive everlasting good there, and anybody who has been contrary to
God such that he has not done His bidding will in accordance with his wicked
deeds receive punishment which can never end. I must say this to you: you have
been placed in this life in order to know the will of God for as long as you might
have the opportunity to do so. Each man must think on this for as long as he
has time and space. May each man think of reforming, for too many questions
can be asked by one who is not prepared to refrain from wickedness but rather
undertakes to inquire how the kingdom of God and His righteousness might be
won: anybody who undertakes this inquiry will be a fool, for he will never reach
a conclusion! Time is short, and we shall all die and will scarcely remain here any
longer. The judgement of God will come, where we shall have to answer for what
we have done here: questions will be of no use then! First of all you must therefore inquire carefully into how to live well, so that we might be spared punishment and come to that place where we can live without suffering woe. (2543–96)

     For if we spend our time in vain on foolish questions, we will surely de-
part from here without having done any good, and when we come before God,
we shall not be able to find any place there if we have not done anything which
pleases or gladdens Him. Everything has its time and place; turn your mind
to this fact. Here is the place to learn goodness; elsewhere will be the time to
claim the reward! Let it not occur to you to thwart yourself by wrongly making
a change which puts things into the incorrect order. It is not reasonable to go
postponing what should come first, or demanding reward beforehand and then
thinking about acting; rather may the good deed come first, and the reward follow thereafter! Let us be supplied with righteousness like a man who has undertaken a voyage, who at the very outset carefully supplies everything required for
the journey. In this way we shall come to the kingdom of God, which is like a
big city: all those who wish to have the final rest are on a journey heading in that
direction. (2597–626)

     One must not be in any doubt regarding God and His power: the world with
all the things in it bears witness to Him. Let us not make any inquiry into God's
secrets; let us strive wholeheartedly to do good! For when we come to God, we
shall know all His secrets; there will be no need to wonder then when we will be
able to see everything. Anybody who turns his mind to what he is completely unable to find will not only not find it, but will also fall into grave error; and when
he does not do what he ought to do, but instead does the complete opposite, he
will be far removed from the kingdom of God, and will not even set foot in the

---

[1] 2553–58 **Everybody must therefore. . .attaining it** *Pur ceo cuvient. . .digne*: Cf. Mt
6:33.

gates! But if somebody wishes to follow the right path so that he might reach a good end, his entire journey is to no avail unless he has a guide to lead him. He must come to the True Prophet, who is completely able to guide properly; he must follow behind Him and keep a straight path behind Him. The True Prophet is Jesus Christ: in order to follow him, it is quite sufficient to do good and abandon evil, without travelling on foot or by horse. Anybody who is willing to follow Him as guide cannot fall into error. If we are prepared to do His bidding, He will lead us to the city in which we shall see with our own eyes everything about which we have been in doubt: as our inheritance He will make us citizens of that city. (2627–64)

Understand what this path is: it is this life, which is drawing to a close! Those who travel this path are those who are in this life, and the gate is Jesus Christ, for through Him one enters and exits.[1] The kingdom of God is the city where God is in His majesty; only those who are pure of heart will be able to come and see Him.[2] Do not consider this labour difficult: you will certainly be able to manage it! Even if there are things which bring discomfort, the repose which then follows is great. Our guide is beside us whenever there is need;[3] He summons and awaits us, for He desires our betterment. He will not fail to guide us along the right path and lead us to the fellowship which lies in eternal life.

I have told you my opinion in the way that I am able to tell it: I learned it from Jesus Christ, the True Prophet of whom I told you. I must remind you often, in order to make you fully aware, that if you wish to know God, you should first grasp righteousness. May anybody who wishes to refute my opinion because he thinks that he has better to say calmly state his opinion and then listen patiently! This is why, when I first greeted you, I reminded you of the peace of God." (2665–700)

St Peter had finished his speech, and Simon presently began to speak: "We want nothing to do with your peace, for we have no need of peace! If there is peace and harmony, little gain will result from this; for inquiring into truth, peace is of less avail than war. Those who are thieves and robbers have love and peace amongst themselves, and every evil fellowship has harmony in its wickedness. If we have come here for no other reason and have sought nothing except peace, we have gathered here in vain if we agree in all respects. Those who listen will not profit from our peace, but will rather be frustrated. Stop asking for there to be peace between the two of us, and instead ask for battle: then the truth will be clearly demonstrated! If you can crush error, you can thereby win love.[4] I very

---

[1] 2669–70 **and the gate. . .exits** *E la porte. . .eist*: Cf. Jn 10:7–9.

[2] 2673–74 **only those. . .see Him** *Pur lui veer. . .avrunt*: Cf. Mt 5:8.

[3] 2679–80 **Our guide. . .is need** *Nostre guiur. . .mestier est*: Cf. Mt 28:20.

[4] 2719–24 **Stop asking. . .love** *Leissez a demander. . .amur*: The image of war as the mother of peace has been omitted from *Rec.* II.23.4.

much want you to know that when two people are locked in battle, then there will only be peace when one of them falls down defeated. Therefore enter into battle with me, and do not seek peace without battle, for it cannot be any other way; or, if it can be, show me how!" (2701–32)

St Peter was not at a loss for words, and did not hesitate to respond. St Peter said: "What I said, I say once more, and I shall say it again: I ask for peace, but in so doing I am pursuing no cause other than a good one, for I do not ask for peace in order to permit all kinds of nonsense, but rather I ask for peace so that we might present our arguments without quarrelling. If we speak mildly, then each man who has listened carefully will be able to understand the truth properly.[1] Some people have the habit, when they begin disputations, that when they lose in their argument, they immediately start quarrelling so that by reason of their blustering they should not be thought defeated. I therefore ask to have peace in order that we might hear well and speak well, so that one person should not propose an objection before the other has finished speaking, and so that if anything is said which is unclear, it might be repeated, and that any argument which is not understood might be clarified by repetition. For it very often tends to happen when one speaks in public that somebody has not fully understood the argument as it was stated, or one person has not spoken clearly, or the other does not understand much of it. I therefore wish to have peace without one person interrupting the other so that we might reach an appropriate conclusion without quarrelling and strife, in no way with the intention of criticising, but rather with a desire to learn properly. In this way it is possible to come close to finding the truth."[2] (2733–74)

St Peter said more about peace than I am prepared to say here, nor am I prepared to write down everything that St Peter said, nor everything with which Simon countered, for both of them spoke a great deal. From the outset I said that I had not undertaken to translate all of the *Book of Clement*, for it could become tedious, and the story would be too long, and I have not promised to translate all the speeches and the long disputations. People tend to be bored by long speeches and long discourses; a few well-chosen words tend to be welcomed. I do not want anybody to grow bored, for I am writing this story to provide enjoyment, and I have especially written it in order to remove solicitude and bring gladness. I shall therefore speak about the speeches as succinctly as I can, and likewise about the disputations, even though they contain compelling arguments, and even though it is possible to profit when one hears people debating. For when somebody asks a question, and the answer follows, the person who hears it can learn from it if

---

[1] 2733–46 **St Peter. . .properly** *Seint Pierre. . .verité*: These lines stand in place of Peter's analogy of two warring kings in *Rec.* II.24.

[2] 2767–74 **I therefore wish. . .truth** *Partant desir. . .truver*: These lines replace *Rec.* II.25.4–10.

he is prepared to pay careful heed: when one person presents an argument, and another responds, those who hear it are improved by it. One should not do everything or refrain from everything, nor be silent about everything nor say everything, for a person in moral decline does not improve if too much or too little is said. It is considered very sensible to heed time and place in all respects; this is why the old proverbs quite rightly say: moderation in everything and temperance in accordance with time.[1] (2775–818)

St Peter easily brushed aside everything with which Simon countered him. St Peter frequently requested peace, and Simon completely refused it; through reason St Peter refuted everything with which Simon could counter. They argued back and forth until they changed their topic considerably: they both spoke at length about the world and the Creator, and Our Lord Jesus, and the law of Moses; they spoke at length about the Scriptures, about the New and the Old Testament. Whenever Simon lost in his argument, he began to quarrel, for he said many slanderous things: he often called St Peter ignorant, often accused him of stupidity, said many base things to him, and made many heretical statements about Our Lord Jesus Christ. St Peter was not greatly concerned by this, and always replied with moderation. The battle was very fierce, but Simon could not prevail. St Peter presented so much evidence from the old and new Scriptures that Simon did not know what to say, which caused him both grief and fury. They debated until it was getting very late in the day.[2] Simon then said: "The day is coming to an end: let further discussion wait until tomorrow! You will come before me tomorrow, and if you can prove to me that the world was made from nothing and that souls are not mortal, I shall thenceforth follow you everywhere and assist you in preaching." (2819–58)

St Peter replied very succinctly: "This will happen whenever you wish."

Simon departed presently, and the third part of the whole crowd which had come with him followed; the others had no interest in him. Those who left with Simon were estimated to number up to a thousand men; all the others stayed and implored St Peter, on their knees and elbows and with great devotion, to perform a miracle for them whereby God might have mercy on them. St Peter said a prayer for them in the name of Jesus Christ and healed the insane[3] and many other sick people, and then he ordered everybody to leave and return the next morning. Once they had all left, St Peter did not go elsewhere; he ordered that the area be made ready and sat down there to eat. All his followers ate with him,

---

[1] 2815–18 **this is why...time** *Pur ceo dient...temprure*: Cf. Morawski, *Proverbes français*, no. 567 and 2250 ("De tout et par tout est mesure," "Selonc le tans la tempreüre").

[2] 2775–850 **St Peter...in the day** *De peis...avant*: This section stands in place of *Rec.* II.26–69, which vv. 2819–50 partially summarise.

[3] 2875 **the insane** *les forsenez*: *Rec.* II.70.4 speaks unequivocally of those possessed by demons.

but Clement, who was a pagan, ate with other companions who had not yet been baptised. And lest Clement suspect anything other than goodness, St Peter said to him: "Clement, my friend, let it not vex you if you do not eat with me before you have been baptised. For the fact that I am accustomed to acting in this way does not stem from pride, for as long as you are a pagan, you will not be able to eat with me. If I were to commune with you, I could harm myself thereby, and you would not profit from that fact that I had been harmed. For it is against the law that a pagan should commune with a Christian,[1] for all those who are pagans and sacrifice to idols and then eat from what they have sacrificed to the idols are, since they commune with devils, companions of devils,[2] from which they will never be freed unless they are baptised.[3] It is not because of me, but rather because of you that you do not commune with us. Everything lies within your power, for I am ready at any time, whenever you so desire, for you to be baptised by me. I am prepared to do this at any time: from now on it is entirely up to you either to act or to refrain, to hurry or to delay, for as long as you delay, you will never commune with us. You are excluding yourself by delaying so long!"[4]

This is what St Peter said. Presently he ate, and then said thanks and retired, and the other companions all retired, for it was night. (2859–928)

St Peter rose when the cock crowed; it was not full day, but rather daybreak. He wanted to wake his companions, but there was no need for this, for he found them all awake, and presently he greeted them. He sat with them, and they with him, and each of them then listened to him.[5] He began to speak, and he presented such arguments about the Father, the Son, and the Holy Spirit and said so much about the Scriptures that everybody began to marvel that the mouth of any man could speak in this way, and that any man might abandon the plain truth in favour of vacuous nonsense. He did not stop speaking until day had broken fully.[6]

Presently a man came who said that Simon was absolutely ready: he had come and was waiting, as was a very large crowd with him. Simon, he said, was

---

[1] 2889–902 **Clement, my friend. . .Christian** *Clement, ami. . .Cristien*: An amplified explanation of the reasons for Clement's exclusion in *Rec.* II.71.2.

[2] 2903–8 **for all those. . .devils** *Kar tut cil. . .sunt*: Cf. 1 Cor 10:20–21.

[3] 2907–10 **since they commune. . .baptised** *Quant commune. . .baptizié*: A substantial abbreviation of the discussion of demons in *Rec.* II.71.4–6, with the comments in *Rec.* II.71.1–4 on inhabitation by demons simply omitted.

[4] 2911–24 **It is not. . .so long** *N'est pas en mei. . .targié*: Relative to *Rec.* II.72.5–6, these lines focus more on Clement, and introduce the idea that Peter himself will baptise him.

[5] 2936 **and each. . .him** *Chascuns. . .entendi*: Following this line, Peter's explanation in *Rec.* III.1.27 of why one should not preach to the unworthy is omitted.

[6] 2946 **broken fully** *partut cler*: After this line, *Clement* does not include the sparsely transmitted *Rec.* III.2–12; cf. Rehm, *Recognitiones*, xcvi.

standing there and had everybody's attention; he was speaking a great deal and saying a great deal, and was endeavouring to deceive the people; he was striving to say as much as he could whereby he might discredit St Peter. St Peter immediately stood up and headed for the square, and stood right in the spot where he had been the day before, and all the people turned to him and listened to him joyfully. Once Simon had seen that the people were joyful at the arrival of St Peter, and how they all appeared, he was absolutely astounded by it, and with anguish he spoke in this way:

"I am quite amazed by the foolish people who love Peter and not me: they show him love and honour, and they consider me to be a sorcerer! Since they knew me for some time before they saw Peter, he is a stranger to them, and I am well-known, and so I ought to be more loved! Anybody with understanding can clearly see that Peter, who has claimed for himself the love and honour due to me, is skilled in sorcery!" (2929–80)

Simon slandered St Peter in this and other ways. St Peter turned to the crowd and greeted them on behalf of God; he looked at Simon and then spoke to him in this way:

"Your wicked conscience, Simon, is quite sufficient for you to be utterly confuted: there is no need for you to seek another explanation! If you are amazed that you cannot be loved and that everybody hates you—if you do not know why, I shall tell you. You have a very wicked nature, for you are very deceptive; you give the impression of truth, of which there is not the slightest trace in you. People have gathered around you in order to learn what the truth is, but since they have found in you nothing from which one might benefit and see that you are completely contradictory in saying one thing and doing another, they all hate you and have abandoned you since they have failed to find truth. Nonetheless those who heard you speak did not abandon you as soon as they had realised that they would be deceived by you, until such time as somebody else came along who pleases them more than you do, from whom there comes to them greater hope of learning the truth through him: from that point on they abandoned you, and now they follow him completely. On account of your magic you thought that you would never be found out, but it cannot be so: you have been a most false teacher to them, for you know nothing of truth, nor are you prepared to hear it from somebody who would certainly tell it to you if there were any reason in you. If you had frequented our school, you would have heard the saying that there is nothing so well hidden that it might not be exposed, nor is anything so well concealed that it might not be plainly revealed."[1] (2981–3030)

Simon did not welcome any of what St Peter said. Simon then said: "I am no longer prepared for you to keep prattling on like this! I demand of you the

---

[1] 3027–30 **nor is anything. . .revealed** *ne n'est chose. . .uverte*: cf. Mt 10:26.

promise that you made here yesterday in front of everybody regarding whether this world was created, and whether the soul is immortal."[1]

St Peter replied: "Were it not the case that somebody else might not be improved by it, I would not open my mouth at all, and would not say a single word to you! Talking to you is fruitless, for no improvement results: you have not come here because you wish to benefit, nor for any reason other than to contradict. But just as the ploughman who wishes to cultivate his land well loses a great deal of his seed—for it does not fall evenly, since part of it lands on earth, and part of it falls on stone where no root can take, and part of it amongst thorns, whereby it is completely choked or trampled on a path—I say exactly the same thing about you, for I do not trust you in any way. I shall waste much of my labour in talking to you, for you will never be improved by any good that you hear. I must nevertheless speak, not for your sake, but for that of the people."[2] (3031–66)

Simon then said: "I understand that you are speaking angrily. There is no point talking with you if you are going to get so irate!"

St Peter replied: "I can clearly see, Simon, that you are seeking an opportunity to depart unscathed and avoid entering into a disputation, for you have well understood that you will then be proved completely guilty. You cunningly accuse me of anger and immoderation and thereby wish to hide the fact that you wish to leave. Identify any scandalous or outrageous thing that I have said or done which might have brought shame upon you or which should be retracted, even though the fact is that you are the one deceiving the people! You have accused me of anger here because you do not know what else to say; you are not prepared to hear reason, nor anything other than what you wish." (3067–90)

They spoke a great deal about one thing and another and broached various subjects, but when Simon saw his opportunity, he did not hesitate to engage in slander. At one point he could not proceed, and then he praised him for speaking well, but soon afterwards he reverted and was quite ready to slander. He called him foolish and ignorant, and harangued him vigorously, and once he had said these base things,[3] he said to him: "Do not think that I am acting out of anger when I speak so bitterly; I feel great pity for those people whom you are leading astray! I have spoken so harshly on account of the pity for them which seizes me, but I am not angry, even if I have criticised you." (3091–110)

---

[1] 3037–38 **whether this world. . .immortal** *De cest mund si. . .est*: Rather than representing what Simon actually requests in *Rec.* III.14.3–5, these lines reprise the offer made in vv. 2853–58.

[2] 3049–66 **But just as. . .people** *Meis sicume. . .gent*: A considerable amplification of the metaphor in *Rec.* III.14.7.

[3] 3091–101 **They spoke. . .base things** *De un. . .vilainie*: These lines replace the discussion of evil in *Rec.* III.15.4–16.4.

St Peter replied to these words: "You are utterly wicked if you are acting so abominably and behaving so outrageously towards me without anger! But it cannot be that there is no fire when one sees smoke rising.[1] I am not prepared for you to be the judge of that with which you counter me from now on; it will not be for you to judge whether I speak well or badly. If you wish to counter me or to ask anything from now on, I want you first to admit that you do not know this very thing. Do not speak in order to instruct me, for you cannot manage to teach me anything, for my knowledge comes to me from elsewhere! I learned from a master whom none can surpass. Therefore admit what it is that you do not know, and I shall make you grasp it very clearly if you are prepared to listen properly, for I have no interest in your teaching or your judgement, for you are not to contradict and adjudicate! But may you counter me, and I shall respond; let there be discussion between us, and let all these good people pass judgement on us!"[2] (3111–42)

In response to this, Simon said to him: "Does it then seem sensible to you that people who know nothing of any value should judge the two of us?"

St Peter replied: "It is not so, for the many people in the crowd here present can understand an argument twenty or thirty times better than can one person, for what is said as a proverb very often tends to be true; what people say has the aspect of prophecy. In addition to all this, all the people who are now present here have gathered to hear us because of the great love that they have for God, so that through us they might be more certain of following the truth. Since they are gathered in such a way that they all have one will, we shall take all of them in place of one, and they will all judge the argument since they have come for no other reason, for the voice of the people is the voice of God. And if you wish to be quite sure that they have gathered here for no other reason, witness their patience, with what peace and silence they stand in order to hear what outcome our discussion will reach![3] I therefore have great hope that God will make everybody realise which of us two it will be who will tell the truth."[4]

Simon then said: "Do you then want there to be a discussion between us, with me presenting my opinion, and you presenting yours afterwards?"

---

[1] 3116 **sees smoke rising** *fumee lever veit*: Following this line, the discussion of evil in *Rec.* III.16.7–17.6 is omitted.

[2] 3117–42 **I am not prepared. . .judgement on us** *De ceo dunt. . .jugement*: These lines render *Rec.* III.18 rather approximately.

[3] 3172 **what outcome. . .reach** *Quel chief. . .parler*: Following this line, *Rec.* III.19.5 is omitted.

[4] 3173–76 **I therefore have. . .truth** *Partant ai. . .dirrat*: These lines omit from *Rec.* III.19.6 the metaphor of securing the palm of victory.

St Peter said: "My opinion is that we should inquire into nothing other than what God Himself commanded when He spoke to the people about knowing His will properly and serving Him willingly and well."[1] (3143–86)

Simon then countered with a great deal, and St Peter did not hesitate to offer a compelling response to each of his questions. They spoke at length about one thing and another until they came to the topic of the world. St Peter proved that it had been created: it came from nothing, and is heading towards nothing. They spent the day discussing this, but it did not end so quickly. When Simon could not proceed, and night was drawing in, and he was unable to say anything else which was not countered by St Peter,[2] he then began to swear that if St Peter could demonstrate that the soul was not mortal and could never die, he would then be satisfied in all respects and would thenceforth do all his bidding. But it was getting late, he said, and so he postponed it until the following day. St Peter wanted to continue speaking, but Simon was not prepared to stay there any longer; Simon departed, and a few of his companions with him. All the others remained there and fell straight to their knees; they all fell to the ground in order to beg mercy of St Peter. Through his prayer, St Peter healed the sick.[3] They all then left joyfully, and St Peter and his followers remained there. They prepared their meal there, sat down on the ground, and ate, and then said their thanks and presently went to bed. (3187–224)

St Peter could not break his habit, for he rose well before daybreak; he found his companions awake and all attentive to him. Since he saw them awake so early, he then said to them very tenderly:

"Dear brothers, I implore you: if any of you cannot stay awake, may he not feel any shame before me, nor do anything whereby he might be harmed, for it is a difficult thing for a man to change his habit suddenly. A man can change his habit more effectively first through small steps and then through larger ones, and in this way nobody will be harmed when he has grown accustomed over a long period; there will be no discomfort or hardship once one has grown used to it. All of us who are here present were not raised in the same way: we are not all from the same land, nor all educated in the same way, nor have we been equal in bearing both good and ill; nonetheless we can in the long run grow sufficiently accustomed to be able to bear everything well, without being harmed in any way. One

---

[1] 3184–86 **when He spoke. . .well** *La u il. . .a gré*: An abbreviation of *Rec.* III.20.2–4; cf. Mt 6:33.

[2] 3187–200 **Simon then. . .Peter** *Simun atant. . .Pierre*: These lines signal the omission of *Rec.* III.20.2–30.5, but the summary of their content is inaccurate, since the discussion concerns less the creation of the world than the nature of evil, free will, and similar.

[3] 3218 **sick** *malades*: *Rec.* III.30.8 also mentions explicitly those possessed by demons.

can be terribly harmed by a change suddenly effected; the person who is willing to refrain gradually will be able to do it more easily and effectively. Neither loss nor harm results when one is willing to observe moderation, for everybody knows full well that it is not beneficial to make excessive haste; a man can grow accustomed to whatever he wishes through practice. A man's nature will not be harmed when a habit is gently changed; habit is a second nature, but great moderation is necessary in all cases.[1] I call God as witness that I shall not be scornful if there is anybody who cannot stay awake and who must sleep all night: by night may he sleep as much as he wants, and by day may he do what pleases God! We must think and keep God in mind: if we keep God in mind, the Devil will find no place in us." (3225–76)

The companions all told him that they were not harmed by staying awake, for they had awoken before him, but did not dare wake him: it was not right that he should be woken or that he should rise before he pleased, for quite rightly it cannot be that the disciple should be above his master.[2] Nonetheless, they told him, they had nearly woken him, for they greatly desired to hear the word of God, but on account of the love that they had for him they refrained from waking him.

St Peter clearly understood what they desired when he heard this. He then repeated to them everything that he had said the preceding day in the whole disputation between him and Simon, and moreover he promised them—whereby he gave them great cheer—that at night he would expound to them everything that he said in disputation during the day, and would recall anything that he might have omitted through forgetfulness; or if he had said little about something, whereby he might have been less well understood, he would explain the argument in the right order, even if Simon had not observed it, for either he did not know how to observe it or, perhaps, he did not wish to do so in order to cause trouble and strife, as a result of which one often tends to omit much of what ought to be said, and to say what ought to be kept quiet. Simon had said nothing from which any profit might be derived, for he would have emerged on top if St Peter had been defeated, be it through arguing or slandering or rejecting reason.[3] St Peter freely expounded everything that he had said the previous day, and did not cease talking until day had fully broken. (3277–322)

---

[1] 3243–66 **All of us. . .cases** *Nus tuz. . .mesure*: A considerable amplification of *Rec.* III.31.3.

[2] 3282–84 **for quite rightly. . .master** *Kar par reisun. . .meistre*: Cf. Mt 10:24.

[3] 3313–18 **Simon. . .rejecting reason** *Simun. . .reisun cuntredire*: This sentence is equally opaque in the Old French, perhaps because of missing lines. *Rec.* III.32.6 does not offer any insights.

The third day had now begun. St Peter came out presently; he had prayed, and he came to the disputation. Many people had come there, and he greeted them all. He saw Simon standing in the square, and so began to speak:

"My lords," he said, "I am very upset and quite amazed by some people who make a pretence of learning and ask many questions. Once we have taught them what they asked of us, they claim to be masters in the very same thing and begin to argue with us about it; they asked as if ignorant, and then contradict us as if they had known beforehand what they have grasped through us!

One of those people who are here may perchance respond to me: 'One asks questions in order to learn, and when one cannot understand, contradiction is necessary, or there will be little profit.' Anybody who believes or has thought this needs to be guided. May anybody who says this listen to me! A question is not a contradiction, even though somebody who inquires vigorously may give this impression. Anybody who asks questions regarding his areas of doubt and cannot understand the answers has to ask frequent questions and make counter-arguments in order to learn. It is not contradiction when one person makes another repeat what he has said in order better to explain and better to prove his argument. Each person who asks questions must observe order and reason; he must be skilled in asking what goes first and what then follows, and thus proceeding in order; then the answer will be appropriate. Anybody who asks questions badly and does not respect the correct order will greatly impair the argument of the person who is to respond."[1] (3323–72)

St Peter said a great deal about this, and more than I wish to say here, and Simon did not hesitate to cut across him.[2] When they had spoken for a long time, Simon then asked him: "Convince me of one thing: whether the soul is such that it never dies. If I have not first understood this, I shall never fully grasp righteousness![3] If you cannot prove this, everything that you say cannot stand."

"It is of greater avail for us," St Peter said, "to endeavour to inquire into whether God is just: may this be the first question! If we inquire into this first of all, we shall thereby gain better evidence of the order of religion." Simon replied to these words:

"You have done plenty of boasting about observing order when debating, but you make a very poor show of knowing how to observe order! I ask one thing, and you reply another: I ask whether the soul is mortal, and you reply that it is necessary to know whether God is just!" (3373–400)

---

[1] 3363–72 **Each person. . .respond** *Ordre e reisun. . .deverat*: An abbreviation of *Rec.* III.34 which omits the conceit of the traveller in search of knowledge.

[2] 3373–76 **St Peter. . .cut across him** *Entur cest. . .traversant*: These lines indicate the omission of *Rec.* III.35–38.

[3] 3382 **righteousness** *justise*: This theme was introduced in an omitted section of *Rec.*

St Peter replied: "I speak rightly."

Simon said: "Then prove it!"

St Peter then said: "There are many people who pay no heed to God; there are many people who do not love God and who do not recognise him as Lord. Their whole life is spent in sinful pleasure; they have abandoned themselves to vice. Many such people have died right in their beds in front of their friends, and their friends do them the honour of burying them finely. There are others who honour God and shed many tears for their sins; they have endeavoured to live well in accordance with righteousness; they are peaceful, chaste, and sober, and have other virtues in them. One of these dies all alone, far from people and in a wasteland, or perhaps he is slain outside and far distant from his country, and cannot have the honour of people willing to bury him. What will happen to rectitude and justice if souls die completely without receiving reward for good deeds, and without punishment being meted out to the wicked?" (3401–28)

Simon replied: "This is why such great doubt holds sway over us, as we see those who do good dying shamefully, and the tyrants who have always wallowed in evil living just as they please, and then eventually dying without shame and without dishonour."

St Peter said: "We are certain that the soul lives and never dies: it is by the very reason why you said that you cannot believe it that we have been assured that God will come at the judgement. We fully understand without any doubt that God is just, and it is therefore necessary and right that there should be another world after this in which each man will through righteousness receive a reward in accordance with his service. If this world were so ordained that each man received his just desserts here, we would thereby be clearly proved not to be telling the truth in what we say about the judgement of God and the rectitude of righteousness. But since each man does not receive here what he has deserved here, we believe and have no doubt that God will pass judgement."

Simon replied: "If this is true, why can I then not know it? Why can you not persuade me to believe you in this?" (3429–62)

St Peter replied: "This is because you do not heed the True Prophet, Jesus Christ, who taught us and told us: 'Seek first the reign of God, and follow His righteousness, and so you will be able to learn everything that you wish to know.'"[1]

Simon then said: "I ask to be excused from this; I am not prepared to do His bidding. I shall not go seeking righteousness before I am sure whether the soul is mortal or not." St Peter replied to Simon:

"And may you excuse me this thing that you wish to know from me! I must do what my master taught, and nothing else."

---

[1] 3467–70 **Seek first. . .know** *Le regne Deu. . .vuldrez*: Cf. Mt 6:33.

Simon said: "I am quite certain that it will never be proved by you that the soul is not mortal; you will never manage this, and therefore all your teaching amounts to nothing, and all your religion amounts to nothing but a sham! You are to be esteemed for knowing how to speak skilfully, but you should not be esteemed for what you are teaching here, for many are abandoning their carnal pleasures because of what you say, for it is your argument that they must practise forbearance; you have given them hope of receiving a great reward elsewhere. As a result they have lost this world and are deceived in the belief that they will gain another, for when the soul departs, it dies just like the body." (3463–502)

St Peter did not welcome the words that Simon said. He rubbed his forehead and ground his teeth, and his face completely changed colour through his anguish; he sighed deeply, and clearly showed that he was upset. Even though there was cause for nothing but anger, he was not prepared to hesitate in replying:
"You are," he said, "full of guile, with the manner of a venomous snake! You have come like a snake, which is more cunning than other beasts: you wish to deceive these people as did the snake which showed its cunning in casting Adam from Paradise.[1] In your very manner you are utterly wicked and deceptive; you wish to be considered wise, and thereby cause great damage. You wished to make the people believe, as did the snake, that there were more gods than one, but I presented you with such an argument that I utterly confuted you with it. Then you fell into the error that when you cannot proceed, you say that there is no god: first you acknowledged more than one, and now you are not prepared to acknowledge a single one![2] Once I had confuted you because you were creating both too many and too few gods, you then took a different track, and now say that the soul is mortal. You lead people into false belief when you take away from them the hope of having better in the next life once this one has finished, provided that they have endeavoured intently and very carefully to live righteously. If one is to hold to the belief there is no other world to come, then there is no need for there to be any virtue if one is to believe it to be thus: each man may then live his life in sinful pleasure and lust; mercy and righteousness will have no place in such a system. (3503–50)
You justify yourself excessively and endeavour to place this mortal life into a state of error from which great sorrow results. You accuse me of wickedness because I have urged people to renounce evil and do good for the love of God, in hope of a better life once the soul has departed the body. You wish to denounce me as evil because I do not wish to allow people to go astray, fight against each other, and destroy and take everything that each man can seize. What will be the condition of this life if each man sets upon his neighbour through hatred and

---

[1] 3513–18 **You have come...Paradise** *Cume serpent...getat*: A rather clearer allusion to Gen 3:1 than in *Rec.* III.42.2.
[2] 3532 **a single one** *neis un*: Following this line, *Rec.* III.42.4 is omitted.

envy, and if each man attacks his neighbour, and if they constantly live in fear through anger and suffering? It is impossible for anybody who does evil not to fear the very same thing, and you can therefore clearly see what life it is that you lead, as you hate peace and seek war, and abandon right to pursue wrong. In no way do I give the impression of anger in order to avoid responding to your inquiry, for I have an answer fully ready! I am absolutely certain, without any doubt, that the soul lives and never dies; I am anxious and very concerned on account of the people whom you are deceiving. Without any compulsion I shall answer your question, for I know full well what to say; I shall answer it for you — I know full well how — and this will be in a manner so clear that there will be no need for any more proof in order to make you understand. As soon as you hear it, you alone will fully understand it; the others will then find out about it as they need to do so." (3551–96)

Simon presently said: "Since I see that you grow so angry with me, I shall ask nothing more of you, nor shall I listen to you any more!"

St Peter then said: "If you are seeking a pretext to leave, you have my permission to withdraw: you do not need to seek a pretext, for everybody has fully understood that you have said nothing of any benefit. You have no idea what to say other than to ask questions in order to contradict, for no other reason than disagreement: anyone can do that! There is no argument so compelling that, once it has been requested, one might not simply respond by saying: 'That is nonsense!' But so that you might know that I am sure of it and that I can show you with just a few words the definite proof that the soul is not mortal, I ask you just one thing that all people know, both great and small. Answer me, and I shall immediately prove it to you in one sentence so that you will be sure and absolutely certain that the soul is such that it never dies!" (3597–624)

Now that he had found a pretext to leave — and he did not wish to remain there any longer once St Peter had grown angry — Simon still remained and stayed there, for he thought that he might hear something which might be a source of wonder of the likes of which he had never before heard:

"Ask me," Simon said, "one thing which is sensible and which all the people, great and small, who have come here can clearly understand, that I can answer for you, so that you can then explain and clarify to me through reason whether the soul is mortal or not."

St Peter replied: "I shall tell you it and shall prove it to you so well that as soon as you hear it, you will understand it better than any other man.

What is it that one should believe more: what one hears, or what one sees?"

Simon replied: "A thing which is seen should be believed more than one which is heard."

St Peter then said: "Why is it then, when one clearly knows what one sees, that you wish to know through me what you yourself have already seen?"

"I do not know," Simon said, "nor do I see what you are saying or why." (3625–54)

St Peter said: "If you do not know, go to your home! Go into the place where your bed stands, and there you will find ready and waiting the image of a child who obeys you completely. You killed him and captured his image in painting; you have covered him with a purple cloth, for he is completely subject to you. Ask him, and he will tell and present the truth both to your ears and to your eyes in such a way that you will clearly understand it! What need is there to hear from me whether the soul is to live or die when you can see one and talk to it yourself? If the soul had no life in it, it would not be able to say a single word. If you say that the situation with the child is not as I say, and if you perchance say that you know nothing of this image, let us go to your home and take with us straightaway ten companions from this crowd that we have here present in order to examine whether the situation is such as I have presented it to you here!" (3655–84)

Simon did not feel like laughing once St Peter had said this! He was extremely distressed by it and considered himself utterly confounded; he was very unhappy to be there, and would very much have preferred to be elsewhere. His conscience shamed him, which gave him a heavy heart; he did not have a drop of blood left in him, for his secret had been revealed. His colour changed greatly, for he was extremely afraid that if he wished to deny anything, St Peter would be so angry about this that he would go to his home and search every corner until he had found that through which he would be proven guilty.

Simon implored St Peter not to bring complete shame upon him: "Have mercy on me," he said, "my lord Peter! I beg you by that good God who is in you not to confound me further. Pay no heed to my wickedness; do me the charity of having mercy on me, for I sincerely repent! Receive me to repentance, and thenceforth I shall consent to you in all respects and shall dedicate all my efforts to helping you in preaching! I have learnt first-hand and understood that you are a prophet of the true God; I have fully grasped that you know people's secrets and hidden affairs." (3685–720)

Once Simon had said this, St Peter turned to the crowd: "My lords," he said, "you have clearly heard how Simon has converted. He has told me that he repents, but I shall show you that he is lying! He promises repentance to me, but he will soon change what he says; you will soon see that he is being deceptive, for he will return straight to his unruly behaviour. Because I know his secrets and have revealed his wicked deeds, he has deemed me a prophet, but he is quite deceived in this regard. He has promised to repent, but I must not lie on his account; in whichever direction he might wish to head, be it towards doing good or evil, I must not lie on account of Simon, whether he be saved or not. I call heaven and earth as witness that what I told you about him I did not say through prophecy, for I am not a prophet. Rather he had amongst his acquaintances some people who have now left him and converted to God: these men told me what I said because they were familiar with his wicked secrets. I did not say anything about him as a prophet; I learned it all from his companions!" (3721–52)

Simon was utterly confounded once St Peter had revealed this. He then began to slander and insult St Peter:

"You wicked scoundrel!" he said. "You are utterly full of wickedness, for you are more deceptive than any other man of woman born! It is by chance that I have been defeated by you; it is not by truth that you have overcome me! I did not seek repentance from you on account of any lack of knowledge: I feigned repentance because I wanted to deceive you so that you might think and believe that I wanted to turn to you. I thought that I would persuade you to trust me enough to reveal all your secrets and private affairs to me, and once I had learnt everything, I would confute you with the very same thing. You cunningly understood this, but gave no indication of it in order to draw me out until I was considered ignorant. You completely deceived me because you were aware of this, and by pretending to be guileless you have inflicted this shame upon me, for you have made these people believe that I am ignorant. (3753–86)

Your cunning manoeuvre caught me unawares and harmed me, for you said at the very outset that I was not truly repentant, and that after my repentance I would return to my original opinion. You revealed this beforehand, and I was therefore caught unawares and am angry that I am compelled to admit before the people here present that I never repented. I said it all as a deception, but you have caught me unawares in such a way that I cannot turn in any direction where I might find a defence. For if I am truly repentant, I am immediately proved to have been in error, and I will be dishonoured; and if I say that this is not the case and that I repent of nothing, and you have forewarned of this very thing, all the people here present will then consider me to be defeated and will consider you to be wise. I did not suspect you, and so was less on my guard against you; I was little prepared for you, and so I have been completely deceived. You are cunning and deceitful, but I did not think this of you. You are very experienced in this kind of matter; you have exposed me, and I have not exposed you at all. It is not through truth that you have managed to defeat me on this occasion; it should not be a source of glory for you if you are victorious, for you have managed this through chance and nothing else. I have nonetheless clearly understood why this has happened to me: I showed great kindness to you, for I spoke to you whilst standing here and was patient with you, and as a result I was less prepared. But now I shall reveal who I am and what I know; I wish to reveal my power and so much of my divinity that you will immediately fall to the ground and worship me as God! (3787–838)

I am the first power, who always is and always was.[1] I placed myself in Rachel's belly and took flesh and blood in her; I became a man in her so that I might be seen by men. I have flown in the air above, placed myself in blazing fire without being burnt or harmed, and merged with it so that my body and the fire became one substance. I have made images move by themselves and caused them to have life; I have then removed life from them, and I have made bread from stone. I have flown from one mountain to the next, and the angels carried me; they took me in their hands and gently placed me from the sky onto the ground.[2] I have done this and much more besides, and can do so again, and so it can be clearly known that I am without doubt the Son of God. I am God, for ever unchanging, and my existence is everlasting. Those who are prepared to believe in me will have everlasting life,[3] but nobody ought to believe in you when you cannot do anything more than could your master, who was unable to save himself from the death to which he was consigned when he was placed on the cross: nothing was of any avail to him then, even though he was skilled in sorcery! Your words are completely vain when you present no deed which might be a truthful proof, for you are full of falsehood!" (3839–78)

St Peter then said: "Do not accuse of foul and outrageous deeds those who are not guilty of them! All those here present know full well that you are a sorcerer from what they have heard you say, for you are proved guilty of it by what you have admitted here. There is no need to start arguing in order to defend our master, for it is well known, and will be more so, that He alone is good and the Son of God. I have spoken about Him at length to those to whom I was supposed to talk, and I shall talk further whenever I see the time and place. But if you wish to deny that you are a sorcerer, let us go to that place where your home stands with all the people here present: there it will become clear without further inquiry that you are a sorcerer!" (3879–900)

This did not please Simon, and so he began to quarrel; he shouted and slandered vehemently and created a huge uproar there so that he might then have a pretext to leave without people denouncing him and judging him to be defeated.

St Peter did not leave, even though Simon said foul things to him, nor on account of any shouting or quarrelling was he prepared to move from the spot, for if he had left on account of any uproar or shouting, somebody who had seen it would judge him to be defeated. St Peter stood very firm lest he should be judged to have been defeated. Simon stood and heckled him a great deal, and St Peter pressed him hard[4] until the crowd grew angry and drove Simon from the square. Simon was put outside the gates, and out of the whole crowd only one followed

---

[1] 3839–40 **I am. . .was** *Jeo sui. . .fu*: Cf. Acts 8:10.

[2] 3845–58 **I have flown. . .ground** *Jeo ai volé. . .mis*: Cf. Mt 4:3, 4:6.

[3] 3865–66 **Those who. . .life** *Cil ki. . .vie avrunt*: Cf. Jn 11:26.

[4] 3909–20 **St Peter. . ..pressed him hard** *Seint Pierre. . .mult le hasta*: A considerable amplification of *Rec.* III.48.3, presenting a far more pugnacious Peter.

him; Simon departed with this man alone, and of all the rest not one departed. St Peter stayed and stood there, and all the people turned towards him. They all listened attentively to him, and he then began to speak: (3901–30)

"Dear brothers," he said to them, "may what pleases God not vex you! Suffer patiently what God suffers: do not be vexed by the wicked! You must suffer everything for the sake of God, for if it so pleased Him, He could easily exact revenge upon those who serve him badly: He could quickly smite them all down, and not a single one of them could escape. Yet God does not do this to them, but rather suffers them in this life in order fully to show His goodness and prove their wickedness; He suffers them and waits until the last judgement.[1] And if God suffers it thus without avenging Himself on those who have opposed Him, but rather has granted them all a delay until it so pleases Him, why can we not suffer it? I do not say this on account of Simon alone, whom devils have under their control, but rather I say it on account of many others, for if the Devil had failed to attract Simon and to do with him as he wished, he would without doubt have found somebody else who would be entirely subject to what he wished. For as long as this world lasts, it cannot be without offences, but all those by whom the offences are caused are utterly damned.[2] Wretched Simon, over whom the Devil exerts such control, is to be greatly pitied; the Devil has entered him and chosen him for his purpose. This is a result of the sins with which he has long been burdened; it is a result of his great sins that the Devil holds him in his power. (3931–72)

What can I say about Simon when he does not reform, but rather becomes worse? He had converted to Jesus Christ and pretended to believe in Him; he fully grasped and knows full well that man's soul never dies. Devils have placed themselves inside him, and by them he has been deluded in such a way that he has murdered a child through whom the devils continue to deceive him. This dead child does what he wants and answers his many questions for him, but he is greatly deceived by him, for he is not as Simon has believed. It is not the dead child who speaks with him in this way, nor is it the soul that he sees, but rather it is the Devil who is deceiving him who reveals himself in this image, and in this way he fools and convinces him and has such a strong hold on him that he cannot repent. He makes him believe that an illusion is the soul of the dead child in order to confirm him in error and in order to make him more certain — even though it is not the truth — that he has the soul in his power.[3] Nonetheless I spoke in accordance with his belief, and so he was caught unawares. It is to be deeply regretted that Simon is not prepared to reform, given that he has thor-

---

[1] 3931–46 **Dear brothers. . .judgement** *Seignurs freres. . .jugement*: God's power to punish is portrayed rather more vividly than in *Rec.* III.49.2.

[2] 3961–64 **For as long as. . .damned** *Kar tant cum. . .esmeuz*: Cf. Mt 18:7; Lk 17:1.

[3] 3979–4000 **Devils have placed. . .power** *Deables se sunt. . .poesté*: A considerable amplification of *Rec.* III.49.7.

oughly understood through the Jews with whom he spent time that when the last judgement comes, vengeance will be taken on those who have done wrong and do not repent of it.[1] Therefore convert, my lords, repent of your sins, kneel on the ground, and turn your minds to begging for mercy!" (3973–4014)

When St Peter said this, all the people fell to the ground. St Peter looked towards heaven, prayed tearfully, and most reverently implored God to have mercy on those people, and to hear them so that all those people might be saved. Then he told everybody to leave and return in the morning. The whole crowd left once they had heard this; not one of the crowd remained. St Peter followed his usual custom: he did not wish to change in any respect, but rather sat down there to eat. He and his followers ate there, and after dinner they lay down to rest. (4015–32)

St Peter rose well before daybreak and found his companions awake. He greeted them and then sat down. Niceta spoke first and said: "My lord Peter, please hear me; give me permission to speak! I wish to ask a question of you, but do not take it as an offence."

St Peter replied: "I permit you to say whatever you see fit, and by no means only you, but rather everybody collectively: may each man now and on other occasions ask and say what pleases him!"[2]

Niceta thanked him sincerely when he had permission to ask his questions, and then he said to him: "Why is it that Simon performs such wonders when he is so thoroughly opposed to God? He places himself in fire without burning; he makes stones look like bread and makes dogs of brass bark; he makes images move by themselves and can even fly through the air. He boasts of this and is in no way lying: he can do it all, although I know not how. If somebody sees this and other things in him, is it any wonder if he believes him? When those in God's service perform great miracles in God's service, and those who are opposed to Him also perform their wonders, how will one be able to know what is false and what is true, and whom one should avoid and in whom one should believe, when His enemies can do the very same thing as His friends? And what blame attaches to the people who have plainly seen and heard the wonders that those men perform—even though they are not aware of whether those who perform them are good or evil, or whether they are true or false—and do not know any reason why they should believe in one and in favour of him reject the other when they do not know their nature? And if one is supposed to believe because one sees miracles being performed, why will that person who believes in God not be just as guilty as one who believes in the Devil when he does not know

---

[1] 4009–10 **on those who. . .repent of it** *De ces ki. . .serrunt*: The part played by the Devil in preventing penance (*Rec.* III.49.9) is not included.

[2] 4046 **pleases him** *lui plest*: Following this line, the rest of *Rec.* III.51.2 and all of III.51.3–6 are omitted, and with them the metaphor of teaching as a means of providing medicine for the sick.

that the situation is any other than that everything is in God's service? What guilt attached to the people of Egypt when they did not believe in the wonders of Moses[1] when they saw the sorcerers who duplicated these wonders? (4033–90)

I can say of myself that perhaps if I had been alive at that time when Moses and Aaron came before Pharaoh, who was king of Egypt and had with him sorcerers who performed many wonders which resembled the deeds of Moses, perhaps I would say, when I was not sure of anything else, that Moses was a sorcerer and had done nothing in God's service, and would believe the opposite of the sorcerers, and that their actions resulted entirely from truth, without any false deceptions. If I could not know by myself what was illusion and what was true, I would judge by what I saw if I were unaware of any deception there. For this very same reason I ask in respect of Simon, who is thoroughly opposed to God: even though he does what pleases him, how is he able to do what he does, and in what way does anybody who believes in him commit a sin?" (4091–116)

St Peter very much welcomed what he heard Niceta asking. It gave him very great pleasure to see him being so inquisitive, for through what he had asked, St Peter was quite aware that he wanted to learn and that he very much desired to know that thing of which he was uncertain, and so he took great pains to answer his question. But I do not wish to recount everything that he said, for he spoke at great length. Nonetheless I shall give the essence of it: "When God," he said, "had created man, he gave him the choice of good and evil without compelling him in any respect. The human race has grown a great deal since man was first created. It is separated into two orders: one order has chosen good, and the other has opted for evil; one of these drags people upwards, and the other downwards. Both orders have in charge of them kings who are the opposite of the other: the good king loves and does good, and the evil one is drawn to evil. The good king performs His wonders by doing good to everybody; the evil one would like to perform wonders whereby he might resemble the good king, but he cannot perform any wonder from which any benefit might be derived. If anybody considers these two kings, and their wonders and their laws, his reason will quickly tell him which one should be believed, and which not, for the wonders that they have performed provide in themselves ample evidence whereby anybody who has any sense will be able to know which one he ought to follow. The bad king does nothing truthful, even if he pretends that it is true: there is no truth there, for everything is illusory and vain. Anybody who considers him closely will clearly understand that no good or benefit will come from him,[2] for what profit will there be from an image if it moves through sorcery, or if one sees it walking by itself, or if one hears dogs of brass barking, or from making mountains jump, or from fly-

---

[1] 4088 **wonders of Moses** *merveilles Moysi*: Cf. Ex 7:8–13.

[2] 4052–162 **He places. . .come from him** *Senz ardeir. . .en surdrat*: This section includes a few elements of *Rec.* III.52–59, with most of the material of less clear origin.

ing through the air above, or from making it appear to people that stone has the appearance of bread?[1] Show me what profit comes from this and from anything else that Simon does! Nothing of what he does is reliable, for he acts through the Devil, who is king, master, and lord over all those who do evil.[2] (4117–76)

The good king always does good, without any illusion or deception; everything that He does is beneficial, for people gain their salvation from it. He restores sight to the blind and restores hearing to the deaf; He makes the mute speak and makes the lame walk properly, and those who are filled with the Devil become healthy through Him. He heals those who are lepers, no matter how hideous they may be; He makes the crippled stand again and restores life to the dead; he cures all sickness. Jesus Christ did this and more besides, and God has done the very same through me, as you have seen. These miracles are reliable,[3] and the Devil cannot perform ones like this. He will not be able to do anything from which any man might benefit until the end is nigh, when the world will be in decline. Around that time he will be granted the power of genuine miracles. Then he will heal the insane[4] and many other sicknesses; this will be a sign, when it happens, that he will be completely destroyed. He will be working against himself by doing good; he will be acting entirely against nature, for he has no interest in doing good. Once he has performed the good for which he never had any desire, his time will come to an end because he will doing good against himself. He will then have turned against himself, and so will be doomed to destruction. Every kingdom loses its standing when it fights against itself:[5] it will be exactly the same with the Devil when he acts against himself, for he never loved anything which might benefit man. The Devil will be utterly confounded when he is thus divided. (4177–224)

When this thing is due to happen, and this world is drawing to a close, the temptation will be so great that the wisest will be in doubt about it. Even those who are amongst God's chosen[6] will, if it is possible, be deceived when they see the miracles that those who are opposed to God will perform. The normal situation will then be completely changed, and so nobody will be able to know what comes through God and what through the Devil, for things will be so easy to believe unless God performs an act of mercy to forewarn his followers. That time has not yet come, but it will come, no matter how long it takes. Anybody who

---

[1] 4169–70 **or from making. . .bread** *U de faire. . .semblance*: Mention of the transformation of bread is found only in the Θ and ∏ᑫ readings for *Rec.* III.60.1.

[2] 4171–76 **Show me. . .do evil** *Mustrez mei. . .malfeitur*: These lines seem to be our translator's invention.

[3] 4195 **reliable** *estable*: This quality appears to be an addition relative to *Rec.* III.60.2; the same term is added in the innovated vv. 4171–76 (see note.)

[4] 4203 **insane** *forsenez*: *Rec.* III.60.4 speaks explicitly of demonic possession.

[5] 4217–18 **Every kingdom. . .itself** *Chescun regne. . .cumbat*: Cf. Mt 12:25.

[6] 4229 **amongst God's chosen** *parfit en Deu*: Cf. Mt 24:24.

loves God will still very easily be able to discern clearly what is in God's service, what should be believed, and what should not; anybody who has faith in God will have no reason for doubt! But if anybody is not prepared to beseech God and has his heart turned entirely towards the earth, God will think little of him when he forgets God. In vain will he have faith in God to give him understanding; his conscience will clearly tell him that he is guilty through his negligence."[1] (4225–54)

St Peter spent so long saying these and other things[2] without taking a rest that day had already fully broken. Presently one of Simon's disciples entered the house. He came in shouting and implored St Peter to have mercy on him: "Have mercy," he said, "on me, my lord Peter, I implore you! I am a wretch; receive me, for I wish to convert to your religion! I was deceived by Simon on account of those wonders that I saw; I thought that he was a powerful god, and so I followed him. I realised to some extent when you spoke against him that he must be evil, and that his magic was wicked. Nonetheless when he left, I was the only one who followed him; I was then still not entirely aware of his depravity. When he saw me coming after him, and nobody else besides me, he was, he said, very glad about it, and I would be very blessed. He made me go to his home and asked me to stay with him. He rose in the middle of the night when everybody in the house was asleep; he made me get out of my bed and secretly told me that if I would stay with him and follow him as master, he would make me greater and more powerful than any other man alive, just as long as I would accompany him and remain with him for the rest of my life.[3] I promised him that I would stay, and he compelled me to swear that I would remain with him and would not leave him. (4255–98)

I swore this, and acted like a fool, and he then placed about my shoulders I know not what mysterious filth,[4] and once he had placed this on me, he ordered me to bear it and head out with him. He headed towards the sea and found a ship waiting; he took the filth from my shoulders and boarded the ship without me. He did not stay there long at all; he soon returned, but did not bring back any of what he had been carrying when he had boarded the ship. As far as I can conjecture, he threw it all into the sea. He asked me to come with him; he wanted to head for Rome, he said. There he would perform so much of his magic that he

---

[1] 4201–54 **Around that time. . .negligence** *Vers cele ure. . .neglegence*: This section expands and innovates relative to *Rec.* III.60.4–5.

[2] 4255–56 **St Peter. . .things** *Tant est. . .dire*: These lines mark the omission of *Rec.* III.61–62.

[3] 4279–94 **When he saw. . .life** *Quant venir. . .demurasse*: Simon's cunning is amplified relative to *Rec.* III.63.5.

[4] 4301 **mysterious filth** *privee ordure*: The identity of this *ordure* is unclear, with *Rec.* III.36.6 speaking opaquely of "polluted and accursed secret things."

would secure great praise and acclaim there; there such honour would be done to him as due to a lord, and there he would cause himself to be considered to be God, and would make himself be served like God. If I came to Rome with him, there, he said, he would make me a rich man: I would have plenty of gold and silver, and if I subsequently wished to leave and return to my country, he would make me have as much honour as I could ask for. When I heard this from him, since I saw in him no proof that he would do what he had said to me and place me in the condition that he had promised, I clearly recognised that he was a deceiver, and in return I offered him this response: (4299–336)

'Excuse me this journey: I cannot leave Caesarea! My feet hurt, I cannot walk, and I have a household to which I must attend. I have a wife, and children who are small and innocent, and I would be abandoning them if I undertook a journey with you. Since it cannot be otherwise, there is no other choice: I must stay.' Simon called me a coward for shirking like this; he began to reproach me harshly for not wishing to go with him. He then turned away, and said to me in parting: 'I shall head straight for Rome, and I shall have such great glory there that you will sorely repent when you hear news of it!' (4337–56)

Once he had said this, he left. He is heading for Rome according to what he said, and I immediately came here, and I beg and implore you for mercy. Receive me, for I was deceived, but now I am truly repentant!"

Once the man who had come from Simon had recounted all this, St Peter told him to sit outside in the square and remain there until he came and apprised him of what he wanted him to do. St Peter then readied himself and headed for the square. He saw clearly that there were many more people there than there had tended to be on the previous days. He chose to stand in the place where he had previously debated with Simon. He gave greetings from God to everybody who had come there on account of God, for this was his custom, and then he presented to everybody that man who had come there from Simon, and while presenting him, he spoke in this way: (4357–80)

"Dear brothers, listen to me! This man whom you see here has come from Simon, and he says that Simon has fled. He has told me that Simon threw his filth into the sea, and that he cast his idolatrous implements[1] right into the sea. He did not do this out of repentance, but rather out of his fear that he would be proved guilty of being a sorcerer: he was not entirely sure of himself, because if he were declared guilty of practising sorcery, he would be captured and bound

---

[1] 4387 **his idolatrous implements** *sun mahumet*: *Rec.* III.64.3 speaks of "the implements of his wickedness," whereas *Clement* uses a word derived from the name of Mohammed which usually denotes an idol. On *mahumet*, see David A. Trotter, "L'anglonormand dans le *Middle English Dictionary*," in *'Ki bien voldreit raisun entendre': Mélanges en l'honneur du 70e anniversaire de Frankwalt Möhren*, ed. Stephen Dörr and Thomas Städtler (Strasbourg: Editions de Linguistique et de Philologie, 2012), 323–37, at 331–32.

and condemned as a criminal.[1] Simon implored this man to leave with him; he promised him a great deal of wealth if he would remain with him. When this man began to make excuses and said that he could not accompany him, Simon called him cowardly and wicked, and set off for Rome alone."

St Peter revealed this to everybody, and then the man who had come stepped forward before everybody and recounted to them exactly how Simon had spoken to him and how he had departed. (4381–410)

Everybody was extremely distressed by this, and it was a cause of very great anger when they heard that Simon had done nothing but deceive and had undertaken nothing that he did not do through sorcery.

St Peter then said: "Good people, desist from such anger. Do not be concerned about the past, whatever might have happened. Do not worry about everything which has been and gone, but rather think about what is to come after! Do not think about the past any more: what was in the past is finished, but what is to come is in danger! Be assured that this world will never be without ignominy until the Devil has power to do his will. Anybody at that time who can be attentive and on his guard so that he can avoid being deceived by the Devil through guile and becoming subject to him will receive a reward that he will never be in danger of losing; and it will be no wonder if those who neglect themselves and are not prepared to remain on their guard are deceived when they have poorly prepared themselves. (4411–40)

You have heard how Simon has fled; he has left to take unawares those who are willing to heed him. He has set off ahead, and I must follow him. He is going in order to deceive people: anybody who heeds him is a fool! I shall journey after him, but I cannot do so immediately, for since it is right that better care should be taken of you who have converted than of others who have heard nothing of what pertains to their salvation and know nothing of God, I wish to stay with you for three months in order to make you steadfast in the truth. For anybody who acquires or gains something and then completely loses it is more upset to have lost it than if he had never had it, for it is a greater loss to lose something which has been gained than something which has not been gained, even if one has endeavoured to do so. It is exactly so with you and me: I have gained you and drawn you into faith, and I have no desire to lose you by rushing to other people until I have done enough with you for me to be sure of you. I shall therefore stay with you, and shall leave after three months. I wish to head after Simon, and intend to reform those whom he deceives, for I could stay so long that by the time that I came after Simon, he would have said so much beforehand that my labour

---

[1] 4392–96 **he was not. . .criminal** *Pur ceo. . .jugié*: This explanation is an innovation relative to *Rec.* III.64.3.

would be entirely in vain if through his magic he had managed to make my words achieve little."[1] (4441–82)

Great were the sorrow and lamentation which could then be heard when St Peter mentioned that he wished to head after Simon, and that he would stay for no more than three months and would then depart. It was out of love that they wept, for they loved St Peter dearly; and St Peter, who was full of sympathy, could not keep himself from weeping, for he was seized by great compassion, and so said this prayer for them:

"Lord God, almighty Father, who created heaven and earth from nothing and created all things, have mercy on these people! Give comfort to them, I implore you. They appear to hold me dear; they have done this for me on account of your love, for they consider you to be their Lord. May pity seize you, Lord God, for there is nobody who might take care of them except you, who are capable of protecting them against the Devil!" (4483–506)

St Peter said prayers of this and other kinds. He then made Zacchaeus bishop to remain there in his stead; he made him bishop of Caesarea, for he was a fine, upstanding man.[2] He ordained four deacons and twelve priests there to be masters in instructing the people in how they ought to behave. He ordered those whom he had ordained to be sensible and wise; to receive paupers and strangers, respectable widows and orphans, and to do to them every good within their power; to endeavour to love God, and to tell the young people to behave chastely; to strive to serve God in such a way that people might follow their example; to instruct the people thoroughly to do good and refrain from evil; to love each other and to help each other, and to make it clear through their deeds that their love was not empty. This is what he ordered of the ordained; he then turned to the people. He told them to believe in God and be baptised; to honour the bishop, as this would be an indication of love; to heed and obey him in all respects, for, he said, he knew Zacchaeus well: he was well educated and loved God, and so he had appointed him to represent God, and anybody who did honour or ignominy to him would be doing the same to God, for he was appointed to represent Him.[3] Each person should think about himself, and before he was baptised, should come to Bishop Zacchaeus and have his name written down;[4]

---

[1] 4449–82 **I shall journey. . .little** *Aprés lui. . .attendreit*: An expanded version of *Rec.* III.65.4–5.

[2] 4507–12 **St Peter. . . upstanding man** *Ureisuns. . .bon afaire*: Compared with *Rec.* III.66.3–4, the consecration of Zacchaeus receives less attention.

[3] 4537–46 **to honour the bishop. . .represent Him** *A l'eveske feissent onur. . .lieu*: This version of *Rec.* III.66.6 should have appeared after v. 4516. As a result, instructions which in *Rec.* are addressed to the clergy are in *Clem.* directed to the laity.

[4] 4547–50 **Each person. . .written down** *Chescun. . .enbrever feist*: These lines place more emphasis on administrative procedure, whereas in *Rec.* III.67.2 Peter encourages

and everybody should fast before they were baptised. After three months — after which time he had said that he would not stay there any longer — all those who so desired would be baptised; there would then be a celebration, and it pleased him to set this date. Once they were baptised and confirmed with chrism, they would receive communion and would thus be saved. He told them a great deal about baptism, and why Jesus Christ established the custom that people must be baptised.[1] (4507–66)

All the people left once St Peter had said this. St Peter went to his lodging; he summoned all his companions, and when they had all gathered, they listened to what he had to say:[2]

"My brothers," he said, "it is right that we should have compassion and help the people whom Simon intends to deceive. Since he has headed off, we must follow him. Simon has headed off with the sole intention of hindering me: if I were free of obligations here, I should be hot on his heels in order to be on hand to respond to him, to expose him, and to confute him. But it would be neither right nor proper to abandon those who have newly converted to God for the sake of others who are far from here, of whom we do not know whether we can persuade them to listen to what we must say to them. We must nonetheless not abandon them without helping them; there can be no question of delay if they are to prosper through us. We could incur loss if we delayed too long, for Simon does not hesitate to perform his deception: he may catch so many people unawares with it that few will be prepared to heed us. Some companions must therefore follow hot on his heels to warn the people that Simon is deceiving them and is lying, and tell them that I shall come as soon as I can. My mind is firm in the intention to remain here for three months in order to make those who have been converted by me steadfast in true faith.[3] Clement, who has newly arrived, will remain with me, for he fervently desires to hear the word of God. He will therefore not leave me, nor will Niceta and Aquila, who have recently converted and will therefore remain with me.[4] Let all the other companions except these three go ahead: through them Simon will be quite sure that he will have me near him wherever he goes! May each one of those who are to leave be ready by tomorrow, for we

---

people to visit Zacchaeus to hear of the mysteries of heaven.

[1] 4564–66 **and why Jesus. . .baptised** *E par quel reisun. . .gent*: This information is an addition relative to *Rec.* III.68.1.

[2] 4567–72 **All the people. . .say** *Parti sei en est. . .escuterent*: The names of the twelve followers given in *Rec.* III.68.1 are omitted.

[3] 4585–612 **But it would be. . .true faith** *Mais ne serreit. . .cunverti par mei*: A considerable amplification of *Rec.* III.68.4.

[4] 4613–20 **Clement. . .remain with me** *Od mei. . .demurrunt*: Some of the names found in *Rec.* III.68.5 are omitted.

may soon incur loss by delaying any longer. In this exchange of opinions I have stated mine; may each man now state his own!"

Everybody fully endorsed this opinion, even though those who were to go ahead were sorrowful, for it greatly upset them that they had to go far away, so dear did they hold St Peter.[1] (4567–636)

On the appointed day the companions who were due to leave were ready. They came before St Peter and took their leave of him, and on leaving said that their hearts were heavy that they were to go so far from him that they would not see him for three months, for the loss that they would experience in the meantime would be very great, and they would miss out on a great deal of benefit by not hearing him speak; nonetheless, even though it upset them, they were willing to do his bidding. They were prepared to go in order to remain obedient, for it was quite right to do whatever pleased him. He gave them his blessing and prayed fervently for them that God should grant them to act so well that their journey would not be wasted. There were twelve companions; I do not know what they were called. They set off, and St Peter remained there.[2] (4637–62)

St Peter was in Caesarea, and he strove vigorously to win people over. He made every possible effort to make great gains for God. Many of those people who heard him speak converted. Within three months he managed to gain ten thousand men there, and all were baptised once the three months had passed; they all became Christians when the day of the celebration came.

In the meantime, the twelve companions went after Simon. They pursued him until they found him in Tripolis; they inquired thoroughly into his situation and wrote it all in a letter. They readied their messengers and sent word to St Peter of how he was deceiving the people who were prepared to listen to him, for he was saying many wicked things throughout the towns and the cities. He was slandering St Peter terribly, giving it to be believed that he was a deceiver: he was, Simon said, wickedly cunning and an extremely deceptive sorcerer. He was entirely opposed to God, and was bereft of knowledge; everything in which he claimed to be a master was false and could not be. His claim that the dead could rise was impossible; it was not credible that the dead could return to life. Anybody due to debate with him would need to be on his guard; he must be on his guard, for if he were not, St Peter would treacherously murder him! He had, he said, debated with him, but when St Peter was unable to proceed and had been

---

[1] 4625–36 **May each. . .St Peter** *Chescun de ces. . .seint Pierre chier*: An abbreviation of *Rec.* III.69.

[2] 4659–62 **There were twelve. . .remained there** *Il furent duze. . .i est remis*: These lines stand in place of the account of Peter's return to the city in *Rec.* III.70.3–71.7. The claim not to know the names of the twelve followers is slyly duplicitous, for they have been quite deliberately omitted from vv. 4567–72 (see note).

completely defeated, he placed his companions in an ambush. Simon had been forewarned of this and fled out of fear; otherwise St Peter would have ensnared him, for either he would have poisoned him, or he would have struck him dead through magic or sorcery or deception.

Every bit of slander that Simon had said was written in the letter, as was the information that he was mostly dwelling in Tripolis. (4663–716)

Once this letter reached St Peter, he had it read out in front of the people. He was not prepared, he said, to tarry any longer: he wanted to head for Tripolis. He would remain there all winter; anybody who wanted to look for him would find him there, and if anybody wanted to follow him, he would, he said, gladly grant permission to do so. Nevertheless, if it were the case that he had a household to look after—such as a wife or children who were dependent on him, or a father or mother or kin who would be discomfited and without support or help—such people should not be abandoned, for anybody who abandoned such people would have committed a foul and sinful act by turning away from them and so leaving them without support: such people should be cared for, for the sake of both God and nature. He vigorously exhorted all the people of Caesarea to act well, and ordered them in the name of God to heed Zacchaeus, whom he had made bishop on account of the goodness that he knew to be in him. He implored them to love God and honour their priests, and likewise their deacons, and to do so for God's sake, and for no other reason. He implored the chaplains to be charitable towards the laity, and implored the other clergy to do likewise, and to behave so well that the laity might follow their example. When he had spoken at length to the laity and the clergy, he said before everybody as he took his leave: "My lords, I commend you to God! If God so wills, I shall depart tomorrow, and shall delay leaving no longer."

This is the essence of the business that St Peter conducted in Caesarea.[1] (4717–62)

The next morning he left there and set out for Tripolis.[2] A faction of the people joined his fellowship; they left Caesarea and followed him towards Tripolis.

There were many people who accompanied him and were upset by his departure. He did not make much progress on that day on account of the people who followed him, for young and old alike frequently approached him for advice; they frequently took their leave and turned back towards their homes, and the same people soon returned and detained him by speaking to him; they felt such great

---

[1] 4717–62 **Once this letter. . .Caesarea** *Quant cest brief. . .Cesaire*: These lines reorganise *Rec.* III.74.1–2, inserting in vv. 4719–38 a version of *Rec.* III.72.2, which was omitted earlier. Following this section, the allusion to the letter to James (*Rec.* III.74.3–4) and the description of its contents (III.75.1–11) are omitted.

[2] 4763–64 **The next morning. . .Tripolis** *D'iloec. . .chemin*: The stop in Dora mentioned in *Rec.* IV.1.1 is omitted.

love for him that they were unable to part from him. So much did they come, so much did they go, so much did they leave him, so much did they detain him, so much did they seek advice from him, so much did they take leave of him, so much did they talk as they went, so much did they stop and stand, so much did they go at leisure, so much did they hate leaving, so much did they keep tarrying in this way that it was approaching evening. Once St Peter had managed to free himself from the people, he came to a town and there took lodging.[1] This was not far from Caesarea, but he could not go any further. Upon leaving there he endeavoured to speed up; he made better progress and passed through several countries. Both through market-towns and through cities he preached a great deal about Jesus Christ, for even though he was passing through, he nonetheless did not forget Him. When he entered cities or market-towns or other places besides, he gladly stopped there if people would listen to him there; if he thought that he could achieve anything, he was not prepared to rush away from there. Nonetheless he said to everybody that when he came to Tripolis, he would stay there until the end of winter, which was just beginning; anybody who wanted him at his leisure could find him in Tripolis.[2] (4763–816)

His fellowship was already very large by the time he was approaching Tripolis, for he could not pass through any place where he said anything about God without a large faction of the people following his fellowship. They accompanied him until they reached Tripolis. When they arrived at the gates, they met the companions who had left St Peter three months earlier and who had written the letter on account of which St Peter had come. They were absolutely delighted when they saw St Peter; presently they entered the city and led St Peter to his lodging. He took lodging at the house of Maro; that was the name of the man to whom the house belonged. Those who had been sent ahead had provided many lodgings, and they made plenty of lodgings available to all those who had come; there was nobody who could complain that he was bereft of lodging. News of their arrival was soon known throughout the city; many people who wanted to see St Peter rushed there. Once St Peter had seen that the people had rushed there to hear and to see him and to hear him speak, he told them very kindly that he needed a delay, for he intended to rest that day and the next; but on the third day they should all come and hear the word of God, for he would definitely come then and present his opinion to them. When it did not please him to say any more, the people remained there no longer. (4817–60)

Presently the companions said to St Peter, who had not eaten, that it was high time to eat, but he informed everybody that he would not and told them that under no circumstances would he put any food in his mouth unless he were sure

[1] 4765–94 **A faction. . .lodging** *De la gent une partie. . .sun ostel*: An amplification of *Rec.* IV.1.2, with rhetorical embellishments.
[2] 4795–816 **This was not far. . .Tripolis** *Ceo n'iert pas lung. . .truver*: The names of the towns included in *Rec.* IV.1.3–4 are omitted.

that all of his followers had good lodgings, for he would not be comfortable if his followers were uncomfortable. The twelve companions then assured him through their response that all his followers had lodgings and were comfortable in all respects; they had made preparations beforehand, and the citizens were in any case glad to open their houses to him and his companions. There were fewer people seeking lodgings than there were people to lodge them; they were unhappy and upset that more people had not come seeking lodgings! They had readied their homes, and very much wished for each person to lodge somebody in his house, and they would gladly find for them everything that they would need without taking anything from them, for they felt very great love towards St Peter, and fervently wished him to come quickly to Tripolis.

When St Peter heard this, he was absolutely delighted by it, and he very much appreciated that they had made such good preparations. He gave his blessing to them, and then told and ordered them not to leave there, but rather to remain there for supper. They then sat down to eat,[1] and partook of what sustenance they had. When evening fell, they retired and slept well that night. (4861–904)

Early the next morning St Peter rose before daybreak in accordance with his custom. All his companions were awake. Including St Peter, there were sixteen: St Peter first of all; Niceta, Aquila, and Clement; and the twelve companions whose names I am unable to recall.[2] If one adds together four and twelve, if one counts properly, that makes sixteen.[3] St Peter gave greetings to everybody, and they all greeted him in return. He sat down, and the fifteen companions sat down around him. He then said to them: "Since we are doing nothing else, let us attend to ourselves today! I shall recount to you what we did in Caesarea, and you twelve will tell us what you have done here: tell me everything about Simon's situation, and whether he is faring well or not!" First of all, St Peter recounted everything that he knew which ought to be said; he told them everything that he knew about Caesarea which ought not to be passed over. Then the disciples recounted all their adventures in Tripolis, and in so doing recounted everything without omitting anything.[4] They spoke at such length that the day began to break. (4905–36)

---

[1] 4901 **to eat** *al mangier*: The information in *Rec.* IV.3.1 that Peter bathed in the sea before eating is omitted.

[2] 4911–12 **and the twelve. . .recall** *E les duze. . .nuns*: A humorous allusion to the translator's earlier deliberate omission of the names under pretence of ignorance (cf. notes to 4567–72 and 4659–60.)

[3] 4913–14 **If one adds. . .sixteen** *Ki met ensemble. . .sedze*: This mathematical epiphany has no equivalent in *Rec.*

[4] 4927–34 **First of all. . .anything** *Tut avant. . .leisserent*: These lines have no equivalent in *Rec.*

Presently a man came in who was well known to the house. He told them that Simon had fled from there in the middle of the night, and on account of St Peter's arrival had headed from Tripolis towards Syria; Syria was the name of the country to which Simon had fled. He then told St Peter that people were coming in great throngs: they had already come to the gate and were waiting there to enter, and they greatly wished to see and hear him. It seemed to all of them that the delay that he had imposed was long; they said again and again that the wait was hard to bear. It would be hard for them to bear spending that day without hearing him, and they strongly agreed amongst themselves that the delay should be shortened. They were not prepared to leave the gates and were hoping to enter: "I do not know," said the man who was speaking, "how it has happened, but there is a large crowd. The more the day has broken, the bigger the throng has become. I do not know from where they got the idea, but they are quite sure that they are due to see you, St Peter, and that they will hear you speak today. And since it is the case that such a large crowd wants you so much and is waiting, they will be willing to hear whatever pleases you, and we shall tell them what you wish. But it will be viewed very dimly if as many people as have come here have to leave upset that you did not first speak: they will not be thinking of the delay, but rather that you are scorning them all!" (4937–78)

St Peter considered what he heard this man saying to be quite wondrous, and he said to his fellowship: "Have you seen how the prophecy told to us by our master, Jesus Christ, has come true? 'The harvest,' He said, 'is very great, but there are very few people working. Ask Him who is Lord of the harvest to ready as many workers as needed and send them to His harvest!'[1] He also told us another thing which we now see with our own eyes: that many will come from the east and west and join the fellowship of Abraham and his line; that is Isaac and his son Jacob, from whom God had chosen that He who would cast the world from danger should come.[2] The prophecy has come true, for we have now seen it with our own eyes. Let us therefore, dear brothers, endeavour to serve God! Strive to learn what you might teach to others, to hear well, to understand well, to learn well about the right order, to speak well, to reply well, and to explain arguments well, to preach well about the way to act well and to speak well, so that through your teaching those people who grasp the reason of our preaching might attain salvation,[3] for you have already clearly seen how the people have come here, and what desire they have to hear what ought to be of benefit to them. Through the grace and power of their Creator they have happened, even before they are able to know Him properly, to begin to love Him dearly, and they most lovingly yearn for the coming of their Lord, and for the means of doing His bidding to be

[1] 4985–90 **The harvest. . .harvest** *Mult est. . .enveit*: Cf. Mt 9:37–38; Lk 10:2.

[2] 4993–5000 **that many. . .come** *Que mulz. . .peril*: Cf. Mt 8:11; Lk 13:29.

[3] 5005–16 **Strive to learn. . .salvation** *De aprendre. . .predicatiun*: The anaphora in this section has no parallel in *Rec.* IV.4.4.

shown to them. It is a fine beginning given by God when God grants people to love and desire something of which they have never heard anything, and to love and honour those whom they have never known, and to yearn to join their fellowship solely from what they have heard.[1] But let this be enough on this topic for now because of the crowd waiting out there, for because of their great devotion I must make a speech!" (4979–5040)

St Peter said this and other things that God placed in his heart, and then he requested a place and location which might accommodate the assembled crowd and in which he might speak to everybody.

In response to this, his host Maro said to him: "I have a very large house! Up to five hundred men can fit into it, and I have within my grounds a large garden suitable for this purpose. You can go there if you wish, or elsewhere if you prefer, outside the gate on the street where the crowd has gathered. And if that were possible, the crowd would be greatly placated, for there is not one man there who does not yearn to see you." (5041–60)

Once Maro had said this, St Peter then stood up and ordered Maro to go and show him his house. Once the house had been shown to him, and he had then gone out into the garden, all the people—I know not how[2]—entered in a large throng. They all passed through the house and came into the garden in droves. The man responsible for watching the gate was very lax in his duty there; he appeared to be very negligent when he let all the people come in![3]

Once St Peter noticed that the people were rushing there, he then looked around and spotted near the house a pedestal which was standing on the ground, and he climbed onto it to make a speech. He began his speech by greeting everybody. As he said greetings to everybody, some of those who had come were unable to remain on their feet without having to fall to the ground, for they were insane, and they had been brought there to be cured of the Enemy's power by St Peter. The Devil could not endure once St Peter had greeted the people: through the mouths of the wretches who were possessed by the Devil the evil spirits cried out that St Peter should grant them a delay so that they might remain in the bodies but for one single day. But St Peter was not prepared to agree to grant their request: he ordered them to exit without harming the bodies; the devils then left, and the sick people were completely cured. Once the people had seen the miracle

---

[1] 5017–36 **for you have. . .heard** *Kar vous avez. . .cumpainnie*: This section bears only a partial resemblance to *Rec.* IV.4.5–6. Following it, *Rec.* IV.5, which involves Moses and the Jews, is omitted, with vv. 5037–40 rejoining *Rec.* IV.6.1.

[2] 5067 **I know not how** *ne sai cument*: This is our translator confessing his own ignorance.

[3] 5071–74 **The man. . .come in** *Mult i dechai. . .gent*: The condemnation is an addition by the translator to *Rec.* IV.6.3.

performed on those who had been insane and had now been purged in this way, they then all implored St Peter to heed their request and help all those who had other sicknesses. St Peter then said: "I shall gladly do so, but first I shall speak to you." As soon as he had promised this, God was not prepared to delay, but rather the sick people there regained their health immediately. Once this had happened, it was impossible for the power of these miracles to be kept quiet, for it was soon known throughout the city. As rumour of it grew, and more people rushed there, all those who had been ill and had regained their health stood to one side on account of the large throng. St Peter had ordered this, and it was done since it pleased him. Then St Peter raised his hand and indicated to everybody to be quiet. He ordered them to listen, and then began to speak: (5061–134)

"My lords," he said, "I shall begin by explaining to you what you ought to believe about those who came here sick and have been cured by the grace of God. First of all you must know that you are not to blame God if people suffer infirmity or fall into adversity: God is not guilty in this, but rather His righteousness and His power, by which the world is sustained, appear all the more reasonable. It is quite right and just that many people suffer misfortune, for the Devil has them in his power on account of their own wickedness. For in the very beginning, when God created the world from nothing, He made man in His image and placed His breath in him. In this way He brought him to life and wanted him to live for ever, and to behave towards God such that God might acknowledge him as His son. He wanted to make him heir to His kingdom, and gave him sense and knowledge to do good, avoid evil, and follow God's commandment. He did not wish to impose on him any compulsion which might harm him, but rather through the rectitude of righteousness He gave him very great freedom, and placed it entirely in his power do His bidding with it. He put him in Paradise; the place in which he was put was beautiful. As long as he was there and behaved well, plenty of fruits came from the earth without it being cultivated, without toiling or expending effort. A simple law was imposed upon him, and he could have followed it without any difficulty; he would have been happy for ever if he had observed what God wanted! But then through wicked covetousness he abandoned the law which had been imposed on him. There was only one commandment: this he transgressed and utterly ignored. (5135–82)

When he turned against his Lord, he thenceforth lost his honour. He was then cast out of the place where he had enjoyed honour; thenceforth he was consigned to pain, toil, and dishonour. The fruits that he used to enjoy came to an end, for the earth yielded nothing unless is was cultivated with toil, and it still rarely returns the effort invested. All that was good had turned bad, and there was no question of regaining it. This was very bad, and then there came worse, whereby God was enraged further, for as soon as man had been cast out of the glory in which he had been, the race which issued from him had neither love for God nor faith in Him. From him there came wicked heirs who brought shame upon their Lord; they renounced their Lord, and the more they multiplied, the more they neglected Him and the less good intention they had. Their false belief was that they did not believe that God was responsible for providence, but rather believed solely in chance: they would not believe that there even was a God, so wicked were they! They did not believe that God took care of heaven, earth, and the world, and the things which are in them, and all creatures.[1] They then entered into such great error that they worshipped the Devil instead of God, and honoured the images that they had made like gods: they worshipped images of men and beasts, and through a most foolish error created great feasts, temples, and altars in their honour. They devoted themselves to making sacrifices to them; they performed utterly filth-ridden rituals which are too vile to mention and more horrible to see. This invention came from the Devil to degrade human nature; by abandoning right and doing wrong, man was consigned to death. It is as a result of this, as has been the case for a long time, that the world was damned, as God had been forgotten in favour of the Devil, who is His enemy. The Devil holds in his power all those who do his bidding, but he gives a very poor reward when he leads them all to perdition. He drives them insane here and makes them behave repulsively; he utterly corrupts their minds to make them live shamefully. Here he keeps them in dishonour, and from here he drags them into suffering which will never end, but rather will last for ever without end. (5183–250)

In order to avoid such great harm and to forewarn you of this we have been sent to you so that you might be saved by us if you are prepared to follow what you hear from us in service of God. We cannot compel you to believe what we say: it will now be up to you to choose whether to do it or reject it. For if you are prepared to do it, you will receive a twofold profit from it: the Devil will have no power over you and will be cast from others by you, and you will moreover gain the life which can never end. As for those who are not prepared to hear, devils will have power over them and will drag them into such great suffering from which they will never be rescued: they will be trapped in the depths of Hell, and there they will suffer unremitting punishment. I warn you of this, my lords: avoid being caught unawares again; remove yourselves from the error through which body and soul are damned; believe in one God and follow Him—through Him you will be saved from death! For the love of God abandon the idols that you have worshipped and honoured through ignorance, for you may be sure of Him. If you are prepared to convert to Him and accept Him as Lord, He will love you as His children and will place you in His kingdom in such joy, such grandeur, such glory, and such nobility that no man's heart can grasp it until He comes to claim it!"[2] (5251–90)

---

[1] 5215 **creatures** *creature*: The term could also denote "creation."

[2] 5135–290 **My lords. . .claim it** *Seignurs. . .al prendre*: This section replaces Peter's three-day sermon in *Rec.* IV.8–VI.14, its content sometimes stemming from *Rec.* (e.g., vv. 5252–71 for *Rec.* IV.14.1–3), but otherwise appearing to be a mixture of conventional doctrine and a distant summary of the missing material.

St Peter said much more there than I can say here. The speech was long and far-reaching, and he clearly proved through reason that everything that he said was completely true, and he had an attentive audience when he spoke. On that day and the next he did not stop, nor on the third or fourth day was he exhausted, nor did he take a rest from preaching during the three months that he spent in Tripolis. Many of those who heard him preach converted to God. He spoke a great deal, he said a great deal, and he performed a great deal of miracles there, for those who were infirm regained their health through him.[1] (5291–306)

When he had stayed in Tripolis until three months had passed, and he had converted a great many people, he then summoned Clement and ordered him to fast and ready himself fully so that he might be baptised. And Clement did not hesitate: he gladly put into practice everything that St Peter told him. After he had fasted as long as pleased St Peter, St Peter baptised him.[2] The companions were happy about it, and St Peter was delighted that Clement had been made Christian by him. On account of the joy that they all felt they made it a day of celebration.

St Peter and his disciples had now been in Tripolis as long as they had intended before they had arrived there. St Peter did not wish to remain there any longer, and wished to head for Antioch. He ordered twelve of his companions to go ahead so that news of his coming might be known through them, and that they might inform the people, once they arrived in Antioch, that when St Peter arrived, he would stay there for at least three months.[3] They remained there no longer, but St Peter still stayed. He gathered the people who had turned to God through him; he summoned all those whom he knew to be of good faith; he baptised them all and then gave them communion. He made Maro, who had been his host, into a bishop, and told him to endeavour to do good and to draw people to God. He ordained twelve priests and instructed them in their duty, and likewise ordained as many deacons as pleased him; he told all of them what they should do, and then prepared for his journey.[4] He wished to stay in Tripolis no longer; he wished to head for Antioch. (5307–58)

---

[1] 5291–306 **St Peter. . .health through him** *Mult plus. . .par lui santé*: An allusion to the preceding major omission.

[2] 5319 **St Peter baptised him** *Seint Pierre le ad baptizié*: The information in *Rec.* VI.15.2 that this is performed in the fonts by the sea is omitted. A similar omission from *Rec.* VI.15.4 is found in v. 5345.

[3] 5335–38 **and that they might. . .three months** *E a la gent. . .demureit*: A change to *Rec.* VI.15.3, in which Peter rather orders his followers to wait there for three months.

[4] 5355–56 **He told all. . .journey** *A tuz dist. . .eire*: These lines omit from *Rec.* VI.15.5 that Peter establishes an order of widows.

St Peter left Tripolis, but on account of the crowd which followed him he could not make good progress that day, and so covered a shorter distance. He was often approached for advice, which reduced the chance of good progress, and they could scarcely travel far, for the crowd of people which accompanied him was very large and was not prepared to part from him on account of the love that they felt for him. Little progress was made on the first day; he barely reached his lodging, which was quite close to Tripolis. He stayed there that night, but the next morning he was not permitted to march on, and had to stay there. The next day he set off and endeavoured to make better progress; that day he went to Antaradus and took his lodging there. He slept there that night, as did such a great number of people that I cannot say how many there were or who they were, for a large throng followed him and kept him company.[1] (5359–86)

Once St Peter had noticed that the crowd was so big, he then summoned Niceta and his brother Aquila, and then said to them: "Since it is the case that our fellowship is growing so much, I quite understand that there will be some who will envy us, but we cannot drive away those who wish to accompany us, as this might distract them from their good intentions. But lest our fellowship should be a cause of envy, you two brothers must go ahead and lead these people with you. Once you have managed to near the city, you must not enter it in droves, but rather with one person first, and then the next; separate yourselves into sensibly divided groups. Ensure that your comings and goings are carefully organised, and likewise ensure that your progress is carefully regulated; do not all enter on one day, but rather make sure that nobody may say of you that we are seeking vainglory, and that there is nothing about us which might be criticised. I am quite aware that you are very upset that I have given you this instruction, for you consider it a great hardship that you must leave me, and that we shall spend two days without seeing each other, so great is your love for me. But I shall tell the truth, and you must believe me: if you love me—and I love you ten times more—and if we are to allow our honour to diminish for the sake of our love, and are prepared to stop doing good in order to stay together all the time, such love will not be reasonable since it is not beneficial." (5387–434)

St Peter spoke for longer there,[2] and the brothers presently replied: "We must be quite glad to do as you command, for you are most provident in everything that you undertake, for through God's providence you have been chosen to do good. It is hard for us to be parted from you for a day or two, but we must bear it. We shall be unhappy on the day that we cannot see you; nonetheless we are prepared to do your bidding immediately. Now we fully understand for ourselves how upset and dejected our twelve brothers are who have gone ahead on account

---

[1] 5359–86 **St Peter left. . .company** *Seint Pierre. . .tint*: A meandering rendering of *Rec.* VII.1.1, with place names omitted.

[2] 5435 **St Peter spoke. . .there** *Paroles plus. . .Pierre*: I.e., the omitted *Rec.* VII.2.2–6.

of the great benefit of which they are deprived when a whole month often passes without them being able to lay their eyes on you."

Once they had said this, they set off ahead, and St Peter clearly told them to remember, when they approached the cities, to go together two by two, to cause no disturbance when entering, and to take up lodgings in the humble hospices. (5435–62)

Everybody had left except for St Peter, who remained behind with Clement. Clement was overjoyed that St Peter had kept him back; he thanked him from the bottom of his heart for not having been sent ahead. Clement said: "I give great thanks to God and likewise to you that you have kept me back with you, and that I have not gone ahead, for I would soon die from grief if I had to be parted from you."

St Peter then said: "If the need for you to travel a short or long way to improve others should befall us, will you then be certain to die from sorrow or from pain because you will not be in my company the whole time? Will you then not compel yourself to undertake a journey without me if the need is such that there is no other possibility? Do you then not know that good friends who have grown very close cannot be separated, even if their bodies are far apart, but rather are always together as long as their hearts are full of love? In just the same way you have often seen that if people do not truly love each other, even though their bodies are subsequently close, their hearts are always far apart." (5463–96)

Clement replied: "Do not berate me or take it amiss if I say anything unreasonable, for I do not do so without good cause. On account of the great love that I have for you I shall never willingly part from you, for—be quite sure!—I love you alone more than I do any other man. I hold you in the place of a father and in the place of brothers and a mother, and moreover—and this is much more significant, as it increases my love for you—you are the cause of my salvation, for I have heard the truth through you. And it should not be forgotten that I am a young man with a fickle heart, and so misfortune might befall me if I had to leave you. I might fear committing a transgression because of some desire that I shall not fear as long as I can be with you: all lust feels shame before you, even though it may pay no heed to reason. Nonetheless, by the mercy of God, I have great faith that His grace will keep my mind from ever being deceived, since I have learnt from you that I must tend towards nothing other than what ought to be done. Besides this I have clearly remembered, for I committed it thoroughly to memory, that you said in Caesarea that if anybody wanted to undertake a journey in your company without upsetting anybody who might depend on him—such as a father, or a mother, or a wife, or a brother, or a son, or cousins, or little orphans, or close friends in need of help, who for reasons of compassion must not be left helpless—if anybody was not burdened in this way, he would gladly have permission to follow you immediately, and I call you as witness to this.[1] I am alone, for I have no father, no wife, no son, no mother, no brother, no cousin, and no relative to worry about. Since I am alone and have nobody else but myself, I wish from the bottom of my heart to serve you, and if it pleases you, I greatly desire this." (5497–552)

St Peter began to smile when he heard Clement say this. He replied with gentle humour: "Do you not then think it fitting for you to attend to my service and take care of my possessions? Who will make my bed better than you? Who will look after my precious sheets? Who can better look after my rings and my frequently changed clothes? Who will oversee my kitchen and my cooks better than you? Who better than you to serve up the many and varied dishes that people are wont to prepare in order to stuff themselves like a ravenous beast which cannot be satiated? Nonetheless, I must not hide the fact that even though you have been with me, you are not familiar with my way of life, for this is my usual food: bread and olives and nothing else, or with cabbage on very rare occasions, and with nothing but water[2] to drink. This is all my clothing: this tunic and this pallium. This is enough for me, and I seek nothing else, for I need nothing else here. This world affords me no pleasure, for my heart draws me to another place where the rewards will be so great that they will never end. But it is amazing that you, who are not used to suffering great discomfort, can follow us and adapt so quickly to enduring our way of life, since you have always been brought up amidst great abundance. You are to be praised for this, and one can greatly wonder at it, and I admire you greatly for having accepted not wishing to seek anything beyond what you need. For my brother Andrew and I grew up in great poverty and have experienced great hardship; we were very poor, and so had to work, and this is why we can walk and travel without difficulty. So if you are prepared to agree for me to serve you, I should much rather do it for you than you for me, for I am a labourer and am used to enduring toil without difficulty." (5553–614)

Once Clement had heard this, he was not just a little upset! He began to tremble all over and to weep great tears, for he took the words that St Peter said to him straight to heart, as he esteemed him more highly than the whole world.

Once St Peter had noticed that Clement was weeping and upset, he asked him why he was weeping. Clement replied and said to him:

"What was my transgression against you which has made you crush me so utterly by saying such harsh words?" In response to this, St Peter said to him:

---

[1] 5527–44 **Besides this. . .to this** *Bien estre ceo. . .guarant*: Clement's claim to have remembered carefully is supported by the similarity of these lines to Peter's speech in vv. 4725–38, but he expands the list of dependents relative to *Rec.* VII.5.6.

[2] 5578 **water** *ewe*: *Rec.* VII.6.4 does not mention Peter's preferred beverage.

"If I have transgressed by saying such words to you, you transgressed first of all by saying the very same thing to me earlier, for you said at the very beginning that you wanted to be my servant."

Clement replied: "That is not at all the case, but rather my service to you is fitting, for you are the messenger to whom the duty of leading souls to salvation has been entrusted: this is why God has sent you, and it is therefore painful for me to hear that you should serve me."

To the words that Clement said St Peter offered this response: "Everything that you say might be true if our master Jesus Christ, who came to earth to lead the world to salvation and who is more sovereign and noble than any creature, had not come to serve and had not ordered us to serve our brothers and not be ashamed of this."

Clement then said: "I am quite dim-witted if I thought that I could ever defeat you by anything that I might say to you. But thanks be always to God, who is so provident, for letting me join you! I have no relative to gladden my heart, and so I came to you: I have you instead of kin, and you have given me comfort in their stead."

St Peter said: "What, Clement? Do you then not have any kin? Are you so bereft of relatives that not a single one is left for you?" (5615–70)

Clement replied: "I have many relatives, for I have come from noble stock. My relatives are the most powerful men in all of Rome: I am of the emperor's line, and so were my ancestors. My father was a relative of the emperor and through the emperor he married my mother, who was of high nobility and had come from a distinguished family. Together they had two twin sons, who according to my father were very handsome and closely resembled each other, and were older than I. I remember very little of them, save for what my father told me, and likewise I remember little of my mother and her appearance. My father was called Faustinianus, and my mother was called Matthidia; one of my brothers was called Faustus, and the other was called Faustinus. When I was barely five years old and at that time knew little of any value, my mother one night dreamed, as my father subsequently recounted, that she had to leave the city and take her two eldest sons with her: she would spend ten years away with them, and if she did not do this, there would be terrible consequences. My father loved his sons dearly and held my mother very dear; he did not want misfortune to befall them, and so gathered for them as many serving men and women as they could want, and a great abundance of wealth. He led them to the sea and put them on a boat, and bade them to sail to Athens; he told them that they should stay there and that his sons should go to school. He kept just me with him in order to have some consolation from me, and he sincerely thanked the one who had warned my mother in the dream that she had dreamt for being allowed to keep me with him. (5671–716)

Within the year no messenger came to gladden his heart in any way, nor a single person to tell him how a single member of his family was faring. He then prepared messengers and gave them plenty of money: he told them to set out to sea and head for Athens, and to spend as little time there as possible before bringing back good news. They set out, but never subsequently returned. My father awaited their arrival, but when he failed to hear anything from them, he was very upset, and readied more messengers and dispatched them. They crossed the sea in the third year and took with them very great wealth; in the fourth year they returned, but they brought back no news of either my brothers or my mother to gladden my father's heart. They had, according to them, been in Athens and had asked many questions there, but they found neither hide nor hair of anything that they expected to discover there: there was nobody who had seen them, for they had not arrived there. They had searched until they were exhausted, but they failed to find out the slightest thing to give them any certainty. (5717–48)

When my father heard this, he was utterly stricken with sorrow, for he did not know where to go in order to find out the truth about his family. He himself headed for the sea and made me go with him. He came to the port and asked the people whom he found there whether they had found two children four years ago, and a woman who was their mother, washed up on that shoreline. He spoke to various people who replied in various ways. He drew little comfort from anything that they said to him. Nonetheless, on account of the very great tenderness that he felt for his family, just as he was in great doubt, he likewise had hope that he might be told some news which might afford him a little more certainty. The wait was long, and so his hope waned. He then took the decision of a man overwhelmed by grief. He handed me over to guardians; I could well have been twelve years old at that time. He gave a great deal of various kinds of wealth to my guardians; he left me in their care, and then departed from Rome to seek his sons, my brothers, and his wife, who was my mother. He came to the port in tears, set out to sea, and then departed. From that time until today I have not received any message from him, and to this day I have not found out whether he is alive or dead. I strongly suspect that he drowned, or died as a man consumed by grief. Twenty years have passed since this happened; I have not received any news from him since then." (5749–92).

Clement had recounted his adventures, and St Peter considered them to be harsh; he could not stop himself from weeping on account of the great pity that he felt for him. He turned to his friends and spoke in this manner:

"If a man of our faith had suffered as much in his life as Clement's father suffered, many people would quickly say that our religion alone was the cause of such great hardship! There are many of those who believe that all the great hardships which occur all happen by chance without God's intervention, and that everything that a man can suffer must come from genesis.[1] Those who err in this

---

[1] 5810 **genesis** *destinee*: The Old French here uses a term which subsequently renders *genesis* from the *Recognitiones* (on which see note to v. 7099). *Rec.* VII.11.1 here actually

way are wretched, since they have no hope of benefit from it. When such hardship befalls people who serve God faithfully, and they patiently take the rough with the smooth for the sake of God's love, they will receive pardon for their sins if they are not bitter towards God because of this." (5793–818)

Once these words had been said, one of those standing there asked St Peter to come the next morning to see a work of art. The craftsman who created this work could not have been lacking in skill: it was made masterfully; such works are not made nowadays! Phidias, who was very skilled in craft, had made it in the past; he who had crafted that work that St Peter was to see was an expert in painting and knew much about carving. The work was in a building full of nothing but wonder: the house was most extravagant, and its columns were made of glass;[1] there is nothing on earth to rival its painting and carving. The building was on an island called Antaradus:[2] the sea completely surrounded it, and a ship was necessary for anybody who wanted to cross. It was six furlongs distant from where St Peter was at that time.[3] St Peter, who was generous, agreed to do what was requested, and told those who were with him and were to cross to the island to make suitable preparations to avoid creating any disturbance. They should come to the ship in the morning and behave very well, not run hither and thither, which might arouse unfavourable opinion, proceed in orderly fashion, and do everything with decorum. In the morning they all gathered quickly, boarded the ship, and crossed; they carefully observed the conduct about which St Peter had spoken to them. They came to the building and saw many wonders there. Once they had seen the columns, which were large and made of glass, St Peter had little interest in anything else that he saw. He did not care even to look at the carving and painting; he was impressed only by the columns when he saw them. He went out presently, while the others continued looking at the wonders which were inside; they had never before seen such wonders. Once St Peter had come out, he saw a woman there; she was sitting at the gates of the building and seeking alms from the passers-by. St Peter looked at her carefully and then addressed her: (5819–80)

---

speaks of *fatum* "fate," but our translator's choice of *destinee* serves to makes it clearer that Faustinianus, who later appears as the principal proponent of the importance of *destinee*, is precisely the kind of misguided individual whom Peter here evokes.

[1] 5836 **glass** *veire*: It is only in the $\Pi\Theta\Phi^{\pi}\Psi\eth$ readings for *Rec.* VII.12.1 that the columns are *vitreas* "of glass," with other branches offering *viteas* "of vine."

[2] 5840 **Antaradus** *Andarad*: This reflects the $\Sigma\Lambda^{dp}\Theta\Phi\Psi$ reading for *Rec.* VII.12.1; cf. Rehm, *Recognitiones*, xcv, and the note to 418 above.

[3] 5819–44 **Once these words. . .at that time** *Quant ces paroles. . .esteit*: The beginning and end of this section stem from *Rec.* VII.12.1, but the description of Phidias comes from *Rec.* VII.12.3.

"Woman," he said, "please show me which of your limbs you have lost for you to be begging like this, for you appear to be hale and hearty! Why is it that you are so poor, and why do you not do any work with the hands that God has given to you, but instead so debase yourself by not being prepared to do any work to earn your crust?"

The woman sighed deeply when she was addressed in this way, and then she replied to St Peter: "I should be happy if I were to have hands with which I might perform labour! It has so happened that I have retained the appearance of normal hands, but they have become so weak and numb through my abuse that they are dead, and I feel nothing from them, so often have I gnawed them with my teeth." (5881–902)

St Peter then said: "Why have you done such great harm to yourself?"

The woman said: "My wretchedness has driven me to what I suffer. There is no other reason, for if it were so that there were any strength in me, I would have cast myself to my death a long time ago or drowned myself in the sea for sorrow, or have done enough by myself to bring an end to my suffering."

"Woman," St Peter said to her, "what profit do you or others who kill themselves reckon to gain from this other than falling from bad into worse? And they will endure greater pains elsewhere than they have suffered in this life, all the more so specifically because they have killed themselves deliberately, for once the soul is cast out, it will suffer more than did the body."

She replied: "My inclination is that I should very much like to hear whether the soul can remain alive once it has left the body, and whether the soul can have life once it has descended into Hell, for I should gladly suffer death or great pain provided that I might have a little time and space to see my dear sons."

St Peter then said: "Why is it that you are gripped by such great sorrow? I should very much like to know this, for if you were prepared to reveal it, I would clearly show you and fully prove through reason that souls have life once they have descended into Hell, and to counter that desire to kill yourself by drowning or jumping that you have held for so long you will receive from me a medicine which will allow you to meet your end without sadness." (5903–46)

The woman was somewhat cheered by the promise that he had made to her, and she began to recount to him the events that she had experienced.

She said to him: "There is no need for me to tell you about my line, my country, and my kin: you would perhaps not believe it; nobody will believe it easily, and so there is no need to speak of it. I shall tell you about nothing other than the cause of my grief, which has left my hands feeble and numb through my gnawing. I come from a powerful family; my relatives are of high nobility. I had a noble man as husband, and the love between us was very great. I conceived two twin sons by him, and after these two I had one more by him. My husband had a brother who loved me most wrongfully; he made improper advances, but I would not consent to him, for I highly valued chastity and everything pertaining to morality. I did not wish to reveal it to my husband as I did not wish to

turn the brothers against each other: disgrace could soon result from this for us
and our family. I was anxious to protect myself, and therefore began to consider
that I would leave my country in order to avoid ignominy, taking my two sons
with me and leaving the third with my husband, and stay away for long enough
to keep my body chaste until the insane lust had cooled through my departure.
The one who was in love with me grew more impassioned by seeing me every
day. (5947–88)

It was my intention to do this, and in order to achieve this more effectively
I fabricated a dream as if it were a vision and then recounted it to my husband.
I told him that it seemed to me that a god had come to me. He had warned me
whilst I slept that my two children and I should leave the country and stay away
for ten years. After ten years, when it so pleased him, he would make us return
joyfully, and if I chose to refuse in any way, I would die first of all, and then all
my children likewise; there would be no chance of avoiding this. Once my husband had heard this, he was very upset and unhappy because of it. He did not
dare to refuse any of it, but rather made preparations for our journey: he summoned serving men and women and entrusted them to us to serve us; he invested
a great deal of money and finances in everything that he thought necessary. He
ordered us to set a course straight for Athens and to head straight there, to stay
there so that the children could attend school, and to remain there until we had
permission to return. Once we had set off to sea, we were soon caught by a storm;
the ship could not withstand it and was wrecked with everything which was in
it, except that I alone — poor wretch! — was cast onto a rock. They all drowned; I
escaped and landed on this island. I came here at night and sat alone, and nothing of mine was left for me; I was in utter anguish, and would have drowned myself if not for the fact that I thought that I might find my sons, whom I loved so
much. (5989–6032)

The next morning I went shouting along the shoreline, seeking my sons
and whether I might find their dead bodies in order at least to have them buried. People came towards the port who saw me disconsolate; they were seized by
great pity for me and began to search with me. But when they failed to find anything, the women who had come there then came to comfort me; they recounted their own experiences to me, and by recalling their own sorrow they wished
to shake me out of my sadness. But I grew all the more upset once I had heard
more of their hardships; my heart was not inclined to find solace in others' loss.
At that time there were plenty of people who insistently offered me their houses.
Amongst the rest there came one who entreated and detained me until she made
me come to her house, for the words that she said to me gave me the wish to be
with her, and therefore I accepted her lodging. She told me that she was a widow,
for she had had a husband who had been a young man when he had drowned in
the sea, and that since this man's death she had not wished to commit herself to
anybody else. She had committed herself to widowhood; even though she had
received many propositions, she would not take another husband, such love did

she feel for the first. She told me to stay with her and to share her house with her, along with any other profit from her labour and mine. (6033–72)

What merit is there in telling a long story? I chose to stay with her, and the reason for this was because she remained faithful to her husband. I could not forget how harsh my misfortune had been: I gnawed my hands so much and wrung them so much, and did so much harm and damage to them that soon afterwards they became so numb that they have never been any use to me since; and the woman who took me in was then struck down by palsy, and she lies in bed at home so that she has done no work for a long time. Those who felt pity for me renounced their generosity a long time ago. We are both reduced to beggary, and what we possessed has been spent. As you see, I sit here asking for anything which might help me; whatever I can acquire is shared by both of us. I have said enough, and you have heard it. And why do you delay carrying out the promise that you made to me when you gave me hope of providing a medicine through which we might pass beyond the torments that we suffer here and soon be able to die?" (6073–102)

St Peter stood quite flabbergasted when he had heard this from the woman; he thought a great deal about the story and had strong suspicions about it. Clement presently came and said that he had been running around the area for quite a while, for when he failed to find St Peter, he had wandered a long distance looking for him.

Clement said: "I have been looking for you everywhere. Now you must tell me your intention: what would you like us to do?"

St Peter replied: "We shall leave soon. Go ahead to the port and wait for us at the ship." Clement did not wish to refuse him, and quickly did as he had commanded.

St Peter forgot nothing of what he had heard the woman say. He thought about it a very great deal, as he later revealed to Clement. He had a certain suspicion about it, and asked the woman where she had been born and from what line, and who her relatives were, and to tell him the name of her country and to do likewise regarding her sons, for if she would say this, he would certainly honour the agreement in which he had promised her that he would give her medicine. (6103–32)

Even though the woman was greatly distressed, she would not reveal the truth; she greatly desired the medicine, but nonetheless dissimulated a great deal. She turned to lies, for she named her land as Ephesus; her husband came from Sicily—I do not know whether she lied about his name;[1] she lied about her sons'

---

[1] 6140 **I do not know. . .name** *Ne sai. . .nun*: The comment is by our author, with no equivalent in *Rec.* VII.19.4.

names, but St Peter did not realise this. He thought that she was not lying, and so replied: "Oh woman, alas! I truly thought that we should experience great joy today, for I recently heard a nearly identical story, with very similar details, about such a woman, and I very much thought from what you have told me that you were that woman."

Once the woman had heard this, she urged him to say more. She said to him: "I beg you: do as I beseech you! Tell me about this woman whom you have briefly mentioned to me. Tell me who she was, and what happened to her; I should very much like to hear about her, and wish to find out through this whether any woman was ever born who is more unfortunate than I." (6133–64)

St Peter was seized by great compassion. He was not capable of lying about anything, but rather said:

"Amongst those who accompany me and follow me for the sake of God there is a young man, a very fine fellow, who according to what he says was born in Rome. He also told me recently that he once had a father and two brothers who were twins and older than he, but none of them was alive. His father, he said, had told him that his mother had dreamt that she had to leave Rome and that she had to stay elsewhere. Her two sons, who were twins, had to leave with their mother, and if they were not prepared to do so, they would all certainly die. She left her country and took her two sons with her, but what became of them could never be ascertained thereafter. Their father set out in search of them, but never again did he return."

The woman was absolutely astounded when she had heard this, and could not stop herself from falling. St Peter picked her up and sat her down. He comforted her as best he could and asked her why she had fallen.

Once she had eventually regained consciousness and recovered her senses, she then began to become animated and to rub her face in anticipation of the joy that she expected to experience from what she had heard. She then said: "My lord, please say where this young man is!" (6165–202)

St Peter now grasped the situation, but he wanted to obtain more from her: "Woman," he said, "you will tell me more before you can see that man!"

The woman then said: "Truth to tell, he is my son, and I am his mother."

St Peter asked what his name was in order to gain greater certainty: "What," he said, "is the young man's name?"

She replied: "His name is Clement."

"He was the man," St Peter said, "whom you just now heard me tell to go ahead to the ship."

The woman presently fell down again and placed herself at St Peter's feet, and she fervently implored him to hurry to the ship.

St Peter replied anew: "I shall gladly do what you request if you will promise to do what I shall tell you."

She replied: "I shall do it all, just as long as you show me my dear son, for through him I have the hope that I shall find my other sons."

St Peter said to her: "When you see him, give no appearance of anything, but rather restrain yourself until we come to him and speak to him together." (6203–32)

The woman said: "I shall do exactly so." Presently they left that place. St Peter held the woman by the hand and went like this; they walked towards the ship until Clement could see them. Clement laughed because they were walking and holding hands like this; he nonetheless headed towards them, and from a distance came to meet them. He held his hand out, clearly showing that he was not ill-bred. He took the woman from St Peter, doing so for his master's honour; he wanted to lead the woman ahead in order to unburden St Peter. As soon as she felt his hand, she immediately let out a loud cry; she rushed forward to embrace him, wanting to kiss him as a mother would her son. Clement knew nothing of the matter and so wanted to step away. He thought the woman insane, and so pushed her away; he was ashamed in his own way, and grew angry towards St Peter. (6233–58)

St Peter then said: "Stop that, Clement, my dear son; behave well. Do not push your mother away; you surely ought to cherish her!"

As soon as Clement heard this, his eyes filled with tears; he bent down to his mother, who was lying on the ground, and kissed her. He stared at her very closely, and the more that he looked at her, the stronger the memory of their earlier acquaintance became. Many people from the area came running there, for the news was soon known of how the woman who was a poor beggar and had been staying there had been recognised, and of how her son, who was considered an upstanding man, had found her. St Peter and those with him made preparations to leave the island; they were about to board the ship and take the woman away with them, but the woman said to Clement: "My dear son, I cannot rightly leave here without taking leave of the woman who gave me lodging. She is sick and infirm, and lying helpless at home."

St Peter and all those who heard this recognised great goodness in her and held her in very high esteem for not having forgotten her companion. St Peter immediately summoned some of his followers and ordered them to go and fetch the woman, and carry her to him in her very bed. They departed quickly and brought the woman there; they placed her at St Peter's feet in front of that whole crowd. (6259–300)

Once everybody had fallen silent, St Peter said: "If it is true that Jesus Christ has sent me to lead you to the truth, and if I do good and speak to you as I learned from Him, in order to strengthen the faith of all those who follow His religion and to teach all those who truly believe without doubt that there is one God in heaven and on earth whose bidding we must do, in the name of His Son, who sees all that there is, may this woman be healthy!"

He said nothing but this, and barely this, when the woman arose completely healthy; she stood up and then fell at the feet of St Peter, who had healed her. She then turned to her companion and asked her what had happened. She told her quickly the end and the beginning in such a way that everybody from the area who had hastened there was amazed. St Peter made a speech to the crowd and spoke clearly about religion; he spoke clearly about the faith for as long as time permitted. He then told everybody that anybody who wanted to hear more should follow; they would find him in Antioch, for he would stay there for three months, and he would say plenty about everything pertaining to people's salvation. As an example he told them about what merchants do: "If people," he said, "often undertake long journeys for the sake of trade, and leave their country and expose themselves to great dangers, both on land and at sea, out of their desire for financial gain, why should it be considered a hardship to leave one's country and go abroad for three months for the sake of the life which will never end?" (6301–46)

Once St Peter had said this and other things there, Clement summoned the woman who had lodged his mother and had been healed by St Peter. He gave her a thousand drachmas from his own pocket and in front of everybody entrusted her to a powerful man from the area who was highly esteemed for his goodness; he accepted her and sincerely promised to do anything asked of him. Clement likewise shared some of his money amongst the other women who had consoled his mother when she had been bereft; he gave thanks and gratitude to everybody who had done any great or small act of kindness to her. They then sailed away from the island and took the woman with them. They had all come to their lodgings, and everybody was comfortable. Then the mother asked her son what had become of his father.

Clement said: "He left in search of you, and I have not seen him since."

She began to sigh, but then began to console herself, for the fact that she had found her son had been a great source of gladness for her; she had forgotten all the other woes, so greatly was she consoled by him.

St Peter had his wife with him, whom he had married in accordance with custom. Wherever he went, she followed, as a woman ought to follow her husband.[1] Clement placed his mother with her, for St Peter had permitted this. (6347–82)

St Peter set off the next day, not wishing to stay there any longer. Through a series of journeys he travelled until he approached Laodicea, a famous city of great wealth and with many inhabitants.[2] He had already come near the gates when Niceta and his brother Aquila, who had come there beforehand, caught sight of him. Once they saw him, they set out towards him, and they were over-

---

[1] 6377–80 **St Peter. . .husband** *Seint Pierre. . .mari*: An addition to *Rec.* VII.25.3 in order to explain why the eminent saint, perhaps surprisingly for a medieval audience, has a wife.

[2] 6383–88 **St Peter. . .inhabitants** *Seint Pierre. . .pueplee*: The more detailed itinerary of *Rec.* VII.25.3 is omitted.

joyed at his arrival. They greeted him with great love, kissing him and all the others. They had prepared his lodging at the hospice, and led him there. St Peter saw that the city was large and that a large number of people lived there; there, he said, he would stay for ten days, or longer if it were necessary. (6383–402)

St Clement's mother had come there, but she was not known by everybody, for Niceta and Aquila had not been there when St Peter had found her helpless and infirm.[1] They therefore asked Clement, who was their companion, to tell them, if he could do so, who this strange woman was.

Clement replied: "This is my mother, whom God has restored to me through St Peter."

Once Clement had said this, St Peter immediately began to tell them all about how he had found the woman. He told them first how he and Clement walked together and how they talked to each other when Niceta and Aquila had gone ahead to lead the large crowd. Clement, he said, had revealed to him from which country he had come, and how he had lost his mother, his brothers, and then his father. Next he told them about the island to which they went on account of the wonders which were there; about how the woman requesting alms from passers-by sat there, and how he spoke to her, and what answer she gave; about all her misfortune up to the time when she had been ship-wrecked and had barely escaped; and about the loss of her sons, who had died in the sea, of whom one was called Faustus, and the other was named Faustinus.

St Peter recounted all this, but he did not say it with such brevity, for he recounted it all in order and freely as he had heard it. I told this at length earlier, and so I have put it here more concisely, for it could become tedious to repeat the same thing too often.[2] (6403–50)

Scarcely had St Peter recounted this when Niceta and his brother Aquila rushed forward, since they could restrain themselves no longer. They stood absolutely flabbergasted and said: "Thanks be to the Lord God! What is this that we hear? Can it be true, or are we dreaming? Can it be that what we have heard here is so? Can it be that it is not nonsense?"

St Peter immediately replied: "What you have heard is true, unless we are insane."

They fell silent for a moment and then said before everybody:

"We are these two of whom you speak, Faustus and Faustinus! We listened to you carefully and wondered, in listening to your speech, whether it concerned us or not. We thought and bore in mind that the same event quite often tends

---

[1] 6405–8 **for Niceta. . .infirm** *Kar Niceta. . .meseisee*: An addition for clarification relative to *Rec.* VII.25.5.

[2] 6429–50 **Next he told them. . .too often** *De l'idle aprés. . .rehercer*: As indicated by its closing lines, this section considerably abbreviates *Rec.* VII.26–27 in order to avoid repeating earlier material.

to befall many people in various places. Even though we had our suspicions, we nonetheless kept quiet in order to hear and understand what the outcome of the matter was to be, in order that we might then speak out once we had learnt the truth." I know nothing of their behaviour or of the joy experienced by Clement and his two brothers when they found each other in this way. My source says nothing about it, but I am nonetheless quite certain that all three were absolutely overjoyed, but I am unable to tell you any more about it. (6451–90)

I likewise do not know whether their mother regained her health through St Peter. My source does not say whether she was healed in respect of her hands, but I shall nonetheless certainly say what I feel: St Peter, who held his disciples so dear, was not so remiss or uncouth that he, who did a good deal more for strangers, did not through the power of God restore health to their mother's hands![1]

The two brothers were overjoyed and wept profusely for joy; they both fervently desired to see their mother and speak with her. They went into her lodging, but found her asleep; they wanted to kiss her immediately as she lay there asleep, but St Peter, who ordered them to step back, would not allow it: "Allow her," he said, "to rest, and do not say a thing to her! Let me speak to her and prepare her mind. Once I have said what I think, I shall then present you to her, for if she were suddenly woken and were not gently roused first, she would immediately be overcome, and from the joy that she experienced she would quickly be bewildered by too sudden an appearance." (6491–524)

Once she had rested until she had awoken completely of her own accord, St Peter said to her before her sons: "I wish first of all for you to know what our religion is; I do not know whether it pleases you or not. We acknowledge no God but one, and we follow Him, and Him alone. He created the world from nothing, and our allegiance is to Him; we trust in Him resolutely and follow His law devoutly. His first commandment is that we should faithfully love Him above all others; we must place all our devotion in His name. We must honour our parents and maintain justice and chastity, and we must guard ourselves carefully against communing with any pagan, both in drinking and in eating, even though he may be a very dear friend to us. We must avoid all pagans, be they our father or mother, wife, son, brother or sister, first cousin or liege lord,[2] until they have received baptism and become Christian: from then on they will commune with us, and we will commune with them. May you therefore be forewarned, and it must not

---

[1] 6483–502 **I know nothing. . .hands** *Ne sai rien. . .fist*: A significant addition by our author relative to *Rec.* VII.28.4, in response to the lack of information in his source regarding the reunion of Clement and his brothers and the fate of Matthidia. In the version of this scene found in Paul Guillaume, ed., *Istoria Petri et Pauli: mystère en langue provençale du XVe siècle* (Gap/Paris: Maisonneuve, 1887), vv. 510–12, Matthidia confirms that her hands have been cured.

[2] 6549–50 **wife, son. . .lord** *Femme, fiz. . .seignur*: The list of those excluded is expanded relative to *Rec.* VII.29.4.

vex you; since our religion is such, reason dictates that it cannot be: even though you are Clement's mother, may such a feeling not overtake you if you do not eat with him before you have turned to his religion." (6525–62)

She replied: "What prohibits me from being immediately baptised in accordance with his religion, without my being delayed in this? For I can tell you in truth that I have long utterly detested those which are called gods, for I never found any good in them: I sacrificed often to them, but I never benefited from this. What shall I tell you about chastity, of which I have always been so fond that I did not consent to wicked vice in order to wallow in sinful pleasure, and did not abandon my chastity through the compulsion of poverty? You must fully believe me in this regard, for you can clearly see how it happened through my great love for, and great fidelity towards, my husband that in order to remain chaste and avoid immorality I fabricated the dream of which I told you and departed with my two sons, and left Clement alone behind to serve as a comfort to his father, for the poor wretch was very fond of his children, whom he held very dear, so much so that he would scarcely grant that I should take the two with me and that Clement should remain with him; he would have him alone, and make do with this much. For I would have achieved nothing if it had not been for the dream, which gave me the authority to have the two as I wished, for if I had not left at least one of the three with the father, he would then have remained without any consolation at all and could have quickly died from this." (6563–602)

Even if it killed them, Niceta and Aquila could no longer restrain themselves once their mother had said this; they immediately embraced her, and both kissed her repeatedly and wept profusely for joy.

The woman was absolutely flabbergasted when they had grabbed her in this way; she then asked them what this could mean, and St Peter revealed everything and said:

"Woman, do not be troubled, but rather feel great gladness in your heart! Be assured that these are your sons who were supposed to have died at sea: these men are Faustus and Faustinus! But now it will be up to you to inquire how it was that God saved them, how they escaped from danger when all the others drowned, and who changed their names so that one is called Niceta, and the other Aquila, and who first named them thus. Inquire into the things which have befallen them, both pleasant and harsh, and we shall listen with you to what we have not previously heard."

The woman was overjoyed once she had heard this news. On account of the joy that she experienced from it she could not say a word at that time; she could not prevent herself from falling. She eventually regained consciousness and then said:

"My sweet children, whom I hold so dear, tell me, I implore you, what befell you in the storm which beset us, which was so powerful and terrible, and from which I have suffered so much sorrow." (6603–42)

Niceta then said: "My dear mother, on that night which was so bitter to us, once our boat had been destroyed and broken into pieces, we two children—I know not how—came upon a plank which had broken off the ship when it was no longer possible to cling on. We clung to it all night and suffered great hardships; we were driven here and there, and could not find any respite. In the morning people came sailing to us who saw us floating there; they were robbers on the lookout for ships which travelled by sea in order to take people's belongings from them, and they did not practise any other profession. They took us on board their ship, but this became the cause of great hardship for us. We found no love there, for we were treated very harshly there; we suffered terribly from hunger, thirst, and beatings. They tormented us very wickedly and changed both our names: they called me Niceta and my brother Aquila. They treated us in this harsh manner in order to scare us so that we would not reveal from which country we came. The storm did not stop them from sailing as hard as they could, and they held their course until they reached Caesarea; there the robbers who had treated us so harshly sold us. A widow of Caesarea, a chaste and very kind woman called Justa, bought us and acknowledged us as her sons. She sent us to school and had us well taught;[1] we endeavoured to study hard, and then focussed our attention on the philosophers. We greatly desired to hear the truth regarding the identity of the religion that one should by reason follow. We debated this often, but derived little benefit from it; we strove wholeheartedly to be masters in debating. (6643–96)

We had a companion called Simon Magus; he was a sorcerer and knew a great deal of wickedness, and so bore the surname Magus. We shared his company, even though he was wicked; we had been raised with him, and so were closer to him. We were so friendly with him that we were nearly deceived by him. We have one True Prophet in the religion that we follow. His arrival had been greatly desired and anticipated: those who belong to His religion have great hope in Him. He has promised eternal life to all those who are prepared to follow Him; those who are prepared to turn to Him and strive to do His bidding will be for ever blessed, for they will live in joy without end. We thought that Simon was the one who could give such life; we would have been completely deceived by him if Zacchaeus, a disciple of my lord Peter, had not warned us. He showed us that this Simon was a deceiver and a sorcerer, and did nothing but lie. We therefore left Simon, and came to St Peter in order to hear the perfection of true religion. Dear mother, in this way we came to St Peter, and we wish for you such good as we ourselves have found so that we might partake together of the good that God gives us, for we greatly desire to eat and drink with you. Dear mother, such are the adventures which befell us up to now; the robbers who treated us harshly and cruelly seized us in this way when you thought that we had drowned in the sea and failed to escape." (6697–744)

---

[1] 6685–86 **She sent. . .taught** *Ele nus fist. . .endoctriner*: The explicit allusion in *Rec.* VII.32.3 to study of Greek writings is omitted.

Once Niceta had said as much as he thought fit, his mother then fell to the ground and placed herself at St Peter's feet and asked him to summon the friend whom he had made healthy and who had lodged her when she had escaped from danger. Once she came, he should not hesitate, but rather should baptise both of them quickly, so that on that very day she might not be separated from the full company of her three sons, and if it pleased him, he should permit her to eat and drink with them. The mother implored this, and the three brothers asked the same.

"Do you then think," St Peter then said, "that I am so unkind that I should wish forcefully to prevent you from eating with your mother? But it is nonetheless necessary for her to fast for one day beforehand, and then she will be baptised: she will not be delayed any longer, for I am quite sure that without any doubt she has very firm belief in God, for I heard her say something whereby I am quite sure of her faith. If this were not so, she would wait longer, for she would be tested for a long time; it would be necessary to talk to her and take pains to teach her."

Clement then said: "Please reveal what you heard her say which made you sure of her firm intent!" (6745–80)

St Peter replied to Clement: "I gained conclusive evidence from what she said when she requested that her hostess be brought to her and join our religion along with her, since she wishes for her to share the good that she believes that she will receive through us. She has shown great love for her when she wishes her to be baptised with her: if she did not believe it to be of particular importance, she would not have sent for her at all. Many are to be reproached—and they very much need to be set right—for the fact that once they have received baptism, they keep it completely for themselves. They do not give any indication that they are sure that they receive great benefit from baptism when they have not striven to draw their relatives and friends into the faith that they have received for themselves. If they believe and are sure that they will receive everlasting life through the faith that they have received, they should then be fully prepared to draw in as many people as they can so that they might be blessed together. If anybody has a relative or friend whom he sees to be sick or in some danger from which it is doubtful that he will be saved, he weeps profusely about it and is sorrowful because of the danger that he perceives there. Likewise those who have received the faith from which they are to benefit, if they believe and are quite certain that anybody who believes in God and serves Him well will escape from the fire of Hell and come to the joy of heaven, should strive most wholeheartedly to admonish their friends to make suitable preparations beforehand to avoid falling into that fire. And as for those who are so cruel that they are not prepared either for profit or for love to convert so that they might be prepared to hear of their salvation, one must feel great sorrow for them and weep fearfully for the fact that they are consigned to pain and will receive everlasting punishment. But now fetch that other woman here for me in order to hear whether our religion pleases her or not, and then we shall see what should rightly be done; for this women who is here, on account of the faith that I see in her, will not fast but for a single day, and then she will be baptised." (6781–840)

The woman there present replied in front of everybody that since she had found her sons, she had not tasted any food. On account of the joy that she felt she had had no interest in eating; she was so happy with finding them that since then she had had no care to eat anything small or big, except that the day before she had drunk a full goblet of water, and St Peter's wife had seen this.

St Peter's wife indeed confirmed that what she had said was completely true. In response to her saying this, Aquila then replied:

"Now that we have heard this, why should we delay baptising her given that she has fasted for so long beforehand?"

St Peter smiled somewhat at this: "That fast," he said, "that she performed was not a baptismal fast as she did not fast for that very reason." (6841–64)

Niceta then said: "Perhaps God has ordained such temperance that since we came together and recognised each other, He wanted the fast to come first before she knew the reason for the fast, so that she should not be separated from us for even one day, nor we from her, but rather that we should share a table and eat together. Just as she remained chaste before she had grasped that chastity was a great virtue, which nonetheless was very beneficial to her, perhaps she likewise fasted before she knew what benefit comes from this in order to be baptised quickly without being kept from it, even though she did not immediately know to what benefit baptism leads, and did everything that she ought to do without knowing the reason for it in order that she might be advantaged thereby and might in no way be hindered from receiving baptism quickly and from eating and drinking with us." (6865–90)

St Peter replied: "Let us be careful lest we be deceived by the Devil by reason of your mother, no matter how much you cherish her! But you and I shall do better, for today we shall all fast together, and your mother will be baptised tomorrow, if God accepts this, for we must not abandon rectitude on account of affection: neither on account of a favour to any person, no matter how good it might be considered to be, nor on account of the request of any friend, no matter how much we might cherish each other, must we forget to observe God's commandments. It must not vex you to fast with your mother today, for abandoning what God has commanded can lead to great sin; we must be careful lest our outer senses, which are full of carnal pleasure, take such firm control of those senses within, which must think only of God, that their freedom may be lost; the inner ones must rather retain supremacy over the outer."

St Peter said a good deal more there, for he presented to them examples which are written in the Gospels—more than I wish to include here.[1] (6891–922).

On that day they all fasted, and once the morning had come, St Peter summoned forth the mother with her three sons watching. He observed order and reason in all respects, and accordingly baptised her in such a font as was available there: it was the sea, which was nearby.[2] Once he had done everything that they wished, they all returned to their lodgings. There he taught the mother a great deal about what ought to be done; he told her a great deal about the reason which pertains to religion. They then ate together and thanked God sincerely, and so did St Peter, who had told them a great deal about how one cannot lose by leading a chaste life, but rather anybody who remains appropriately chaste will derive great benefit from this; and likewise in respect of the contrary, anybody who wishes to abandon chastity and live his whole life in filth and lust will suffer terrible punishment for it; be it sooner or later, he will not escape it. Although chastity is a great virtue which very much pleases God, nonetheless those who err so greatly that they do not hope for any benefit from God will receive no benefit from their chastity if they are not chaste for God's sake,[3] but rather those who are prepared to serve God willingly and behave chastely once they have received baptism will be blessed. (6923–60)

St Peter had said this to them because of their mother. He then told them to take careful note of, and take as an example, what had befallen their mother, who had behaved chastely, and to note well what the benefit had been which had come to her through chastity. Anybody who wishes to live chastely will have to guard himself very wisely; he will not be able to restrain himself on his own, but rather he must take flight as soon as he recognises that temptation will beset him. He must be entirely prepared to withdraw as if from fire, and to guard himself as well as he would from a rabid dog, for anybody who places himself in a burning fire or approaches a vicious dog may soon be burnt by the fire and soon bitten by the dog. May nobody trust that he will be able to do anything by himself alone: one cannot save oneself by fighting and resisting. In order to extricate oneself, no other way of thinking or any effort is of any use except for fleeing immediately, for one cannot restrain oneself otherwise. Their mother had acted in this way in

---

[1] 6919–22 **St Peter. . .here** *Seint Pierre. . .vueille*: An allusion to the omission of *Rec.* VII.37.3–7, which deals with the excision of sinning members (cf. Mt 5:28–29.)

[2] 6929–30 **in such a font. . .nearby** *Ceo fud la mer. . .esteit*: The explanation that the sea is a substitute for a font is an addition relative to *Rec.* VII.38.1.

[3] 6953–56 **nonetheless those. . .for God's sake** *Nepurquant cil. . .sunt*: These lines replace Peter's contentious argument in *Rec.* VII.38.3 that the chastity of nonbelievers can accrue temporal benefit. In *Rec.* VII.38.5, Matthidia's good fortune confirms what Peter has claimed, and so when this section is rendered faithfully in vv. 6961–68, it loses some of its effect as an example.

order to remain chaste—and she acted rightly—when she so hated immorality that she abandoned her country for this reason, wherefore God looked upon her in such a way that she was rediscovered by her sons and recognised her sons, whom she believed that she had lost for ever. Mother and sons are together and experience great joy together; after this they will receive the life in which their joy will never come to an end.

St Peter detained them with his speech until evening fell, and when it was time to retire, everybody went to rest. (6961–7006)

Morning came, and presently St Peter and those who were with him rose. He took with him only Niceta, Aquila, and Clement; he took these three brothers with him and summoned them to the sea. They washed in the sea in order to be more refreshed[1] by this; they then moved to one side into a place which was secluded. They said their prayers there, choosing the secluded place for this purpose.

A poor and quite old man had stepped to one side; he was very poorly attired, and it was quite clear that he was a labourer. He stood secretly and watched their conduct; he clearly saw that they were praying and that they were intent in this. He did not wish to accost them whilst they were at prayer. He watched their gathering carefully and awaited their arrival. When he saw them come, he headed towards them; he first greeted them, and then he said to them: (7007–32)

"If it does not vex you that I have come to you here, and if you do not consider it an offence or deem me boorish, I should gladly speak with you, if I did not think that I might offend you so much that I should be accused of importunity by you. I would say what I think to you as people whom I see to be deceived: I felt great pity for you, as for people whom I see to be duped; you have what seems to be truth, but you are without any doubt wrong. Therefore I shall, if it pleases you, tell you what I think about that which is nothing. I shall tell you what I understand, and then I shall listen to you in case you are able to tell me anything whereby I might be improved. If you are prepared to bear it patiently, and if it pleases you to hear what I think, with just a few words you will, if it is not yet in your possession, know what is right and just; or if you are disturbed by the fact that I have detained you, tell me so, and I shall leave and carry out my tasks elsewhere."

St Peter replied: "It is agreeable to us that you should say what pleases you; say everything which pleases you, and we shall listen to you carefully: be it falsehood or truth, tell us whatever you wish! For you are to be highly esteemed for wishing to teach us and for being anxious for us to be improved by you, and for wishing us to be educated in what is right by saying what you think, just as a father teaches his sons in order to improve them." (7033–74)

---

[1] 7014 **refreshed** *legier*: The precise sense of *legier* here is not certain.

The old man replied: "I saw you washing in the sea; you moved to one side and placed yourselves in a secluded spot. I secretly stayed, and watched carefully to see out of what necessity you remained there, and I noticed that you were praying. I felt very great pity for you when I saw you in such great error. I waited until you had finished, and then came over to you in order to explain to you that you err in worshipping in this way, and so that you might be set straight lest you continue toiling in vain, for there is no way that any God exists or that He has created any of the world. No good comes from serving God, as is the case for one who does not exist; there is no providence in the world, but rather all things which exist in the world are governed by chance, for there is nobody who takes care of them; and each person will without question have to suffer the genesis[1] which has befallen him, for he will not be able to avoid it. Genesis and chance make and unmake everything. I tell you this for I know it well, as I have experienced it for myself, for I am well versed in that discipline called mathesis;[2] I am more familiar with it than any other man and so know a great deal about it. Therefore refrain from your praying since you cannot experience any benefit from it, for whether you pray or refrain from it, you will never experience anything except what was destined for you from the hour that you were born." (7075–116)

Clement looked at the man very carefully, for his appearance seemed very familiar to him, and it very much seemed to him that he must have seen him elsewhere. Of this a cleric highly steeped in learning once said:

"When a person is born to somebody else, even though there may subsequently be separation, and they may be kept apart without seeing each other for a long time, nonetheless the nature of their family bond, which does not forget the former acquaintanceship, comes to the fore."[3]

Clement asked the old man who he was and from where he came, but no matter how much he tried to inquire, the old man would not say anything about it. He nonetheless said this much in response: "In what way is your request relevant to what we discussed before? Let us discuss that first of all! Thereafter we can, if necessary, speak of our families, and we can state our names and countries as friends do." (7117–42)

He was extremely eloquent and most commendably patient; he spoke very reasonably and behaved very wisely, so much so that all those who spoke with him esteemed him very highly indeed.

---

[1] 7099 **genesis** *destinee*: The first of many instances in which *destinee* renders from *Rec.* the term *genesis*, a concept central to Faustinianus's belief that a person's fate is determined by the stars under which s/he is born.

[2] 7108 **mathesis** *mathesis*: A mode of philosophical enquiry involving mathematics, music, geometry, and astrology.

[3] 7121–30 **Of this a cleric. . .fore** *De ceo dist. . .cunuissance*: These lines replace the metaphor of the igniting spark found in *Rec.* VIII.2.4. The source of the wisdom in *Clem.* is unclear.

St Peter walked calmly ahead and spoke as he walked. He looked carefully here and there until he spotted a quite beautiful location by the sea where people tended to come to shore. He went towards that spot because it was very secluded. Once he reached it, he sat down there, and asked the others to sit. He did not scorn the old man, whom he saw to be so poor; he did not consider him ignoble because he was dressed like a pauper. Once they were seated there, St Peter addressed him: (7143–64)

"You appear to be very learned, and appear to be very noble of heart since you were prepared to come to us in this way to reveal your thoughts. You have said what you think; now hear what we think, and if you wish, we shall tell you what we believe to be right. Once we have presented what we think, even if it does not please you, do not be any more angry with us than we are with you: accept from us exactly the same intention as you have towards us."

As they sat and talked, a very large crowd gathered there.

The old man said: "Perhaps these people crowding around us in such numbers will disturb us."

St Peter replied that they would not: "Let us pay no heed to these people around us unless it be on your account, for we fear that when we debate with you, if we can offer you evidence which is not contrary to reason and which you cannot deny, you may be ashamed by it and may not be prepared to acknowledge the truth in front of the crowd."

To this the old man replied: "I am not so senile or hardened in stupidity that I should deny you in any way. Once I grasp the truth of a thing that I hear from you, I shall never deliberately refute anything on account of the crowd." (7165–202)

Once he had said this, St Peter then spoke and began like this:

"What I think," he said, "is thus. Those who have learnt to speak truly and by telling the truth enlighten men's minds—those who do so clearly resemble the rays of the sun, which are bright, and which no man can extinguish for as far as their brightness can reach; and they are not so bright for their own sake, but rather in order to give enlightenment to others. Of those who go preaching the truth in this manner to the people who are in error, a wise man once said: 'You are the light of the world. It is impossible for a city built on a mountain to be hidden. Nobody who lights his candle hides its brightness under a bushel or hides it elsewhere once he has lit it, but rather he who lights it places it on a candlestick from which it can spread brightness through the house and give light to everybody.'"[1] (7203–28)

The old man said: "Whoever said these words expressed them very well! But let one of us speak first and allow us to hear more, and let us direct our discussion towards a definite aim. Let us not go back and forth, but rather let us keep

---

[1] 7218–28 **You are the light. . .everybody** *Vus estes. . .aver*: Cf. Mt 5:14–15.

to one subject in order to attain truth regarding the thing about which there has been doubt. For when it comes to disputation, it is not satisfactory that one man should present what he feels unless the other does likewise, for the kind of disputation in which one man proposes objections and the other fails to do so is of little value unless another aim is agreed whereby the truth might be investigated. In order that our disputation might be in accordance with order and reason, may one man say what he thinks first, and the other what he thinks thereafter, so that one might make the other understand the proposition that he wishes to defend. In this way they will be able to have material with which they might better question each other; and if it pleases you, I shall tell you first what I believe.

I say that there is no providence in the world, but rather everything is subject to instability and chance, as in a world for which nobody is responsible, for I see many things in the world which are completely contrary to justice; much of what one sees is contrary to what is just and right. I therefore say with confidence that genesis encompasses everything, and that nothing will exist without proceeding entirely according to genesis." (7229–68)

St Peter wished to respond at this point, but Niceta stepped forward and asked to be allowed, if it pleased him, to respond to the old man; St Peter should give him permission to speak, even though he was a young man, and the other man was advanced in years, and should not take it amiss if he wished to speak to him, for he would behave as well as a son ought to behave towards his father, without saying or doing anything unseemly.

The old man said: "Dear son, I gladly grant that you should say what you see fit; may both you and your companions freely present your arguments to us! And likewise as regards the others who are hastening here I gladly grant that each person who knows anything should say what he thinks; I shall listen carefully to it, for when many inquire into a thing about which they have doubts, the resulting instruction is better when it comes from many rather than from few people, for the truth will be found more quickly by a crowd than it will be when there are few people: a group of many has greater wit than one of few." (7269–96)

Once Niceta had permission to speak to the old man, before he spoke of anything else and started his speech, he first began to justify himself lest it be viewed askance that he deprived St Peter of the argument that he was about to make:

"Dear father," he said, "do not think it an act of foolhardiness that I have intervened in this way and not waited until my lord Peter said what he knew that it was appropriate to say: I do it for no other reason but through love and in order to preserve his honour. He is a man filled with God and he knows everything which might be expected of a Greek; the Holy Spirit has filled him, whereby all knowledge is in him; he knows everything and lacks nothing, for God has placed all good in him. It is not fitting for him to speak of anything other than celestial matters, and therefore I wish to speak to you in accordance with the manner of speech of the Greeks. Once we have debated to the point that we are unable to proceed any further and are obliged to halt, it will then be for him to speak as one who through God knows all knowledge and clearly sees everything pertaining to truth. Through him we shall attain the truth, and not only we, but rather all those here present, once they have heard him speak, will know the truth through him. He is to be judge over us, and when one of us is defeated, we shall entrust our entire business to him and shall abide by his opinion." (7297–338)

Once Niceta had said this about St Peter in front of everybody, the people who had hastened there discussed it excitedly amongst themselves. Each man turned to the next and each asked the next whether this St Peter was the one of whom they had so often heard that he was so righteous and esteemed and had been a disciple of Him who had been in Judaea and performed great miracles there. They then turned to St Peter in order to listen to what he would say; they treated him with the same honour as do good servants their lord.

St Peter clearly perceived this and asked for attention, and then said to everybody: "Let us listen carefully and devote all our attention to judging carefully in accordance with what is just which of these two is more right. Listen carefully to what they say, and when they have debated for some time, we shall then do what is appropriate for us and say what is necessary."

The people were overjoyed when they had heard this from St Peter. Niceta presently began and spoke to the old man in this way: (7339–68)

"Dear father," he said, "you have told us the opinion that you hold. You have stated before everybody that nothing in the world exists through God; there is no providence in the world, but rather all things on earth and everything that one may say or do are subject to genesis. I could answer this quickly, but because it is right to respect the order and manner which pertain to our topic, we shall tell you our opinion in order to show you what we believe; we shall tell you exactly what we think, as you asked of us.

I say that the world exists through God, who ordains everything as it pleases Him. The whole world is sustained by God, who has ordained everything well; through providence all things are governed which require it. Everything which exists in the world, God created, and as God wishes, so does everything proceed. The world cannot last for ever; when God wishes, it must end. After its end there will then appear the world which will never end and which has been created in order to receive all those who are prepared to serve God. None will enter that world except for those who have fully deserved it, for there is one most just God—there is no need to have any more—and He will render everything to each person in accordance with what he has done.[1] You have heard our opinion; now you will say what pleases you. It is now up to you to prove that my opinion

---

[1] 7391–404 **Everything which exists. . .has done** *Quanque est. . .feit avrat*: There are additional comments on the last judgement relative to *Rec.* VIII.6.7.

cannot be valid, or to demonstrate the legitimacy of your opinion, and in accordance with what you say, you will soon receive my response; or if it pleases you that I should say more, there will be no question of me hesitating." (7369–414)

"Dear son," the old man then said, "we have stepped to one side, and so the matter of who is to speak first need not be of great concern. We should not be bothered about who speaks first, or who speaks thereafter, since our disputation is being conducted in purely amicable fashion. But may you nonetheless speak first, and I shall listen to this very gladly, and I should be glad to hear from you everything that I should say to you, so that by saying your opinion and by revealing mine thereafter, by first presenting the arguments and then by indicating the deficiencies, you might after the difference of opinion attain the truth."

Niceta replied: "If you wish, I shall gladly tell you the points of your argument. I shall gladly state your contentions and respond to them." (7415–36)

The old man said: "First reveal how it is that you know the thing of which I have not yet spoken, and I shall then better believe that you can state the elements of my argument, even though you have not yet heard them."

Niceta said: "The proposition that you have professed is well known, for those who have turned their minds to studying your doctrine are quite aware of the conclusion which results from the proposition. I spent much time with philosophers, and as a result I know in some detail the opinions which follow the definitions. Since you have revealed which proposition you hold, I am well aware of its conclusion, for I have studied this proposition. My brother Aquila and I devoted a good deal of effort in the past to carefully listening to, studying, and understanding philosophers. Our other brother who is here has heard a great deal about their writings, and has heard many a lesson about Aristotle and Plato.[1] May you therefore be fully forewarned of the kind of people to whom you have come, for those who will hear you speak are well versed in these writings!"

The old man said: "I fully understand what you have reasonably said. You have clearly demonstrated through reason that through my proposition you may know the conclusion of what pertains to my argument. But I am one step ahead of you in that I said somewhat more, for I said that nothing, be it good or bad, can exist without genesis, and so said more than your master."[2] (7437–80)

Clement then said: "Hear, dear father, whether my brother Niceta can manage to prove to you that God through His providence sustains the world and all

---

[1] 7463 **Aristotle and Plato** *Aristotle e Platun*: Further allusions to Epicurus and Pyrrho in *Rec.* VIII.7.5–6 are omitted.

[2] 7480 **your master** *vostre meistre*: The allusion to Christ is added relative to *Rec.* VIII.7.8, while mention of Epicurus is suppressed.

things which are encompassed in this world. After this I shall be able to talk to you about genesis, for I know about it."

Once Clement had spoken in this way, Aquila said: "What is the purpose of calling the old man 'father'? We must not call him 'father,' for we have specifically received the instruction not to call anybody 'father' except for God above." He then turned in the other direction and spoke to the old man: "Dear father," he said, "do not take it amiss that I spoke thus and chastised my brother for calling you 'father,' for we have been instructed not to call any man by this name."[1] (7481–504)

The whole crowd laughed a great deal when Aquila said this, and the old man and St Peter both began to laugh a great deal.

Aquila then asked urgently what had caused their laughter.

Clement replied: "We are laughing because you gave us cause to do so, for you criticise others for something of which you yourself are guilty: you called the old man 'father,' for which you first criticised me!"

Aquila was deeply ashamed when he was unable to justify himself, and then he said: "Truth to tell, I do not know whether I called him 'father.'"

Whilst this was taking place, St Peter, who had seen it all, had some suspicions regarding the scene that he saw there, as he subsequently revealed to the companions whom he had with him. He then looked at Niceta and instructed him to continue speaking, lest he tarry in such a way that his purpose should be further delayed.

Niceta began to speak once St Peter had so instructed him. (7505–32)

I cannot write down all the arguments that he put forward. He presented a good deal of what each philosopher said: what their opinions were, and what the proposition of each one was. He carefully explained what Pythagoras said, and what Anaxagoras had said; what Diodorus said, and what Anaximander said; what Asclepiades said, and Zenon, and Empedocles. He spoke about Epicurus and Plato, about Thales and Cameleun;[2] about what Democritus, Diogenes, and Callistratus said; what Parmenides had said, and what Aristotle said. He presented these philosophers, and what each one had to say about what the origins of the world and the four elements were. He clearly proved through reason that there is no God but the one who created the whole world from nothing and governs and sustains everything, and who through His providence maintains every substance in a good condition. For if there were no providence, there would be no reason for anybody ever to do any good; there would be no reason for anybody to toil in order to seek and maintain righteousness if there were no God who rewarded everything in accordance with the good that each person did. (7533–66)

---

[1] 7502–4 **for we have been. . .name** *kar cumandé. . .nun*: Cf. Mt 23:9.

[2] 7546 **Cameleun** *Cameleun*: A confused rendering of the name of Alcmaeon of Croton, influenced by the *Calemeon* found only in the Θ reading for *Rec.* VIII.15.1.

He proposed many arguments and offered many examples involving various creatures and the path that their nature follows, the sky and the firmament, the sun which shines so brightly, the moon and the stars, the planets and the wonders which there are in astronomy, about which I do not know what I should tell you. He clearly showed that men and beasts which are alive exist through God. He offered examples involving trees and plants from which fruit comes, and others which have nothing; the seasons which change so frequently that one hour never waits for the next; how winter passes, and how summer follows it, and when winter subsequently returns, how summer lasts no more. He clearly stated that not one of all the things on the land and in the sea could exist if God, who ordains everything as He is able, had not first of all created it. He presented many different methods of argument in order to set the old man on the right path; he himself asked so many questions and himself provided so many solutions that the old man had no need to ask a single thing. He spent so long saying this that the day advanced a long way, for I have summarised everything briefly and have provided here the mere essence of the whole disputation. And once he had endeavoured to say as much as was certainly bound to suffice, the conclusion was thus:[1] (7567–604)

"It is God," he said, "who created and ordains everything which exists in the world, but He Himself was not created by anything which was or which is: He always was and always will be, and His condition will never change. Those who place before God the nature that God has bestowed upon His creatures, and have relegated God so far that they dare to say that there is no other God but nature which does or is responsible for anything, err most grievously; they are in need of guidance, for it is terrible when they do not grasp their folly and their error. They are being quite outrageous when they say that nature has no reason in it, and then through great foolishness say that nature itself creates rational creatures. It is utterly preposterous when a man persists in the erroneous belief that reason can come from something in which one is certain that there is none. And if it is true that it is through reason—which is God Himself by another name—that all things are well created and maintained and preserved, I do not know for what purpose one should change the name of God and say anything other than the truth about what has always been when one knows and is sure that everything comes from the Creator.

Dear father," he said, "this is what I had to say to you. You will now respond, and I shall hear whether I have omitted any aspect of anything that I should have told you."

This is the essence of what he said. Presently the old man replied: (7605–46)

---

[1] 7533–604 **I cannot. . .was thus** *Ne puis pas. . .suffire*: These lines summarise a few elements of *Rec.* VIII.9–34.5, with the list of philosophers from *Rec.* VIII.15 conspicuously reproduced.

"Dear son, you have spoken very well, for you have omitted nothing nor failed to say most skilfully everything pertaining to providence; no man could, I believe, speak better about it than you have done. But the day has greatly advanced whilst we have been talking here; it is therefore necessary to take a break, and if it pleases you, I shall postpone until tomorrow. I want you to tell me more then, and if you can do as I wish, I shall be greatly in your debt and shall be extremely grateful to you for this."

Once the old man had said this, Peter stood up and sat there no longer. (7647–62)

The most powerful man in the city had been there amongst the others; he was the chief of Laodicea and without doubt had a noble heart. What he did came from a noble heart, for he implored St Peter and likewise his disciples to allow him, without incurring their displeasure, to change the old man's clothes and give better ones to him, for his clothing was utterly filthy and tattered.

St Peter gladly received the offer that the powerful man made; those who were with him likewise very warmly welcomed him, and for his good intention, which came to him from great honesty, they held him in high esteem, and said that they would gladly permit this, for, they said: "We are not so full of foolishness as not to wish for that man whom we esteem so highly that we speak carefully to him in order to bring him to salvation, even though he is not well dressed, to have what is necessary for his body; and we shall gladly give to him of such possessions as we have, and firmly believe that he will welcome this and will behave with us like a father with his sons. We shall have him lodge with us, and as far as concerns what else we have, we want him to share with us everything that God gives to us." (7663–98)

The powerful man who was there and had made the request, when he heard them say this, wanted either by force or by entreaty to drag the old man from there and take him home with him. St Peter likewise implored the old man to come with him, and the brothers who were there very much wanted to have him with them; they wanted to take him with them, and the powerful man wanted to have him. Presently the whole crowd cried out: "Let it be as the old man wishes!"

The old man began to speak as soon as he could make himself heard, and he said in front of everybody: "Today I shall stay with nobody. Today I shall not partake of anything, for I shall upset one person on account of the other; I do not wish to make some people happy, as a result of which the others might be sad. I have now decided to act in this way, and afterwards shall do just as I see fit." (7699–722)

When St Peter saw for certain that the old man had refused and would not under any circumstances acquiesce to accompanying any of them, he turned to the rich man and spoke to him in this manner:

"It is an act of goodwill that it pleased you to come to us to listen to us speaking here, and we thank you for it; and on account of the love that you show to us you should not leave unhappy. We certainly ought to reward the honour that you do to us to the best of our power: show your house to us, and prepare it for tomorrow so that we might gather there and debate with this old man, and we gladly permit all those who wish to hear us to come there."

The rich man was very gladdened that St Peter said this to him, and the crowd there present agreed to go there. The whole crowd presently departed, and the powerful man showed his house. The old man left, but Clement did not forget him, for he summoned one of his servants and ordered him to follow the old man with utmost stealth and to ascertain with great discretion where he went to stay, and to inform Clement of this quickly. St Peter returned to his lodging, with him being the fourth man beside the three brothers; they told their companions how they had debated with the old man. They told them all about one thing and another, and then sat down to eat. Then when night began to fall, they all retired. (7723–64)

The next day St Peter rose early in the morning and woke his followers. He roused all his companions, and then they set off to pray at the place where they had been in seclusion the day before. When they had finished their prayers, they headed toward the house to which St Peter had decided that he wanted to go on that day. On the way, St Peter said: "Listen to me, servants of Jesus Christ! It is good for each of us to do as God gives him grace to do. May each man take pains to advise those who need advice; may each man strive so that we might convert to our religion all those who come to hear us so that they might all profit from having come to us. I tell you all together, in accordance with the wisdom that God gives us, that you must not be vexed by speaking the good that you know so that the ignorant might be improved by your teaching. Add your eloquence in order better to explain the teaching that you have heard from me, but do not include anything of your own invention; beware of proposing anything that I have not advocated. Say as much as I have said to you, and say nothing beyond this, even though it might seem to you that it is true, for misfortune could quickly result from it. May none of you propose anything except what the True Prophet taught to me, and I to you! Keep to this without saying anything else, even if it might appear that there is something which is not completely comprehensible, for it has often happened to some who are ill prepared that by proposing from their own invention something for which they have no master or advocate, they turn completely from the truth by speaking their own thoughts. By thinking of something other than what they have learnt, when it comes to speaking, they then speak worse, for they have no authority other than of their own invention." (7765–818)

Those who were with St Peter and who heard him say this gladly assented and said that they would do nothing beyond what they had learnt from him; nothing would ever be added by them.

St Peter said in turn: "May each of you learn the practice of disputation. With me listening practise until you can speak without danger; may one man state his argument, and then the other, until you have all spoken in accordance with the wisdom that you have. Niceta spoke yesterday in accordance with what was necessary; Aquila will speak there today, and we shall entrust our business to him. Clement will speak after this once Aquila has spoken, and if there is any need afterwards for anything more to be discussed, I shall say something as I deem appropriate." (7819–42)

St Peter had now proceeded so far and spoken so much about this that he had reached the house, and he was joyfully received there, for the master of the house welcomed him very kindly and heartily, and he likewise welcomed his companions with great honour. He led them all forth into a fine and suitable spot; it was made in the form of a theatre and was of fine craftsmanship. There they found a large crowd of people who had hastened there; many of those there present had been there long before daybreak. They had awaited St Peter there; amidst the others was the old man, who had arrived there a while before St Peter and stood completely quietly amidst the crowd. St Peter's followers, who were well trained, positioned themselves around him; they all entered with St Peter in the middle, doing so out of respect for him. They stared in all directions to see whether the old man had come. St Peter saw him first of all, hiding amongst the crowd; he had clearly recognised him amongst all the others as soon as he had seen him. He called to him with the others listening and told him to come forward: (7843–74)

"Come forward!" St Peter said. "Why are you standing so far back? Why are you hiding like this and concealing yourself for shame? You should not stand back, for your soul is brighter than are those of many people who think very highly of themselves. Come forward, and you will tell us whatever your heart inspires you to say!"

Once he had said this, the old man no longer hesitated to stand up; the crowd made space for him so that he could take up his position. As soon as he had come forward, he immediately said:

"I am quite sure of the sense and the order, but I have not remembered all the words of everything that the young man and I discussed together yesterday. But it is fitting, I think, that everything which was said between us yesterday should be briefly repeated today so that if I have forgotten anything, I might be reminded of it by the man here present who spoke yesterday. There are furthermore many people here who were not present then and did not hear the two of us speak, and so it is quite right to repeat it.

The essence and sense of what we discussed at length yesterday is that one should believe without any doubt that everything that one sees in which there is a certain proportion and art and form and appearance results entirely from great power and was created through great intelligence. (7875–912)

And if everything which exists originates from reason, and all things are in their condition through the power of a right-thinking mind, it must surely follow that the whole world, with everything which belongs to it, is maintained by providence, even if we have not grasped this and even if we think that there is no reason in many things that one sees.

And if mind and reason have joined together as one so effectively that through this union everything is created, it surely follows that it is God who creates all things through reason.

And if every creature follows its nature through God, He who ordains and provides everything must be just.

And if He is just, it follows from this that He must judge, for it befits His reason that He must have discretion in order to pronounce the right judgement on everything which is done well or badly, and He will judge all men in accordance with what each one does. There will then be a division so that the good and the wicked do not receive the same, for those who are good and the wicked should not be equals.

This was the essence, to my mind, of our whole discussion. (7905–46)

But proof of this is required in order to convince me. If someone can prove to me and by reason cause me to believe and know for certain that mind and reason create everything that there is on earth and in the sky, and that this reason is nothing other than God alone, who has encompassed all things in His power, from there it surely follows that the one who creates everything ordains everything through justice and reason; providence must surely come from the one from whom creation comes.

But if nature is blind to the extent that it is completely without reason and that every creature comes from nothing but chance, then I can say quite confidently that there is no judgement, but rather everything, whether good or bad, will be completely equal, since for a good deed no reward will be given, and for a bad deed nothing will be lost, nor will there be any judge who understands anything or who awards anything for good or evil. This is the crux of everything that there is, and everything depends on this, and so do not take it amiss if I endeavour to talk with you and if I desire that this be discussed so thoroughly for me that I might acquire understanding of it through clear explanation. The door is closed to me since I have such doubt about this thing; I fervently wish for this door to be opened for me. Through this doubt I am prevented from tackling a different topic; little will be achieved by discussing anything else unless I have first heard about these points. May one of you who is qualified to respond to this offer a response! I am not ashamed of learning if I am made to hear reason; I shall gladly listen to anybody who tells me the truth, and I shall gladly assent to reason. I am in no way persuaded by anything which was discussed yesterday, and I have in particular not yet been convinced that the world remains in its condition through any reason which resides in a mind, for I see many things in the world which are without doubt awry. It is therefore quite clear that genesis is prevalent throughout the world; everything which can exist must exist through genesis. I shall prove this by my own case if I have no other argument." (7947–8008)

Once the old man had said so much that it was necessary to respond to him, all were silent save for Aquila. He replied and spoke thus:

"Since we have your permission to say what we wish, and your word that you are prepared to listen to what you hear us say, I have been appointed by my brother to respond today, for Niceta, who spoke yesterday, has today permitted me to speak with you."

The old man said: "Dear son, speak, and say whatever you wish!"

"Remember," Aquila said, "how my brother Niceta presented you with plentiful arguments when he spoke with you yesterday, as gently as a son with his father, and explained exactly why things which never appear to be of benefit were created."[1]

The old man said: "I should like you to set me right on this matter. I should like to understand why this supreme mind, of which you say that it creates everything with both great reason and justice, created in this world such things from which no good or profit ever comes, such as lizards, mice, fleas, and plenty of other pointless little creatures, in which there is no beauty and which are completely without goodness. Explain the reason why that which is neither good nor fine is created!" (8009–44)

Aquila fully understood the question, and he replied:

"If we can persuade you to believe us that everything that you have mentioned here was created by reason, I could then tell you and set you right regarding why those things which place you in such doubt were created, and I would prove to you by reason that they are not created other than justly."

"I cannot believe," the old man said, "nor rightly understand that anything is created by reason or by a mind which has intelligence on account of many things which exist in the world and proceed contrary to justice and order."

Aquila did not hesitate, for he replied immediately:

"If you," he said, "do not believe that there is anything in this world that God has created and ordained and maintained through reason, and cannot believe this because you see many contrary examples in which there is no order or reason or anything which causes anything but ill, why will you not believe that everything which proceeds in accordance with reason is through God, and that nature, which has no reason, will never produce any rational work? (8045–76)

I am quite certain, for truth to tell we cannot rightly deny that many things go very much askew and awry, but not everything proceeds in the same fashion, neither everything well, nor everything badly.

---

[1] 8023–30 **Remember. . .created** *Menbre vus. . .ne funt*: These lines jump from *Rec.* VIII.41.1 to VIII.43.5, omitting a complicated discussion.

Regarding the things which go well, believe that they have come from reason, and that God has so ordained them that they are maintained by Him.

As for everything which goes awry, do not believe that God ordains any of it, but rather that this is by chance in accordance with the weakness of nature. But I have been astonished by people who have not noticed that things which have sense can change their intention, and anybody, whether foolish or wise, changes his mind accordingly. In accordance with the sense that each man has, he will accordingly act well or badly; where there is no sense, there is neither bad nor good, as is the case with something which understands nothing, for it comes entirely from reason that a thing follows the right order. But when the right order goes so far from its course that the thing goes awry, it will then never proceed in accordance with reason as long as the order remains disturbed." (8077–106)

The old man replied: "I wish this thing to be better explained to me."

Aquila said: "Without delay I shall offer the proof through an example. We see two things in the sky above which are both bright and beautiful: these are the sun and the moon, and both provide great brightness. And there are many stars which keep their proper course; through these one knows the season and the hour, and one knows the temperature of the seasons. As long as these remain in their proper course, men on earth benefit from them, but when it pleases God that men should be punished for their sins, everything changes and becomes entirely the opposite, for the sun withdraws its rays, or it burns most excessively, or it is so covered by cloud that it is completely obscured from view; and the moon does likewise, for it provides no brightness, and the stars which used to be so visible are covered. Then the winds change, and many storms arise; wind and rain and hail destroy and devastate everything, and pestilence completely obliterates the crops and fruits of the earth. A terribly damaging year results when everything on the earth perishes; the year is immensely harsh when such an event occurs. Every time that such an instance of pestilence comes upon the earth, the proper order is disrupted at the same time as it is kept, for there is no man who is not well aware of what great benefit the sun brings to all the things in the world, for everything needs the sun. At all times its course is ordained, for God alone has so assigned it, and the moon likewise always remains on its proper course. The stars which always remain on their proper course act likewise: even though they are not always seen, they have remained on their proper course. (8107–58)

But nonetheless, even though it is the case that there is nothing but what I have said, when God as punishment casts his scourge upon the people so that the sun becomes burning hot or withdraws its light, or the moon, which used to be bright and pure, becomes dark, or the stars, which were so bright and beautiful, do not appear in the sky, as a result of which the winds change so much that great damage arises from them, and the world falls into danger through pestilence which destroys everything—when such a thing is seen in the sky and such a scourge comes upon the earth, this does not result from chance, but rather God is punishing the people in this way. Nothing of the proper order changes, but rather God withdraws from people the goodness and benefits that they were accustomed to having as long as they did His bidding. He wishes to chastise them in this way so that they do not become attached to sin; nevertheless when such an event befalls the earth on account of sin, on the one hand order is kept, and on the other it is disrupted. The proper order is well maintained as long as the proper course is not changed, and it at the same time appears disrupted when the benefit is lost on account of sin. From the same place that the benefit came, the loss comes, and people suffer this by their own just desserts." (8159–92)

Aquila said a good deal more there, for he spoke with great freedom. He said plenty about good and evil, and from where their origin stems. Of good he said that it comes from God, who creates all good and nothing evil, but rather He tolerates it and waits, for He very much wishes for improvement. He presented many examples by which he convincingly proved that anything which has reason will never be created by that which does not have reason. From good, nothing will come but good, and a rational thing comes from reason; from evil, good rarely tends to come, and so it should be avoided.

The old man was very resolute and for his part stood very firm. He asked a great deal and enquired a great deal, and strove greatly to propose objections, and Aquila did not hesitate to respond when he saw his opportunity. About the questions and answers and their proofs and arguments I should be quite inclined to say more, but I do not dare, for I am avoiding to the best of my ability saying so much that it might become tedious.[1] (8193–220)

When they had spoken to each other until they presently had to pause, the old man said: "Do not, dear son, take it amiss that I say this to you: even though you are very worthy and skilled in speaking, I cannot nonetheless force my mind to believe anything other than that everything proceeds through genesis, and that nothing exists without this, for I know full well that everything has befallen me as was destined for me. I shall therefore never be made to believe that it lies in our power to do good or evil, for we cannot intend or do anything unless genesis proposes it. And since it is the case that all our deeds, be they fair or foul, do not lie within our power, but rather proceed in accordance with genesis, under no circumstances will the hope be conceived that judgement will ever come to bestow a good or bad reward; nobody should expect it under any circumstances. But because I have clearly seen that you are well educated and are very learned in the discipline that we are discussing, I shall, if you wish, say briefly what I know of this discipline." (8221–52)

Aquila replied to the old man: "If you wish to speak about this discipline, my brother Clement, who has learnt more about it than I, will respond to you. I

---

[1] 8119–220 **As long as. . .tedious** *Tant cume. . .ennui*: As the final two paragraphs of this section indicate, *Rec.* VIII.45.3–56 has been omitted, with a few elements of it included in Aquila's speech and the concluding summary.

can find an argument via many other approaches through which I can prove to you that we have it entirely in our power to do whatever we wish, for I shall not engage with a topic about which I have learnt nothing."

Once Aquila had acknowledged that he not well versed in that discipline, Clement, who knew a good deal about that discipline, immediately replied to the old man:

"Dear father," he said, "you will come tomorrow and tell us what you wish, and in accordance with what we hear we shall then respond to you, for I think that you welcome the fact that you are speaking to such people as are not ignorant of the discipline in which you are well versed."

The old man was very pleased by what Clement had said to him. They agreed to meet there again in the morning in order to debate and ascertain whether it was possible for anything to exist through genesis, or whether one has it in one's power to act according to one's will.

Once they had agreed to come to that place the next morning, St Peter stood up and spoke and pronounced in this fashion: (8253–86)

"I am absolutely and utterly astonished that people wish to wrestle with a simple thing as vigorously as if it were very difficult, and spend so much time splitting hairs and inventing propositions that through extensive discussion they complicate what in itself is plain and simple — and those doing this are precisely the people who appear to be wise! For they think of God as nothing other than a mortal man, and they think that they can investigate His intention as if it belonged to a man who is their peer. And at the same time they think even less of God, for there is no man born on earth who can investigate the intention of other people as long as the one from whom the intention originates keeps it hidden to himself, for nobody can know the thoughts of other people without the help of the one who thinks them. Likewise nobody can manage to learn any discipline in which he can be proficient and confident unless he has learnt it from a master. And since it is the case that one cannot know any intention which originates from a man unless the one from whose mind the thought originates has first revealed it, the intention and will of God will be understood much later, for no man has ever been born who has seen God in this world. Therefore no man can know what God has in His thoughts unless God sends the True Prophet, who reveals His desire and says as much about His intention as pleases God, and nothing more. When people presume through the nature that God has placed into any creature to judge God and His power without having had a master for this, this kind of transgressive and outrageous behaviour can be seen as quite laughable. One can laugh wholeheartedly at those who presume through their intellect to find what can never be, and claim to be so expert in this that they dare to pass their judgement on everything that God has created in accordance with such reason as He knows — of which they are completely ignorant — and say of His won-

ders: 'This is good, and this is not beneficial; this is small, and this is greater,' and
do not know the slightest thing about it. It is quite outrageous when people who
have no justification whatsoever dare in this way to judge God, who is true and
just! God knows everything that there is, and they know nothing, and so their
judgement is worth less.[1] (8287–350)

The philosophers spend a great deal of time thinking and inventing words;
they invent so many new words that they should be considered fools! Their inven-
tions cannot be rightly understood, so obscure are they; they have gone so far in
splitting hairs that they have turned completely from the truth. The knowledge
which originates from and ends with God is simple and brief: there is no difficulty in learning it, for it is very easy to understand, but nonetheless it is necessary to have guidance from the True Prophet, for those who learn without Him
will never be fully proficient in it. The philosophers with their intellect have
completely wasted their time: they have not had a guide and so have lapsed into
error; they have left the right path, as a result of which their labour is completely
wasted.[2] But the ones who are following the right path are those who started in
simple fashion; they do not go astray, for the True Prophet is guiding them. Anybody who wishes to have this guide can easily find Him; in whichever land one
might be, if one has turned to Him wholeheartedly, one can readily find Him,
for He will be present for all who call Him when in need, be they near or be they
far away. But those who are so arrogant that they have started the path without
a guide to lead them the right way—everything that they do achieves little, for
God, who does not deign to come to them, appears to sleep, since they are so deluded that they do not seek His guidance." (8351–92)

More words were said there than can be written here. St Peter delivered a
long speech, speaking about the True Prophet.[3] Once he had finished his speech,
the whole crowd departed; St Peter asked the old man to come and lodge with
him, but he did not wish to do so, and instead left, saying that he would return
the next morning. St Peter followed his usual custom when he returned to his
lodging, for he and his followers ate, and then, when it was time, they all went
to bed.

St Peter rose early in the morning as he was accustomed to doing; he very
soon headed off in the company of his followers until they reached the place

---

[1] 8327–50 **this kind of transgressive. . .less** *Mult poet estre. . .jugement*: These lines
render *Rec.* VIII.58.6 rather loosely, and following them, *Rec.* VIII.59–60 is omitted, removing discussion of the True Prophet.

[2] 8372 **wasted** *perdu*: Following this line, *Rec.* VIII.61.3–13, with discussion of the
True Prophet, is omitted.

[3] 8393–96 **More words. . .Prophet** *Plus paroles. . .dist*: An allusion to the preceding
abridgement of roughly *Rec.* VIII.59–62.14.

where they had been and debated on the previous day. There they found many people who had arrived there considerably earlier, and the old man, who had arrived much earlier, was quite ready. As soon as St Peter saw him, he said to him in this fashion:

"Remember the agreement which was made before us yesterday. You should remember that Clement is to speak to you today, and you are to speak to him; this is how today was fixed yesterday. You are to prove that nothing can exist other than by genesis, or Clement is to prove to you that genesis achieves nothing and that good or evil—whichever pleases us—lies within our power." (8393–430)

The old man replied: "I remember the agreement clearly and gladly assent to it. I have likewise clearly recalled the content of your speech yesterday, for yesterday you stood up once we had reached our agreement. You then spoke about a wise man, whom you called the True Prophet. Nothing into which one inquires will, you said, ever be known without Him."

St Peter said in turn: "You have not yet fully grasped what I said yesterday, but I wish to remind you of it more clearly in order to give you greater certainty.

I spoke of the will which has always been in God and of the purpose that God fixed before He created any of this world; with what purpose and with what sense God created the world and appointed the seasons; of the reason that He has in Him through which He established the law and promised various rewards in accordance with what each person deserves, for those who wish to persist in goodness will receive a great reward from Him, and those who have chosen evil will receive what they have deserved: for evil He will cause them to have pain and suffering which will never end. No man should strive for any reason to discover this purpose for himself, for there is no man so worthy that he will not fail to find it by himself unless he receives guidance in this from the Prophet, who completely understands the purpose and will of God, and whom God sent to earth in order to reveal the truth of God and of His will. Nobody should toil away at this for any reason, for conjecture is of no use; anybody who presumes to ascertain by himself what pertains to God is completely wasting his effort, for God leaves him to his own devices. He fails in his speculation because God pays no heed to him, for unless the Prophet teaches him, his study achieves nothing. Nevertheless I do not say this about everything in the world, for one can study hard and through intelligence discover much pertaining to this life without the power of prophecy, for many arts and disciplines and professions are invented through the intelligence and intellect of people who turn their minds to it without the True Prophet intervening in their thoughts: a man's intellect can grasp a great deal, and one man can learn a great deal from another. (8431–94)

But since you have told us that you know so much about the stars and the course of the firmament, whereby you will prove to Clement that everything is begun and comes to an end through genesis, and since Clement has promised you that he will prove through reason that all things exist through God and proceed in accordance with His will, and that man has in his power to speak and do His will without experiencing any interference from any star or the firmament, and that genesis is not a thing through which either evil or good comes to pass, it will now be up to both of you to say what pleases you." (8495–512)

The old man presently replied: "There is no need for any objection to what I have heard from you, or to raise major questions regarding whether it can be true that one can through the Prophet of truth attain certainty about one's areas of doubt, and that we have entirely in our power everything that we wish to say or do. Your speech has affected me greatly since I heard the argument for the power of prophecy yesterday, for I cannot prevent myself from saying that I fully understand your proposition and without doubt fully assent to it, and I fully acknowledge that no man can be certain without a master. He will never be sure by himself unless he receives teaching from elsewhere, for the period and the length of a man's life is very short, and the breath through which one lives in this world is very slight. But even though I promised to tell Clement what I think regarding how all the things in the world are subject to genesis, or to hear from him how genesis achieves nothing, may Clement nevertheless be so kind as to state his proposition first, for if he begins first, I shall have material for my response from what I hear him say. For I fully admit that I have been quite bewildered since I heard you say so much about prophecy yesterday; as a result of this I do not know what to say, for I clearly see that conjecture will never produce anything certain. Conjecture and speculation create all the doubts which exist in the world, and so I am inclined to the belief that everything proceeds through providence." (8513–58)

Once the old man had admitted this, Clement, who knew a great deal about the relevant disciplines, immediately responded to him, but his response was long and vast. He chose his words very well, but I cannot say all that he said; he spoke very appropriately, but I must pass over it briefly lest people who hear it should grow bored and so stop listening. Nonetheless I must not fail to mention some of it; I must briefly include the essence of what he said to the old man. I shall record as much as might be fitting for the story:[1]

"God," Clement said, "created the world; when and how, God alone knows. The world has been created like a house which has two levels, and it is erected in storeys in order to accommodate two households, one below and the other above, since they are not of one fellowship and are separated from each other either by a vaulted ceiling or by planked flooring. In this very manner God created heaven and earth, with the earth below and heaven above, but they have a large space between them, for heaven and earth are separated by the firmament which is in

---

[1] 8559–74 **Once the old man. . .story** *Quant tant out cuneu. . .histoire*: An acknowledgement that most of *Rec.* IX.3–14 is about to be omitted.

the middle. The angels are in heaven above, where their joy never ends; men are placed on earth below, where they experience both good and evil. (8559–94)

But not all men on earth are equal or of one nature; the world contains and always has contained great diversity. Not all are kings, nor all lords, nor all holders of great fiefs; nor all rich with great wealth, nor all masters of great knowledge; nor all lay, nor all educated, nor all skilled in one profession; not all are grammarians, nor all dialecticians; not all are trained in the seven arts, nor all to be equally esteemed; not all know how to farm land, nor all how to fish in the sea; not all are smiths, nor all craftsmen, nor all accustomed to hard labour; nor all poor, nor all powerful, nor all wealthy with great possessions. There is no man on earth who knows everything nor who has all grace in him, but rather each person is proficient in the discipline to which he has devoted his attention. Nobody can be king unless he as a result has people subject to him; anybody who has no power of lordship cannot be a lord. Those who do not have subject to them any people who are at their command and who respect their rule are kings and lords of nothing. (8595–626)

The world is completely varied because all men are not equal; God has likewise ordained various professions amongst people so that they do not remain idle, but rather so that each person might earn his living by working and by practising an honest profession. For all the professions that people practise are invented out of necessity in order to support our existence through drink and food and clothing, without which a man cannot live, no matter how upstanding or free he might be. For if a man could live without working or having costs, never would so many professions have been invented, for people would not have paid so much attention to this. This is why people work for clothing and food; and when a man cannot continue without being obliged to work, it will then be clearly proved of what intent he is when God does not apply any compulsion to prevent him from favouring and choosing the thing which most pleases him. Since anybody who serves by compulsion and unwillingly completely loses His goodwill, and since one does not tend to esteem anybody who serves through obligation, God does not wish to compel, but rather provides plenty of time and space for one to decide and choose whatever one wishes to do and say. And when a man puts into practice what he has been intending, the deed, when it transpires, makes the intention completely clear, for anybody who breaks the law on account of hunger or thirst or cold and seeks his livelihood by being a robber and a thief, or a murderer or a perjurer or anything else which is outrageous, clearly proves that his mind is far distant from its proper condition when through his foolish desire he turns to wickedness. And anybody who turns his intention to good, and loves what is right and hates what is wrong, and has set his mind on justice and righteousness, and feeds himself through his honest work, and seeks garments with which to clothe himself, and practises his profession honestly so that he can earn what he needs — this man clearly demonstrates that his aim and intention have come from great intelligence, and God considers him to be His friend because he has chosen good. (8627–88)

The other man, who has chosen to do evil, is opposed to God: he has fixed his mind on evil, and so God neglects him. A prince full of treachery has a firm grip on this world; all those who deliberately do evil belong to his household. This prince is their leader, for they do what pleases him; this prince leads them into error and draws them away from their Creator. He beguiles and deceives them in everything that he says or does to them; he makes them believe that there is such power in the course of the stars that the whole world proceeds through their course and exists through nothing else, and that there is nothing in accordance with reason unless it is in accordance with genesis. This prince holds all those who believe such folly in his grip; he makes them wallow in sin and does not allow them to repent, for in order to prevent repentance he has induced them into the false belief that God is not responsible for the world, but rather that everything proceeds by chance. They wish in this way to excuse themselves in order to have freedom to sin, but those who believe this are deceived, for they have lost God because they have turned to the one who is His mortal enemy. (8689–722)

We see clearly how much variety there is in the world; the diversity is so great that there is little equality. All are not equal: some are good, and others bad; some are of high, and others of low standing; some are thin, and others fat; some are young, and others old; some are faithless, and others loyal; some are poor, and others rich; one man speaks the truth, and the other deceives; one man is a lord, and the other a servant; one man is indolent, and the other industrious; one man buys, and the other sells; one man gives, and the other takes; one man seeks one thing, and the other something else: such is this mortal life. All this diversity occurs in accordance with the will either of God or of man, for God ordains and organises everything, or He tolerates everything which occurs without genesis, for this in no way exists. God wants it this way, and He has ordained that one person should be supported by the other: the needy man by the wealthy man, the weaker man by the powerful man, the low-ranking man by the high-ranking man, the sick man by the healthy man, the less intelligent man by the wise man, the younger man by the older man. The craftsmen likewise through their professions support those who have not turned their minds to learning a profession; what one man makes in order to earn, another man buys or gives a reward for. (8723–60)

This is the way of things, and this is the custom, and in accordance with this man's life proceeds: God has ordained that it should be so without having applied any compulsion, for the sake of righteousness and rectitude, and that each person should help the next and bear him love and faith in order to maintain balance in all respects. Neither through the stars nor through anything else on earth or in the sky will there ever be any obstacle to prevent what is pleasing to God from being. Our nature requires us to love goodness and justice: there is no point in anybody being half-hearted, for nature teaches us what to do and what to avoid if we are prepared to think about it carefully. For nature clearly requires that one person should not do to another anything other than that which he wants to be done to him and for which he might receive both gratitude and thanks.[1] Above all else he must bear faith and love to his Creator, who brought him from nothing to the point of placing His image and His appearance in him and making him such that he should always honour Him. Making excuses achieves nothing, for it comes from one's true nature that one should serve God and love God, do good and avoid evil, and that each person should love and support his neighbour as he does himself. No man ever need go beyond this; it can suffice for him if he does this much, for anybody who follows this mode of conduct is certainly being true to his nature. But since many have gone astray and so betrayed their nature that they renounce good and do evil, they have abandoned their Lord God in order to serve the enemy of God, and through their wicked life they ally themselves to the prince of treachery. God, who is most gracious, has said and done a great deal in order to draw His servants back to Him, and has offered so many examples that those who have left Him should certainly return to Him. But the prince of evil drags them back and keeps them in vice; he does not wish them to leave their sin, so firmly does he keep them tied to himself, and so they will suffer torment with him if they do not change their intention.[2] (8761–818)

Just as dried tow, when it is coated with pitch, is easily ignited as soon as it is placed in fire, the same thing happens with sin when a man turns from God: just as the pitch coats the tow, in exactly the same way sin pollutes. A man who through covetousness[3] abandons justice and righteousness will be quickly ignited by the fire of Hell when he is placed there.

And just as moistened tow cannot be coated even if pitch is placed on it, since it is protected by the moisture and is not easily ignited even if it is placed in the fire, in just the same way a baptised man will not be coated by sin nor will he be harmed by the fire which burns for ever and lasts for ever, as long as he retains in himself the moisture of baptism.[4] (8819–42)

The birth from which we have all descended was very high, but through the fire of covetousness the birth has been brought very low. In order to extinguish the heat of that fire which is so harsh, God ordained baptism against the fire which is so cruel, so that through the water of baptism the fire might lose its

---

[1] 8779–82 **For nature. . .thanks** *Kar nature. . .grace*: Cf. Mt 7:12, Lk 6:31.

[2] 8693–818 **A prince full of treachery. . .intention** *Un prince plein de felunie. . .entente*: The source for this section is unclear, although parts of it appear inspired by *Rec.* IX.6 and IX.7.1–4.

[3] 8827 **covetousness** *cuveitise*: Here and following, *cuveitise* renders the sin of concupiscence evoked in *Rec.*

[4] 8819–42 **Just as dried tow. . .baptism** *Sicum estuppe esuee. . .baptesme*: These lines expand and simplify the simile in *Rec.* IX.10.5–7, but suppress the role played by demons in igniting the tow.

substance. For God has ordained such power and such strength in baptism that those who receive it will experience a new birth, for that old birth, which was lost and cast aside in most ancient times, is recovered through baptism. Those who receive baptism and keep it faithfully will be children of God through this very thing: such is the power of baptism. (8843–64)

There are many things which prove that all things in the world proceed by nothing other than God, and anybody who thinks otherwise of them is without reason.

There is one thing which is very commonly experienced and so is more easily proved: this is fear, which often strikes, often of something and often of nothing, for there is no man who does not at some time experience fear of something or other.[1]

The rich king and the emperor are never fully secure: they constantly fear losing something, and so are rarely in a state of security.

Counts, barons, and knights, even if they are brave and fierce, nonetheless greatly fear angering the king, their lord.

When a king or prince raises his army, they all ready themselves and come quickly: nobody dares to respond slowly, and all fear tarrying too long. And once they have all gathered, even though they may be brave and worthy and all armed for battle, they are nonetheless not so bold that they undertake to enter battle without the permission of their leader.

In just the same way those who are servants very often have firmer nerves and have greater strength and greater valour in themselves than their lords, and nonetheless they are not so daring that they neglect anything or deliberately violate what they have been commanded to do. (8865–900)

The covetousness which has seized this whole world is very great, and were it not for the great judgement which is appointed for the wicked, each man would by sheer force take from the next what he had. But on account of the laws which are imposed people inflict less harm on others; they are afraid to do harm on account of the harsh judgement which follows.

It is the same case with wild animals, with beasts which survive through violence: even though they are very cruel, we very often see the camel and the elephant tamed, even though both are big; and also the bull and the lion, even though they are fierce and vicious, and other beasts that it would take too long to mention are often tamed. Wild animals are commonly tamed by being subject to a master who subdues them through fear and harsh treatment.

There is no need to seek examples of men and beasts on earth; there is no need to think very much when one can find so many reasons which offer such compelling proof that it is not necessary to invent anything. Look at how the earth behaves when it bears so much that it supports there; when it trembles, it

---

[1] 8869–74 **There is one thing. . .other** *Une chose. . .que que seit*: After omissions and abridgements, *Clement* rejoins *Rec.* here at IX.15.1, albeit rather loosely at first.

very much appears that this happens to it as a result of great fear, and so it clearly reveals that it fears God when it shakes through an earthquake.

The sea rises and falls; as much as God wishes, it advances. The pleasure of God comes and goes, and nothing passes beyond this.

The angels of God, who are in heaven, have peace and harmony amongst themselves; with pure loyalty and pure love they carefully serve their Lord God. (8901–44)

The entire course of the firmament, and likewise of the stars, and also the rains and the winds are entirely ordained by God.

The demons in Hell, who bear neither loyalty nor love to their Creator, nonetheless fear Him so greatly that they do not dare to transgress His command. They very much appear to fear God when they do not dare to come near Him, but rather constantly flee from Him: the fear that they have is clearly visible through this. There is no need for a long speech or to search very far in order to present more proof, for anybody who looks carefully at one thing and another on earth, in the sky, on the sea, and elsewhere will clearly see that no creature changes its nature: it remains in its proper condition because it fears God, from whom it originates. It is a quite evident fact, since fear restrains and represses and hinders and dissuades men and beasts from transgressing, that man can and should better restrain himself from transgression on account of love and honour for, and fear of, the Creator, for man certainly has it in his power to transform his will and avoid doing anything which he thinks might be despised by God. He should have such fear of God that if the Devil places into his heart anything which might be against God, he should certainly refrain from it for God's sake, for if he so wishes, he can avoid it; he need never do it on account of the Devil. It certainly seems right for man to have such fear of God that he should always pursue good and not do anything against God when the Devil, from whom all evil comes, is so afraid and fearful of God that he does not dare to do as much evil as he would have in mind.

I have done as you requested, for I have told you what I know. It is now up to you to respond, and you will tell us what pleases you." (8945–96)

Once Clement had said this and more than is written here,[1] the old man, who had understood him clearly, replied to him:

"My son Clement," he said, "has presented his argument most wisely; his arguments are so fine that there is no need for a response. The essence of everything that he said is that the nature placed in man has such freedom in itself that it can refrain from evil and can also do plenty of good if the heart is so inclined. Everything that pleases it lies completely in its will and choice; there is no compulsion or obstacle to either acting or refraining. Even if there is cause for evil, one can certainly refrain from evil, and he provides an example of this, for people

---

[1] 8997–98 **Once Clement. . .here** *Quant Clement. . .seit*: Cf. note to vv. 8559–74.

certainly refrain from doing evil on account of fear, for nobody is constantly secure; and when one begins to think about something which could result in evil,
one can avoid the sin without particular effort by driving from oneself the Devil
who places evil in man's heart.

This is the essence of the matter, but nonetheless, even though his argument
is convincing, I cannot change my mind or compel it so that I might agree, for I
have clearly seen through what has befallen me that when one does good or evil,
it comes and goes through the stars: it originates and arises from there, and one
is obliged to do it without any chance of avoiding it. From there stems the entire
cause of murder and adultery, and likewise whether a woman conducts herself
chastely and well comes from there; and if she has not preserved her honour, she
is not to be criticised for this, for she cannot do anything else if she does that towards which her genesis drags her." (8997–9044)

On this topic the old man said a great deal, but I am not disposed to say it
all, and little profit would come from it even if I wrote it all down here, for he
presented his proposition and said a great deal about the planets, all of which he
identified by name: there are seven of them, the sun being one, then the moon,
Jupiter, Venus, Mars, Mercury, and Saturn. All good and evil comes from these
seven; everything proceeds through them and arises from them: whether a man
is killed or kills another, or is full of deception, whether he is a drunkard or a
lecher, or whether he is a madman or a reprobate stems entirely from the seven
planets, and through these seven, he said, everything proceeds. All the differences and all the qualities that men and women have in themselves, and everything that they say and everything that they do, and all events whether pleasant
or harsh cannot happen through anything else; he could not, he said, believe
anything else.[1]

When he had spoken at length, Clement then replied to him: (9045–72)

"You have spoken very well, dear father, about what pertains to this subject,
but reason invites me to respond to you forthwith, for I have had much practice
in the discipline of which you speak. It pleases me to speak to you, for I see from
what you have said that you are well educated. Listen carefully to my response,
for I can present to you an argument through which I think that I shall convincingly prove that genesis does not arise through stars, for there is no way in which
anything which causes evil or does good might stem from any planet, for anybody who desires good can do good and can certainly refrain from evil. For anybody who wishes to turn to God can overcome the assault of the Devil, for, as I
told you earlier, there are many people who would do worse than they do if they
did not fear being caught in their transgression. On account of the great fear that

---

[1] 9045–70 **On this topic. . .anything else** *Entur cest. . .tenir*: As its opening lines indicate, this section abridges *Rec.* IX.17.

people have of God and men, they do less evil and refrain from transgression, for they are afraid of being caught. Each country has its laws[1] which are imposed by kings or by princes who were or still are in power. There are many laws and many customs which are imposed by powerful men; each country has its practice, and anybody who violates it incurs harm. (9073–108)

There is a country at the end of the world,[2] and the people who live there are called Seres, and they have the law that they must behave well amongst themselves. In that country they are not accustomed to worshipping idols or having a temple; no robber or thief lives there, nor any woman who fornicated; nor is there any man who ever knew that murder was committed there; nor are women or men adulterous there. Such are the laws, and such is the custom that the whole country observes, and nonetheless it cannot be that the stars in which you say that the wonders and the woes on earth have their source and cause are not there as well.[3] In this it is quite clear that the laws which are imposed there have greater power to cause people to refrain from evil than the stars have to cause evil. (9109–30)

The land of India is long and broad, and there is another country there called Bactria. There are many people there who have their own laws amongst themselves. These people are called Brahmans, and since most ancient times they have always adhered to the ordinances that their ancestors imposed there. No man kills another there, nor will adultery ever be committed for the sake of carnal pleasure, nor will any man be seen drunk. They do not worship any idol, but rather follow God alone. They live and eat in such a way that they never kill any animal for food. They have no evil amongst them, but rather have good: such is their law.[4]

In the aforementioned country called India there is also another region, but I have found no indication of its name.[5] The people who live around there are extremely wicked hosts, for they take and hold captive the guests who come to them; they are cruel when they kill them and monstrous when they eat them. (9131–58)

The people of Persia have the custom that they contract marriages with close relatives; there the son marries his mother, and the sister takes up with her broth-

---

[1] 9101 **Each country has its laws** *Chescun pais ad ses leis*: This marks the beginning of a section in the *Recognitiones*, running to v. 9482 of *Clement*, derived from Bardaisan's *Book of the Laws of Countries*.

[2] 9109 **at the end of the world** *al chief del mund*: That is, the furthest point to the east, rendered in *Rec.* IX.19.2 as *initio orbis terrae* "at the beginning of the world" (270.4).

[3] 9120–26 **Such are the laws. . .as well** *Tels sunt les leis. . .mateire*: The allusions to Mars and Venus in *Rec.* IX.19.4 are omitted.

[4] 9148 **their law** *lur lei*: Following this line, *Rec.* IX.20.2 is omitted.

[5] 9152 **but I have found. . .name** *Mes ne ai. . .nun*: The uncertainty stems from *Rec.* IX.20.3, which speaks vaguely of a certain region in India.

er, and the father takes his daughter if she appeals to him. The people of Persia
who act in this way often leave their country, but they do not change the custom
that they have acquired on account of changing their country.[1]

There is a tribe called the Gelonians in a far distant region. There women
work the ploughs, and have no interest in being clothed or adorned in accordance
with the custom of other countries; they have no care for ointments or appropriate footwear. They perform the labour and endure great toil and hardship; the
women do everything on the land that the men ought to do; and when they wish
to be intimate with a man, in accordance with their law and by custom they will
allow themselves to be most intimate with whichever man they desire. But they
prefer all those who are strangers and visitors: they gladly consent to them, for
they love and yearn for them more than the men from their own country, and
they will never be reproached by any man from their country for having acted
badly. The men of that land do the opposite of the women, for they have their
hair finely styled and have themselves adorned in fine clothes. They are bedecked
in gold and silver, and smear themselves plentifully with ointment; they are
physically strong and are fine hunters, and are very fierce in battle.[2] (9159–200)

A large country in Persia differs greatly from this custom. This country is
called Susis, and the women there are highly esteemed; they take great pains to
be beautiful and to keep themselves so at all times. They take great care of their
hair[3] and laden themselves with so much clothing that they cannot carry it all, as
a result of which they require help, for their maids accompany them and support
their clothing for them. The women there heavily adorn themselves with gold
and silver and jewels. They allow themselves to be intimate with whomever they
wish, and have permission to do so: they accept visitors, servants, and strangers alike. There is never any complaint from their husbands, for they all know
the custom; their husbands do not reproach their wives, for the latter hold the
power.[4]

In the distant lands of the east there lives another race. Such is their law that
if a young man so utterly debases himself that in contravention of the reason of
nature he wallows in such filth as to let himself be defiled like a prostitute,[5] his
relatives themselves will seize him once they are fully aware of the truth of the

---

[1] 9165–68 The people. . .country *Cil de Perse. . .apris*: A very abbreviated version of
Rec. IX.21.

[2] 9200 in battle *en esturs*: Following this line, *Rec.* IX.22.3, which deals with astrological matters, is omitted.

[3] 9207 hair *chevelure*: *Rec.* IX.23.1 does not mention this feature.

[4] 9222 power *seignurie*: Following this line, *Rec.* IX.23.3, with its astrological content, is omitted.

[5] 9225–30 Such is. . .prostitute *Tele est. . .femme de mestier*: The condemnation of
homosexuality is more virulent than in *Rec.* IX.23.4.

matter: they will put him to death without delay, paying no heed to kinship; they will not extend him such honour as to permit him to be buried. (9201–36)

There is another country[1] elsewhere where the laws go drastically awry, for there the young men who are fair and fine of body are taken and given to a husband in the same way as are women here, and never will there be any protest, or criticism, or reproach.

In the country of the Britons one woman has many husbands.

In the country called Parthia many women have one husband.

The Amazons have no husband, and amongst them there is nobody but women. They do not permit men amongst themselves; their law has been thus for a long time. For the whole year they remain chaste until the equinox comes which is in the season called spring; towards the end of March in this season they leave their land as if heading in search of a celebration. In the neighbouring lands where men reside, they celebrate; the men who live there are very familiar with their manner and are very familiar with their custom of coming there to be intimate with men. The men come to their celebration and celebrate with the women: they have their way with the women, who have stayed there for no other reason. Once the women have conceived, they return to their country, and when the time comes to give birth, they keep the female offspring; they remove all the male children, but I do not truthfully know whether they kill them or whether they send them elsewhere to be raised outside the country. Yet it is well known that they will never have such compassion as to allow a single one to return and stay with his mother.[2] (9237–80)

By custom the people of Media, when a man comes to the country who is so certain to die that he has no chance of survival, do not allow him enough time to give up the ghost, but rather throw him alive to dogs which kill and eat him.[3]

The people of India do wait until their sick give up their soul, but they burn their bodies when they are dead, and do so by custom. Through the great love that the wives have felt for their husbands, they offer themselves to be burnt with the husbands whom they held dear. The people of the country gladly accept it when the women offer themselves; they are utterly foolish and wretched when they let themselves be burnt alive.[4]

---

[1] 9237 **another country** *un autre pais*: Our translator suppresses from *Rec.* IX.23.5 the information that the people involved in this practice are the Gauls.

[2] 9249–80 **The Amazons. . .mother** *Amazones. . .demurer*: An amplification of *Rec.* IX.24.2, after which *Rec.* IX.24.3–5, with allusions to astrology and other peoples, is omitted.

[3] 9281–88 **By custom. . .eat him** *La gent. . .manjuent*: The astrological content of *Rec.* IX.25.1 is omitted.

[4] 9299–300 **they are. . .alive** *Mult sunt. . .vives*: This opinion is added by our translator to *Rec.* IX.25.2. Following this, *Rec.* IX.25.3, with its astrological content, is omitted.

The Germans are another people; they often hang themselves.[1]

There are many peoples who have given no thought or care to learning, for there are peoples and countries in which no cleric has ever been taught.

There are many countries and lands over the sea and in other distant parts, and islands surrounded by the sea to which there has never come any minter, or carpenter, or architect, or poet, or painter, or any cleric skilled in geometry or who might write a tragedy.[2] (9281–314)

If anybody looks at these facts, given that they are such and so varied, his reason will surely tell him that it is nothing but nonsense to think that genesis has any power from which bad or good might stem, and likewise in respect of the stars he will quite clearly see that they have neither power nor strength other than in accordance with the will of God. It is quite clear that genesis is worthless when it cannot endure in the land of the Seres, who never commit murder, since it cannot persuade a single one of them to abandon His laws.

When the Brahmans and the Persians likewise respect their laws, genesis is extremely weak since it has not had the power to make the Brahmans eat meat and the Persians change their custom so that fathers and sons restrain themselves and are no longer intimate with their daughters and mothers.

It is the same case with the other lands cited as examples here: genesis cannot prevent them from constantly wishing to follow the ordinances and ways that their ancestors established there.[3]

Those who first supplied laws began a very long time ago. Laws have been significantly changed, and customs altered since then, for the most recent people often undo what the first did. Wise people with careful thought change laws in accordance with the times. The world is not such that all people observe one law, or that everything which was established in the past should always be kept. The people of the present day do not have the power or strength to maintain everything, and so it very often happens that things are changed. (9315–60)

There is an example very close at hand which amply proves this, and since we see it with our own eyes, we cannot rightly deny it. Consider what laws and how many changes have often been made by the emperors who are lords of Rome and who have conquered the entire world, for as soon as they have conquered and overcome their enemies, they make them change their custom completely and abide by the laws of Rome: they have to change completely by force, and genesis cannot prevent them. The stars of as many countries as have been conquered by

---

[1] 9301–2 **The Germans. . .hang themselves** *Germani. . .suvent*: The astrological content of *Rec.* IX.25.4 is excised. Following these lines, *Rec.* IX.25.5–27.3 is mostly omitted.

[2] 9307–14 **There are many. . .tragedy** *Mult ad. . .tragedie*: These lines stem from the earlier omitted *Rec.* IX.24.5, but with astrological content and names removed.

[3] 9315–44 **If anybody. . .there** *Ki bien. . .ancesurs*: This section bears some resemblance to *Rec.* IX.25.7.

the Romans have lost much of their power when they have not controlled the people to the extent of keeping their laws without accepting others upon themselves.

I wish to tell you even more which should certainly by reason suffice. All the Jews have one law and observe this amongst themselves; Moses gave it to them as God taught it to him. In this law it is prescribed to them that they should all be circumcised; they are circumcised in childhood on the eighth day after their birth. They have observed this law in such a way that it cannot be transgressed, for all their sons, when they are eight days old, are circumcised without delay; this law will never be so brought forward as to begin before the appointed day, nor will it ever be so postponed as to be delayed until after the day. There are many lands and many places where many Jews reside, but wherever they reside, they do not transgress this law. The Saracens and the pagans pay no heed to this law: never will one of them be circumcised in the manner of the Jews, even if they reside in the same country or even in the same place. (9361–408)

All the Jews likewise respect Saturday; they take special care that whole day to stop all their work. On that day they are not prepared to undertake as much labour as selling or buying, or setting a fire, even if it is cold, even to cook food on it, or doing anything else strenuous enough for it to be counted as work. In all places the Jews take great pains to observe the Sabbath, but other people who live beside them carry out their work. On Saturday they perform tasks as on any other day of the week; they pay no heed to that law that the Jews follow amongst themselves.[1]

Genesis has lost much of its force and power, and the stars have likewise greatly failed in their proper course when they do not make all people living in one country observe one law, but rather they have their own laws and customs which differ greatly from each other.[2]

In order to draw everything to a close more effectively I shall say one more thing so that you might be more completely persuaded.

Scarcely seven years have passed since people from all over the world converted to Jesus Christ, who is the truthful and righteous and almighty Prophet. Rumour of Him came from the land of Judaea; many people turned to Him on account of the miracles that He performed. Through what they saw and heard of Him, they have abandoned their paganism: they have forsaken their foolish practices such as sinful marriage; they have forsaken adultery and take care to do it no more; they have forsaken all their fornication, through religion and solely through the teaching of the Prophet, from whom all good comes. (9409–56)

---

[1] 9409–26 **All the Jews. . .themselves** *Le samadi. . .sei*: The allusion in *Rec.* IX.28.5–6 to the Jews' abstention from exposure of children is omitted.

[2] 9427–34 **Genesis has. . .other** *Destinee ad. . .cuntraires*: These lines have no clear source, but may reflect some of the material earlier omitted from *Rec.* IX.28.4.

The report on how He is faring has already come from St Thomas, the apostle of God, who is preaching in India. He has sent a letter through which he reports and describes his situation: he has already preached so much in Parthia that people have largely forsaken being intimate with many women there, as they were wont to do, and those who live in India are largely refraining from throwing their sick to the dogs and being intimate with their mothers or daughters, and brothers are refraining from improper relationships with their sisters. And the women of Susis, who used to be so lustful that they allowed all those who most appealed to them to be intimate with them, are refraining from the fornication in which they so often used to engage. This does not come from genesis, but is rather caused by God and St Thomas, who through his preaching brings them to this religious conviction. All this ought certainly to suffice for you without speaking any more about such matters: if you have turned your mind to it and look at the places and times, you will, if you pay careful attention, draw conclusions from all this, given that on account of the mere rumour which has come from Judaea regarding the Prophet who came and performed miracles and wonders, many people have already converted who have abandoned their foolish error and fervently wish for St Peter to come in order to bring them certainty regarding the one of whose miracles they have heard so much. (9457–98)

I shall say one more thing in order to provide such a conclusion that there will be no need to say any more or to toil over any more evidence.

With great rectitude and righteousness God created man and his nature; God is good and He made him good, and He did not wish there to be anything other than goodness. How can it then possibly be true that He subsequently introduced genesis for the sake of trouble and vexation and in order to drag into sin the one who was created for goodness, and will subsequently exact revenge for every wicked deed that he has done? By reason this cannot be so when God wants nothing but good, for we are absolutely sure that no sinner will ever be harmed or suffer any punishment except on account of the evil that he has done and from which he could refrain if he would truly strive to do so. God knows man and his capability, and what he can do and what he can avoid; He gives reward for this in this world, and likewise in the next He will reward each man in accordance with what each has deserved.[1] In this world God exacts revenge upon those who do not keep God in their thoughts, but rather have completely forgotten Him just as the world did in the past when it utterly perished before it knew a thing about it through the onset of the Great Flood. All those who were drowned then had not been born at the same time, and nonetheless they all unavoidably met their death on the same day; nobody could save anybody else when they all drowned at the same hour. It did not come from genesis that so many people were drowned there, since all those who died at the same hour had not been born at the same

---

[1] 9523–28 **God knows. . .deserved** *Deu cunuist. . .chescun*: An amplification of the theme of reward and punishment in *Rec.* IX.30.3, rendered by the preceding sentence.

hour. This is nothing but foolishness, and it is utter nonsense to say that terrible events befall man through nature, but rather when sins precede, harsh punishments will follow. (9499–550)

We must therefore be prepared, if we desire our salvation, to strive to know what can be of use to us, for when it comes to answering for ourselves at the time when each person is to receive his reward, anyone who does not know what is good will receive no good there, nor will God ever acknowledge him: he who knows nothing will not be acknowledged; he will be there in vain, and will receive no good there, but rather he will be crushingly burdened with the ill and harm that genesis, according to what you said, was supposed to inflict, both inside and outside, both on the soul and on the body. So many devils will assail him that he will not be able to save himself from them if he has not paid heed to God and on account of fear of God's judgement does not strive to resist and to remove wicked desire from himself.[1] There are three things which draw man into error and make him a sinner: the flesh, which constantly seeks delight and very much wishes to experience pleasure; then the habit of doing wrong, when one is not prepared to refrain from evil; and the Devil, who draws people towards evil and is always waiting to ambush. These three things assail man and goad him to do evil. But he who is prepared to pay heed with all his heart will certainly be able to defend himself from all of them by hearing and knowing the truth, and by fearing God and the judgement which will come, for anybody who does this will overcome in all respects.

I must surely have said enough with this, without for the present saying any more about the fact that we have in our power everything that we desire. It is now up to you to respond, and you will tell us what pleases you." (9551–94)

Clement fell silent once he had said as much as his argument required, and the old man, who was not slow to respond, said to Clement:

"My dear son Clement, you speak very well and do not fail to say anything well, but nonetheless I cannot manage to persuade my mind to relinquish its habit: it constantly remains in the same state. I absolutely cannot force myself to believe anything other than what I first said, for I am utterly convinced that everything comes and goes through genesis and through nothing else. I have it firmly in mind to hold this proposition, for everything has befallen me as was destined for me. I have likewise fully grasped that genesis led my late wife into what she experienced. I shall not abandon my proposition on account of anything which might be said to me since I have discovered for myself that everything that I say has been proved to be true. But since I fully understand that you are skilled in this discipline, I shall describe my own genesis to you as I have experienced it, and the nature of the genesis that my wife encountered. Genesis caused her

---

[1] 9551–72 **We must. . .himself** *Partant estoet. . .oster*: A lengthy version of *Rec.* IX.31.1, stressing the horrors of the judgement, after which *Rec.* IX.31.2 is omitted.

to fall in love with one of her servants: the planets passing at that time and the signs were so configured[1] that they made women fornicate and fall in love with their own servants. They were bound to drown in water, and genesis did all of this to them. This is what happened to my wife, for she lapsed into adultery: she fell in love with her servant, but was afraid of reproach. She therefore pretended as a pretext that great peril would befall us if she did not leave her country; she therefore departed, and I remained. Once she had departed with the servant and had had her pleasure with him, she sorrowfully drowned in the sea with the very servant whom she so loved." (9595–648)

Clement then said: "How do you know that what you have said is true — that your wife fornicated with her servant and drowned?"

"I am so sure of it that I have no doubt about it, but, truth to tell, I was nonetheless unaware that she had such base love for her servant before she had left the country. But once she had left the country, I learned it from a brother of mine who told me, once she had gone, exactly how she had acted. She was so in love with my brother that she absolutely could not stop herself from coming to him and begging him to fornicate with her. But my brother was an honest man as he would not dishonour me: he immediately spurned the improper advances that she was making. That poor, wretched woman was then utterly dismayed, for she feared me terribly and was afraid of reproach. But no blame should be apportioned if she acted wrongly, for she could not do any different: her genesis was such that it forced her to do this. She then fabricated a dream and told it to me, causing me great anxiety; someone had come to her, she said, but she was unable to say who it was. This man had told her at night, as she slept in her bed, that she should leave the country and make preparations to stay elsewhere; she should take two of our sons with her, and leave the third, the youngest, with me. Once I had heard this from her, I was very saddened and upset by it. I saw to it that they were saved and did not incur any harm. I loved my wife and children very dearly, and so did not allow them to tarry for long: the two eldest sons departed with their mother, but the third brother, who was the youngest, remained with me; the man gave me very great consolation by granting permission for this son to remain with me." (9649–700)

Clement began to weep when he had heard him say this, and he thought it quite possible that this old man was his father. Likewise Niceta and Aquila, who were Clement's brothers, wanted to rush forward immediately and reveal the whole affair. But when St Peter realised this, he ordered them all to stand back: "Be patient and do not rush," he said. "Wait as long as I see fit."

St Peter turned in the other direction and addressed the old man: "Please name for us," he said, "the child who was the youngest of these three."

The old man said: "The boy who was the youngest was called Clement."

---

[1] 9631–32 **the planets. . .configured** *Les planetes. . .furent*: These lines replace the more precise astrological details in *Rec.* IX.32.5.

In response to this, St Peter said to him: "If today I return to you your wife, healthy and chaste, together with your three sons, and do so quickly, will you then believe it true that the heart of man which tends towards goodness can refrain from evil without there being any compulsion to do so, and that anybody who desires good will certainly do good, and that there is no such thing as genesis? And that everything that we say is true, and that the faith that we hold is good?"

The old man said: "It is not to be believed that you can manage this; it is impossible for you to fulfil the promise that you have made to me. I therefore tell you what I am certain of: just as what you are promising will never be realised, in the same way there will never be anything great or small which might avoid genesis, for it must be followed in all respects."

St Peter then said: "I shall offer to you these people whom you see here present as witnesses that I shall this very day return to you your wife, alive and chaste, and your three sons together with her. Listen to what I shall say and heed the truth! I shall tell you the whole truth, for I know a great deal more about it than you do. For the sake of both you and this crowd I shall tell the truth, for I am aware of it, so that you might as a result be better known and that I might thereby be better believed." Presently he turned to the crowd and spoke before everybody in this way: (9701–56)

"Good people, look at this man who is dressed so poorly! He was a citizen of Rome and a close relative of the emperor; he was once a very rich man, for he held great honour in Rome. He is called Faustinianus, and in the past he had great wealth. The emperor gave him a wife who bore him loyalty and love: she was called Matthidia and was born of a noble family. Together they had three children, of whom the two eldest were twins; the third, the youngest, was called Clement, and he is standing here with us now." When St Peter named Clement, he pointed to him with his finger. He then turned towards the twins, who were older than Clement: "And these are," he said, "your two sons, who are twins and who departed when little advanced in learning and years, and from that point until now they have not seen you. One of them is called Niceta, and the other bears the name Aquila, but they had different names in the past when they were with you during childhood: one was called Faustus, and the other bore the name Faustinus."

The old man was utterly amazed when he heard his sons named. He did not have a single limb which could hold him upright and he could not prevent himself from falling over; he had in him neither strength nor power, so surprised and astonished was he. His three sons waited no longer when they saw him fallen to the ground: they took him and hugged him and kissed him as their father. The old man lay in a swoon without moving for so long that his sons greatly feared that they might lose their father and that he might never regain consciousness, but rather might give up the ghost in their midst. The whole crowd which was there at that time and saw this was astonished; great and small alike were utterly amazed when they had seen this. (9757–806)

St Peter, who was watching all this, instructed the brothers to stand up. He made them all stand back lest they suffocate their father; he did not want them to hug him any longer, and thus tax him further. He then took the old man by the hand and very gently helped him up. He arose utterly bewildered, like a man who had slept for a long time. St Peter began to comfort him, and then in turn began to tell the essence of the whole story before the crowd: how the old man's brother had desired to have his way with Matthidia, but she would not debase herself by being willing to consent to him; she did not wish to be unfaithful, for soon such rumour would arise from it as would dishonour both him and her husband. She did not wish to reveal this to her husband or to turn the two brothers against each other. She did not wish to be the cause of blame and strife, and did not want disgrace or harm to fall on their family through her, but instead she very cleverly fabricated a dream in order to remain faithful. She had dreamt, she said, that she had to leave Rome. Her eldest sons, who were twins, were to leave Rome with her; the youngest was to remain behind and stay there with his father. (9807–42)

Once they had departed, misfortune befell them on the distant seas, for they were shipwrecked by a storm, rescuing nothing other than their three bodies. The woman was cast on her own onto an island called Antaradus; there she sat on a rock, utterly bereft of useful help and assistance. But her two sons were elsewhere, for once their ship had been wrecked and completely broken into pieces, pirates sailed up, having noticed how the two children clung together so firmly that they did not wish to be separated. The pirates hauled them on board and took them to Caesarea; they sold them to a woman, but had both their names changed. They called one of them Niceta and named the other Aquila; the woman loved them dearly and kept them as if they were her own sons. She took care of them and had them well educated, and they had the intellect to study well; they devoted a great deal of effort to becoming steeped in learning. They had a companion with them by whom they were very nearly deceived, for he is exceedingly wicked and treacherous, and is called Simon Magus. But when the two of them noticed that they had nearly been deceived by Simon, they left Simon because of Zacchaeus and turned to St Peter. (9843–78)

And Clement, who was in Rome, abandoned most of what he owned once Barnabas had visited there, and departed from Rome to search for the truth regarding what he had long doubted, and came to Caesarea on account of what Barnabas had previously told him. In Caesarea he found St Peter, who warmly welcomed him. Clement stayed with him from then on, and he took great pains to ask questions and strove vigorously to ascertain what was a lie and what was true, and St Peter gave answers to everything regarding which questions were asked. After this St Peter recounted how he had found their mother sitting on the island of Antaradus and begging for her daily bread, and what joy was experienced by all those who lived on the island that she who had been so lost had been recognised there. He did not wish to forget the nature of the mutual friendship that the two women had so faithfully kept, and how the woman who had welcomed the other had been cured, and how Clement thanked and gave plenty of his money to all those people who had done good to his mother. (9879–911)

St Peter recounted all this, and he also told about Niceta and Aquila, who had not been there when the shipwrecked woman had been rediscovered on the island. But then once all were gathered, and they looked at the woman who had come with St Peter and whom they had not previously known, they asked Clement exactly who she was, and learned that it was Clement's mother, whom he had lost a long time before. And when the names that they had previously had during childhood were revealed, they cried out aloud that they were Faustus and Faustinus, and recounted the tale of all that had befallen them. And once they had realised that the woman was their mother, St Peter would not allow them to reveal themselves, but instead ordered them to refrain lest their mother be overwhelmed by the joy which would wash over her once she had found her two sons. He therefore wanted to speak to her in order better to investigate her mind, and then summon her sons in order to introduce them to their mother. He himself presented them, which pleased him very much indeed. (9912–44)

St Peter recounted this summary in front of the sons together with their father, and all the people who heard it listened to it very gladly. The story was very pleasing, and so they all listened to it more attentively; many who were there wept, and could not keep themselves from joy.

The news of this was soon known and had already spread so far that the woman who was the mother of the three brothers had heard it; she had already heard of the whole affair, but I do not know how or through whom.[1] She hesitated no longer once she had heard the news, for she came running at full speed and shouting in a loud voice like a madwoman in front of the whole crowd: "Where is," she said, "Faustinianus, who is my rightful spouse and husband, who began his toil long ago, and has crossed so many countries and experienced so many woes as a result of seeking me in towns and in cities and in market-towns, and in many other places near and far?" (9945–72)

When the old man heard the shouting and understood the words, and beheld exactly how she appeared to be behaving in front of the crowd, and how she looked around to see whether she could recognise her husband, he no longer remained sitting or stayed there, but rather ran towards the woman; weeping for joy he hugged her and kissed her again and again.

St Peter then told the whole crowd to leave immediately, for, he said, it would be most shameful if any of them stayed there any longer, but they should rather let them have enough space to speak to each other and to say whatever

---

[1] 9958 **but I do not know. . .whom** *Mes ne sai. . .ki*: Our translator takes on himself the ignorance professed by Clement in *Rec.* IX.37.1.

they wished to each other in absolute privacy; and anybody who so wished should come the next morning and hear the word of God.

No man or woman remained there once St Peter had said this to them; everybody returned to their homes, and St Peter wished to do the same. He was about to return to his lodging with as many followers as he had with him, but the master of the house then addressed St Peter: (9973–10000)

"It would," he said, "be base and wicked to accommodate in a lowly hospice such people as we see here, and of whom we have heard so much good, when my house, which is large and empty, stands ready for you here. In my house I have beds and much more besides ready for you."

But when St Peter refused and tried to avoid staying, the lady came out of the house when her husband achieved nothing; she brought some of her children with her, but I cannot say which ones or how many. She threw herself at St Peter's feet and began to implore him: "Dear lord," she said, "stay here! Please heed this request of mine." But St Peter did no more for her than he had done for her husband; she could not secure his agreement to stay there. He remained steadfast in his refusal until one of their daughters came there, who had been insane and tormented by the Devil and had, on account of her insanity, been bound in chains; she had been carefully kept under lock and key, for she was completely wild. This woman came there completely cured of the Devil who had held her in his power, for the doors of the house in which she had been imprisoned had been unbarred all by themselves, and the locks had been unlocked without a key. She had come out of the prison in this way when she felt herself fully cured, but even though her sanity had been completely restored to her, she was not free of the chains with which she had been bound as long as she had been insane. She immediately threw herself to the ground once she had seen St Peter; she fell to his feet and asked him to stay there, and said to him: (10001–46)

"You will be acting against what is just and right if you leave here today: you must not leave here since I have been thus cured today. You must not upset me now, nor sadden my parents today: it is right that you should stay here on account of the joy of my recovery!"

St Peter inquired who the woman was who had addressed him in this way, and asked the reason why she was in chains.

The father and mother were overjoyed when they had seen this of their daughter, of whom they had never had the slightest hope of the possibility that she might regain her health and be freed from the Devil. They were so astounded by this that they could not even reply, but their servants who were there apprised him of the truth: (10047–68)

"This girl," the servants said, "was no more than seven years old when the Devil took her so firmly in his grasp that he completely robbed her of her sanity. No man could come near her without her wanting immediately to grab him; she would bite and tear apart with her teeth everything which came near. Twenty years have passed since the time when she first lost her mind; no man has been able to cure her since then, for nobody has dared to come near her. She has maimed many men and consigned several to their death: no man could prevail against her during the whole time that she was insane, so powerful was the Enemy who had taken up his home in her. But he has fled through you, for he could not remain there any longer; the doors which were firmly barred and shut with locks were made to open by themselves, for they could no longer hold. The maiden has been cured, and this has happened to her through your aid, and so she asks you to remain here and not lodge elsewhere; make this a day of celebration for her, or if not, you will greatly upset her. You ought not to disappoint her, but rather greatly rejoice with her; you should be overjoyed on account of the health that she has through you, and you should also bring great joy to her parents by lodging here." (10069–104)

Once the servants had recounted what they knew about the maiden, the chains broke by themselves and fell from her; both her hands and feet, which had long been bound, were free. St Peter was then quite sure that it had all happened through him; he was quite certain that God had cured the girl through him. He therefore heeded her request and did not leave that house; he stayed and lodged there, and sent for all his companions who had remained at the lodgings that they had previously taken. All those who had remained behind there came with St Peter's wife, and once they had arrived there, they all lodged there. Each person took his own bed—nobody with anybody else, but rather each person separately. They ate and drank there as they had previously been accustomed; after dinner they thanked God, and then retired to their beds. (10105–30)

The night passed, and the next morning St Peter rose when day broke. The three brothers slept no longer when they saw St Peter awake; the four of them went to the place where the old man had gone to bed. He had his wife beside him, but both of them were sleeping; they were not lying in the house where each person had his own bed.[1] St Peter did not wish to wake them, and so did not wish to intrude on them; all four went away and waited outside the door. All four of them sat on the ground, and St Peter then said to the three brothers:

"My dear friends, who serve God together with me, please listen to me. You love your father very dearly, and this is no surprise; you feel very great love for him, but I am extremely worried that you, because you love him so much, might overly rush him to convert to our religion before he is firmly settled in true faith. If he is not first prepared, he should not be pressed into joining our religion for any reason other than God, for it may well happen that he will be willing to convert quickly solely on account of the love that he feels for you. But he will never be firm in his faith in this way, for anything that one does either for a man's gratitude or for his thanks is not to be very highly esteemed since it cannot

---

[1] 10139–40 **they were not lying. . .own bed** *Ne jeurent pas. . .chescun*: An addition relative to *Rec.* X.1.1 in order to clarify the parents' location.

last permanently: it will quickly and easily collapse, for there will never be any good without God. I shall therefore give you my advice if you wish it to happen, as I do: in my opinion it is good and right that your father should have a period of grace to accompany us for a year us in order both to hear and to observe our conduct and what we shall say to the people. Let him live just as he will without being bothered by you! And if he wishes to heed what is good, he can certainly learn it with you by hearing what we shall say when we speak before other people. For if he wishes to stand firm in the right intent by hearing us, he will then ask us to do to him whatever we see fit for him, and to allow him to become part of our religion; and if his heart tends in another direction since he does not wish anything better, let him be our friend! Those who come to religion unwillingly and without devotion not only abandon it when they can no longer bear it, in order to cover up their weakness effectively and excuse themselves lest people should harshly criticise them, but also slander it to people, for they say that true religion is completely without reason. Other people are harmed by this when they are discouraged from converting and moving towards good by those who do not wish to do good." (10131–206)

In response to this, Niceta said to him: "My lord," he said, "I do not deny that your advice is good, but I wish to say my opinion in order to hear more that I have not heard and to know more that I do not know. If our father does not live as long as the period of grace lasts, and dies before the year has passed, precisely what will become of him? Then there will be nothing to prevent him from going straight down to Hell; there he will remain in suffering and pain, and there will never be any possibility of anything good."

"It is very pleasing to me," St Peter said to him, "that you are thinking so much about your father, and I am very happy and glad that you have such concern for him; and since you are asking about this for no other reason than that you do not know it, you are to be completely forgiven for having asked me about it. But do you think that every man who grows accustomed to doing good, since he does good in front of people and conducts himself well, attains salvation because he appears to behave well unless God, who understands people's conscience properly, first passes His judgement? He will have no other chance of salvation unless God, who sees the thoughts of all hearts, passes judgement on him, for there is nothing which is hidden from Him. Those who behave well amongst people do not all do it purely for God or out of any righteous intention, and for this reason God has paid no attention to it. Some people do it perchance either through some pretence, or because of some ancient custom initiated by pagans, or because of some teaching which often passes from one person to the next, or because of the love and companionship of a good friend or cherished partner, or for some other reason for which it would take a long time to provide examples. (10207–54)

But those who through love of God and righteousness set their minds on serving God and loving God and leading a good life will for this experience the everlasting joy which will for ever be their legacy. The power and favour of men are of no use in securing this: nothing other than faith can be of any use in pursuing this. Through faith and goodwill one can attain salvation, and by gladly serving God freely and lovingly. You must certainly believe in addition to this that God knows everything which exists, and knows beforehand the truth of whether your father is one of His. And what will happen if God has understood that your father is not one of His? Who will be the one to deny anything which comes from His ordinance, and which He ordained so long ago when the world first began? But nonetheless I shall give you such advice as I am able. When your father rises and comes to you, we shall all sit down together and ask questions as if to inquire into and learn what seems difficult to understand, so that your father might profit and be improved by listening; it may bear fruit if he can be instructed through listening. But nonetheless be patient if he wishes to say anything to us first: we will be all the more able to respond if he asks questions of us. And if he asks nothing of us, it then seems to me that it will be advisable for us to give the appearance amongst ourselves of being people who are anxious to learn properly by asking; I know no better advice to give in this regard. You have heard what I have said; you will now say what you think."

What St Peter had said to the three brothers pleased them greatly; they fully assented to the advice and said that it was very good. (10255–306)

Clement nonetheless replied: "As far as concerns our father, the end is very much consonant with the beginning, and as for the outcome for it that I envisage, I trust in God and believe that after such a fine beginning, God will not wish him to be lost, but rather He who has protected him in this way until now will cause him to have a good ending. But nonetheless I wish to say this: if we follow the advice that we should ask questions and give the appearance of being in doubt, you, my lord Peter, should not act as our equal, for you ought not to ask anything which might give the impression that you are in doubt. For if it perchance so happened that our father noticed from your pretence that you were in doubt about anything, he would be very offended by it, for he would think himself deceived. You must certainly avoid this, for at present he thinks and is certain that there is nothing about which you are in doubt and of which you are not fully certain, and if you begin asking so many questions that you seem to be in doubt about anything, he will no longer truly believe any of us when he sees everybody in doubt. From then on he will pay no more heed to you than he does at present to one of us, for he will think that we are all equals and that we have no master here when he sees everybody in ignorance and no hope of certain knowledge. Rather be patient, and we shall speak, and you listen to what the three of us say. We shall ask many questions, and when we are unable to continue, we shall seek from you a solution to every question that we have asked." (10307–50)

St Peter said: "Let us leave things as they are. There is no point in talking about this any more, for if God, who ordains everything, wishes your father to be saved, He will give us a most propitious and appropriate opportunity for this; without any human agency, we will, if God intervenes, have a fine beginning. For this reason I state my opinion again as I stated it before: allow him to accompany us and hear us debating, and do not mistakenly rush him until God gives such an opportunity as pleases Him, and then let me decide. Keep to what I have said and act in accordance with my advice!"

Each man had said what he thought when a boy arrived; he said that the old man was awake and preparing to rise. Those who had been waiting outside then wanted to enter and see him; they had already stood up, but the old man arrived presently. Once he had seen them, he greeted them and kissed his sons in order. They all sat down on the ground there, but the father spoke first of all:

"Can each man," he said, "who wishes to speak and ask questions of somebody else do so freely, or will it be necessary to remain silent the whole time, as Pythagoras said and wrote in the past, and as those who follow his teachings still say?" (10351–88)

St Peter replied: "We have no interest in forcing anybody to ask questions or to be silent, but rather we leave him completely to do as he wishes: may each man do as he will, for not a single person will ever be compelled by us! For we are quite sure that those who are inclined to reflect carefully on how they might manage to attain salvation will under no circumstances be able to keep themselves from feeling obliged to reveal what they hold firmly in their heart, and so will not be able to remain silent about it. But he who neglects what might bring his salvation, even if he takes pains to ask how he might profit, will never derive any benefit from any question other than that he will gain some praise thereby and will be esteemed amongst people for asking so much in order to learn; he will be considered diligent for this, but there will never be any more gain than this. Now it will be up to you whether you wish to hear anything from us, and you will ask it." (10389–414)

The old man said: "There is a saying which is very common in the school of the philosophers who used to be highly regarded in Greece. The philosophers at that time had concluded that nothing in itself is either good or evil, but rather good and evil alike exist in accordance with how they are perceived; everything should be considered good or evil in accordance with each man's custom and practice, as each person sees fit. For according to them it will be neither evil nor wrong if one man puts another to death; nobody should accuse the one who commits murder of evil, for he has freed the soul which was burdened by the flesh.[1] And they also in turn give it to be believed that it is not evil to commit adultery if it is done so secretly that the husband knows nothing of it; or if it is perchance the case that he knows about it, if he is not concerned by it, it is not evil since no harm ensues as it does not matter to the husband. (10415–42)

---

[1] 10429–34 **For according. . .flesh** *Kar a lur dit. . .encumbree*: This rendering of *Rec.* X.5.2 omits the second part, which deals with the topic of just men putting others to death.

In respect of theft they likewise say that there should be no sanction for those who have their eye on other people's belongings and then take them: one should not criticise it as evil when privation makes them do this; through need they have taken from other people that which they themselves lack, for he who cannot acquire it from his own possessions must take it from other people's, and if he cannot do this openly, he must take it secretly. Many people are thieves for no other reason than lack of belongings. The thief who steals for no reason other than necessity is less blameworthy than is the man who loses what should have been made available as a gift: the one who does not have it must steal when the one who has it is not prepared to give it. The one who amasses wealth should therefore give him enough that he might not do evil on account of privation and not take anything from other people, for all the possessions that people gather should be shared, and each person should take quite openly the wealth which people stock up. Everything ought to be shared, but the world is full of discord because each person takes so much for himself and claims as his own what should be shared: the conflict which there has been in this world has stemmed from the fact that one person says that 'This is mine!' and the next says that it is his.[1] A wise man living in Greece[2] said very convincingly, albeit a very long time ago, that everything that friends have should be shared, and they are not friends if they do otherwise with it; even wives are counted in this, for they are not excluded from this when everything is included. Just as the sun and moon share their brightness with everybody, and just as the air is shared by all so that each person has an equal amount of it, every other thing should likewise be shared, and this would be good! I wanted to say this because I have taken it upon myself to do good, but I know little about it, and I do not know how I should do good if I do not know beforehand what is good, for if I have first of all managed to ascertain what is good, I shall then understand the opposite, and I shall be able to refrain from evil. (10443–98)

May one of you three respond to this—and may my lord Peter hold his peace! It would be quite unreasonable if he were to debate with us, for he cannot be gainsaid in anything as soon as he has said it, nor should one then question it, but rather everything that he says is to be firmly believed. He must therefore hold his peace and listen to us as a judge, and once we have debated until we are unable to say any more, through him we will achieve certainty regarding the matter about which we are in doubt. Through his word alone I would, if I so wished, accept his proposition, as I shall do in the end, for I shall submit entirely to what he says. But first of all I should like to know whether one will be able through disputation to find anything that one is seeking through enquiry, and whether

---

[1] 10455–78 **Many people. . .is his** *Plusurs ne sunt. . .esté*: A considerable amplification of *Rec.* X.5.5.

[2] 10480 **A wise man living in Greece** *Uns sages huem manant en Grece*: Namely Socrates speaking in Plato's *Republic*.

one will thereby attain certainty. May Clement respond first of all: I should like
him to show whether anything comes from nature which is either good or evil
or nothing, and may he likewise show whether what one does is good or evil."
(10499–526)

Clement responded without hesitation when he had heard this from his father: "Since your desire is such that it should please you to hear from me whether
anything which is good or evil comes from nature or deed, or whether good and
evil exist solely through the custom that people have — as a result of which the
world experiences such discord since each person takes for himself and claims as
his own what should be shared, just as the air is shared, as is the sun which gives
light — it seems to me that I should not draw an example to prove my case from
anywhere other than from those disciplines with which you are conversant and
of which I hope that you know more, so that you might have no doubt about anything that I say to you.[1] Behold the evils of which nobody doubts that they are
bad, such as gout and fever and serious illnesses by which we see many gravely
afflicted; consider betrayals, anger, and quarrels; witness what woe it is to be in
tears, at war, in turmoil, in pain, and to languish bound in prison, and to suffer
great torments. Do you not agree that these and other things that one frequently
sees are evil?" (10527–58)

The old man said: "It is not wrong that these are very great evils, and if there
is anybody who does not believe this, may he find out through experience that
this is so!"

To this Clement said: "As you are certain of and acknowledge this much,
then I must tell you more in accordance with the discipline of astronomy with
which I have clearly perceived that you are very conversant: I must therefore
speak about it more clearly in order to present the argument to you more clearly,
and you will understand the argument more clearly through the discipline in
which you are well versed. You fully acknowledge that fever and other things that
I mentioned previously are very evil things, frequently experienced throughout
the world. Through the stars, according to you who are very conversant with this
discipline, these evils arise, and evil are the stars which cause such evils; those
stars which do good are good according to the astronomers. Can what I say to
you be true?"

In response to this, his father said to him:

"Everything is thus, my dear son Clement, for it cannot be otherwise."[2]
(10559–86)

Clement then said: "All the evils which affect the individual or the community have their origin in just one place: in the stars which are evil. Those same

---

[1] 10546 **that I say to you** *que jeo vus die*: Following this line, *Rec.* X.7.3–6 and X.8.1–
2 are omitted.

[2] 10573–86 **You fully acknowledge. . .otherwise** *De fievre estes. . .autrement*: This
rendering of *Rec.* X.9.2–3 omits names from Roman mythology.

stars which cause a man to have fever cause a man to be unruly, and those which cause the onset of illness cause treachery, and everything that you have acknowledged as being evil has, according to you, originated from them; and those same stars are the cause of both murder and adultery, of theft and other evils that we consider to be most sinful. It must therefore stand to reason, seeing that they cause nothing but evil, that murder is an evil thing, and likewise theft and adultery, since the stars responsible for evil works are striving to do this: everything that they do is evil since they themselves are evil, and they lead you into such practices which cause you to be considered a fool."[1] (10587–610)

"You have proved to me," the old man said, "succinctly and well and skilfully that many things which are done are very evil in themselves, but answer me regarding those who do evil and cannot do otherwise on account of the genesis which compels them to it and forces them into evil. How can God blame them and justly condemn them on account of evil when compulsion and necessity force them to commit the evil? I ask you the reason for this since you are speaking in this way."

Clement replied to his father: "I am extremely concerned about speaking harshly with you, for I am bound to honour you in every way; were this not the case, I should tell you some of what I have in mind."

The old man said: "My dear son, speak, and be sure not to omit anything on my account! Even though it might seem like a transgression, be sure not to omit anything for this reason, for it is the one who asks badly who commits the misdeed, and not you, nor are you to be criticised any more than a wife who grows angry with her husband and chastises him when he has given himself over to lecherous behaviour." (10611–40)

Clement then said: "When you and I are debating amongst ourselves, if we then start distancing ourselves from what we have previously accepted and contradict ourselves so much that today we deny everything that we said yesterday, it will then be the same with us as with the spider which spins and weaves a complex piece of work: it takes great pains, toils a great deal, and wastes a great deal of its innards, and once it has woven its web, it frequently changes and alters it. It will be just the same with us who change our points so frequently: we will not be able to complete something which is constantly being remade.[2] We must therefore take care not to refute or accept anything before we see which argument is to be believed, and which not, and once we have managed to establish our opinion, we should not renounce this under any circumstances, but rather we should adhere very firmly to it. In this way we will come to a more effective conclusion re-

---

[1] 10587–610 **Clement then said. . .fool** *Clement dist dunc. . .musarz*: A version of *Rec.* X.9.4–7 which omits all mythological content.

[2] 10647–56 **it will then be. . .remade** *Dunc iert de nus. . .refaire*: These lines replace the metaphor of Penelope undoing her weaving in *Rec.* X.10.4.

garding the things that we discuss; once we have examined one thing thoroughly, we shall then examine the next more effectively." (10641–68)

"My son," the old man said, "you speak well, and I am quite aware of why you have said it, for yesterday, when you debated with me, you stated and presented to me many fine and fitting arguments which were very compelling; you offered me many fine proofs regarding many things in nature. You mentioned a power from which I did not believe there to be any benefit, for it is evil and does evil and constantly draws people towards doing evil. It often changes and disguises itself in order to draw people into covetousness; it takes great pains and offers great enticement in order to cause people to fall into vice. But even though it has the desire to do this, it cannot have the power; it can beleaguer a man greatly without compelling him to sin. Anybody who is not prepared to consent to it will not experience any compulsion or obligation, for anybody who strives to resist will certainly be able to overcome it."[1] (10669–92)

"It is once again good," Clement said, "that you remember, but nonetheless despite everything that you recall of it you have still erred."

"You must not reproach me," the old man said, "or overly criticise me; if I have erred, please forgive me, for I have still had little practice in this. For I have found myself confounded since we spoke to each other at such length yesterday; I understood the truth and so assented to it, but nonetheless I cannot yet strengthen my resolve so that I might fully believe what pertains to my salvation. I cannot free my mind; it constantly holds me like a fever which has greatly taxed a man and then relaxed its grip a little, but nonetheless has not left him in such a way that he has fully recovered, as chills remain in him which very frequently cause him discomfort.[2] In just the same way I am tormented because I have for a long time believed in the proposition which constantly draws my mind towards genesis, for I have so clearly perceived in nearly everything which has befallen me that I have experienced it exactly as it was destined for me, as a result of which my mind constantly moves in the direction of genesis, so firmly does it believe it." (10693–726)

"Father," Clement said to the old man, "now pay careful attention to that discipline with which you have dealt so much, in which your mind is so set. Pay careful heed to the nature of those who are conversant with this discipline, for the most skilful goes awry in it through lack of knowledge: they do nothing but lie; hear the reason why! Take one of those who practise this discipline to one side and talk to him; reveal to him that an event befell you at a certain time, and then ask him to tell you in accordance with the discipline of astronomy which stars caused this, and he will tell you that he knows it full well. If you reveal to

---

[1] 10669–92 **My son. . .overcome it** *Fiz. . .cuntrester*: A bloated rendering of *Rec.* X.10.6 which still omits astrological content.

[2] 10710–16 **it constantly holds. . .discomfort** *Tuz tens me tient. . .ennuis*: An elaboration on *Rec.* X.10.8

him an event by which you were harmed, he will immediately present you with the evil stars, and will tell you that everything which befell you was caused by them.[1] (10727–50)

Then go to another and take him to one side, and reveal to him some matter which is completely different from the first. Tell him the time and the hour of some agreeable event which benefited you in order to ascertain from where it came, but take care not to change the hour that you said to the first man; that very same hour that you revealed when you spoke to the first one about the evil event you must then reveal to the other one in respect of the good event, and he will immediately know all about it. He will straightaway say which stars are good and will name them; he will take great pains to reveal causes of good by speaking at great length. Everything that the one said about the evil event, the other will wish to turn to good; even though the hour is the same, and the event different, the second man will want to say so much about the stars which are good by bringing the hour and time together so that they fall into alignment with the stars, and he will cover so much ground in presenting his arguments that by sheer force he will manage to make you believe that all the good which befell you came from good stars, and that it was reasonable and right that everything had to happen in this way. The second astronomer will say as much about good as the first one told you earlier when offering you his proof regarding evil, and so it can be recognised that they do nothing but deceive people.[2] (10751–90)

Be fully aware that no profit can come from such a discipline: it is too greatly given over to falsehood and very much resembles a dream, for when a man has dreamt a great deal and then awakes from sleep, if he does not understand on his own what the dream means, he thinks about it when he does not know what the dream must betoken. But if an event then befalls him to which he might relate it, he then for the first time understands the dream, and understands and explains it in accordance with this. It is just the same with genesis: there will never be any man who by reason of any star in the sky or any planet or anything else might be certain of anything which is to happen; rather it is necessary to see or to hear it." (10791–810)

Clement proposed other arguments there which must be abridged; it would take a long time to recount them all, and somebody might grow bored.[3] What he said pleased his father so much that he was unable to refute him in any respect, but rather admitted to him that everything that he said was right. They sat there

---

[1] 10745–50 **If you reveal. . .them** *Si aventure. . .avenu*: An abbreviated rendering of *Rec.* X.11.2–3 which omits astrological detail.

[2] 10765–90 **He will straightaway. . .deceive people** *Des esteilles. . .genz trechier*: The rejection of mathesis eschews the technical details found in *Rec.* X.11.6–9.

[3] 10811–14 **Clement proposed. . .bored** *Autres reisuns. . .ennuiereit*: An allusion to the abridgement of *Rec.* X.12.2–7 in the preceding sentence.

for so long and talked there for so long that people who very much wished to enter gathered at the gates, for they very much hoped to experience great benefit inside, and so very much wished to enter. A man came and told them this, and St Peter let them all enter; the place was large, and there were many people who all entered it. When he saw so many people entering, St Peter then said to his followers: "Whichever of you three most wishes to do so will speak before this crowd about the religion that pagans follow, for many people have come here on our account." (10811–34)

"My lord Peter," Clement said, "I see and recognise great goodness in you; I esteem most highly everything that you do, for you appear extremely gracious to me. You are a kind and gentle man, and you are clearly demonstrating this to us now; you are most charitable and patient since you are prepared to allow us to dare to speak in front of you and ask whatever pleases us. For nowhere else have I ever seen nor have I ever heard of any other man such as we have seen here in you, for you have no envy in you; you are extremely humble and are not disdainful, and the fact that you are always cheerful has drawn us to you. Our desire to heed your teaching increases greatly as a result of this." (10835–54)

St Peter said: "It is not entirely from disdain or envy that some people are not prepared to allow questions to be asked of them, but rather a large part of this comes from the fact that they feel themselves to be so ignorant that if they were asked a question, they would not be able to say much in response. And if they were seen to be incapable of responding well, they would inevitably be ashamed if they were to lose any of their reputation by being considered ignorant, and this is why they are so evasive. But they ought not to be ashamed of this, even though they could not know everything, for there is no man who knows so much that he does not need to learn more. If our master, who knows everything and through whom the whole world was created, was not prepared to say that He knew everything—He could nonetheless certainly have said it, but rather attributed everything to God the Father and said that He alone was to be believed[1]—how is it that any man dares to boast and say that he knows everything in order to cause people to talk about him and to gain a little prestige? Through the example of our master we clearly understand that it is impossible for any man alive to know anything other than what God allows him; God alone knows all that there is to know, and there is none but He who knows everything. We have nonetheless learnt as much as it befits us to know and as much as God has provided for us, which will certainly be enough for us. The knowledge that our master taught to us is quite enough for us; there is no need to seek anything beyond this, for what He told us is enough." (10855–96)

Clement said: "My lord Peter, when we were in Tripolis recently, what I heard you say there caused me no little surprise. Nobody speaks anything other

---

[1] 10873–78 **If our master. . .believed** *Si nostre meistre. . .creire*: Cf. Mt 24:36; Mk 13:32.

than Hebrew in the country from which you originated. You were raised with this as a child, but I nonetheless noticed that you spoke Greek as well as if you had used it frequently. You spoke most compellingly then and touched on the stories that those in Greece often tell when they have celebrations for their gods, but you have nonetheless not learnt very much about their tales. Their tales are quite full of filthy and wicked material, and if it pleases you, I shall tell you a little of what I have heard about them. I am prepared to start from the very beginning if you wish to listen to me talk about them." (10897–918)

"You act most commendably!" St Peter said. "We shall gladly hear what you wish to say about them, and you deserve much praise for helping us to preach."

"I shall talk about them," Clement said, "since I understand your pleasure in this matter, but I shall not say anything in order to teach other than to demonstrate the way in which the pagans err and how foolish their understanding is."

Clement presently wished to continue speaking, but Niceta, his elder brother, bit his lips as if it displeased him, and gave him a sign to be quiet.

St Peter clearly noticed this, but what he saw did not please him in the slightest. He then turned to Niceta and tackled him regarding what he saw: (10919–36)

"Niceta," he said, "why is it that you wish to impede Clement? You should not do this on any account, for what he is doing comes from a noble heart. Why do you do injustice to his nature, which is the result of noble nurture? And do you think that you might honour me by making him be silent? I have no interest in such honour, for it is insignificant and quickly passes. Do you then not know that if all those who have been given to God by me and have received our faith could, after their conversion to God, be of such merit that they might all be able to preach the faith of God and draw others to God, as they would have seen me doing and would have learnt through me, they would do me honour and great glory? Do you perhaps think that I am seeking glory? What glory can be greater than preparing for our master Jesus Christ worthy disciples who do not remain overly quiet so that they might save only themselves, but who rather bravely reveal through both good deeds and true words what might be of benefit to many, and in accordance with what they have learnt reveal what they know? It would greatly please me if you, Niceta, and you, my dear son Aquila, would help me to preach and would say the word of God, all the more so because you know full well the way in which the pagans err and because you can speak more effectively about what you have directly experienced. I do not say that this would please me solely regarding the two of you, but rather I say exactly the same regarding all those who have converted to God, for I should like for everybody to know enough that they might instruct others with it. The world is full of great errors and has need of great help; there must be great assistance in order to turn the world towards good." (10937–86)

Once St Peter had said everything which occurred to him at that time, he turned back towards Clement and in front of everybody gave him this command:

"Clement," he said, "continue with what you had in mind!" Clement had no desire to hesitate once he received this instruction:

"As," he said, "I was saying earlier, when I was in Tripolis with you, I heard you speak most compellingly there about the gods that the pagans worship, and I shall say some more about them in your presence as you so wish it. I shall reveal to you the nonsense of their fictional tales and ridiculous stories in order to make these people understand how wickedly they err, and in order that you might become more familiar with them through what you hear me say about them. (10987–11006)

Those who are considered amongst pagans to be wise and worthy and are so steeped in learning that they are esteemed for their knowledge say that before the sky and earth had been created, and before any light appeared, everything was mixed together without anything being given form there; there was no design in the world, but rather everything was in chaos. There was no separation of things, for fire and water and earth and wind and other things lay together, for everything was completely mixed together. The mixture lay together until it adhered together and became solid. It took the form of an egg, but it was very big, for it comprised everything which was to exist; it was solid on the outside and formed a shell, but inside it remained completely soft. Everything lay together in this way until it cracked, and there came out from it a beast which was very big and which had the appearance of a man. It had a twofold form in it, for it was a man and a woman together; with this form light emerged once that big egg had cracked. This beast bore offspring from which other creatures then originated. It first conceived Substance, and Prudence was its next child; the third thereafter was called Motion, and the fourth was called Coition; from these four came the matter from which both sky and earth are wholly created. From the sky came six males who had no father but the sky, and from the earth six females who took up with the six males.[1] (11007–46)

The pagans claim that a vast line descended from these.[2] One of the six who was born in the sky was called Saturn; the female born of the earth whom he took was called Rea. This Saturn had learnt that he was destined to conceive a child who would be more powerful than him and who would take his honour from him. Saturn was very afraid of this, and in order to evade this danger he thought that he would devour his sons as soon as they were born so that they would not have any more power than he. His first son was called Orcus, and the next was named Neptune, but they could not be born quickly enough for their father not to eat them: he took them and devoured them, and no longer feared those two. Orcus was the eldest child and was devoured first of all. Neptune was conceived afterwards and seized as soon as he was born; he was devoured after

---

[1] 11043–46 **From the sky. . .males** *Sis madles. . .pris*: The numerous names in *Rec.* X.17.5–6 are omitted.

[2] 11047–48 **The pagans claim. . .these** *Li paen. . .grant*: A summary of *Rec.* X.18.1–3.

his brother, and neither love nor entreaty was of any avail. A third son was then conceived who was called Jupiter. Once his mother was pregnant with him, she felt pity for her child, and she began to consider how she might save the child. Once the time came when she was due to give birth, on account of the child, who would cry, she summoned performers to strike cymbals and drums so that when the child cried out, he would not be heard on account of the noise. (11047–86)

Once Saturn had noticed that his wife had delivered on account of her belly, which was thin and protruding less than before, he urgently asked where the child was and that he should be brought before him, for he wanted to do with him as he had done with the first two. The mother had conceived a plan, and she held forth a stone: "I have," she said, "no other son than this stone to which I gave birth." Saturn thought that this was true and that his wife had not had any other child; he placed the stone in his mouth and made it slip down his throat. Once the stone reached his belly, the two brothers who had previously been devoured were so heavily laden that they could remain there no longer. Orcus came out first of all, and Neptune followed after him; both who had previously entered from above exited from below. Orcus, who came out first, remained below, for he fell deep down. Orcus remained completely beneath the earth, but Neptune settled somewhat higher: he fell onto the water as he came out, and then did not wish to leave there. Jupiter was the third brother, and his mother Rea seized him. She had him mount a goat which was to carry him up to the sky; he stayed on the goat until he reached the sky above. (11087–122)

There he is a god, so say those who perform sacrifices to him. Such are the tales that pagans tell, and they tell others as well. This Jupiter had for his entire life given himself over to lecherous behaviour. He took his sister as his wife, but bore her neither loyalty nor love; Juno was his wife and sister, and in this he was no better than a dumb animal which does not understand what law obtains for kin. He started very wickedly in his youth, for no daughter, niece, or female relative could avoid being defiled by him. Any wife, spouse, or girl, or any other woman in his vicinity, had to yield utterly to him, or he would take her by force; he was never tempted by any woman without fully possessing her, if he so wanted.[1] But even though he was of great power, he was nonetheless very concerned that his father might have another son who would be more powerful than he, and so he waged war against his father and did not allow him to have peace on earth, and he pursued his elder brothers together with his father until they had been driven back, and then he concentrated his efforts against his father. He pursued him until he captured him and placed him in very tight chains. He removed his genitals, not wishing any further heir to come from him, for he feared offspring which might then wish to attack him. Jupiter was still afraid that his father might recover, and wishing to feel more secure in respect of the things of which his fa-

---

[1] 11135–44 **He started. . .wanted** *Mult cumençat. . .eust*: An abridgement of the account of births and intermarriage in *Rec.* X.20.4–7, with names omitted.

ther had been deprived, he threw his genitals into the sea, and from then on felt more secure about them.[1] But once the blood which flowed out on account of the excision entered the sea, it was thrown here and there so much and struck by such great waves that a foam developed and arose from it from which, they say, Venus, who is called goddess of love, was born; the tale about it is written thus. And Jupiter brought forth this woman and many others that it would take very long to describe or even to imagine, and little benefit would come from describing them.[2] (11123–78)

He would often disguise himself and often change his form when he found a woman or girl who would not yield to him. Once the husbands who had beautiful wives were away from home, he would then make himself appear as if he were the husbands. He would come to the wives in this way and fornicate with them; they did not notice until they had finished fornicating. He took many other forms, as the story-tellers recount, through which he deceived maidens and other women whom he found attractive. He would become a dragon or a serpent, and very often a bird or animal; he turned himself into an eagle, a vulture, a swan, and often took the form of a bull or a bear. He performed many such transformations and thereby deceived many people.[3]

He had many sons and daughters, but he was very cruel and harsh to them: he killed and condemned many of them, and thus showed that he had little love for them; he consigned the women to disgrace, and the men to ruin. This is what the pagans acknowledge regarding the god whom they consider almighty; they acknowledge in him many evils for which it is right that he should be reproached, and for which men would be condemned if they were proven guilty of such evils, and nonetheless they make their god of him, whereby it is quite clear that they are blind.[4] (11179–214)

Plenty more could be said about him, for there is a great deal of material. This Jupiter who is above all others, and the rest who are beneath him but are nonetheless called gods, have changed both men and women into such and so many forms that it would be difficult to enumerate how many there are. Very many were changed: some into plants, and some into flowers; some into animals, some into birds, and some into springs or streams; there were some changed into trees, and some others into stones. They changed many into stars and transported them up to the sky; there is scarcely a sign or planet or star of which the poets

---

[1] 11158–66 **not wishing. . .them** *Ne vout que. . .aseurat*: This explanation is added relative to *Rec.* X.20.9.

[2] 11175–78 **And Jupiter. . .them** *E ceste. . .surdreit*: These lines stand in place of the name-laden genealogy in *Rec.* X.21.

[3] 11179–200 **He would often. . .people** *Il se sout sovent. . .deceveit*: An abridgement of *Rec.* X.22, with names suppressed.

[4] 11201–14 **He had many. . .blind** *Fiz e fidles. . .avegle sunt*: An approximate version of *Rec.* X.23–25, with names omitted.

have not said in their writings that they all were once men, or beautiful women, or something else which brings a fine ending to the tale, for in order to make the tales more appealing they tend to finish with such things."[1]

Clement said a great deal about this, but he spoke at greater length than I have done, for he named which women Jupiter loved. He identified by name a good number of those with whom he had fornicated; before anybody who wanted to hear he named the sons and daughters, of whom there were many; he described the manner of conception, for he knew a great deal about the subject. Regarding Jupiter's children he likewise identified by name which ones he put to death, and he identified by name which ones and how many their father disgraced, and who was turned into a star, be it his son or be it his daughter, and who into an animal, who into a bird, who into a tree, and who into anything else.[2] Once he had said so much that he did not wish to continue, St Peter then replied: (11215–58)

"If everything that they have said and everything that they have written down is true—that both men and women were changed into a different form than they previously had, such as into stars, birds, animals, and into other things of which you have taken great pains to apprise us here—it must according to their claims seem that dumb animals and birds, flowers and springs and streams and the other things of which you spoke did not exist before men were changed into such forms in this way, but rather they came into being from that time onwards. Until that time the sky above was completely without stars, and it was a wonder that the men who lived back then could survive in that life when they had neither the comfort nor the profit from the benefits that they should have had from them, for a man's life does not last if it is not helped by such things."[3] (11259–80)

"It is a great wonder," Clement said, "that people persist in such error and consider to be a god one who was brimming with all kinds of evil. Jupiter was a wicked lecher, and did not care about adultery. He committed a terrible crime against his father when he maimed him most painfully; he did not care about murder and was accursed in all his deeds. The pagans do not deny any of this, but rather celebrate it. Anybody who was caught committing such deeds now would be condemned and put to death! Why is it then that they honour him for being like this, and given that he was like this, worship him as a god? If he is a god by committing so many evil deeds which it is foul even to mention, by the same token all those who commit such evil deeds will have to be considered to be gods, for murderers and lechers, adulterers and deceivers should therefore be

---

[1] 11215–38 **Plenty more. . .things** *L'um en porreit. . .finir*: A rather loose version of *Rec.* X.26.1–2.

[2] 11239–56 **Clement said. . .anything else** *Asez de cest. . .el*: An acknowledgement both of the omission of *Rec.* X.26.3–4 at this point and of the preceding abridgement of *Rec.* X.17–26.

[3] 11280 **by such things** *ne est aidee*: Following this line, *Rec.* X.27.3–7 is omitted.

considered as gods, hailed as gods, and served as gods. But nonetheless I cannot grasp how they can honour the so blatant evil in him which they would very much criticise and very much condemn in other people if they knew them guilty of such crimes." (11281–310)

St Peter said: "As you do not know why, I shall explain it you, and you may learn it. First of all they do it because by talking about him, they believe that they will endear themselves to the god by celebrating his deeds. There is likewise another reason why so many people gravitate towards these gods, for the poets who in the past earned praise and esteem for their writing composed these tales in verse; there were such people who wrote about them, and some of their writings have survived and are popular because of their fine composition. Those who wish to acquire learning focus on these writings in their childhood and youth, and then they will scarcely be able to avoid always believing what they learned in their youth."

Once he had heard this, Niceta replied to these words:

"My lord Peter, do not believe that those who were educated and considered to be wise people at that time did not have other reasons for this, for they added allegories with which they paint over the ignoble elements. They have little interest in the tales other than that they have used them as examples. Through analogies they wish to prove what in itself cannot be; they add embellishments to these tales, but nonetheless they are all liars. And if it pleases you that I should talk about the meaning of their allegory, I shall explain their arguments in accordance with what I have remembered. But nonetheless I do not wish to explain them because I should wish to affirm them, but rather in order to explain their sense to you. God forbid that I should agree with them!"[1]

St Peter granted permission for this, and so Niceta began: (11311–54)

"In Greece," he said, "there used to be two masters who were very highly esteemed: one of them was called Orpheus, and the other Hesiod. The masters who came subsequently all followed these two. Orpheus said nothing other than what Clement told you. Hesiod spoke about it in a different way, for he gave a meaning to the tales; he expounded on them, but his argumentation is very weak.[2] Saturn is the earliest one about whom the ancient writers wrote in their books. Hesiod said that in Greek he was called Chronos, the sense of which is nothing other than 'time,' for there is no other meaning in this word. Saturn was so old that nothing before him is known; in the same way nobody can extend his thought to before time. Saturn claimed Rea for himself; he stayed with her and made her his wife, and through their union they conceived many children. The allegory of this is that this Rea represents the matter from which everything is conceived

---

[1] 11349–52 **But nonetheless. . .agree with them** *Mes nepurquant. . .i asente*: While the preceding sentence renders *Rec.* X.29.3, these lines represent the delayed *Rec.* X.29.2.

[2] 11361–66 **Orpheus said. . .weak** *Orpheus. . .reisun*: An approximate version of *Rec.* X.30.2, after which *Rec.* X.30.3–31.3 has been omitted.

and then released: everything that the sky and earth hold comes from time and matter. Orcus, Neptune, and Jupiter were their sons, but I cannot recount and explain here everything that I find written about these three.[1] But nonetheless I shall say this much: that Orcus, who was the eldest child, was called Aides in Greek, and he was called Pluto; this Pluto represents hell, which is below earth and is not visible. The second son was Neptune, and this is the element which is called water. And Jupiter was the last, but he was the highest of the three: he represents the air above; the others are cold, and he is hot.[2] (11355–404)

By Juno, who was their sister, is meant the lower air which is intermediary between the sky and earth. Juno represents this air; Vulcan, fire; Phoebus, the sun; Mars, great burning;[3] Venus, beauty; and Mercury, who can fly, represents speech. And to explain things briefly so that one might better understand them,[4] everything which is in the sky and everything on the earth originates from time and matter; earth and water and air and sky originate from this, as does everything in anything else. Jupiter had great power, which was a great source of displeasure for his father. Jupiter chased him until he captured him and deprived him of his genitals so that he could no longer conceive; he bound him tightly and kept him restrained. This means that the higher air is strong because it is very hot; through the heat which comes from the air, time has lost all its power. Nothing more can come from time, and it must remain as it is. Never again will time and matter come together; never again will they create anything which has not previously existed, nor does anything else new originate from them. The world has been created, and all the things in the world have been created; even if time and matter come together, they will never again be able to create a new world. Hesiod explained it thus, and others subsequently said more about it; there are plenty of their writings which are still popular today, but why should I say any more about this and continue talking? For the pagans cover up nearly all their

---

[1] 11390–92 **but I cannot recount. . .three** *mes tut cunter. . .truis*: Depending on whether one reads the lines as direct speech or not, the translator may here place his own ignorance in the mouth of Niceta.

[2] 11389–404 **Orcus, Neptune. . .hot** *Orcus, Neptunus. . .chaud*: An abridgement of *Rec.* X.32, after which *Rec.* X.33 has been largely omitted.

[3] 11409–10 **Vulcan. . .Phoebus. . .Mars** *Vulcan. . .Phebus. . .Mars*: In a section which draws some of its content from *Rec.* X.34, Vulcan alone is imported from an earlier list of gods in *Rec.* X.27.4, thus creating, since he represents fire, a partial overlap with Mars, who represents a burning which, in *Rec.* X.34.4, is more clearly related to the fires of passion. The allusion to Phoebus shows our translator's mythological knowledge, since *Rec.* X.34.4 speaks of Apollo.

[4] 11413–14 **And to explain. . .understand them** *E pur briefment. . .entendre*: The translator here places in Niceta's mouth the acknowledgement of, and justification for, his own abridgements. The following paragraph contains a summary which includes the earlier omitted *Rec.* X.33.5–6.

errors with such embellishments, and through such allegories they turn fictional tales into philosophies." (11405–48)

Niceta's brother Aquila heard everything that he had said; he had said more there than I have said, and to this Aquila replied:

"Whoever first invented and wrote that from which no benefit comes," he said, "was exceedingly wicked and impious, and gave himself over to folly. For there is no need for the truth to be proved by falsehood in something which is quite clear and quite appropriate in itself; and when something is beautiful in itself, there is no need for any vile creation[1] or base invention in order to prove beauty through filth. Turning beauty into filth and truth into lie stems from nothing other than folly since there is no reason in this, for never will any man be bettered in his life through such an allegory. There is no morality or benefit, and everything is vain, but nonetheless I shall say what I feel about this for your betterment. Everything that people say about their gods was entirely true; they were all thus mired in filth and ignobility without any allegory being added. To my mind the pagans are not lying in the slightest in everything that they say about them; simple people who lived back then and had little intelligence commemorated their children, and they themselves were honoured.[2] There then came more intelligent people who noticed the error, but even though they were wise, they could not free themselves from their custom. And when they could not manage to undo the custom, they turned the tales, which are brimming with shameful filth, into allegories so that they might thereby be made more beautiful.[3] (11449–94)

But nonetheless no profit stems from everything that they have said: those whom the pagans worship as gods were exceedingly evil and wicked. But even though their conduct was disgusting, more deserving of accusations of folly are those who know that they were like this and nonetheless make them into their gods. It ought to seem quite logical that each person should take great pains to be like those gods whom they so invoke and honour. Saturn is one of their gods; may those who serve him become like him! May they have themselves castrated,

---

[1] 11462 **vile creation** *tritevele*: The word *tritevele* most often denotes dogs and hell-hounds; cf. *AND*, s.v. *tritevele*; Lewis Thorpe, "Tristewel et les autres chiens de l'enfer," in *Jean Misrahi Memorial Volume: Studies in Medieval Literature*, ed. Hans Runte, Henri Niedzielski, and William Hendrickson (Columbia, SC: French Literature Publications, 1977), 115–35. Here, however, this literal sense seems unlikely. *Tritevele* rather seems synonymous with the following *vilaine cuntu[v]ure* "base invention" and *ordure* "filth," forming part of the argument that there is no need to add any ignoble new elements to something which requires no alteration.

[2] 11449–84 **Niceta's brother. . .honoured** *Quanque Niceta. . .onurance*: These lines draw on *Rec.* X.35, but with significant modifications, with the final sentence having no clear equivalent in *Rec.*

[3] 11494 **more beautiful** *enbelies*: Following this line, *Rec.* X.36.2–5 is omitted.

and then they will be bound to earn his favour when they are as was he who had lost his genitals! As the lord, so the servant: the pair will be all the better suited for this! May they do likewise in respect of the other gods: may they strive to become like them, for as the god, so the one who worships him; anybody who acts thus honours his god![1]

But all this is nothing but jest, for our reason clearly tells us that anybody who wrote such errors in a book was given over to folly; such foolish writings should not have been accepted, but rather thrown into a fire. Young people should not see them and thereby be given a wicked foundation, but they should rather be instructed and through reason turned towards good. My lord Peter, if it so pleases you, you will say what you think of this."[2]

Aquila said this much and more.[3] Once he was silent, St Peter, who had ready everything that he was to say in response, then spoke: (11495–534)

"Be certain," he said, "and sure, my dear son Aquila, that there is no reason in the error that the pagans believe, nor anything but fabrication! God has ordained that it should be so and that there should be no reason, and that there should be no beauty in that which is contrary to the truth. Their cause is base and brimming with falsehood and baseness, and so cannot survive without always being proved to be wrong. For if their cause were such that it had a convincing appearance of truth and that one could make it such that there were any compelling reason in it, scarcely a man would be found who would abandon his habit and forsake falsehood in order to turn to the truth. For even though their cause is extremely base, it is very difficult to find anybody who is prepared to convert to God in order to serve Him; and what would happen if their cause were such that it had a reasonable defence? Which man would abandon the error whilst he could vouch for it? A man's mind holds firmly to what it learns during his youth; what he has learnt during youth will be removed from his mind with difficulty, and this is why God has so ordained it that it could easily be recognised that the error is foul and base and brimming with monstrous filth, and that it could be easily grasped that any reason to defend it is lacking. God has ordained this very well, and He does likewise with everything else. Everything that God does is beneficial, even if we have not grasped it; in everything that He does there is nothing but good, even if we do not see the reason for it." (11535–78)

St Peter said this much at this time, but the brothers said considerably more, for each of them said a great deal about what he had previously learnt about the

---

[1] 11495–518 **But nonetheless. . .honours his god** *Mes nepurquant. . .sun deu onure*: These lines draw on *Rec.* X.37, but there the castration of the followers of Saturn is a statement of fact, rather than the ironic recommendation that we find here.

[2] 11519–30 **But all this. . .of this** *Mes tut cest. . .a cest*: These lines reflect the essence of *Rec.* X.38.

[3] 11531 **Aquila said this much and more** *Tant e plus i dist Aquila*: An acknowledgement of the preceding abridgements.

tales and allegories; after that about the philosophies, and the kind of glosses which embellished the filth; and about the masters who had lived back then who had transformed the material and taken pains to harmonise the gloss and the literal sense; and how each one had said such reason as he was able to say, and presented meaning as far as he could find harmonious support for it. Clement, Niceta, and Aquila spoke a great deal about this, and in everything that they said they demonstrated the error of the pagans.[1] (11579–98)

St Peter had listened carefully to everything that each one wanted to say. Niceta had spoken last because Clement had asked him to tell them what he had heard read in school about a wedding at which all the gods had come to a supper. According to the pagans, all their gods gathered when Peleus took a girl called Thetis as his wife. Niceta told and recounted the whole tale, and then explained it all and turned it into philosophy, but I shall not do you the service of telling you any more about the wedding, for it is all falsehood and nonsense. And nonetheless St Peter listened to him when he recounted this; it was, he said, skilfully composed, even though no betterment was to be had from it.[2] (11599–620)

The three brothers fell silent presently, and directed their attention to St Peter. He then said to them: "It certainly seems to me that those who fabricated such things back then were very ingenious. They strove and took great pains to invent and present something which might appear true in order to transform into something acceptable what in itself is nothing but vile; they wanted thereby to redeem their writings, which had no merit in them. But one must not act in this way when one is to present and propound the law of God, for then it is appropriate that one should treat it wisely. No man should by himself undertake to understand it through his own wit; it is necessary to have a different teacher, for one's own intelligence achieves nothing unless there is also another master who is educated in the Scriptures. One can find many writings which are easy to transform by imposing various interpretations without altering anything of the letter, but there is no need to change interpretations in the Scriptures. One must not overly transform Holy Scripture by imposing interpretations which did not exist through an understanding conceived of individual will in order to hold it as an authority in contravention of reason and truth. The understanding to which one must hold must come from the Scriptures; one should not propose anything which does not have from Scripture the guarantee and firm support that what has been presented is true. It is therefore essential to have a good master who is to teach others well; but when he has subsequently learnt enough to be stable and

---

[1] 11579–98 **St Peter said. . .pagans** *Tant aparmeismes. . .mustrerent*: It is *Rec.* X.40 which is omitted at this point, but the content of the summary in this section stems rather from earlier chapters whose omission had already been signalled.

[2] 11599–620 **St Peter had. . .from it** *Escuté i out. . .amendement*: As the penultimate sentence suggests, this section is a brief summary of *Rec.* X.41.

secure from this, he will thenceforth be able to debate more freely, if the desire should so seize him, as reason will invite him to, about disciplines or anything else of which he has heard in his childhood or youth. But he must in all respects keep his mind from affirming anything other than that in which truth and rectitude exist with reason. May he beware of worshipping idols and confirming falsehood!"[1] (11621–74)

St Peter finished his speech with these words and then turned and looked at Faustinianus, who had listened to him very carefully. He spoke to him and asked how his mind stood, and said to him:

"Old man, if you care enough for your soul to be able to attain lasting peace when your soul is to leave your body, ask whatever so pleases you if there is anything about which you are in doubt! For it is by no means certain that a young man will have a long life, and one can be quite certain that an old man will not be long in this life. Young and old alike must therefore turn their minds to reforming. As much of this life as there may be left to come passes quickly; this respite will soon pass, and however it might be, it is very brief. Old and young alike must therefore think about being truly repentant: each person who wishes to save himself must turn to God, and must devote all his efforts to making his life good. He must take care to provide fine clothing for his soul; its clothing must be such as to have the knowledge of truth. He must clothe it in the purity of righteousness and chastity; he must have compassion and pity together with charity. With such and similar clothing the soul will be pure and bright and beautiful; a mind which understands reason must certainly have such clothing. (11675–714)

He must keep himself from any fellowship by which his clothing might be tarnished: he must associate with upstanding men and flee wicked men. He must cherish those fellowships and frequent those gatherings in which people speak of righteousness and how one is to flee vice, in which people talk about having pity and maintaining humility; about living well and chastely and about praying to God devoutly; about asking God for what is necessary and thanking Him in every way; about purging the conscience properly by performing worthy penance; about wholeheartedly renouncing past sins and giving alms to the poor—and may the alms be such as might be beneficial to penance! For one can quickly secure forgiveness by giving alms gladly: he who gives well will receive well, for God will have mercy on him. One should frequent such gatherings by which one might save souls, in which nothing is discussed except things which lead to good. (11715–42)

If the one who turns his mind to God and wishes to abandon all sins by receiving penance is a man greatly advanced in years, he must give great thanks to God for casting him out of danger, and all the more devoutly because once he

---

[1] 11673–74 **May he beware. . .confirming falsehood** *Guard sei. . .mençunge cunfermer*: An odd addition relative to *Rec.* X.42.5.

has lost the desire and pleasure which come from the flesh, he abandons falsehood and holds to the truth. God has done a great favour to that man by giving
him enough time, once carnal desire finds no substance in him by which it might
be ignited, to grasp what the truth is without being in any way distracted by the
temptation of the flesh, which greatly drags people towards perdition, for he does
not need to experience vexation or toil in order to tame his flesh. It is therefore
essential for him to remember deeds of mercy; he must persevere in such deeds
in order to perform penance well. May he not think that penitence consists solely
in abstinence and belabouring oneself for a long time with lengthy fasts and extended periods without sleep! Everything will be completed well if the heart is
firm in its purpose; the conversion is good when the devotion is good. God sees
the heart and understands it fully, and He takes it in accordance with how it is;
He pays more attention to the heart than He does to time, and it pleases Him
when He sees firm purpose there. He sees and knows full well who the people are
whose hearts are firm in their devotion to Him, and it pleases Him greatly when
a man turns to Him wholeheartedly and does not go seeking a delay whereby
much time may pass by, but rather has immediately recognised God as soon as
he has heeded Him, and is horrified by the past in which he persisted so long
in error, and then sets his desire entirely on being able to reach the kingdom of
God. (11743–90)

    We must therefore not delay, but rather let us strive to come near to Him.
Let us not neglect this; let each one of us with firm purpose set our hearts on the
kingdom of God so that we might joyfully reach it! May he who is poor not say:
'I cannot turn to God straightaway, but rather I shall convert to God when I am
a man rich in possessions.' It is not wise to speak like this, for God seeks no possessions other than a heart of mercy and such deeds as befit it. Likewise may the
man who is rich not refrain on account of his wealth and his worldly possessions
from converting and doing good. He must not delay or wait until he has managed to spend all his wealth or until he has managed to divide up all the grain
that he has amassed in granaries. May he not say in his heart: 'What shall I do
with my wealth? And what shall I do with my grain; in which place shall I store
it?' May he not have such faith in his wealth, and may he take care not to forget his soul! May he take particular care not to say to it: 'Great goods have been
stored up for you; eat, drink, be merry!' Anybody who says this shows little fore-
sight, for to him will be said: 'You stupid fool! You will have no respite beyond
this night! Your soul will be taken from you this night, and what will become
of your hoard then?' For this reason each person, whoever it may be — man or
woman, whatever his or her age; whether rich man or beggar, whatever his profession — must rush to convert so that he might expiate his sins and reach that
life which lasts for ever without end. It pleases God greatly, and He welcomes it,
when a young man gives himself to Him and puts his youth behind him in order
to have God in his mind, and turns his heart to God to the extent that he completely subjects himself to discipline. And the old man is to be praised when he

is prepared to abandon old habits and forsakes long-held customs in order to set his mind on God, and when he has such fear of God that he completely extricates himself from foolish error. (11791–846)

May there therefore be no hint of hesitation, nor may any more delay in this matter be sought! What cause is there to prevent a man from doing good deeds immediately? Are you afraid that for a good deed a great reward will not be given? How much worse off will you be if you strive to do good when good conscience alone is enough to present at the judgement? Do you then doubt the argument that when it comes to the reward, the great one will not be given for little, and because the deed passes quickly that a reasonable reward will not be given in that everlasting life? I have said this on account of those of false belief; everything is just as I have said, and it will in no way differ from what the prophecy says of it. (11847–66)

What is achieved by mentioning the philosophers or their books? In what way is any man bettered in his life through all their philosophy? Given that they themselves were mortal, how did they dare to speak of God and about how God is not mortal by guesswork and nothing else? How did they dare to speak about what cannot be seen? Why did it occur to them to speak through conjecture about how and when the world was created when not a single one of them was there when it was created? How and why did it occur to them to say what will be and what once was when there is no man who knows anything about it unless he has the gift of prophecy?[1] One should not speak about this through guesswork and supposition; in order to attain the truth, one must have the authority of prophecy, to which the entire doctrine that we propound is subject. In everything that we propose we say nothing of our own invention; we say nothing to you through speculation which might result in criticism of us, for to say anything which cannot be warranted is nothing other than to deceive people. We present nothing but patent things, comprehensible things, clear things for which we have authority from the Prophet of truth. Anybody who wishes to hear about the power of this Prophet and who He was, and about His prophecy, will find with us somebody to tell him about it: may he come to us without delay and be attentive in listening! For we shall promise to offer him such proof of the power of prophecy that as soon as he has heard it, it will seem to him that he can see it with his own eyes and even touch it. And once he has become so convinced that he turns to true faith, from then on everything that he has previously heard will seem simple to him. He will gladly turn to righteousness and pity once the love of God is fully aflame in his heart, and he will experience great sweetness from it. There will no longer be any labour which is in any way difficult or burdensome,[2] but rather the more that he hears of good, the more he will wish to hear of it." (11867–924)

---

[1] 11867–84 **What is achieved. . .prophecy** *Les philosophes. . .grace*: These lines reflect some elements of *Rec.* X.47–51.2.

[2] 11921–22 **There will. . .burdensome** *Puint de. . .fes*: Cf. Mt 11:30.

St Peter said a great deal about this and a lot about other matters resembling it. Some of those who were there present at that time and were afflicted by illnesses were cured by St Peter, who prayed for them; even the insane[1] left there fully healed. Then St Peter made everybody leave and told them to return there in the morning, for in that place he would tell them more about God. At his bidding, they departed and praised God with great joy; each went to his home, and St Peter did likewise. (11925–40)

St Peter had returned to his lodging, as did the three brothers with their father. It was high time to eat; all were ready to go when a man came and entered the house who bore this news:

Simon Magus, he told them, had arrived in town. Simon had with him two companions, both of whose names the messenger stated: he said that one was called Anubion, and the other he named as Appion. They had come there from Antioch and were lodging together with Simon.

When Faustinianus heard this, he was delighted by the news, for he had known those two previously and therefore wanted to talk to them. He sought leave from St Peter to greet them, and said: "Anubion and his companion Appion are friends of mine; I should like to go and greet them if I can secure your permission for this. And perhaps Anubion and I shall be able quickly to agree for him to come here with me and debate with Clement, specifically regarding genesis, for he is well versed in this topic."

St Peter said: "I very much commend you for thinking well of your friends, and I certainly grant that you should see them. But nonetheless you should consider how everything is happening for you: everything is turning out well for you! God has most favourably ordained for you this and everything which has befallen you: God bestowed a great gift on you when you found your wife and children; in addition to this He has caused your friends to come, and so you should appreciate them all the more." (11941–82)

"Everything that you say," Faustinianus said, "is true; I can see it clearly." He presently departed on his own without taking any companion with him. He sought the lodging of Anubion, who was staying with Simon. Once he had found it, he stayed there and did not return that night.[2] His sons remained with St Peter, and they spent their time asking many questions. They did not stop during the whole night, and considered it a pleasure to stay awake on account of the sweetness of the teaching to which their minds were turned. They spent the night learning and asked of St Peter many things about which they were uncertain, and they carefully noted his answers. The night passed, and dawn came, and presently St Peter looked at the three brothers and spoke:

---

[1] 11931 **insane** *desvez*: *Rec.* X.52.1 refers explicitly to the possessed.

[2] 11987–90 **He sought. . .that night** *Il quist. . .repeirat*: An addition relative to *Rec.* X.52.5 to clarify Faustinianus's absence.

"I am," he said, "quite bewildered as to why your father did not come back to us last night." (11983–12006)

Presently Faustinianus arrived and found St Peter there first, and his three sons sitting with him and talking about him amongst themselves. As he entered, he greeted them all in order and explained the reason why he had been unable to return the previous night. The sons looked at their father, but were anything but welcoming to him: they grew exceedingly afraid the more they looked upon him. They did not behave like sons towards him, so crestfallen and aghast were they, for it seemed to all three that their father's face appeared to be that of the Simon who bore the surname Magus, and he seemed identical to him in his appearance! It was nonetheless still the case that he had his own voice. To anybody who stared at his face he would look exactly like Simon Magus, but anybody who had been acquainted with him previously would recognise him by his speech. But nonetheless his sons did not consider him to be their father on account of that face; all three considered him to be Simon, for his appearance presented him as such. Only St Peter was not deceived by this; he saw clearly that this man was their father.[1] (12007–36)

Faustinianus was astonished when he saw and heard his sons behaving so harshly towards him and showing him no love, but rather fleeing from him and cursing his face. Only St Peter, who saw nothing on him but his real face, addressed the three brothers together: "Why," he said, "are you acting like this? Why do you step back and curse your father?" The mother was there with her sons; as they were, so was she, for they were all utterly astonished, and they replied on the basis of the appearance that they saw:

"This man's face seems to be Simon's, but his voice appears to be our father's!"

St Peter said: "You can clearly hear that his voice has not been changed in the slightest; sorcery could not change his voice, for today it is as it was yesterday. You cannot perceive any of his other features, but I can see his real face: I can clearly see that this is Faustinianus and that he has his old face, but you and others who see him believe to be seeing Simon in him. Through sorcery Simon has managed to impose his appearance on him; he appears to you and others to be Simon, but I can see his true face clearly."

He looked at the old man, who was unaware of all this:

"Both your wife and your sons," he said, "are very upset because of you, for the face that you used to have is not to be seen on you, but rather you have a different one: the wicked and deceptive Simon has imposed his face on you!" (12037–76)

---

[1] 12015–36 **The sons. . .was their father** *Les fiz . . . lur pere fu*: A substantial amplification of *Rec.* X.53.4 in order to enhance the drama.

As he said these words, a messenger came and brought to them what had been entrusted to him from Antioch, from where he had come. St Peter had sent some of his companions, of whom this messenger was one, to Antioch, and this man had now returned from there; the companions who had remained there had sent him back to St Peter. The messenger delivered his message to St Peter, and described what outrageous things Simon was doing in Antioch and how he was slandering him:

"My lord Peter," he said, "Simon is causing great harm to you! I very much wish you to know that he has already sought to do a great deal of harm to you. He has remained in Antioch and performed many wonders there; in front of the people he has said and done enough to draw their hearts to him. He has given the people there to believe that you are skilled in sorcery; he calls you nothing other than an enchanter and is causing you to be considered a sorcerer; he is taking great pains and striving greatly to cause as much trouble for you as possible. He has caused you to be so hated by everybody that if you were to come there, they would tear you to pieces with their very teeth; never would they let you leave with your life! We who had gone there on your behalf, when we saw and recognised that there was no point in your coming to the city with it being so agitated, gathered in secret and had a long talk about it. We discussed what was to be done, but we saw nothing but obstacles. (12077–116)

We had reached a point where we had run out of ideas when, at just the right time, Cornelius the Centurion[1] arrived, having come from Caesarea, saying that he had been sent on behalf of the prefect of Caesarea to carry out his business there. We summoned him to speak to us and explained our woes to him; we asked him to help us and give us honest advice. He responded very readily: 'If,' he said, 'you trust my advice and do what I shall tell you, I believe that I can indeed help you. I shall drive Simon, who is so deceptive and wicked, away from here.' We promised to do everything and follow his advice in all respects. He then said: 'The emperor Caesar has ordered us to search everywhere, both around Rome and elsewhere, for those who are considered to be sorcerers, and that those who are engaged in sorcery should be arrested without hope of release. Many of them have already been arrested, and many have been put to death. I shall give everybody here to believe that I have come here for no other reason than to capture this Simon and those whom I can find with him—that my men and I have come here to place him in tight shackles—and that I shall take him away with me, bound in shackles, to the place where I shall have him condemned. I shall give my friends to believe that I have come here for no reason other than to arrest him, and you must spread the very same news to all those with whom you speak. May your men secretly give his followers to believe that I am waiting here for no other reason than because I wish to arrest Simon here, for I am quite certain that

---

[1] 12120 **Cornelius the Centurion** *Cornelius Centuriun*: On his association with Peter, cf. Acts 10.

once he hears this, he will immediately take flight; or if you have a better idea, you may state your opinion to us now.' (12117–64)

What more should I say? We all immediately agreed to do what he had told us, for his advice pleased us greatly. Some of our men joined up with those who were on Simon's side; they put on a pretence to them and recounted what news they had heard. Once the news had spread far enough to reach Simon, he was very grateful that he had been forewarned of this and immediately fled from there; he left in this manner and is now here, as we have heard say. When we who were there saw this, we all decided together to apprise and warn you not to hasten your arrival. Do not come near Antioch until you hear further news from there, and whether the fact that he has fled from there has caused things to be forgotten somewhat, and that the hearts of the people who have conceived such hatred for you have changed." (12165–88)

Once the man who had come from Antioch had delivered his message, St Peter had thought carefully, and he looked at Faustinianus:

"Faustinianus," he said, "listen! You have been disguised by Simon. He would like to harm you, and so has imposed his face on you, for he believed that the emperor had instigated a search for him in Antioch in order to condemn him for practising sorcery, and out of fear he fled from there once he heard news of this. He has altered your countenance and imposed his face on you, for he would like you to be captured and put to death in his place. He would like to bring about your death in this way and cause sorrow to your sons." (12189–208)

Once the old man knew what had become of him, he wept bitterly about it and lamented terribly; he considered himself utterly confounded and disgraced, and with tears in his eyes he replied:

"My lord Peter, you have said it: it is true that I have been duped in this way! I have been most cruelly deceived. Anubion wanted to warn me in secret precisely to beware of Simon. He wanted to warn me of his plot, for he had known me for a long while, but I, wretch that I am, did not believe him in this regard, for I had never done any harm to Simon; I did not suspect his plot at all, for I had done him no wrong. Woe is me, ill-fated wretch! What sorrow I have consigned myself to! I heard it said a good while ago that Simon was a most redoubtable trickster, but I was not prepared to believe of him that he was such a wicked man. Woe is me, wretch! What has happened? How have I been so confounded that as soon as I have found my children and my wife after so many years, I could not have the opportunity to experience joy with them for one day, but rather have plunged myself back into the misery in which I was before, or even worse?"

The old man was utterly anguished, and wanted to leave, if only he knew where to go. But even though he was utterly crestfallen from this, even more crestfallen was his wife: she tore at her hair and had lost all control of herself; she wept disconsolately, and was unable to curb her sorrow. Their three sons were likewise extremely upset about their father once they had seen him with a completely different face than he had previously had and did not know how he had acquired that appearance.[1] (12209–52)

Presently Anubion arrived, saying that Simon had fled; he had left there that night and had fled in the direction of Judaea. Anubion saw how they appeared and how they were behaving; pity seized him, for the sorrow that he had seen amongst them was very great.

St Peter looked at the brothers, who appeared utterly dispirited. He said to them: "Stop all this grieving! I assure you: believe me that this man is without any question your father! Do not step back because of him, but rather I strongly urge you to step towards him and do as good sons should. God will give you an opportunity for him to lose Simon's face: he will return to his true appearance and will be exactly as he was before."

He then turned to the old man and accused him of a transgression: "You had," he said, "my permission to greet your friends Anubion and Appion, but in no way to talk to Simon!"

"It is true!" Faustinianus said. "I have acted wrongly in this regard; I freely admit it." (12253–80)

Anubion then spoke in order to seek forgiveness for the old man: "Peter," he said, "I implore you to pardon this man for everything that he has done wrong in this matter, for I know him: he is a noble man. But this good man was unsuspecting, as a result of which the poor wretch was deceived. Simon duped him; hear how, for I was there and wish to tell you everything that happened. When he came to greet us, it so happened that Appion and I were with Simon. Simon revealed to us that he wanted to flee the next night, for he was afraid of the news that he had heard and on account of which has fled from here. He informed us that he had been told that people had allegedly come to Laodicea to arrest him, and so he did not dare stay there any longer. They had come on behalf of the emperor, and so he wanted to effect a transformation and impose his face on the man who had come there at that very moment; through this he wished to deflect onto him all the wrongs that he himself had committed. He said to us in secret: (12281–309)

'All I ask of you is to make this man stay and join us for supper, for I shall make a certain ointment which, after eating, he will immediately smear all over his face and thereby resemble me in such a way that all those who subsequently see him will truly believe that I am he. But beforehand I shall have you smeared with the juice of a plant that I know such that if you are smeared with it beforehand, you will then be unable to be deceived in such a way that his face is not

---

[1] 12225–52 **Woe is me. . .appearance** *Las mei. . .chiere*: These lines are out of sequence in that they render most of *Rec.* X.57.2–3, placing the despair of Faustinianus and his family immediately after Peter's revelation, whereas in *Rec.* X.57.1 it is preceded by the arrival of Anubion.

visible to you; none of his appearance will be hidden from you. All except for you will believe that he is Simon on account of this juice.'

I replied to what he said: 'What is the benefit to you of doing this? What will be the gain that you will secure by doing what you are intending?'

'I have,' he said, 'planned this in order to secure the gain and profit that when those who have been seeking me come and look him in the face, they may arrest him, and then stop looking for me. And if he were condemned to death, I would thereby be avenged upon his two sons who abandoned me and defected to Peter. They have completely turned against me and are helping Peter in all respects, and so it would be a great comfort to me if their father were ignominiously killed, for they would without doubt grieve terribly if they lost their father ignominiously.' (12309–46)

I have told you the truth of how everything transpired, but I was afraid to speak of it in order to apprise Faustinianus. Simon did not permit me to leave so that I might warn this man; I could not even find an opportunity to speak with this man in secret so that he might beware of being deceived by Simon. Simon fled the next night, and Appion went with him, together with another companion by the name of Anthenodorus. These two went with Simon and accompanied him in the direction of Judaea, but I lied and pretended that an illness had overcome me, and by saying this I strove to remain, and have stayed in order to make all haste to come here so that you might hide this man away until those men who were supposed to arrest Simon have left the country, lest he be arrested in Simon's place because he appears through his face to be him and be taken to the emperor to suffer a dishonourable death. I was very preoccupied by this matter and hastened to come here in order to find Faustinianus here, but I must return immediately before the return of the companions who left to accompany Simon." (12347–80)

Anubion recounted all this, and then said to the three brothers: "Be sure," he said, "in all truth, without any deception or dishonesty, that I recognise and see without any deception your father in his true appearance, for I clearly know and clearly see that he has nothing on him but his true face. In no way does he lack his true face; I am not deceived by this, for I was smeared with the juice of a plant by Simon before he changed his appearance, as a result of which I cannot be deceived, but rather I see him as I have known him; I have known Faustinianus for a long time, and I still see that face on him. But I am astonished that you can be deceived about your father by Simon's magic, but it is quite clear that he is a sorcerer when on account of his magic you do not recognise your father, even though you see him." (12381–402)

The weeping to which the father and mother and their three sons were reduced on account of what had happened was harrowing and heart-rending; so much did they wail, so much did they weep that Anubion felt pity for them and could not keep himself from weeping.

Great pity seized St Peter on account of the grief that he saw, and he promised them that he would return the father's true face to him and would remove Simon's face: "Faustinianus," St Peter said, "I shall cause the true face that you have lost through Simon, who has deceived you, to be restored to you, but nonetheless let us see to it that we will first of all benefit from it! I shall return it to you as long as you do as I command."

Faustinianus promised to do whatever St Peter wanted as long as he would cause him to have his true face, in return for which he would do anything. (12403–24)

St Peter kept to his promise and so began to say:

"You heard clearly with your own ears, if you paid any heed to it, that that man who had been sent to Antioch and came on behalf of those who have remained there in order to say what they found there described how Simon Magus was there and had agitated all the people. The city is completely incensed, and he has incited it against me; he says that I am a sorcerer and a murderer and a deceiver. He has caused me to be so hated by everybody that if they could seize me there, they would be very much inclined, if they had me in their power, to tear me to pieces and devour me with great fury. But do as I tell you: Clement is to remain here with me, and you are to proceed to Antioch, taking your wife with you. Your sons Faustus and Faustinus will also depart with you, and others who will show you the right way will accompany you, for I shall send with you people who will execute my commands properly. When you arrive in Antioch, as you resemble Simon you will explain in front of the people there that you are most repentant. With the people listening you will speak thus: (12425–59)

'I, Simon, have returned here in order to tell you that I have erred in what I said against Peter: I admit before you all that everything that I said about him is false! Be quite sure that he is not a deceiver or a murderer or a sorcerer, nor anything of what I told you, but rather everything that I said about him resulted from anger; the evil that I spoke of him came from rancour, from a madness which possessed me. I have taken great pains to cause trouble for him so that you should not listen to him, but you should rather not listen to me if I say anything more which might cause you to be angry towards him. Do not feel any hostility towards him, for I tell you truly and honestly about him that everybody can benefit from the goodness on account of which he has come. He is the disciple and messenger of a Prophet who is so wise and in whom there is no falsehood, for he is completely honest. I therefore come to urge you in all good faith and to entreat you to listen to what he will say and to trust his advice in all respects, for if you do not do so, you will be at risk of experiencing a calamity through which the city will be destroyed if his word is not received. I tell you this because the angel of God came to me in a vision last night, and through him I now stand in true faith. He harshly reproached and rebuked me and punished me through a sound beating for having opposed that man who is principled and a friend of God. I therefore implore you: if I ever come again and oppose Peter in any way, flee from me and do not listen to anything that I might say against him! For I freely admit that I was a sorcerer and a deceiver, but I have changed and am utterly repentant. One should renounce evil; one can expiate great transgressions by repenting in worthy fashion.'" (12460–508)

Faustinianus was by now quite aware of everything that St Peter sought from this: "I am quite aware," he said, "of what you seek; do not trouble yourself further! I am quite aware of what I am to do when I see the time and place for this purpose."

St Peter said: "When you arrive in the city to which you are going and see the people coming ready to convert on account of what they hear you say, and that their desire for me is such that they abandon the anger with which they so mortally hate me, summon me immediately, and I shall come; I shall delay no longer thereafter. As soon as I come to you, your true face will be restored to you; I shall cause you to be fully recognised by everybody and shall remove Simon's face."

St Peter did not want him to linger, but rather ordered him to depart, and likewise his wife and his two sons, who were very upset because of him; he also dispatched with him many people whom I am unable to name.[1] (12509–34)

Matthidia, who was his wife, was very anxious about this journey. She refused outright to accompany him as long as that face was to be seen on him: "I shall not," she said, "accompany him, nor shall I ever associate with him, for I would consider myself an adulteress if I were to walk a single step with him! He will never associate with me as long as Simon's face is to be seen on him, and if anybody wishes to compel me to travel with him, his body will not come anywhere near mine, nor will he lie in a bed with me. But I do not yet accept that I shall walk a single step with him."

She objected loudly and refused loudly, and said that she did not dare to accompany him as long as he had Simon's face. In response to this, Anubion said to her:

"Trust Peter and me: it is your husband whom I see here. This is your spouse Faustinianus; hear his voice, which clearly identifies him! Do not inquire any further than this, for I love him no less than you do; do not be afraid to go with him, for I shall accompany you!"

She then begrudgingly assented to go with him.[2]

By the middle of the night those whom St Peter had ordered were ready, and well before daybreak they set off from there, with Anubion accompanying them. (12535–68)

---

[1] 12533–34 **many people . . . name** *tels que . . . Plusurs*: Our translator's ignorance of the names stems from their absence from *Rec.* X.62.4.

[2] 12564 **go with him** *aler od lui*: Following this line, *Rec.* X.63.1 is omitted.

St Peter, who stayed behind with Clement, was in Laodicea. In the morning Appion, who had left with Simon, appeared there. Before St Peter came
out of the house where he was staying, Appion stood at the door, and with him
Anthenodorus; they asked those who were going in and out for Faustinianus.
St Peter did not wish them to be refused entry to his lodging; he ordered that
they be shown in, and when they entered, he asked them to sit down. As soon as
they were seated, they inquired whether anybody could tell them anything about
Faustinianus: "Where," they said, "is Faustinianus?"

St Peter said: "We do not know. Not a single one of his acquaintances whom
we have with us has managed to see him in the last three days since he headed
to you in the evening. But yesterday Simon came here looking for him. He came
in the morning, but to little avail: we did not wish to speak to him, and he could
not obtain the slightest useful response. We did not know what he had in mind at
that time, but he kept telling us and claiming that he himself was Faustinianus,
but we did not believe him a word of this. When he saw that he could not persuade us to believe what he was saying, he was utterly dejected and upset by this,
and he wept bitterly. He threatened that he would leave and kill himself. Once
he had said this, he stayed here no longer, but rather headed off in the direction
of the sea." (12569–606)

Once they had heard this reply, Appion and his companions all began to
wail loudly and to give every appearance of being upset: "Alas!" they said. "What
have you done? Alas, the poor wretch! Why did you not keep him there as he
was and believe him?"

Anthenodorus presently wanted to speak and tell Clement more, for he
wanted to admit openly to him that the man of whom they were speaking was
his father Faustinianus. Appion clearly noticed this, but cut off his speech by
speaking before him:

"Faustinianus," he said, "has turned to Simon and has joined him. One of his
men told us this, for it vexes him greatly that his sons have changed their religion
and become Jews. He hates them so much and is so fearful of them because of
this that he does not even wish to see them with his own eyes, and therefore he
has asked to be Simon's companion. We were told this, but in order to ascertain
whether it was falsehood or truth, we came here in order to ascertain for sure
whether he had come here or not. But it certainly seems, since he is not here,
that what we have heard is true, and that he talked to Simon so much that he has
departed with him. We wanted you to know this and so came here." (12607–42)

Clement had clearly recognised why St Peter had replied guardedly to Appion and the others who had likewise come there with Appion and had sought
Faustinianus there, for he wanted them to harbour suspicions which would cause
them to stay there no longer, but rather flee from there through fear and seek
Faustinianus elsewhere. Clement did not want them to notice enough that they

might discern anything of their secret, and wishing to hide it from Appion, he therefore began to speak:

"Appion," he said, "my dear friend, we wish to tell our father the good that we have learnt, and then it will be up to him to choose what he wishes to reject or accept once we have explained it to him. And if it is the case that it vexes him to hear good, and he flees from us, we will pay him no more heed from that moment on, for we shall care for him no longer."

Appion was aghast when Clement spoke to him in this way, for both he and the others who were with him judged him to be a very harsh man. They all cursed his cruelty and did not stay there from that moment on; they set off after Simon, as St Peter learned the next morning. (12643–74)

Faustinianus continued his journey until he reached Antioch; he entered there with his companions and presented himself as Simon. All the people came running to him when they saw him entering the city; nobody, poor or rich, hesitated to hurry there. They all gathered around him and all saw him as Simon; they all thought that he had come there in order to do what Simon did. They expected to see his usual wonders, but they found something completely different in him, for he admitted in full public view, because he had his present appearance, that everything that Simon had done or said was nothing but a lie:[1]

"For a long time," he said, "God has permitted me to be wicked, and this is clear to me. I am Simon the wretched; too long have I lived, too long have I survived! Everything that you have seen in me and considered to be a wonder is neither true nor a reliable thing, but rather I have done everything through the Devil's magic. Through lies I wanted to cause you to stray from true faith; I have consigned myself to a terrible fate, for my soul is damned and lost. Before all of you here I admit that I have lied about Peter in all respects, for he is not a murderer, nor was he ever in his whole life a sorcerer or a deceiver or anything of what I have often told you. He behaves very honestly and conducts himself very faithfully; he has come for no other reason than to lead people to their salvation. He has very great power in him, and so be certain not to feel any more rancour towards him, for if you trouble him in any way, a calamity may befall you from which this city may perish. In no way reject him, but rather welcome him! It is not for no reason that I say this to you, for the angel of God has rebuked me harshly. Very bitterly did he reproach me and very harshly did he beat and chastise me because I took such pains to cause all manner of harm to Peter. (12675–728)

---

[1] 12675–92 **Faustinianus continued. . .but a lie** *Faustinien. . .si mençunge nun*: The first of a series of changes as *Clement* reaches *Rec.* X.65–72. The content of the present section is derived from the speech delivered by a messenger in *Rec.* X.65a, with X.65 proper omitted for the moment.

Good people, I now beseech all of you together to expel me forcefully from here if my mind should subsequently change so that I conceive hatred for Peter, nor to tolerate me amongst you if you hear me saying anything more to besmirch him! For the Devil, who hates all good, strives to hinder good. It causes him great grief and great sorrow when he sees any man who persists in anything which might bring his salvation; such a man does not bring any peace to the Devil. The Devil made me say so much against Peter in order to prevent you from reaching the life which cannot end. That I made dogs of brass bark and images move by themselves and that I often changed my appearance, I managed entirely through sorcery. You should certainly have realised this when you saw no benefit in it; you should not have paid any heed to it when it was entirely vain. I deceived you through the magic of the Devil, to whom I had entirely surrendered myself in order to turn you away from Peter and prevent you from listening to him. You may derive very great benefit both from his deeds and from his words. He performs incredible miracles: lepers are cured by him; without any evil deception he cures those who are stricken by palsy; he causes the insane to regain their sanity and those who are dead to rise; he causes them to return to life completely, and he cures all illnesses. He performs such miracles in full public view in the name of the one whom he professes and who sends him as His messenger. If you listen to him, you will be acting very wisely!"[1]

Faustinianus said this and other things,[2] and he expressed everything that he said very well. (12729–74)

The people were aggrieved and very unhappy when they heard this; they wept bitterly and lamented when they saw themselves deceived in this way. It upset them terribly that they had done wrong to St Peter in hating him so much on account of Simon, who had slandered him; all their minds changed so that they greatly desired St Peter. The anger that there had been was now completely removed from their hearts; they felt nothing but warmth for him, but they were angry at Simon. There were many who were so furious that they were very much inclined to seize the man whom they saw there, and very nearly captured him in most ignominious fashion. They intended to hurt him because he admitted that he had sought to cause so much harm to St Peter, and so they had nearly seized him. Faustinianus had recognised that they did not wish him well; their appearance was such that he was afraid that he might be seized there and treated harshly. He clearly saw that they greatly desired for St Peter to come there, and he clearly recognised that they were all extremely angry at him. He therefore

---

[1] 12693–772 **For a long time. . .very wisely** *Pose ad. . .que sage*: These lines render *Rec.* X.66, but by omitting the messenger turn into unmediated direct speech the messenger's delivery of the address by Faustinianus.

[2] 12773 **and other things** *e el*: Despite what the line suggests, there have been no significant omissions.

summoned a messenger to dispatch immediately for Laodicea in order to send word that St Peter should hurry there. The messenger was to describe all that had happened to Faustinianus, and to instruct Peter to come quickly to rescue him before the people harmed him, for there was nobody there who wished him well. The messenger whom he summoned had come there with him; he was one of his companions, and so he was not afraid of him. The messenger fully understood everything that Faustinianus said to him; he immediately set out for Laodicea as fast as possible.[1] That very same day, in the late evening, the old man regained his true face; he completely lost the appearance of Simon so that it was no longer to be seen on him. The power of Jesus Christ did this, for human agency played no part in this. (12775–826)

I do not know[2] where Simon was at that time, but nonetheless news of this event reached him where he was, and it vexed him greatly. He felt utterly confounded and disgraced that he had failed in his objective when what he had done to harm St Peter resulted in his glory. He plotted desperately like a man stricken by anxiety. I do not know whether he sought the opinion of anybody else or whether he took the decision by himself, but he immediately headed back towards Antioch at high speed. Before St Peter arrived there, Simon came and strove to restore the old man's true face to him, who had regained it completely without his help. He strove to do this through sorcery, but he had arrived too late, for before Simon had come, the old man's face had been restored to him. It was restored to him without any sorcery, for Jesus Christ had restored it. (12827–50)

Once Niceta and Aquila, who had come there with their father, noticed that their father had regained his face, and that he had said enough to the people that nothing more needed to be said, they did not allow him to speak any more or keep showing himself to the people, but rather they praised God profusely for restoring his true face to him.

Simon spoke in secret to those who had previously been his supporters and allies, but he found them completely changed. He engaged in even more vicious and hateful slander of St Peter than he had done before, but all who heard him, great and small, spat straight in his face. They cast him from the city in utter shame and ignominy. With one voice they all said to him: "If you are ever seen

---

[1] 12775–820 **The people were aggrieved. . .as possible** *Dolenz en fud. . .demeintenant*: The initial part of this section (vv. 12775–82) follows *Rec.* X.67.1 quite closely, but X.67.2 does not begin until v. 12821. The second part of the section (vv. 12783–812) derives from *Rec.* X.65.2–4, although the information delivered by our narrator is in *Rec.* a report from a messenger. The arrival of the messenger in the final sentence (vv. 12813–20) stems from *Rec.* X.65.1.

[2] 12827, 12837 **I do not know** *Ne sai*: The profession of ignorance on both occasions is our translator's.

here again having come with evil intent and to say anything against Peter, you will certainly meet your death: no other payment will be sought from you!"

Simon, who had gained little honour there, presently departed. (12851–78).

St Peter, who had striven to preach diligently and to turn people to God, had remained in Laodicea; he had very much devoted his effort to this. More than a week had passed since the old man had left, as had many companions with him.

Nine days had already passed. On the tenth day the messenger who had come in order to describe the old man's situation to St Peter arrived at full speed. The messenger recounted exactly how things stood for the old man, and precisely how he had behaved when he arrived in Antioch. He presented himself, he said, to the people and spoke at great length to everybody there; he immediately spoke against Simon because his face was to be seen on him. He said many terrible things about Simon and admitted to them that the bad things that he had said about St Peter were entirely false, and he spoke in a completely different way. He said very good things about St Peter, and freely admitted that he was a good man; he had praised him before everybody until he had put their minds at rest. Their anger had been entirely removed; he could come there in safety, for he was very much desired there, but they were so furious at Simon that, on account of the countenance which was to be seen on the old man, they wished to harm him because he looked like Simon, as a result of which the old man was very afraid. And because he was so afraid, the messenger urged St Peter to hurry: "Hurry!" the messenger said. "There is no reason for you to delay! Do not hesitate to come there, so that you might find Faustinianus alive! The people are utterly furious at him, and so I have come here as fast as possible so that you might hurry there quickly enough to find him alive. Hurry likewise for the sake of the people who so greatly desire and expect you: hurry to fulfil their desire; hurry to come there immediately!"[1] (12879–928)

Once the messenger had said everything which had been entrusted to him, St Peter, who had listened to it all, was overjoyed by it, for it pleased him greatly. The next day he gathered together as many of the people as he could muster. He made one of his followers into a bishop and baptised many of the pagans. He ordained many priests, and stayed there for three days thereafter. All the sick who were there regained their health before he left; the insane were cured there, and St Peter restored health to everybody. He was not prepared to stay in Laodicea any longer; after the third day he took his leave and departed; he headed for Antioch once he had done all that he had to do, time and space permitting, for everybody in Antioch greatly desired his visit. (12929–50)

---

[1] 12879–928 **St Peter. . .immediately** *A Laodice. . .chaudpas la venir*: If the content appears familiar, it is because *Clement* has returned to *Rec.* X.65.1–4 (cf. note to vv. 12775–820), this time following the source more closely.

Niceta and Aquila in the meantime went announcing through the city that St Peter was coming there, which gave the people great joy. The powerful and wise men, the most noble and the oldest, indeed the vast majority of the city came in great humility and gathered together; all of them bore ashes on their heads. They went out of Antioch on account of the news that they had heard about St Peter, who was on his way there and was close to entering. When he arrived, and they saw him, they acknowledged their guilt to him; they clearly demonstrated that they regretted that they had been hostile to him when they had been deceived by Simon, who had caused them nothing but harm. St Peter entered the city, and the humility and the warm welcome that all of the people extended to him pleased him greatly. Presently the city's sick were brought before him, some stricken by palsy, some of the others lame or mute, and many feverish or insane, or sorely beset by other ailments. There were many infirm there once they had all gathered. (12951–82)

Once St Peter had seen exactly how they had behaved, what penance they were performing because they had been deceived by Simon, and moreover that they had such faith that they clearly knew and clearly believed that he was of such great power that he could restore health to those who had been brought there stricken by serious illnesses, he raised his hands towards heaven with tears in his eyes and praised God. His devotion grew as a result, and so he offered this prayer:

"God, Our Father, may you be blessed by me and by everything that you have created! We should indeed all praise you and profess your name everywhere, for you make real the claims and promises of your Son. Through you everything that we learned from Him is completely fulfilled for us; you clearly show us that in heaven above and on earth below there is no God but you, and you wish every one of your creations to be sure of this." (12983–13008)

St Peter prayed in this way, and once he had said his prayer, he climbed up and stood in a place from which he could be seen. He ordered that the sick be brought before him. He had them placed in a line before him, and then he spoke to them and said:

"I have come here to you just as you all see me. You must not believe me to be anything other than a mortal man: I am a man just like one of you once I am no longer in the body of a man.[1] You must not believe that I can give health to you, but rather He who came to earth for the sake of sinners can help you. He came down from heaven to earth for the benefit of man, and in order to teach to those prepared to heed Him a medicine through which they will never experience any more sickness, but rather their soul and body will be saved. Therefore pay careful heed, if you wish to regain your health, to demonstrating here in full public

---

[1] 13017–22 **I have come. . .a man** *Tel cume. . .plus*: Cf. Acts 10:16, 14:15.

view that you are firm of faith. May there be no delay or any excuse! I wish all the people whom I see here to witness that you believe in good faith and with all your heart in Jesus Christ, who offered Himself in order to redeem sinners. May you do this so thoroughly that these people might derive from you an example to think about themselves so carefully that they might save themselves before God!"

Presently all the infirm there present cried out with one voice; each of them, great and small, said: "The one of whom Peter speaks is the true God!" (13009–50)

Presently there came a light which was very bright and beautiful and great: the grace of God appeared there and lingered amongst the people. The brightness came suddenly and remained there for a long while. At that very moment those who had previously been unable to walk arose; suddenly all the lame and crippled stood upright; those who had previously lost their sight regained it and use of their eyes; each of those who was stricken by palsy arose. They all ran to St Peter's feet as soon as they regained their health. Some of them had been carried there, so afflicted by illness that they could barely draw breath, and then a breath which was feeble and shallow; these people likewise were immediately cured, and all jumped healthy to their feet. Anybody who had been insane regained his sanity, and the Devil no longer had power over him. All those who had arrived sick were fully cured; they greatly rejoiced over their health and praised God greatly for this. The Holy Spirit demonstrated such grace and such power in that place that the great and small there present hailed God with one voice. Within seven days, to state it briefly,[1] ten thousand men were converted by St Peter, and they believed in God and were all baptised. (13051–86)

A nobleman from the city who had the most power there and was called Theophilus owned a house in the city which was sufficiently broad and long to hold a gathering of many people. Theophilus turned to God and gave up his house; he donated it to be a church, for it was well suited to this purpose, and in accordance with his donation St Peter consecrated it as a church. The people fashioned a chair there and placed St Peter on it; this was done to honour him, and the honour which was done to him on that day is still commemorated in Holy Church. It is celebrated seven days before the first day on which March begins: on that day there is a celebration for St Peter on account of the chair on which he was placed that day; it is still commemorated.[2]

---

[1] 13083 **to state it briefly** *pur briefment dire*: The abbreviation is not by our translator, but by Clement narrating in *Rec.*

[2] 13101–10 **this was done. . .commemorated** *Ceo lui fud feit. . .endure*: The allusion to the Feast of the Chair of Peter (February 22) is an addition by the translator relative to *Rec.* X.71.3.

St Peter was in that church where the chair had been placed for him. He preached about God and spoke about God to those who came to him there. The people came in throngs and listened to him very willingly; they converted in throngs on account of the miracles that they saw there, for the sick who came there were all cured by St Peter.

Clement, Niceta and Aquila, and their mother Matthidia spoke to the old man in a secluded spot. By asking questions the sons wanted to ascertain their father's state of mind, and if anything remained in his heart which was leading him more to bad than good. (13087–128)

The old man had quickly reached a decision when asked about this: "Come with me," he said, "to St Peter straightaway, and you will see how my belief has grown. There I shall give you definite proof of it!" Faustinianus went to St Peter and placed himself on the ground at his feet. Lying completely stretched out, he spoke to him and revealed his thoughts to him:
"The seed that you sowed," he said, "has yielded a fine harvest! Everything that I heard said about God is flourishing and has grown well; the words that you sowed have taken firm root in me. The crop from them is already so ripe that it awaits nothing except one to reap it. Remove from me whatever chaff there is, and then place me in God's granary; make me one who shares in God so that I might dine at His table!" (13129–50)

St Peter was absolutely overjoyed once he had heard this. He himself took him by the hand like a man who felt no disdain. He handed him to his three sons, who felt very reassured by this, and as he handed him to them he said very briefly to the old man:

"Just as God has watched over you so that you have found your sons, may your sons likewise see to it that you are given to God by them!"
As he said these words, he imposed a fast on all the people; he made all the people fast, and he himself was the first to begin it. The week was near its end, and when the next began on the Sunday, Faustinianus was baptised, and St Peter made him a Christian. From this he then drew material for a speech, and he began to recount before the people there present exactly what had happened to him. He recounted and said so much about it and conveyed his story so well that all the people turned to the old man and gazed at him as if an angel of God had descended from heaven and come there. The citizens showed him great reverence and honoured him just as much as they did St Peter, all treating him in the warmest way. (13151–84)

St Peter remained in Antioch until he had caused all those to convert who were prepared to consent to him. Once he had done as much as he could there and won over as many people as he could, he headed off towards Rome, and once he arrived, he stayed there. There he went about preaching to everybody and he performed many great miracles. He converted a great number of people to Jesus Christ, seeking nothing else there; those who were converted by him made him pope of Rome. St Peter stayed there preaching constantly about Jesus Christ until that Lord whom he had served wished to reward him for his service.[1] (13185–202)

God apprised St Peter that he was soon to leave this world; he had travelled until he reached Rome and learned from God that he would die there. The days passed until that day was coming very near on which he knew for sure that he was certain to die. One day he sat down in the company of those whom he had in his brethren; all those seated around him listened to him. Once he had everybody's attention, he then rose and stood up, and then seized Clement and made him rise and stand beside him. He made him stand in full sight of everybody, and then with everybody listening he said:

"Brothers who serve God together with me, now heed me! My Lord and master Jesus Christ, who summoned me here and sent me both here and elsewhere to do what he entrusted to me, has informed and apprised me that I am to remain here no longer; and because the day is near, and I do not have much longer to live, I ordain this man Clement as bishop as a man whom I know well. I entrust my chair to him, for I have known him well for a long time; I entrust all my preaching to him and his name alone. From now onwards I entrust to him my teaching and my entire duty, for he has remained with me constantly since he first came to me. He has remained in my company constantly without any outrageous or ignoble behaviour. Since he has remained with me, he has heard and seen everything that I have said and everything that I have done, and he knows exactly how I am. He has clearly heard and remembered what the power and strength of all my preaching are and the reason to which it leads, for when we have stayed in one place and when we have travelled, and when we have been at rest and at work, he has always been near me and at hand, and he has taken great pains to learn. I tested him thoroughly a long time ago and I have found him to be more faithful than all others. He loves God very faithfully and his neighbour as is appropriate; he has devoted himself entirely to doing good, for he is chaste and very sober. He pursues righteousness in all respects, and is kind and so patient that he wishes no harm or hurt against anybody, even somebody who wrongs him. (13203–64)

Since I know him to be such and understand him to be such, I give all my power to him: the power to absolve and to bind as he sees fit, just as I received

---

[1] 13185–202 **St Peter. . .his service** *Seint Pierre. . .lui vout*: This transitional narrative joins the translation of the *Recognitiones* to that of the *Epistula ad Iacobum*, and stands in place of Clement's salutation to James in *Ep.* 1.

it from Jesus Christ, I hand to him. And in order that everything that he sees and wishes on earth might be fixed in heaven, in accordance with what he deems appropriate it will be his duty to bind and absolve as a man who clearly understands everything which pertains to Holy Church. He has carefully listened to and carefully learnt all aspects of the governance of Holy Church, and so I tell you to listen to him and to heed him. For you should be quite sure that anybody who disturbs the teacher who speaks the truth will sin most grievously against Jesus Christ and God the Father, who created and ordained all things as pleased Him: anybody who opposes God in this way has lost any chance of living with Him. The one who is to be above others and to be a leader and master in order to guide others well must have the same manner as doctors have in order to work effectively; he must not be like a cruel and fierce beast." (13265–94)

Clement fell at St Peter's feet, utterly astonished by what he had heard from him, and he implored mercy from him. He made many excuses and begged him sincerely to choose somebody else for this honour. He had no interest in the chair, and Peter should take somebody else to place on it; he should hand all the power and all the honour to some worthy man, to someone who was better able to avail himself of it and was worthy to receive it!

"Your efforts are in vain," St Peter said. "There is no use in requesting this! You will be finding excuses in vain, for God has promised me that the more you refuse to be bishop, the more surely and the more quickly you will become one. The chair demands to have someone able to govern it, for the chair demands not the one who schemes so much that he desires and covets it, but rather the one who shrinks away from it, and somebody of pure life who will keep it well and guide it well, and who is very capable of speaking of God and can be of profit to many. If I knew a worthy man other than you who was better and had stayed with me as long as you have, and who knew as much, and who had striven to listen until he had learnt more and better, and who knew as much about my teaching and the reason to which it is subject, and who knew as much about the governance of Holy Church as I am sure that you, who heard exactly what I said and how I said it, know—if I could find such a man other than you for this duty, you would not be chosen by me when you shrink away so much and refuse this good work! (13295–339)

But it is not right that this work should remain undone, nor is there any need to look elsewhere for any other worthier man since we have you here at hand, who know everything that is required. I insist on you specifically all the more wholeheartedly because you are a Roman, born in Rome, and you will be the first man of whom I shall make my offering to God of all the Romans whom I have won over, and of the other people who have completely abandoned paganism and accepted baptism: you will be offered first of all, before the others, by my hand. But beware of another thing: that if you are so afraid of the danger of committing a sin if you take over the support and leadership of Holy Church, which cannot be without a guide, I can tell you in absolute certainty that you will commit a far greater sin if you abandon Holy Church by not helping her in her hour of need, and on account of seeking benefit only for yourself you do not think of others' salvation, and are not prepared to share the grace that God gives to you. It is a grave sin to abandon and fail to help the people of God, who are as if in great danger of being shipwrecked at sea. If you are quite capable and quite able to help the people and are not prepared to do so, you therefore remain in danger by failing to help them. But be sure that you must not make any more excuses: you will have to accept Holy Church with all the dangers that there are, because as long as I live, I shall not stop asking and constantly urging you on account of the salvation of all. The sooner you do my bidding in this, the sooner you will save me from anxiety, and the sooner I shall be relieved of that by which I am so troubled; you will have freed me from sorrow so that I will then be able to live joyfully. (13340–90)

I am quite aware, Clement, that you will experience vexation and will suffer great hardship; you will not avoid having to suffer tribulation and great criticism from people who are poorly educated and feel great animosity towards good. But by suffering patiently anybody who slanders and anybody who quarrels, and by striving to have firm hope in God, who repays and rewards all good deeds and places a crown on those who suffer, I am quite certain that you will overcome everything and will thrive nobly. Through patience you will triumph in all respects; I am so sure of this that I have no doubt about it whatsoever. Likewise also pay heed to the reason that I have in mind. When does God have greater need of you and your service: now, when the Devil has begun a battle again Holy Church, the Bride of Jesus Christ, who won her by suffering death—but she has remained on earth without enjoying any peace, constantly embattled, and seeking to receive help against the Devil, who defies her—or at the end of this life, when the battle will be over, and the Devil will be disgraced and routed and defeated, and the Son of God with His great victory will lead His Bride to glory? There will be no need of help once this time and hour have come! What man is so feeble-minded that he cannot fully understand and clearly see that now is the time and now is the place that the Son of God requires you? You must act now; attend to His service now. In no way does He forget anybody who serves Him; be sure that you do not fail Him! Do not fail Him in this hour of need; take great pains to serve Him! Provide Him with help which will aid Him in winning His battle; He is a good king and will reward everything as soon as He has won. Therefore accept this duty with glad heart, for He awaits you; accept the duty of bishop all the more because you have learnt from me how to protect Holy Church properly and are capable of governing it properly. Accept Holy Church for the sake of the salvation of the people who have entered God's faith through us, and make sure not to cause their faith to falter and sway as if on a swing. (13391–452)

But nonetheless I wish briefly to inform and instruct you; before all the people who are watching us and listening I shall very briefly describe to you the governance of Holy Church. You must first of all be of good conduct and strive to live such that you are free from the world. Strive to divorce yourself from all secular concerns: do not be a guarantor or lawyer to support any case or argument; do not engage in any quarrel or conflict for temporal gain, no matter how much it may be worth. God has not prepared you so that you should be ordained bishop in order to listen to and deal with legal cases and abandon the word of God; God does not wish you to be involved in secular business in any shape or form, which might prevent you from performing your duty well. Do not be so wrapped up in the world that you lose the sense that God has granted to you, such as recognising truly which people are good and which are bad, which truthful and which false. If anything should happen through which a legal case arises, the laypeople are to discuss it; the laypeople should strive hard to maintain justice and keep the peace. They should resolve amongst themselves whatever is committed against the law in their midst; they are to spare you from it in such a way that you do not even have to think of it. Just as it is a grave sin if you neglect to preach the word of God as befits your duty, the laypeople will also commit a grave sin if, as soon as a case arises amongst them, they do not take pains amongst themselves to ensure that there is peace and that strife is avoided without you being informed of it and in any way becoming involved. And if the laypeople perchance do not understand enough of justice and are not sufficiently skilled in law to resolve it themselves, then let the deacons step forward and deal with it. They are to teach the laypeople and free you from concerns so that you can devote your attention exclusively to Holy Church and to nothing else. And if you are capable of governing Holy Church appropriately and guarding her as worthily as you must, then you must pay careful attention to serving only God by speaking the word of God and preaching His truth everywhere, all the more wholeheartedly and diligently because your attention is not diverted elsewhere. (13453–519)

For if you are distracted to the point of being given over to the world by paying greater heed to extraneous cases than to the common and supreme good, you first of all will be deceived, and neither you nor anybody else will then benefit from it: both they and you will be deceived by this, and so you must be all the more mindful of this. You will not be able to do everything required of you fervently, and then, when you cannot do everything for everybody, great damage will befall you. You will experience harm from it first of all, for you will fall into such suffering on account of the transgression that you have committed that you will not escape without punishment, and on account of your lack of teaching your followers will likewise fall into utter damnation through ignorance and nothing else. Therefore be mindful to speak of God whenever you have the opportunity so that all those who are prepared to hear you might attain their salvation. They must listen to you frequently and show you great reverence; they must listen carefully to preaching about God in order to grasp what they do not know. They must know, if they are truly wise, that you have come as a messenger, for you come as the messenger of God when you preach of God and His power, and you will have from God such power that everything that you bind on earth will be bound in heaven above; no man will have power over you.[1] You will likewise be the power in respect of everything that you loose, for it is necessary for various reasons to bind and loose in accordance with what is just and right, and frequently to restrain and release." (13520–62)

Through this and other teachings St Peter showed Clement how he should first of all guide himself, and then others.

He then dealt with the priests, and described every aspect of their life to them. He told them clearly that each priest must lead a very pure life:[2] "It is part of their duty," he said, "to advise girls well. They must strive assiduously to marry them off in their youth before their passion becomes too inflamed; they must be compelled lest they head into dishonour because of the strength of their heat. (13563–78)

They must likewise not neglect to marry off older women in honest fashion lest they debase themselves. It very often happens that even in old age a woman cannot cool down from the heat with which she was inflamed during her youth. It is a grave sin and a disgrace to lapse into fornication, and the more often it is performed, the more heinous the sin will be. It is therefore necessary to act, and to ensure by marrying them off that all opportunity to indulge in fornication is removed and that no cause for lapsing into adultery should arise in them.[3] Adultery is a grave sin; none will be judged more harshly than this, with the sole exception of denial of God, which cannot be expiated, for those who deny God will have no further share in Him, no matter how soberly they live, for everything that they do will be worth absolutely nothing. And therefore you who are priests and are ordained to be masters in the good leadership of Holy Church, may your attention be turned to ensuring that Holy Church is well protected and finely adorned by you; keep it chaste so that there is nothing there but purity! She is the Bride of Jesus Christ; He offered Himself in order to save her. He saved her, He redeemed her, and He therefore holds her all the more dear. The Bride thus named is the congregation of God's faithful who move to Holy Church and persist in the service of God. If you devote such care and attention that the Bridegroom finds no blemish in her, and make her so beautiful and bright that nothing ignoble is seen in her, she will be greatly honoured for being found to be

---

[1] 13553–56 **and you will. . .power over you** *E tel poesté. . .poesté ne avrat*: Cf. Mt 16:19, 18:18.

[2] 13563–70 **Through this...pure life** *Par tel. . . chescun prestre*: A transitional narrative added by our translator. The final sentence, urging sacerdotal continence, has no basis in the source at this point.

[3] 13587–96 **It is a grave sin. . .in them** *Pechié est grant. . .en avuilteire*: In *Ep.* 7.3, the warning against adultery is addressed to the priests, not women.

pure, and you will experience joy and benefit from this, for you will be fully rewarded for everything that you devoted to the Bride, as from that time onwards you will be placed with both the Bridegroom and the Bride. Love is good, and for anybody who practises it properly the joy will be great and the love will be great, and the sweetness will never come to an end. And if by chance the Bridegroom should happen to find any stain in her and that she is not completely pure and untainted, as she should by rights be, He will quickly turn against her and hold her in such disdain that she will never come near Him and will never lie in the royal bed. He will not accept her into His presence as soon as He discovers baseness, and you who have not protected her better will experience punishment with her. All the blame will be placed on you for protecting her poorly; you will bear a very harsh sentence if you are proved guilty of such sloth and negligence that what ought to be in the Bride is not there.[1] (13579–652)

May the Bride be sure not to slacken, but rather may she strive and take pains above all else to behave soberly and chastely at all times. May she keep herself from fornication, from which nothing but evil can come: it is a most criminal sin which consigns man to the abyss. Anybody who lies in fornication places his soul in utter perdition; anybody who engages in such a sin is acting most foolishly, for God hates it, and so one should avoid it all the more, for it is an utterly wicked thing.[2] There are many kinds of fornication, of which Clement will apprise you, but above all others and in first place is adultery, which God hates the most. It displeases God above all else when a married man leaves his wife, or the wife leaves her husband; both of these are utterly deplorable. Anybody who is prepared to remain chaste may attain other virtues: mercy will follow from this, from which a person will become kind, and he will acquire charity because he will take pity on his neighbour, and in accordance with the good that he does to him he will discover mercy from it. Just as the person who is poisoned with adultery falls into grave sin, for it is like a poison which spreads everywhere and takes people quite unawares, by the same token anybody who has charity and demonstrates pure brotherly love places himself so high by maintaining this that he cannot climb any higher than this, for anybody who loves God and man has encompassed the essence of all goodness. I therefore tell you: make sure to love your brothers after God; remain in perfect harmony, in sweetness and mercy! The religion will be most wonderful if you act harmoniously; you absolutely must be prepared and must take care of everybody. If you see a poor orphan, do good to him as you would to a cousin; support him tenderly, as would a father and mother their child. Do good to poor widows: comfort them most tenderly, and find for them what they need. Avoid any ignoble behaviour: make sure that

---

[1] 13605–52 **And therefore. . .is not there** *E pur ceo. . .estre i devreit*: A considerable amplification and clarification of the metaphors in *Ep.* 7.5–7.

[2] 13659–66 **it is a most. . .wicked thing** *Ceo est un pechié. . .malveis afaire*: A strengthened condemnation of adultery relative to *Ep.* 8.1.

whatever charity you give them is entirely respectable, and above all else may whatever good you do to them be performed chastely.[1] Marry off young widows, and thereby save them from danger. Place those who are not skilled in a profession in a suitable duty; have them do whatever might benefit them in which there is no ignominy, so that they might earn for themselves what they need in order to survive. Do not let those who are skilled in a profession sit around idly. Take great pains to comfort the weak and the infirm. (13653–724)

I am sure that you will do everything that I have said well if you persist in love and charity and remain loyal to everybody. Always be mindful to affirm charity in your hearts; God will help you greatly in this regard if you seek it wholeheartedly. It can be very helpful in this regard if you are prepared to gather together often and to partake together often of the good that God gives to you. Eat bread and something else with each other, and if you have nothing better, bread and salt. If you gather together often in this way, you will have all goodness in charity. Those who adopt this custom will have great peace in their heart; all goodness will be where there is peace, and it will all lead to salvation. Invite often those brothers who especially love God; share with them charitably the good that God has given to you. May they come to dine with you often, and God will grant you your reward: by summoning such people to your table you will obtain everlasting joy. Feed the hungry for the sake of God, and strive hard to provide clothes for those who have none; provide for the poor everything that they need. Be sure not to fail those who are afflicted by sickness, and help the wretches who have been captured and placed in prison; use all your power to free them. Always be prepared to welcome strangers; receive them into your houses and extend them every comfort that you can. And lest I dwell on this any further, there is no use in enumerating all the good things which ought to be done, and so I wish to draw to a conclusion. I shall nonetheless briefly say that charity encompasses all that is good, and if you have charity, you will be abundantly sure of what to do and what to avoid, without need of any other instructor: charity teaches one to do all that is good, just as hatred does the contrary. Anybody who harbours hatred in his heart moves himself away from his salvation; hatred always distances from good, and charity teaches all that is good. (13725–82)

If one cleric wrongs another, and they cannot achieve reconciliation on their own, may they seek arbitration from Holy Church without turning to secular justice; may they go and present everything to the priests and entrust their business to them, and then follow their judgement and do as they command. Always avoid avarice, which is the root of all vice; no good comes from avarice, for it seeks nothing but earthly gain. Avarice is a covetousness from which utterly wicked actions often originate; terrible evil comes from avarice, and anybody who

---

[1] 13705–12 **Do good. . .chastely** *A povres vedves. . .bien*: A significant amplification of the brief exhortation of chastity in *Ep.* 8.5.

persists in it loses the kingdom of God.[1] Take special care to ensure that there are accurate measures everywhere; maintain everywhere accurate scales and accurate weights which are free from deception; be honest, and return everything that you have taken into your keeping. You will do this and other things very well if you always remain mindful of God, and if it often crosses your mind how the last judgement will be: if you consider how harsh it will be, you will be seized by utter horror of it; you will then be afraid to do wrong, and this will make you heed what is good. How can any man who is prepared to think carefully about this commit a sin? May no man think that it is nonsense that the judgement will surely come; may everybody be sure that it will come, but this world will come to an end before then. Both good and evil acts which have been previously committed will be revealed in full view there; all those who have done good will be well rewarded there, and those who persist in evil here will head into merciless punishment. Each man will receive his just desserts there, but some will receive gain, and others loss, and anybody who is not prepared to believe this here will become aware of it when it is time to receive. The True Prophet Jesus Christ told us everything that I have said here; he clearly apprised us of this and of the judgement which will come. (13783–832)

I therefore say to you who wish to belong to the school of our good master: listen to Him like good disciples and remove discord from your hearts. May nobody harbour animosity towards anybody else, from which no good arises, but rather evil comes; be simple and humble, and then all your affairs will go well! And if by chance it should happen that one of you were to feel himself beset by a wicked sin such as envy, may he not permit it to become fixed and remain in his heart or take up residence there. May he do likewise with any other sin if he feels himself in any way troubled by it: may he immediately go and reveal it to his prelate without feeling any shame; may he admit everything to him without hiding anything, and may he seek counsel until he finds good and healthy advice of avail against the sin troubling him. The one who is to steer his soul by speaking the word of God will offer him comfort in good faith which will benefit him greatly; he will lead him to true faith which will certainly cause him to come to his senses. Through good faith he will do good deeds which will cause him to leave behind that suffering that he had in his heart through the sin, and so he will escape the fire which always burns, and will secure the great joy which never ends." (13833–66)

St Peter instructed the priests by telling them this about their affairs. He then turned to the deacons and taught them about their duty:[2]

---

[1] 13791–98 **Always avoid. . .God** *Tut tens vus guardez. . .tient*: The condemnation of avarice is an addition relative to *Ep.* 10.2.

[2] 13867–70 **St Peter. . .their duty** *Seint Pierre. . .les asensat*: This transitional narrative between *Ep.* 11 and 12 has been added by the translator.

"May those who are deacons," he said, "perform well the duties for which they have been ordained. As soon as they are ordained, they are to be like the eyes of the bishop. May each man strive his utmost to behave in religious fashion and to inspect Holy Church thoroughly so that there may be nothing to criticise. And if it should so be that they see anything which causes them to suspect something other than good, especially if there is anybody whose conduct is such that he is set to fall into sin, may they immediately go and warn the bishop so that he might be prevented from falling, or if he has fallen, that he might be lifted back up. They must apprise the bishop of everything that they see going awry; they must warn him and act so that he might draw the sinner towards goodness. (13867–90)

If they see any man being negligent, and that he comes to church rarely and has no interest in coming there in order to hear the word of God when the bishop is delivering a sermon—for everybody should go there—they must summon him politely and urge him to reform. Those who go there regularly to listen and carefully remember what they hear will experience comfort not only in that life which awaits them in the next world, where God will give them the life which will never end, but also in this world they will be comforted in the face of every adversity, even if an incident which causes them great suffering should occur, such as by being upset if they are hurt or angry, or on account of temporal harm such as loss of their possessions through pestilence or in other fashion, as often happens in the world, or if something is said to them in a base and outrageous fashion which causes them as much grief in every waking hour as if they had in their heart an arrow which were firmly lodged there and which could not be extracted from it. They will be easily freed from such woes and many others by which people are often troubled if they let themselves be properly advised by their bishop, who will tell them things to comfort them. His preaching will manage, if they obey him properly, to relieve them of everything by which they had been troubled. Those who are not prepared to believe me in this regard may experience great harm: as long as they stay away and do not hear the word of God, they will remain completely without comfort in all their adversity. They will be unhappy and upset and brimming with sin; they will lose the kingdom of God in this way and will burn like bramble bushes and thorns. If any ground responds badly and yields thorns instead of wheat, or is so deficient in itself that it bears nothing but bramble bushes, it is right, when nothing of any benefit comes from it, that it should be set on fire so that what grows on it might be burnt and destroyed since no good comes from it. May the deacons do their duty without neglecting anything. (13891–950)

May they take special care of the infirm and strive to help them. They must apprise the people of who the sick are and that they should visit them, and in accordance with what their circumstances permit, may they share with them what they have. For the sake of God may each person share his possessions with them in such a way that their prelate knows about it; and nonetheless it will not be a sin even if they have not apprised him of it. May they inform the bishop when a stranger comes to stay; they must apprise him of it so that he might be ready to receive the stranger who has need either of drink or of food. The deacons must be prepared in this and other matters with all that they know; may they not be slack or slow in what pertains to Holy Church.

It is their duty to strive to improve others both through examples and through words that they have learnt in a good school. They must be very well educated before they become instructors to other people; they must be learned enough to be able to care for souls. They must know when and how they are to speak to people; they must be very discrete and be aware of the capabilities of each person. They must speak to all in such a way that all might profit from it. They must be well prepared in advance so that they might be understood by everybody; they must adapt to everybody and cause themselves to be loved by everybody. May each man be sure, when it is time to speak, to observe order in his material. The one who is to teach others must behave responsibly; he must pay sufficient attention to himself that no cause for reproach might be found in him. In addition to the obligation to know a great deal, he must fear nothing on earth, but rather he must speak bravely about everything that he knows which pertains to God, just as I believe and am sure that you will see from Clement: everything that you hear from me here you will perchance see in him.[1] If I wished to say everything here that I could say about how each person should behave, it would amount to a great deal. But nonetheless it is my wish above all else to hear that you are behaving sensibly and well and that you are maintaining harmony and peace so that when you are to leave here, you might reach the city of which the King of Kings is Lord. All who are there experience joy and peace. (13951–14014)

To anybody who considers the situation in which Holy Church is placed, she very much resembles a ship which is at sea that people have boarded in order to make a crossing. They have come there from various places, and the ship that all enter who wish to reach the place where nobody can die from death is large. He who is Lord of that land is more powerful than any other king; in that land is the city where all good things are in great abundance. The ship travels well with its sail raised as long as the weather is favourable, and it very often lists when the wind is not to its advantage. And when the wind blows wildly, and the waves crash into it, and there is a great risk of being wrecked, it then needs a good guide. May God, who has heaven and earth in His hand, be its supreme guide, and may Jesus Christ Our Saviour lead the ship safely towards land; may the leadership be entrusted to them, the Father and the Son who are one God. May the bishop who watches over the whole ship sit at the prow; may the priests

---

[1] 13971–14002 **It is their duty. . .see in him** *Lur mestier est. . .en lui verrez*: In *Ep.* 13.1, this instruction is directed towards catechists with charge of catechumens. There is considerable amplification in the translation of the importance of education for the clergy.

sit at the oars, ready to row when they are summoned; may the deacons not be idle there, but rather they must be diligent in watching over and organising everything which is necessary in the ship; may those in lower orders make sure that they do not slacken in weighing anchors, tending ropes, and taking care of everything which is necessary: may each do all that he can, for all will be needed in the ship. May those who have boarded the ship who have learnt nothing of the sea — that is to say, the laity — remain completely quiet in it.[1] This is the nature of the ship, and this is the nature of those who perform one duty and another in it. (14015–60)

The sea represents this world, which is brimming with wicked malice. The winds which blow wildly and the waves which cause damage represent the temptations which beset Holy Church. The storms and great floods which combine vigorously resemble the persecutions, dangers, and tribulations by which Holy Church is troubled and very often harmed. The winds which come in great gusts from the valleys and the waters resemble the false prophets who go breathing the lies by which many are often so deceived that they are induced into error by them. The rocks which are in the sea can clearly represent those who show themselves to be extremely harsh once they have risen to great power: they are merciless in doing wrong and condemning people to death; both by threats and by other means they cause themselves to be considered cruel and wicked; they destroy so much and persecute so much as they do not care what harm they do. That the waves come together and often crash into the ship — they disintegrate when they reach it and do not stay together any longer — represents those who are very weak in their belief: as they are not of firm faith, they spend a great deal of time debating amongst themselves in order to seek reason and provide proof for what one can only believe. Those who are mendacious and hypocritical resemble robbers who roam the seas. The danger called Charybdis which so vigorously drags towards perdition, which swallows everything and consumes everything which comes near it and happens upon it — what can this better represent than the grave and criminal sins which drag people towards everlasting death without hope of remedy or redemption? These dangers are to be greatly feared, and each person should guard very carefully against them. Those who have boarded the ship and are heading silently towards the land and the desired city where there is neither quarrel nor strife — but rather there are peace, love, and joy which always last and never diminish — must pray to God wholeheartedly that they might pass through the dangers and land at the place where there is neither danger nor obstacle: namely at the city where there is every goodness and no trace of evil. God will gladly hear their prayer if they strive to be such that their works are good and they refrain from doing evil; their prayer will be heard by Him when it is supported by good deeds. (14061–128)

---

[1] 14055–58 **May those. . .quiet in it** *Cil ki. . .coement*: This element has been brought forward from *Ep.* 15.1, and is repeated in its proper place in vv. 14129–34.

May those who have boarded the ship remain quiet and calm. They should not move from their spot, but rather remain silent and make sure not to disturb the sailors from doing their duty. They must not run or rush or scuffle or tussle there, as a result of which the ship might capsize, and they might all sink. May those who have a duty and have been designated as masters, namely as deacons and priests, and likewise all the others in orders who have been prepared to do a duty, each say and act as his duty demands; may each man firmly exhort the next to behave well and act with decorum. May those who watch over the rigging neglect nothing of their task: may they make sure that they have ready everything needed for guiding the ship; may each one make sure in timely fashion that he has ready everything that he ought to have. The bishop, who sits at the prow and can oversee everything from there, must steer the whole ship by speaking the word of God. May all with great love heed Jesus Christ the good Saviour. All must heed Him since he steers the ship safely. He guides the ship of Holy Church, and nobody who trusts properly in Him can perish. Everything that He commands must be done, and everything that He says must be firmly believed; all must follow Him and must obey Him in all respects. And God, our supreme Father, must also be implored to protect the ship and provide such a wind that it might sail well, without being wrecked or fearing the great dangers which lie in the sea. (14129–72)

This world is often in turmoil and is rarely in a settled state; as the sea rises and falls, it makes it difficult to be there in a storm. The world is very dangerous; it is very changeable and very unpredictable. Those who live there for a long time gain greater experience of this. It is often in great commotion: there is frequently both famine and thirst, and it is necessary to eat and drink frequently, for anybody who does not do this cannot survive there; those who have no clothes suffer from the cold there, and many people are sick there; people lie in wait for others, and those who are afraid take flight. Very many in the world experience great anguish and great fear: there are many in exile, many very sick and infirm, but God, whenever He so wishes, will reunite the exiled. Those who travel by sea often relieve themselves by vomiting; the sickness which weighs on their heart exits from their body through their mouth. This represents the good confession that many in this world offer for the sins with which they are burdened. They confess by mouth everything for which their heart causes them remorse and which leads them to everlasting death, and they admit everything that they have done, and through that confession God grants them true forgiveness for it. Just as the body recovers because the bile comes out through vomiting, in the same way the conscience recovers both from the evil deeds and from the consent to wickedness by which it felt burdened as long as it had the sickness inside it. Many are often nauseated by whatever it is that they have consumed, and the soul is wont to grow sick when it takes pleasure in wicked desire. Vomiting cures the body, and confession cures the soul, but those who have been purged through vomiting need a diet. May they be very careful of consuming anything which must subsequently be to their detriment; may those who have confessed likewise keep themselves very strictly from wicked thoughts and wicked desires and from anything which can harm them![1] (14173–228)

But nonetheless be aware that the bishop, as he is at the front, must suffer and toil more than those whom he has to steer. When God comes to grant rewards, each man will be ready to claim for himself. The reward will be given in accordance with each person's labour, but to the bishop will be given the just desserts of everybody, together with his own. Both will be awarded to him, but in accordance with what he deserves."

St Peter spoke at length both to those in orders and to the other people, and then he turned to Clement and strove hard to teach him:[2] (14229–44)

"Clement," he said, "be prepared; be aware that you are above everybody else! You must regularly bear all the toil and all the burden of everybody; devote all your attention so that each person might feel well. I entrust my duty to you here, but I am losing nothing in handing it over: I have hereby entirely entrusted to you the grace that God granted to me; I give it all and have it all, and you will have it all, and I shall have it. Take comfort in God; I trust in Him that you will do it well. From the tribulations that you suffer here you will secure great reward when you land safely with the ship of God that you are guiding. When you lead it safe and sound and undamaged to the shore, your reward will be ready for you; it will be first for you yourself, and then for the ship and for each person who is in it you will receive a reward. If perchance you are hated, and even the brethren conceive hatred for you on account of your doing what is right and remaining strict, may such hatred be of no concern to you precisely on account of righteousness. Have no fear of this, for God will give you His love; you must not be concerned by this, for it cannot greatly harm you. Have no interest in being praised or criticised by a wicked man; have no interest in gaining the hatred or love of a wicked man, for the love of wicked people rarely leads to any good. As their hate is, so is their love; in both of them there is little honour. It will be much better for you to love righteousness and to observe moderation in all respects: by maintaining this you will be praised and well loved by Jesus Christ." (14245–90)

St Peter turned to the people once he had said this to Clement. He spoke to the people and said to them:

"Dear brothers and servants of Jesus Christ, be obedient in all respects to Clement, whom you see here! I am placing him above you in order to protect you and teach what is true. Be aware that anybody who upsets him will have done wrong to Jesus Christ, who entrusts his chair to him, and will have a lot with which to deal; and anybody who transgresses against Jesus Christ greatly offends

---

[1] 14195–228 Those who travel. . .harm them *Suvent se soelent. . .nuisir*: These lines clarify the analogy between vomiting and confession in *Ep.* 15.5

[2] 14241–44 St Peter. . . to teach him *Seint Pierre. . .se penat*: This transitional narrative has been added by our translator.

God His Father: His Father is not ready to receive anybody who is not ready to cherish Jesus Christ; a harsh judgement will be meted out for this, for he will not be accepted into God's kingdom. May each person therefore be prepared for this and do what he ought to do! Gather on appointed days and hear the word of God. Keep yourself from negligence and remove sloth from yourselves, for if you are negligent, damnation awaits you for this, and if you are slothful, the door to God's kingdom will be closed for you, for Jesus Christ will shut you out and will never let you enter thereafter. Return to Clement often and strive to earn his grace; you must not forget him, but rather should be there on his behalf in all places. Do not permit anybody to do him wrong, and then you will deserve his grace. He is facing a powerful enemy by whom he will be most viciously attacked; he alone will stand on all your behalf, and he must be valiant and brave. He must make sure not to falter when he enters battle on all your behalf, and so it is essential that you should always be near him with great love: hold firmly to him and be obedient to him. If you and he are of one mind, both you and he will be secure; the Devil will not be able to harm him, but rather Clement will be able to destroy him. (14291–340)

He cannot pay attention to everything when he offers himself in order to defend you, and so you must undertake certain things on your own; you must know many things by yourselves without having a master. If it should be the case that wicked people are slandering Clement and he himself cannot attend to this or defend himself against them—namely if somebody hates him and is seeking to do as much harm as he can, and when he cannot do any worse, he disparages and maligns him for the good things that he does—those of you who hear this must be prepared and must strive to be his shield. You must not wait until Clement comes and orders you or asks you himself; be there for him without any request whatsoever. You must not hold dear those people who are not prepared to follow him; you must know his intention, even if he is not acquainted with you. You must flee their company for as long as they persist in malice; you must not even speak to them when you do not see Clement speaking to them. You are not to keep away from them for the sake of causing harm or disgrace to them, but rather so that those who are guilty, when they lose their friends, might repent of their folly when you no longer associate with them, and out of shame or for other reasons might refrain from continuing to act in that way and reconcile themselves with their prelate by renouncing all wicked strife, and so that when they see themselves without support, they might abandon their wicked purpose and cease what they had undertaken once they see themselves without backing and alone, and once they no longer have any associates, they might come in order to humble themselves and be obedient towards that man whom they had previously been slandering. He who associates with such people whilst they harbour such rancour and who is prepared to speak to them when they are not prepared to reform and when Clement is not prepared to speak to them is exactly like one of them: he wishes to destroy Holy Church once he has associated himself with them. Even if this man goes in and out with you, his heart is not there, but rather his body: his heart is completely against you, and you must be all the more watchful of him. He is a considerably more powerful enemy, and it is necessary to be more careful of him than of one who quite openly persists in hostility, for he who comes and goes with you and pretends to stand with you through the friendship that he is feigning is destroying Holy Church." (14341–406)

Once St Peter had said enough to suffice for everybody, he cast his hand forth and grasped Clement in full view of all the people. He seized him from his chair; Clement very much wanted to step away, but St Peter compelled him and, with everybody watching, placed him on the chair.

Once Clement was seated on the chair, he was extremely ashamed; had he not greatly feared St Peter in this regard, he would have utterly refused. St Peter was joyful and happy when he saw Clement sitting on the chair. He then made a request of him, and in front of everybody there he said:[1] (14407–22)

"I ask one thing of you, Clement, in front of those here present: that it should not be forgotten, once you know that I have passed on, that you should write down what you know that I have said. Briefly write down everything that you have seen of me since you came to me, and in writing apprise James, brother of Our Lord, of it; of the two James, this is the Less.[2] Write down the beginning of your faith, when and how and at what age you came to me, and how you then remained with me without ever leaving me thereafter, but rather you then followed me loyally and in good faith and always accompanied me. You have seen my comings and goings in all my travels; you have clearly seen my conduct in market-towns, towns, and cities; and you have clearly heard the sense of my preaching, and you have always listened carefully to everything about which I debated; both day and night you have carefully observed how I have conducted myself, how I behave in private, and how I behave when I am amongst people. Nothing of what I have done or said has in any way been hidden from you: you know and have seen all this, and should briefly write down exactly this. In a short while you will learn more, and will clearly hear what end I shall meet; once this happens, write it all down, and send the letter to James. (14423–62)

Do not be afraid that he will be upset or terribly troubled when he hears word of my death; for a good while he has been quite aware of what I seek: I have not sought personal gain, but rather the common good.[3] He will be greatly com-

---

[1] 14407–22 **Once St Peter. . .he said** *Quant seint Pierre. . .dist*: *Ep.* 19.1 is amplified for dramatic effect.

[2] 14434 **of the two James. . .Less** *dé dous Jacobs. . .Menur*: This clarification relative to *Ep.* 19.2 is added by our translator.

[3] 14467–68 **I have not. . .good** *Jeo ne ai pas. . .utilité*: This rather odd comment seems to stem from an attempt to integrate an isolated variant ($\Delta^{ef}\delta$) in the transmission of *Ep.* 19.3, which in place of *pro pietate* offers *proprietate*, whence *Clement*'s *propriété* "personal gain" and, as a consequently innovated antonym, *cumune utilité* "common good."

forted as soon as he hears that a man has been appointed in my place who is wise and devoted to God, and that a man of little knowledge has not been appointed, but rather that I have appointed to my chair a man who clearly understands what is to be done and has fully learnt the rule of Holy Church together with its organisation. For he understands full well that any time at which he who knows little receives the task of watching over and teaching others is to be feared in all respects: when the teacher is ignorant and understands little of his duty, his followers will be misled and will remain as if blind, and so they must fall over when they cannot see anything. When the teacher is ignorant, he himself stumbles; his followers, when they have not learnt the right path, follow him. Together they head towards a miserable fate since they have not understood the law of God; since they do not sow[1] well, they will not obtain any good, and all will head together down the same path."

Clement understood the request and clearly understood St Peter's desire. He completely accepted it and promised sincerely to do everything that he requested.[2] (14463–15000)

I do not know how long it was, nor do I know whether few or many days passed, but I am quite sure that at that time Nero was the leader of the Romans and was acknowledged as lord of everything which belonged to the empire. Nero was a cruel emperor, and his nature was terrible to bear; he did much evil and little good, and in fact I believe that he never did any good at all.

St Paul the apostle, in the time of Nero, was an upstanding man and of great renown. He had travelled a great deal for God; he had preached a great deal and spoken a great deal through cities and through countries, and he had journeyed round a great number of lands. Once he had done what he could elsewhere, he decided to head to the Romans. He came to Rome in order to preach and speak the word of God; he had set his heart entirely on managing to convert people to God. (14501–22)

St Peter was in Rome before him; St Paul, who was very knowledgeable, arrived later. They were both very highly regarded, for they were very renowned; of their knowledge and their virtues many spoke both near and far. They had travelled for God, but had not gone together; they carried out their preaching in completely different regions. They were not cowardly or reticent, and converted many people to God; they had already completed very many journeys before they

---

[1] 14495 **sow** *sement*: While the manuscript may read *sement*, it should probably be read as *seivent* "they know," whence: "Since they do not know any good, they will not obtain any good."

[2] 14497–500 **Clement understood. . .requested** *Clement entendi. . .requist*: These lines render Clement's acceptance of his election in *Ep.* 20, but replace the valediction to James.

had come together in Rome.[1] St Peter had arrived there first and converted many of the Romans; he converted noble ladies, amongst whom there were some who left and never went near their husbands again, such as Libia, the wife of Nero. Many of the other women likewise conducted themselves chastely and abandoned their husbands in such a way that they no longer went to their beds, as a result of which their husbands, when they realised, were extremely angry at St Peter; they would very gladly cause him harm if they found the opportunity and saw the chance. This did not make St Peter desist so that he refrained from his activities; he wandered freely through the city and preached just as he wanted. It was quite a different situation with St Paul; he could not wander freely, for he had been arrested and detained and had arrived there under guard. He could not have the freedom to speak with anybody who came unless he had permission from his guards; he could speak to those whom they permitted. But nonetheless he was not prepared to desist, when he found a man to whom to speak, from talking about Jesus Christ and saying many good things about Him. As a result it happened that soldiers willingly came to see him; even from the emperor's retinue many came to see him. Many of the soldiers who came had no interest in their duties thereafter; those who had previously performed very reckless deeds in the name of their military service converted to Jesus Christ and no longer served the emperor.[2] (14523–76)

St Peter came to see St Paul, and their joy was great when they met. They hugged each other with great love and kissed each other with great joy; they wept many tears when they saw each other, and everything that they did was full of joy. St Paul recounted the great woes that he had suffered previously and subsequently, and the woes that he had experienced because he had travelled by sea. Those who remain at sea for a long time often tend to grow weary, and lying in a ship for a long time often causes hardship; and when a storm besets them, such as with heavy rain and strong winds, they are all the more at risk the stronger that the storm becomes and the longer that it lasts.

---

[1] 14501–36 **I do not know. . . Rome** *Ne sai. . .furent*: This section marks the beginning of the translation of the *Passio sanctorum apostolorum Petri et Pauli* attributed to Pseudo-Marcellus, although the account of the saints' travels stands in place of their debates with Jews and Gentiles in *Pa.* 1–9.

[2] 14537–76 **St Peter. . .the emperor** *Seint Pierre. . .servirent*: This section omits the beginning of *Pa.* 10, which explains that Simon is present at the behest of religious authorities, but renders much of the remainder. The mention of Paul's imprisonment and preaching is, however, an innovation.

After St Paul had said what he wished to say to St Peter, St Peter recounted to St Paul the great woes that he had encountered at the hands of Simon Magus, who sought to do him harm in every way that he could.[1] (14577–600)

That same Simon had come to Rome and was with the emperor Nero. He performed many wonders before him. He changed his appearance frequently: now he was an old man and then a child; now he was small and thereafter big; now he appeared with the face of a man, and soon thereafter with the face of a woman; he made dogs of brass bark and made images move by themselves. Through these and other things of which he did a great deal he had often deceived many. He had already persuaded the emperor into believing him truly to be the Son of God,[2] for Simon had said to him: "Noble emperor, hear what it is that I wish to tell you: I am the Son of God, who have left heaven and come down to the earth! I shall prove to you that this is true: I shall allow my head to be cut off in some secluded place, which should be dark, and I shall remain dead until the third day. I shall rise from death on the third day and shall appear before you completely healthy. If I do not do what I have said, no longer consider me to be true; if I rise again, believe me all the more because of this, and if not, there is no danger of you hearing anything more from me thereafter. It will now be up to you to test this in such a way that you might be quite certain of it." (14601–30)

Nero wanted to know whether it was true that Simon could rise up from death. He ordered that he should be beheaded in a dark place where there was no light, and that he should then remain in the dark place until he rose again on the third day; no light was to enter there, for there was no truth there. Simon knew a great deal about sorcery and had a sheep brought there. With this sheep he made it so—I do not know how, other than by a wicked spell—that anybody who looked at the sheep would truly believe that he saw Simon. The one who was to behead Simon received the sheep in place of Simon. He put the sheep in a dark place and slew it there in place of Simon; he thought that he had slain Simon, but he had slain the sheep! Nonetheless the man who had slain him wanted to be sure that he had truly killed him. He moved the head towards the light, but found the face changed: Simon's head was not to be seen, but rather the head of

---

[1] 14577–600 **St Peter. . .could** *Seint Pierre. . .pout*: Some of this section may derive from the earlier omitted *Pa.* 3–4, but the comments on the dangers of sea-travel are an innovation.

[2] 14601–14 **That same Simon. . .Son of God** *Venuz a Rume. . .le teneit*: The first miracles in this section draw on *Pa.* 14, whilst the animation of brazen dogs and statues seems to come from *Pa.* 11. Whereas all of the miracles in *Clement* are performed before Nero, those of *Pa.* 11 occur in front of the people. *Pa.* 12–13, omitted by our text, describes Peter's miracles, and then the support granted to Simon by the religious authorities, securing him an invitation to Nero's court, where in *Pa.* 14 he performs the miracles which persuade Nero that Simon is the son of God.

a sheep was to be seen; the spell had been completely broken once the head had been cut off. He did not dare tell the emperor of this, for he was extremely afraid because he had investigated and seen that which had been forbidden to him. Simon was in hiding, but I do not know where,[1] and was not seen until the third day. He presented himself when the third day came and showed himself to the emperor; there was no sign of death in him, nor that he had suffered any harm. The deceiver had experienced no harm because the sheep had been killed in his place! He ordered that his blood be collected and venerated as a relic. Nero then believed that it was certain that Simon had risen up from death; he subsequently believed him to be the true Son of God and honoured him from that time on.[2] (14631–76)

Simon was wickedly cunning, for he thought nothing but evil. He had ample opportunity to do evil once Nero considered him to be the Son of God. He slandered both St Paul and St Peter as does one who was a liar. He took great pains to do them harm, for he did not stop calumniating them; he denounced them to the emperor and defamed them as much as he could.[3] One day he visited the emperor once he was quite certain of him. He spoke to him as do all those who are sure of their friends:[4]

"Noble emperor," he said, "you have clearly seen what I have done. I am the Son of God, and have proved it convincingly: I was dead, but I have risen again! But a certain Peter has opposed me, and night and day he has sought to do me a great deal of harm. He claims to be the apostle of a certain Jesus, who according to him was his master. This Jesus was from Nazareth, and He had many more disciples; there is no need to pay much heed to them, for they are of very little importance. I have suffered a great deal on account of this Peter, and even now he still seeks to do me all kinds of harm. In addition to the fact that he has caused me woe, my woe has recently been doubled: a companion from his band called Paul has come to him. Both have come to Rome, and they will harm your em-

---

[1] 14641, 14663 **I do not know** *ne sai*: In both cases, the ignorance belongs to our translator.

[2] 14615–76 **for Simon had said. . .time on** *Kar dit lui out. . .le onurat*: Simon's first sentence represents the claim that he voices at the beginning of *Pa.* 15, but while he there continues to complain about the apostles, in *Clement* he offers to prove his divinity through the deception described in the rest of this section. In the *Passio*, this deception does not appear until *Pa.* 31–32, in the form of a retrospective account to explain Simon's boast in *Pa.* 31 that he had previously risen from the dead. As a result of *Clement's* re-organisation, the miracle is presented as performed specifically in order to substantiate the claim in Simon's first sentence, and the description of it precedes both Simon's boast about it (vv. 14691–94) and Nero's allusion to it (vv. 14887–90), whereas when Nero mentions it in *Pa.* 25, the narrative has yet to detail the miracle.

[3] 14677–86 **Simon was. . . he could** *Mal arteillus. . .les empeirat*: These lines convey the essence of Simon's calumny earlier omitted from *Pa.* 11 and 14.

[4] 14687–90 **One day. . .friends** *Un jur. . . sunt*: This information comes from *Pa.* 15.

pire unless you think about this more quickly and save the country from them."[1] (14677–712)

Nero, who was very ready to do evil, had word sent to St Peter and St Paul, once he had heard this from Simon, that they should come and speak to him. People who carried out his order were very quickly found; they brought with them St Peter and St Paul, who gladly agreed to come. Once they came before Nero, they found Simon there to oppose them, and he immediately greeted them and attacked them with animosity. He gave the emperor to understand that they were utter reprobates:

"These men are disciples," he said, "of Jesus, who was once their master. This Jesus came from a city which has greatly opposed you and is called Nazareth, but the country is called Judaea. They are in a very bad situation, for they are utterly hated by their own people; through their shameful and outrageous behaviour they have been exiled from their own race. They have been driven from their country, and all their friends have abandoned them. Even though they were born in Judaea, there is no chance that they will be seen in their country; they have no home or refuge there, so greatly does their entire race hate them."[2]

To these words Nero said: "I wish to know why it is, Simon, that you so hate these two men and so persecute them. God loves and cherishes all people without wishing them any harm, and so why do you seek to do such harm to these men whom you see here?" (14713–50)

"Noble emperor," Simon said, "regarding these two men and their entire fellowship I can give you the answer that they have greatly envied me. They have wandered through Judaea so much and done and said so much there that all the people have abandoned me, and nobody there believes in me any more."

The emperor then turned to both St Paul and St Peter, and said: "Why is it that your people and you behave so treacherously, and that your dealings are such as this man gives us to believe?"

St Peter turned to Simon before he replied to Nero, and said: "Simon, those who have heard and believed you have been greatly deceived. You managed to catch many people unawares and deceived many of them, but certainly not me. But those who were deceived by you then repented through me; they were converted to God by me and have utterly abandoned you. You have found me in many places and have often put me to the test; I have very often proved your guilt, from which your whole face has been reddened. I am therefore amazed that you dare to speak to me before the king when your actions are worthless and when your sorcery entirely fails you. Do you think us so helpless, so ill prepared,

---

[1] 14691–712 **Noble emperor. . .from them** *Sire emperiere. . .delivrez*: Simon's opening boast stems from *Pa.* 31, while what follows renders the rest of *Pa.* 15.

[2] 14733–43 **They are in. . .hate them** *A ces estat. . .les het*: These lines appear to some extent inspired by *Pa.* 16.

so little forewarned that any of your sorcery could be of any avail to you in our presence, and that you could manage to make us two go astray?"[1] (14751–88)

St Peter then turned to Nero, and said: "Listen, noble emperor! We are disciples of Jesus Christ; He is our master, and He taught us. He is the Son of God; He came to earth and descended from heaven to draw us to Him. He who has heaven and earth in His control deigned to humble Himself to the extent that He became a man and suffered death, and thereby overcame the Devil. The Devil had man in his power, but Jesus Christ cast him out from him; since He gained the victory, He placed man, who was a servant, into glory. This victory lasts for ever, and our nature is saved by it; the human race was damned, and was saved by the Son of God. Simon, who is here present before you, claims to be the Son of God, but he is lying to you: he is filled with the Devil and so has failed before God. He is an apostate and a liar; he is a thief and a sorcerer. There is no reason or moderation in him, for he is brimming with all kinds of filth; he has done much evil and deceived people, but God will take revenge on him. The time is approaching, and it is quite right that the deceiver should be proved guilty: his deception will be revealed, and all will know of his treachery."[2] (14789–820)

Simon then said: "Noble emperor, you must not believe this man! It is quite astonishing that you are prepared to listen to him when you do not see a distinguished person here, but one who appears nothing other than worthless. He has come from very lowly stock, and used to subsist from his fishing. It may dishonour you to be listening to a fisherman; it is quite apparent that he knows little of value, and this proves that he is capable of little. He is mendacious and ignorant; do not believe anything that he says! He has been a very bitter enemy for me, but I am not prepared to suffer this from him any more. I shall summon my angels down from heaven and say that they should come and capture him; they will immediately avenge me as soon as they have seized him." (14821–40)

St Peter said: "I fear neither you nor your angels in any way whatsoever: the power of Jesus, my Lord, makes me secure in all respects. Through the trust that I have in Him I shall scare your angels so much that as soon as they see me, they will not dare even to touch me. In full public view you will be proved and demonstrated to be wrong in calling yourself the Son of God, for in all truth you are lying."

In response to this, Nero said to him: "Are you then not afraid of Simon, of whom we are quite certain that he is the Son of God, for it is quite apparent? Through his deeds he has demonstrated so much of this that it is quite sufficient as a testimony to him."

---

[1] 14788 **go astray** *forsveer*: Following this line, our text omits *Pa.* 18–21, in which Peter suggests that Nero read the letter from Pontius Pilate, which is then reproduced.

[2] 14789–820 **St Peter. . .treachery** *Vers Nerun. . .felunie*: These lines draw on *Pa.* 22, but amplify considerably Peter's comments on Christ as leader and Saviour and on the eschatological context.

In response to this, St Peter said to him: "If he has divinity in him which can examine a man's mind and is able to see his thoughts, he will be able to demonstrate his skill in this regard if he guesses what I am thinking, and I shall whisper into your ear the very thing that I have in mind so that Simon might not lie to you by saying something other than what I say." (14841–68)

To this, Nero said: "Come here and tell me what you are thinking."

St Peter went very close to Nero and quietly said to him what he was thinking:

"Have brought here immediately," he said secretly, "a loaf of barley bread; have it quietly handed to me, without any fuss and without excessive talking."

Nero had the bread brought to him and deftly placed into his hand, and St Peter quietly took it, placed it beneath his clothes, and said:

"I have now had my thought and have now acted here accordingly. May Simon tell us what it is!"

"How," Nero said to St Peter, "do you think that you can make me believe that Simon could not know this, given that he was able to bring the dead man back to life[1] and himself was able to rise up from death once he had had himself beheaded, and on the third day came before me without having any trace of death in him? Since he has done before me everything that I wished to ask, do you believe that he does not know what you are thinking and will not say it?" (14869–94)

"I did not see," St Peter said, "the good that you say that Simon did. He never did any of it in my presence, and yet I have often seen him elsewhere."

"I myself saw," Nero said, "everything that I just said about Simon."

St Peter said: "If he did the greater thing, may he do the lesser thing before us here. May he say what it is that I said to you, and what I did and what I shall do!"

Nero presently looked round and said: "What do you say, Simon? Why are you not answering? I am quite bewildered by you now; I do not know what to do other than to wait and leave you to your own devices."

Simon said: "May Peter say first what it is that I am thinking!"

"I shall clearly show," St Peter said, "that I know exactly everything that Simon is thinking of doing once he has done the thing that he has in mind."

Simon then said: "Noble emperor, Peter is lying; you must not believe him! God alone knows what a man is thinking; no other man can know it."

"You claim to be the Son of God," St Peter said, "and since you are audacious enough to say this, it is right and proper that you should know the mind and thoughts of a man. Show your divinity and say what I did in secret! He

---

[1] 14886 **bring the dead man back to life** *le mort resusciter*: An allusion to an episode commonly found in narratives involving Peter, in which Simon pretends to bring a dead man back to life, only for Peter to come and do so in reality. This episode is absent from both *Clement* and the *Passio*.

who is Son of God must surely know everything that a mortal man can think."
(14895–928)

St Peter had taken the loaf of barley bread and quietly put it beneath his
clothes. He had covered and hidden it well, and had divided it and broken it into
pieces; he secretly blessed it once he had divided it in two. He had hidden it in
both his sleeves; he had placed one half in his right hand and the other in his left
hand, but he had done all this in secret.

Simon, who felt himself caught unawares and was at a loss for a reply, grew
very angry at St Peter when he could not find anything more to say. He wanted
to show his power though action, and so he cried out aloud:

"May dogs," he said, "come forth here and devour St Peter immediately before the emperor and his followers!"

At these words there came running outrageously hideous and enormous
dogs, and they ran at St Peter. Such dogs had never been seen in the country,
and those who saw them were afraid of them. They were supposed to devour St
Peter, but he knew how to save himself from them quickly, for he immediately
threw back his clothes and stretched out his hands in prayer. He showed to the
dogs the consecrated bread that he had placed in his sleeves. As soon as the dogs
saw the bread, they were so afraid that they fled; as soon as the bread was shown
to them, they neither stayed nor remained there. So they came and so they went
without doing any more harm to St Peter. Nobody knew what became of them;
they could not endure there. They came there suddenly and fled immediately.[1]
(14929–68)

St Peter then said to Nero: "Before you I have proved Simon's guilt. I have
shown you that I knew everything that he was thinking and wanted to do. In
full public view I have proved what he wanted, not by word, but by deed. He had
promised that he would make his angels descend from heaven. Now he summoned his dogs here in place of angels in order to seize me, and so it is quite
obvious that everything that he tells you amounts to nothing and that he is lying to you. There is nothing of any merit in his angels; they are not angels, but
a pack of dogs! It is quite clear how powerful they were when they were afraid
to stay here; they clearly showed, whatever anybody else might say, that they did
not come from God."

To these words, Nero said: "We are defeated, I think, Simon."

"Peter," Simon said, "has seen me often and has known many of my secrets.
He has often opposed me, both in Palestine and in Caesarea, and also in Judaea,
his country, for he turned against me a long time ago [. . .]" (14969–94)

---

[1] 14959–68 **As soon. . .immediately** *Li chien. . .erraument*: The translator's interest in
the dogs is reflected by the length of this version relative to *Pa.* 27.

APPENDIX 1
EXTRACTS FROM *LA VIE DE SEINT CLEMENT*

Passage 1: Peter confounds Simon

	Simun, atant que truvé out	(fol. 178v)
	Acheisun par quei partir se en pout—	
	E mes remeindre n'i vuleit	
3628	Quant seint Pierre curucié esteit—	
	Remist uncore e arestut,	
	Kar tel chose oir quidout	
	Que a merveille peust turner	
3632	Dunt il ne eust einz oi parler:	
	"Demandez mei," ceo dist Simun,	
	"Un mot ki seit de reisun,	
	E que bien le entendent tuz	
3636	Petiz e granz ci venuz,	
	Dunt jeo vus peusse respundre,	
	E vus partant a mei espundre	
	E mustrer peussiez par reisun	
3640	Si la aume est mortel u nun!"	
	Seint Pierre respunt: "Jel vus dirrai	
	E si bien le vus pruverai	
	Que quel ure que vus le orrez,	
3644	Mieuz de autre hume le entendrez.	
	Que est ceo que l'um mieuz creire deit:	
	Ceo que l'um ot, u ceo que l'um veit?"	
	Respunt Simun: "Chos[e] veue	
3648	Mieuz que oie deit estre creue."	
	Dunc dist seint Pierre: "Ceo que deit,	
	Quant l'um seit bien ceo que l'um veit,	
	Que vus par mei saver vulez	(fol. 179r)
3652	Ceo que vus meismes veu avez?"	
	"Ne sai," dist Simun, "ne ne vei	
	Cument vus parlez ne purquei."	

Ceo dist seint Pierre: "Si nel savez,

3656 A vostre ostel vus en alez!

Entrez la u vostre lit est,

E la truverez trestut prest

La figure de un enfant

3660 Ki tut vus est obeisant.

Oscis le avez e sa figure

Retenu avez en peinture;

Cuvert le avez de un drap purprin,

3664 Kar il vus est del tut enclin.

Demandez lui, il vus dirrat

E la certé vus musterrat

Tant par oie, tant par veue,

3668 Que bien la averez entendue!

Quel mestier est de mei oir

Si la aume deit vivre u murir

Quant vus veer la poez

3672 E vus meismes a lui parlez?

Si la aume en sei vie nen eust,

Neis un sul mot parler ne peust.

Si vus dites que ceo ne est si

3676 De l'enfant sicum jeo di,

E si vus dites par aventure

Que rien ne savez de cel figure,

A vostre ostel nus en alum,

3680 Dis cumpainnuns od nus menum

Demeintenant de ceste gent

Que nus avum ci present

Pur cerchier si il est si   (fol. 179v)

3684 Cum jeo vus ai mustré ci!"

Simun ne aveit talent de rire

Quant cest dit aveit seint Pierre!

Mult en fud ja anguissus

3688 E mult se teneit a cumfus;

Mult lui pesat que il la esteit,

Mult mieuz aillurs estre vudreit.

Sa cunscience le huni

3692 Dunt il esteit el queor marri;

Gute de sanc ne aveit en sei,

Kar descuvert fud sun secrei.

Mult i chanjat sa culur,

3696 Kar mult aveit grant pour

Que si rien veusist desdire,

De ceo se desdeinnast seint Pierre,
Par quei a sun ostel alast
3700 E les angles tuz cerchast
Tresque tant que il eust truvé
Ceo par quei il fust cumpruvé.

Passage 2: Peter refuses Clement's offer to serve him

Seint Pierre en prist a suzrire   (fol. 208v)
Quant il oi Clement ceo dire.
Il respundi en suef heit:
5556 "Dunc ne quidez que mestier seit
Que a mun servise entendez
E mes choses en guarde eiez?
Ki frat mun lit mieuz de vus?
5560 Ki guarderat mes dras precius?
Ki poet mes aneaus mieuz guarder
E mes robes a remuer?
De ma quisine e de mes cus
5564 Ki prenderat guarde mieuz de vus?
Ki me frat mieuz de mes plenté
E la grant diverseté
Que genz se soelent aprester
5568 Pur sei meismes engruter
Cume beste afamee
Ki ne poet estre saulee?
Nepurquant celer nel dei,   (fol. 209r)
5572 Tut aeiez esté od mei,
Nen estes acuinté mie
De mun estre e de ma vie,
Kar tel viande ai en us:
5576 Pain od olives e nient plus,
U od cholet asez relement,
E le ewe a beivre senglement.
Ma vesture est ci tute,
5580 Cest mantel e cest cote.
Cest me suffist, e el ne quier,
Kar ci de el nen ai mestier.
De cest siecle ne ai puint de heit,
5584 Kar mun queor aillurs me treit
U les luiers si grant serrunt
Que jameis fin ne prenderunt.

Meis merveille est de vus,
5588 Ki nen avez eu en us
De meseise trop suffrir,
Cument vus poez a nus tenir
E vus si tost afurmer
5592 A nostre vie endurer
Ki avez tuz tens esté
Nurri en mult grant plenté.
En ceo feites a loer,
5596 E mult se en poet l'um merveiller,
E jeo vus mult de ceo pris
Que vus estes en ceo mis
Que rien querre ne vulez
5600 Ultre ceo que mestier avez,
Kar jeo e Andreu mun frere
Des enfance enariere
De grant poverté sumes venu   (fol. 209v)
5604 E granz meseises avum eu.
Busuinnus esteium mult,
Partant uvrer nus estut:
De ceo nus vient que de legier
5608 Errer poum e traveillier.
Pur ceo, si vulez assentir
Que jeo peusse a vus servir,
Mult mieuz a vus feire le dei
5612 Que vus nel devez feire a mei,
Kar uvrier sui e custumier
De travail suffrir de legier."
Quant cest aveit oi Clement,
5616 Lores ne iert pas petit dolent!
Tut en cumençat a trenbler
E a grosses lermes plurer,
Kar la parole mult a queor prist
5620 Que seint Pierre avant lui mist,
De ki il plus grant pris teneit
Que tut le siecle ne valeit.
Quant seint Pierre se iert aparceu
5624 Que cil plurout e dolent fu,
Purquei plurast de lui enquist.
Clement respundi, si lui dist:
"De quei me sui mespris vers vus
5628 Que vus me avez tant cumfus
Par si dure parole dire?"

A ceo lui respundi seint Pierre:
"Si jeo ai en ceo mespris
5632   Que jeo vus tel parole dis,
Vus tut premier en mespreistis
Quant vus ceo meisme einz me deistes,
Kar vus deistes tut avant   (fol. 210r)
5636   Que estre vuliez mun servant."
Clement respunt: "Ceo ne siut nient,
Meis mun servise a vus avient,
Kar vus estes le messagier
5640   A ki est baillié le mestier
Des aumes mettre en sauveté:
Pur ceo vus ad Deus enveié,
E partant me est grief a oir
5644   Que vus deussiez a mei servir."
As paroles que Clement dist
Seint Pierre tel respuns fist:
"Quanque vus dites porreit estre
5648   Si Jesu Crist, nostre meistre,
Ki en terre est venu
Pur mettre le mund a salu
E ki plus haut e plus noble est
5652   Que tute creature ne est,
Pur servir venu ne fust
E a nus cumandé ne eust
Que noz freres servisum
5656   E de ceo hunte nen eussum."
Dunc dist Clement: "Trop fol sens ai
Si vus unkes veintre quidai
Par rien que a vus voise disant;
5660   Meis Deus, qui tant est purveant,
Mult gracié seit a tutdis
De ceo que me sui a vus pris!
Jeo ne ai parent ki me heit,
5664   Pur ceo me sui vers vus treit;
En lieu vus tieng de parenté,
En lur lieu me avez cumforté."
Ceo dist seint Pierre: "Cument, Clement,   (fol. 210v)
5668   Dunc ne avez vus nul parent?
Estes de parenz si esquis
Que nuls nen est de tuz remis?"

Passage 3: Clement proves the folly of astrology

"Pere," dist Clement al vieillard,   (fol. 289v)
10728   "Ore entendez bien a cele art
        Dunt tant vus estes entremis
        U vostre queor est tant asis;
        La nature bien esguardez
10732   De ces ki sunt en la art usez,
        Kar li plus cuinte en mesprent
        Par faute de l'esperement:
        Il ne funt si mentir nun,
10736   Si oez purquei la reisun!
        Mettez a reisun a une part
        Un de ces ki usent cele art;
        Mustrez lui que une aventure
10740   Vus avint e a tel ure,
        Puis enquerrez que il vus die
        Sulung la art de astronomie
        Queles esteilles unt ceo feit,
10744   Il vus dirrat que bien le seit.
        Si aventure lui mustrez
        Dunt vus eiez esté grevez,
        Il vus mettrat demeintenant
10748   Les esteilles males avant,
        Si vus dirrat que par eus fu
        Tut quanque vus iert avenu.
        Puis a un autre vus turnez
10752   E autre part celui traez:
        Mustrez lui de aucune afaire
        Ki al premier seit tut cuntraire;
        Dites lui le tens e la ure
10756   De aucune bone aventure
        Ki vus est turné a pru   (fol. 290r)
        Pur saver dunt ceo est avenu,
        Mes bien vus guardez de changier
10760   La ure dunt deistes al premier;
        Meimes la ure que vus mustrastes
        Quant al premier del mal parlastes
        A l'autre aprés del bien mustrez,
10764   E cil en iert tost cunseilliez.
        Des esteilles chaudpas dirrat
        Ki bones sunt, sis numerat;
        Mult mettrat peine de mustrer

10768 Reisuns de bien par mult parler.
Quanque li uns del mal parlat,
Li autre a bien turner vuldrat;
Tut seit une meisme ure
10772 E diverse la aventure,
Tant vuldrat dire li secund
Des esteilles ki bones sunt
Par la ure e le tens acupler
10776 As esteilles pur acorder,
E tant irrat envirunant
Par ses reisuns mustrer avant
Que tut a force vus mettrat
10780 A tant que creire vus en frat
Que de bones esteilles vint
Trestut le bien ki vus avint,
E que par reisun e par dreit
10784 Tut avenir issi deveit.
Autant dirrat devers le bien
Li secund astronomien
Cumme li premiers des einz vus dist
10788 Ki ses proeves del mal vus fist,
Partant les poet l'um entercier   (fol. 290v)
Que il el ne funt forz genz trechier.
Bien de tel art seez purveu
10792 Que ne en poet surdre puint de pru:
Trop est turnee a mençunge
E mult ad grant semblant de sunge,
Kar quant hume ad mult sungié
10796 E puis de sumne est esveillié,
Si il par sei ne entent mie
Que le sunge signefie,
Pensif en est quant il ne seit
10800 A quei le sunge turner deit.
Mes si lui vient puis aventure
U il le peusse mettre sure,
Dunc a primes le sunge entent
10804 E sulung ceo le espunt e prent.
De destinee tut ausi veit:
Ja ne iert hume ki seur seit
Par esteille ki seit el ciel,
10808 Ne par planete, ne par el,
De chose ki seit a venir;
Veer le estoet einz, u oir."

Passage 4: Simon convinces Nero that he is the Son of God

	Venuz a Rume iert cil Symun	(fol. 350r)
	E fud od le emperur Nerun.	
	Mult fist merveilles, lui veant:	
14604	Sa chere alat suvent chanjant,	
	Ore iert vieillard e puis enfant,	
	Ore fud petit, aprés ceo grant,	
	Ore se mustrat en vis de hume	
14608	E tost aprés en vis de femme;	
	Chiens fait de areim feseit baer,	
	Ymages fist par sei muver.	
	Par cest e el dunt mult feseit	
14612	Deceu plusurs suvent aveit.	
	Vers le emperur out ja tant feit	
	Que Fiz Deu pur veir le teneit,	
	Kar dit lui out: "Sire emperiere,	
14616	Oez que ceo est que vus vuil dire:	
	Jeo sui Fiz Deu, del ciel eissu	
	E desque en terre descendu!	
	Que ceo veirs seit vus pruverai,	
14620	La teste couper me lerrai	
	En privé lieu que seit obscur	
	E morz serrai desque a tierz jur;	
	De mort al tierz jur leverai	
14624	E devant vus tut sein vendrai.	
	Si jeo ne faz ceo que dit ai,	
	Puis ne me tenez a verrai:	
	Si jeo relief, mieuz me en creez,	(fol. 350v)
14628	Si nun, mar puis de rien me orrez.	
	De ceo espruver sur vus ore iert	
	Que bien en peussez estre cert."	
	Nerun vout saver si veir fust	
14632	Que Symun de mort lever peust.	
	Il le cumandat decoler	
	En lieu obscur u rien ne eust cler,	
	E puis remeist el lieu obscur	
14636	Desque il relevast al tierz jur;	
	Ne i deut entrer puint de clarté,	
	Kar puint ne i out de verité.	
	De males arz sout mult Symun	
14640	E fist la venir un multun;	

Del multun fist—ne sai cument,
Fors par malveis enchantement—
Que ki reguardast le multum
14644 Pur veir quidast veer Symun.
Cil ki decoler Symun deut
Le multun pur Symun receut;
En obscur lieu le multun mist
14648 E pur Symun iloec le oscist:
Oscis quidat aver Symun,
Mes il out oscis le multun!
Cil nepurquant ki oscis le out
14652 Si bien le eust mort cert estre vout:
La teste traist vers la lumiere,
Mes changee truvat la chiere;
Ne parut pas teste Symun,
14656 Mes parut teste de multun;
Le enchantement fud tut desfeit
Quant la teste coupee esteit.
Ne l'osat dire a l'emperur,   (fol. 351r)
14660 Ke mult esteit en grant pour
De ceo que il out cerchié e veu
Ceo dunt il out le defens eu.
Symun tapi, mes ne sai u,
14664 Desque al tierz jur ne fud pas veu.
Avant se mist quant vint tierz jur
E se mustrat a l'emperur;
Signe de mort ne out nul en lui,
14668 Ne que il eust suffert puint de ennui:
Li trechiere ne out mal sentu
Kar li multun pur lui mort fu!
Il cumandat sun sanc cuillir
14672 E cum relike chier tenir.
Dunc quidat cert estre Nerun
Que levé fud de mort Symun;
Verrai Fiz Deu puis le quidat
14676 E puis cele ure le onurat.

Appendix 2
Concordance with Latin sources

The purpose of the following tables is to complement the information provided in the footnotes by summarising the correspondence between sections of *Clement* and its principal Latin sources, down to the level of chapters. Brief comments on omissions, abbreviations, and approximate renderings aim to convey an impression of the degree of similarity between target and source text at the point in question. The following symbols and abbreviations are used:

−	no corresponding element in text
?	questionable affiliation
/	apparent lacuna
( )	section with no or extremely weak correspondence to *Clem.*
abb.	considerable abbreviation (general or specific)
app.	approximate resemblance
del.	specified section delayed until later appearance
inn.	innovated material (general or specific)
om.	section of *Rec.* omitted by *Clem.*
summ.	omitted or very extensively abridged, but mentioned in summary

Table 1: The *Vie de seint Clement* (*Clem.*) beside the *Recognitiones* of Rufinus (*Rec.*), the *Vita sancti Clementis* of Johannes Hymmonides and Gauderic of Velletri (*Vita*), and the *De origine beati Clementis* of Leo of Ostia (*Orig.*)

Rec.	Clem.	Vita	Orig.	Clem. to Rec.
–	1–118	(Prol.)	(Prol.)	inn.
VII.8.2–3	119–158	I.1	1	app.
VII.15.3–16.2	159–272	I.2	2	app.
VII.12.1, 16.3–4	273–312	I.3	3	app.
VII.32	313–374	I.6	6	app.
VII.33.1–2	375–420	I.7	7	app.
VII.17, 18.1	421–502	I.4	4	app.
VII.18.2–3	503–542	I.5	5	app.
I.1?	543–552	–	–	app.
VII.9.2–3	553–602	I.14	8	app.
IX.32.4–6, 33.2	603–642	I.16	10	app.
VII.10.1–2	643–666	I.15	9	app.
VII.10.2–3	667–682	I.17[1]	11	app.
I.1?	687–714	I.18?	12?	app.
–	715–736	–	–	inn.
I.1	737–752	I.18	12	abb.; app.
I.2	753–762	I.19	13	abb.; app.
I.3	763–766	I.20	13	abb.; app.
I.4	767–790	I.21	–	abb.; app.
I.5	791–852	I.22	–	om. I.5.3–4
I.6	853–894	I.23	14	
I.7	895–988	I.24	15	
I.8	989–1050	I.25[2]	16	
I.9	1051–1146	/	16	
I.10	1147–1194	/	17	
I.11	1195–1252	/	18	
I.12	1253–1324	I.31	19	

---

[1] *Vita* and *Orig.* innovate a brief narrative of Faustinianus' quest.

[2] *Vita* breaks off during this chapter, its editor indicating an omission.

Rec.	Clem.	Vita	Orig.	Clem. to Rec.
I.13	1325–1368	I.32	20	
I.14	1369–1394	I.33–34	21[3]	
I.15	1395–1420	I.34	–	
–	1421–1616	–	–	inn.
(I.16–18)	–	(I.35–37)	–	
I.19	1617–1652	I.38	–	
I.20	1653–1684	I.39	–	abb. I.20.4–11
I.21	1685–1750	I.40	–	
(I.22–26)	1751–1754	(I.41–45)	–	
(I.27–69)	1755–1824	(I.46)	–	
(I.70–74)	1825–1832	(I.26–30)	–	
II.1	1833–1846	I.47[4]	22	om. c. II.1.3–9
(II.2)	–	–	–	
II.3	1847–1854	–	–	abb.; om. II.3.1, 4–5
II.4	1855–1882	–	–	
II.5	1883–1926	–	–	
II.6	1927–1988	–	23[5]	om. II.6.9
II.7	1989–2004	I.48	23	
II.8	2005–2036	I.48	–	
II.9	2037–2120	I.48	23	om. II.9.7
II.10	2121–2144	–	–	
II.11	2145–2183	I.8	–	
II.12	2184–2204	I.9	–	om. II.12.2–3
II.13	2205–2312	I.10	–	om. II.13.6, II.13.13
II.14	2313–2368	I.11	–	
II.15	2369–2406	I.12	–	
II.16	2407–2450	I.49	–	app.
II.17	2451–2484	–	–	om. II.17.5–6
II.18	2485–2494	–	–	om. II.18.1–10
II.19	2495–2542	I.50; I.13	24	

---

[3] *Orig.* 21 covers *Rec.* I.14–72.

[4] *Vita* and *Orig.* break off at roughly the same point as *Clem.*

[5] Only *Rec.* II.6.11.

Rec.	Clem.	Vita	Orig.	Clem. to Rec.
II.20	2543–2596	I.50[6]	24	
II.21	2597–2644	–	–	abb. II.21.4–6
II.22	2645–2700	–	–	
II.23	2701–2732	–	25	
II.24	2733–2746	–	25	app.
II.25	2747–2774	–	25	om. II.25.4–10
(II.26–69)	2775–2850	–	–	abb.
II.70	2851–2886	–	–	om. II.70.1
II.71	2887–2910	–	–	abb. II.71.4–6
II.72	2911–2928	–	–	om. II.72.1–4
III.1	2929–2946	–	–	om. III.1.2–7
(III.2–11)	–	–	–	
III.12	2947–2980	–	–	
III.13	2981–3030	–	–	
III.14	3031–3066	–	–	om. III.14.3–5
III.15	3067–3090	–	–	om. III.15.4–8
III.16	3091–3116	–	–	om. III.16.1–4, 7–8
(III.17)	–	–	–	
III.18	3117–3142	–	–	om. III.18.4
III.19	3143–3176	–	–	om. III.19.5
III.20	3177–3186	–	–	app.; om. III.20.3–4
(III.21–29)	3187–3196	–	–	summ.
III.30	3197–3224	–	–	om. III.30.1–5
III.31	3225–3276	–	–	
III.32	3277–3322	–	–	
III.33	3323–3362	–	–	
III.34	3363–3372	–	–	abb.; om. III.34.1
(III.35–38)	3373–3377	–	–	summ.
III.39	3378–3402	I.51[7]	–	
III.40	3403–3436	–	–	
III.41	3437–3502	–	–	

---

[6] *Vita* and *Orig.* include only *Rec.* II.20.1.
[7] Only *Rec.* III.39.1.

Rec.	*Clem.*	*Vita*	*Orig.*	*Clem.* to *Rec.*
III.42	3503–3596	-	-	om. III.42.4
III.43	3597–3640	-	-	
III.44	3641–3684	I.52	-	
III.45	3685–3752	I.53[8]	-	
III.46	3753–3838	I.54[9]	-	
III.47	3839–3878	-	-	
III.48	3879–3920	I.54[10]	-	
III.49	3921–4010	I.54[11]	-	
III.50	4011–4032	/	-	
III.51	4033–4046	/	-	om. III.51.3–6
III.52.1	4047–4051	/	-	
(III.52.2–59)	4052–4162	/	-	abb.; app.[12]
III.60	4163–4254	/	-	app.
(III.61)	-	(I.55)	-	
(III.62)	-	-	-	
III.63	4255–4362	I.56	-	
III.64	4363–4416	-	-	
III.65	4417–4482	-	-	
III.66	4483–4532	-	-	om. III.66.3; del. III.66.6
III.67.1	4533–4536	-	-	
III.66.6	4537–4546	-	-	
III.67.2–4	4547–4562	-	-	
III.68	4563–4624	I.57[13]	27	
III.69	4625–4636	-	-	abb.
III.70	4637–4662	-	-	om. III.70.4–5
(III.71)	-	-	-	
III.72.3	4663–4674	I.57	-	del. III.72.1–2

---

[8] *Vita* abbreviates *Rec.* III.45.4–7.

[9] Only *Rec.* III.46.1.

[10] Only *Rec.* III.48.3.

[11] III.49.8–9 missing; editor indicates lacuna.

[12] Only *Rec.* III.52.4–5, 57.1–2 are rendered more closely.

[13] A few details from *Rec.* find their way into *Vita* and *Orig.*.

Rec.	Clem.	Vita	Orig.	Clem. to Rec.
III.73	4675–4716	-	-	
III.74	4717–4722	-	-	
III.72.1–2	4723–4738	I.57	-	
III.74 cont.	4739–4754	-	-	om. III.74.3–4
III.75	4755–4762	-	-	om. III.75.1–11
IV.1	4763–4834	I.58[14]	-	
IV.2	4835–4892	-	-	
IV.3	4893–4978	-	-	inn. 4927–34
IV.4	4979–5036	-	-	inn. 5017–36
(IV.5)	-	-	-	
IV.6	5037–5074	-	-	
IV.7	5075–5134	-	-	
(IV.8-VI.14)	5135–5306	-	-	summ.; inn.
VI.15	5307–5358	I.58[15]	28	om. VI.15.1
VII.1	5359–5418	I.59[16]	29	
VII.2	5419–5434	I.59[17]	29	om. VII.2.2–6
VII.3	5435–5462	-	-	
VII.4	5463–5496	I.59	29	
VII.5	5497–5552	I.60	29	
VII.6	5553–5614	I.61	-	
VII.7	5615–5666	I.62	-	
VII.8	5667–5700	I.63	30	
VII.9	5701–5748	I.64	31	
VII.10	5749–5792	I.65	32	
VII.11	5793–5818	I.66	-	
VII.12	5819–5862	I.67–68	33	
VII.13	5863–5912	I.68	34	
VII.14	5913–5946	I.69	35	
VII.15	5947–5988	I.70	36	
VII.16	5989–6032	I.71	37	

[14] Only a few key elements of *Rec.* IV–VI.
[15] *Vita* also omits *Rec.* VI.15.1.
[16] Element of *Rec.* VII.1.1 only.
[17] Element of *Rec.* VII.2.4 only.

Rec.	*Clem.*	*Vita*	*Orig.*	*Clem.* to *Rec.*
VII.17	6033–6072	I.72	38	
VII.18	6073–6102	I.73	39	
VII.19	6103–6164	I.74	40	
VII.20	6165–6188	I.75	41	
VII.21	6189–6233	I.76	42	
VII.22	6234–6258	I.77	43	
VII.23	6259–6324	I.78	44	
VII.24	6325–6364	I.79[18]	45	
VII.25	6365–6414	I.80	46	
VII.26	6415–6430	I.81	47	om. VII.26.2–4; abb. VII.26.5–6
VII.27	6431–6450	I.82	48	abb.
VII.28.1–4	6451–6482	I.83	49	
-	6483–6502	-	49?	inn.
VII.28.5–6	6503–6524	I.83	49	
VII.29	6525–6562	I.84	50	
VII.30	6563–6602	I.85	51	
VII.31	6603–6642	I.86	52	
VII.32	6643–6696	I.87	53	
VII.33	6697–6744	I.88	54	
VII.34	6745–6776	I.89	54	
VII.35	6777–6840	I.90	-	
VII.36	6841–6890	I.91	-	
VII.37	6891–6922	I.92[19]	-	om. VII.37.3–7
VII.38	6923–7006	I.93[20]	55	
VIII.1	7007–7074	II.1	56	
VIII.2	7075–7148	II.2	57	
VIII.3	7149–7202	II.3	58	
VIII.4	7203–7268	II.4	59	
VIII.5	7269–7338	II.5[21]	-	

---

[18] Om. VII.24.1–2.
[19] *Vita* also omits VII.37.3–7 (but also part of VII.37.2).
[20] Om. closing narrative of VII.38.8.
[21] Om. VIII.5.7.

Rec.	Clem.	Vita	Orig.	Clem. to Rec.
VIII.6	7339–7414	II.6	60	
VIII.7	7415–7480	II.7	61	
VIII.8	7481–7530	II.8	-	
(VIII.9–33)	7531–7604	-	-	summ.
VIII.34	7605–7644	-	-	om. VIII.34.1–5
VIII.35	7645–7722	II.10	63	
VIII.36	7723–7764	II.11	-	
VIII.37	7765–7818	II.12	-	
VIII.38	7819–7884	II.13	-	
VIII.39	7885–7946	II.14; II.9	62	
VIII.40	7947–8008	II.14[22]	-	
VIII.41	8009–8022	II.15[23]	-	om. VIII.41.2–3
(VIII.42)	-	-	-	
VIII.43	8023–8030	II.15[24]	-	om. VIII.43.1–4
VIII.44	8031–8108	II.16	-	
VIII.45	8109–8118	II.17[25]	-	om. VIII.45.3–6
(VIII.46–56)	8119–8220	II.18–22[26]	-	summ.
VIII.57	8221–8262	II.23	63	
VIII.58	8263–8350	II.24[27]	-	app.
(VIII.59–60)	-	-	-	
VIII.61	8351–8372	II.25[28]	-	om. VIII.61.3–13
VIII.62	8373–8406	II.26[29]	-	abb. VIII.62.1–4
IX.1	8407–8494	II.27	-	
IX.2	8495–8558	II.28	-	
IX.3	8559–8594	II.29	-	om. IX.3.2–3
(IX.4)	-	(II.30)	-	

[22] Only VIII.40.6–8.
[23] *Vita* also omits VIII.41.2–3.
[24] *Vita* also omits VIII.43.1–4.
[25] *Vita* also omits VIII.45.4–6.
[26] *Vita* abbreviates, but includes more extracts than *Clem.*
[27] Om. VIII.58.6.
[28] Om. VIII.61.1–4.
[29] Om. VIII.62.6.

Rec.	Clem.	Vita	Orig.	Clem. to Rec.
IX.5	8595–8626	II.31	–	app.
IX.6	8627–8722	II.32[30]	–	om. IX.6.6; inn.
IX.7.1–4	8723–8782	–	–	v. app.?
–	8783–8818	–	–	inn.?
IX.10	8819–8842	II.33[31]	–	om. IX.10.1–4
IX.7.5–6	8843–8868	–	–	
(IX.8–9)	–	–	–	
(IX.11)	–	(II.34)[32]	–	
(IX.12–14)	–	–	–	
IX.15	8869–8996	II.34[33]	–	
IX.16	8997–9044	II.35	–	
IX.17	9045–9070	II.36	–	abb.
IX.18	9071–9100	II.37	64	
IX.19	9101–9130	II.38	65	
IX.20	9131–9164	II.39	66	om. IX.20.2
IX.21	9165–9168	II.40	67	abb.
IX.22	9169–9200	II.41	68	om. IX.22.3
IX.23	9201–9244	II.42	69	om. IX.23.3
IX.24.1–2	9245–9280	II.43	70	del. IX.24.3–5
IX.25.1–4	9281–9302	II.44	71	om. IX.25.3
IX.24.3–5	9303–9314	II.43	70	abb.
IX.25.5–8	9315–9344	II.44	71	app.
(IX.26)	–	(II.45)	(72)	
IX.27	9345–9380	II.46	73	om. IX.27.1–3; app.
IX.28	9381–9434	II.47	74	om. c. IX.28.3–4
IX.29	9435–9482	II.48	–	
IX.30	9483–9550	II.49	75	
IX.31	9551–9588	II.50	76	om. IX.31.2
IX.32	9589–9648	II.51	77	
IX.33	9649–9700	II.52	78	

[30] Om. IX.6.6.
[31] Only IX.10.2–4.
[32] Only IX.11.3–6.
[33] Only IX.15.9.

Rec.	*Clem.*	*Vita*	*Orig.*	*Clem.* to *Rec.*
IX.34	9701–9754	II.53	79	
IX.35	9755–9806	II.54	80	
IX.36	9807–9944	II.55	81	
IX.37	9945–9992	II.56	82	
IX.38	9993–10130	-	-	
X.1	10131–10206	II.57	83	
X.2	10207–10302	II.58	-	
X.3	10303–10350	II.59	-	
X.4	10351–10414	II.60	83	
X.5	10415–10498	II.61	-	
X.6	10499–10526	II.62	84	
X.7	10527–10546	II.63	-	om. X.7.3–6
X.8	10547–10562	II.64	-	om. X.8.1–2
X.9	10563–10610	II.65		abb.
X.10	10611–10726	II.66	85	abb.
X.11	10727–10790	II.67	-	abb.
X.12	10791–10814	II.68	-	abb.
X.13	10815–10854	II.69	-	
X.14	10855–10896	II.70	-	
X.15	10897–10928	-	-	
X.16	10929–10992	-	-	
X.17	10993–11046	-	-	om. X.17.6
X.18	11047–11086	-	-	abb.
X.19	11087–11122	-	-	
X.20	11123–11175	-	-	abb.
X.21	11176–11178	-	-	abb.
X.22	11179–11200	-	-	abb.
X.23	11201–11214	-	-	abb.
(X.24–25)	-	-	-	
X.26	11215–11256	-	-	abb.; om. X.26.3–4
X.27	11257–11280	-	-	om. X.27.3–7
X.28	11281–11330	-	-	
X.29	11331–11354	-	-	
X.30	11355–11366	-	-	abb.; om. X.30.3–5

Rec.	Clem.	Vita	Orig.	Clem. to Rec.
X.31	11367–11388	-	-	abb.; om. X.31.1–3
X.32	11389–11404	-	-	abb.
(X.33)	-	-	-	
X.34.1–4	11405–11412	-	-	abb.
(X.33.5–6)	11413–11438	-	-	app.
(X.34.5)	11439–11448	-	-	app.
X.35	11449–11472	-	-	app.
-	11473–11484	-	-	inn.
X.36	11485–11494	-	-	om. X.36.2–5
X.37	11495–11518	-	-	app.
X.38	11519–11530	-	-	abb.; om. X.38.1
X.39	11531–11578	-	-	
X.40	11579–11598	-	-	app.
X.41	11599–11620	-	-	abb.
X.42	11621–11674	-	-	
X.43	11675–11742	II.71[34]	-	
X.44	11743–11790	-	-	
X.45	11791–11846	-	-	
X.46	11847–11866	-	-	
X.47–51.2	11867–11884	-	-	abb.
X.51.3–6	11885–11924	-	-	
X.52	11925–11990	II.72	-	
X.53	11991–12076	II.76	-	
X.54	12077–12114	II.77; II.73–74	-	
X.55	12115–12178	II.78; II.74	-	
X.56	12179–12224	II.79	-	
X.57	12225–12272	II.80[35]	-	
X.58	12273–12326	II.74–75	-	
X.59	12327–12408	/	-	
X.60	12409–12454	/	-	

---

[34] Only X.43.1–2.
[35] The fragmentary copy of *Vita* ends at this point.

Rec.	Clem.	Vita	Orig.	Clem. to Rec.
X.61	12455–12508	/	-	
X.62	12509–12564	/	-	
X.63	12565–12606	/	-	om. X.63.1
X.64	12607–12674	/	-	
X.65a	12675–12692	/	86	app.
X.66	12693–12774	/	-	
X.67	12775–12782	/	-	
X.65.2–4	12783–12812	/	-	app.
X.65.1	12813–12820	/	-	app.
X.67.2–4	12821–12860	/	-	
X.68.1–2	12861–12878	/	-	
X.65.1–4	12879–12928	/	-	app.
X.68.3–4	12929–12970	/	86–87	
X.69	12971–13008	/	-	
X.70	13009–13078	/	-	
X.71	13079–13120	/	-	inn. 13101–10
X.72	13121–13184	/	87	
-	13185–13202	/	87?	inn.

Table 2: The *Vie de seint Clement* beside the *Epistula Clementis ad Iacobum* of Rufinus (*Ep.*) and the *Passio sanctorum apostolorum Petri et Pauli* attributed to Pseudo-Marcellus (*Pa.*)

Ep.	Clem.		Pa.	Clem.	*Clem.* to *Pa.*
[1]	-		(1–2, 5–9)	-	
2	13203–13294		-	14501–14536	inn.
3	13295–13390		10	14537–14576	app.; inn. 14551–66
4	13391–13452		3–4	14577–14600	app.; abb.
5	13453–13520		14, 11	14601–14614	app.; abb.
6	13521–13566		(12–13)	-	
7	13567–13652		15	14615–14618	app.; abb.
8	13653–13724		31	14619–14630	app.
9	13725–13782		32	14631–14676	app.
10	13783–13832		11, 14	14677–14686	app.
11	13833–13870		15	14687–14690	
12	13871–13970		31	14691–14694	
13	13971–14014		15	14695–14712	
14	14015–14128		16	14713–14742	inn. 14733–42
15	14129–14228		17	14743–14788	
16	14229–14290		(18–21)	-	
17	14291–14340		22	14789–14820	app.
18	14341–14406		23	14821–14852	
19	14407–14496		24	14853–14882	
20	14497–14450		25	14883–14916	
			26	14917–14938	
			27	14939–14986	
			28	14987–14994	

LIST OF PROPER NAMES

Line numbers refer to the edition of the *Vie de seint Clement*. French forms have been provided in parenthesis where they might facilitate identification. Where the name appears more than six times, only the first five occurrences have been listed. * draws attention to an entry in the Notes.

Aaron, first high priest of the Israelites 4093
Abraham, Old Testament figure 1768, 4996
Adam, Old Testament figure 1767, 3518
Aides, Greek name of the god Orcus 11395
Amazons, tribe of female warriors 9249
Anaxagoras, Greek philosopher 7540
Anaximander, Greek philosopher 7542
Andrew, St Andrew, brother of St Peter 1844, 5601
Antioch, ancient city 5330, 5336, 5358, 6331, 11953, etc.
Antonius (*Antoine*), father of Simon Magus 1991, 2327, 2331
Anubion, companion of Simon Magus 11951, 11961, 11965, 11987, 12217, etc.
Appion, companion of Simon Magus 11952, 11962, 12277, 12293, 12358, etc.
Aquila, brother of Clement, born Faustinus, 352, 1315, 1928, 1931, 2408, etc.
Aristotle, Greek philosopher 7463, 7550
Asclepiades, Greek philosopher 7543
Antaradus, both the Phoenician colony of Antaradus and Aradus, the island that Anta-
    radus faces 418*, 5381, 5840, 9849, 9897
Athenodorus (*Anthenodorus*), companion of Simon Magus 12360, 12576, 12615
Athens, ancient city 255, 568, 590, 597, 5708, etc.
Bactria, area in central Asia 9133
Barnabas, St Barnabas the apostle 951, 1013, 1052, 1062, 1159, etc.
Blessed Virgin 120
Book of Clement (*Livre Clement*), *Liber Clementis*, one of the titles of the Pseudo-Clem-
    entine *Recognitiones* 58*, 2783
Brahmans, Hindu caste 9135, 9331, 9335
Bride (*Espuse*), the Bride of Christ, Holy Church 13413, 13424, 13613, 13617, 13629, etc.
Bridegroom (*Espus*), Jesus Christ 13622, 13631, 13636
Britons 9245
Caesar, Nero Claudius Caesar Augustus Germanicus 12137; see also Tiberius
Caesarea (*Cesaire*), Caesarea Stratonis, ancient city 336, 338, 353, 1263, 1274, etc.
Callistratus (*Calistratus*), Greek philosopher 7548
Cameleun, Alcmaeon, Greek philosopher 7546*
Charybdis (*Caribde*), sea-monster 14101

Christ *see* Jesus

Christian (*Crestien, Cristien*) 1632, 1638, 2526, 4673, 6552, etc.

Clement, Pope St Clement I, St Clement of Rome 45, 47, 61, 104, 155, etc.

Chronos (*Cronos*), father of Zeus 11372

Coition (*Asembler*), allegorical figure 11040

Cornelius the Centurion, Roman soldier converted by St Peter 12120

Creator, God the Creator 1049, 2000, 2391, 2464, 2827, etc.

Democritus, Greek philosopher 7547

Devil (*Deable, Diable*) 2457, 2461, 2467, 2474, 2479, etc.

Diodorus, Diodorus Cronus, Greek philosopher 7541

Diogenes, Greek philosopher 7548

Dositheus, Dositheus the Samaritan, heretic 2006, 2007, 2011, 2015, 2146, etc.

Egypt 795, 4087, 4095

Empedocles, Greek philosopher 7544

Enemy, the Devil 5090, 10085

Ephesus, ancient city 6138

Epicurus, Greek philosopher 7545

Father, God 2939, 4495, 10877, 12997, 13284, etc.

Faustinianus (*Faustinien*), father of Clement 125, 159, 225, 235, 267, etc.

Faustinus, brother of Clement, later named Aquila 154, 5692, 6442, 6467, 6617, etc.

Faustus, brother of Clement, later named Niceta 153, 5691, 6441, 6467, 6617, etc.

Flood *see* Great Flood

Gelonians (*Geli*), tribe of North-Western Scythia 9169

Genesis, book of Old Testament 1758

Germans (*Germani*), people of Germania 9301

God (*Deu, Dam(p)nedeu*) 32, 65, 112, 380, 403, etc.; *see also* Father

Gospel (*Ewangeile*) 6921

Great Flood (*Grant Flot*) 9534

Greece 10418, 10480, 10909, 11355

Greek, language 1993, 10905, 11371, 11395; Greek, person 7314, 7322

Hell (*Enfer(n)*) 799, 1465, 5271, 5940, 6819, etc.

Hesiod, Greek poet 11358, 11363, 11370, 11439

Holy Church 13103, 13276, 13277, 13332, 13358, etc.

Holy Spirit 723, 1803, 2939, 7315, 13079

India 9131, 9150, 9289, 9459, 9468

Isaac, Old Testament figure 1769, 4997

Jacob, Old Testament figure 1769, 4998

James (*Jacob*): James, St James the Less (*J. li Menur*) 14433, 14462; the two James (*les dous J.s*), St James the Less and St James the Great 14434

Jesus, Jesus Christ (*Jesu(s, J(h)esu Crist*) 64, 119, 414, 716, 1579, etc.

Jew (*Jueu*) 732, 869, 953, 1807, 9383, etc.

Job, Old Testament figure 1770

Joseph, Old Testament figure 1770

Journey of Peter (*Petri Itinerarium*), one of the titles of the Pseudo-Clementine *Recognitiones* 60

Judaea 729, 868, 919, 957, 1180, etc.

Juno (*Juno, Junein*), goddess 11131, 11405, 11408

Saturn, planet and god 9054, 11050, 11053, 11058, 11087
Saviour (*Sauvur, Sauver(r)e*) 715, 14157, 14037
Scripture(s (*E)scri(p)ture(s)* 1756, 1779, 2940, 11642, 11648, etc.
Seres, inhabitants of Serica 9111, 9327
Sicily 6139
Simon, Simon Magus 376, 381, 406, 407, 1272, etc.
Sinai (*Sina*), Mount Sinai 1772
Syria (*Sir(i)e*) 4942, 4943
Son (*Fiz*), the Son of God 715, 730, 919, 976, 1784, etc.
Standing One (*Vertu Estant*), title of divinity assumed by Simon Magus 2004*, 2173
Stratonis *see* Caesarea
Substance, allegorical figure 11037
Susis, region of Persia 9203, 9473
Thales, Greek philosopher 7546
Theophilus, resident of Antioch 13089, 13093
Thetis, wife of Peleus 11610
Thomas, St Thomas 9458, 9480
Tiberius Caesar, Tiberius Caesar Augustus 862; ~ of Lombardy 860
Tripolis (*Triple*), ancient city 4678, 4715, 4720, 4764, 4768, etc.
Venus, planet and goddess 9053, 11172, 11410
Virgin *see* Blessed Virgin
Vulcan, god 11409
Zacchaeus (*Zacheu*) follower of Peter, Bishop of Caesarea 404, 1316, 1656, 1665, 1685, etc.
Zenon, Greek philosopher 7544